Fyodor Dostoevsky

Fyodor Dostoevsky

A Life in Letters, Memoirs, and Criticism

IN THE BEGINNING
1821–1845

Thomas Gaiton Marullo

NIU Press / DeKalb

Northern Illinois University Press, DeKalb 60115
© 2016 by Northern Illinois University Press
All rights reserved

25 24 23 22 21 20 19 18 17 16   1 2 3 4 5
978-0-87580-746-1 (cloth)
978-1-60909-206-1 (e-book)
Cover design by Shaun Allshouse
Composition by BookComp, Inc.

Library of Congress Cataloging-in-Publication Data
Names: Marullo, Thomas Gaiton, author.
Title: Fyodor Dostoevsky—in the beginning (1821–1845) : a life
   in letters, memoirs, and criticism / Thomas Gaiton Marullo.
Description: DeKalb : Northern Illinois University Press, 2016.
   | Includes bibliographical references.
Identifiers: LCCN 2016008325 (print) | LCCN 2016010226
   (ebook) | ISBN 9780875807461 (cloth) | ISBN
   9781609092061 (ebook) | ISBN 9781609092061 (Ebook)
Subjects: LCSH: Dostoyevsky, Fyodor, 1821-1881—Childhood
   and youth. | Dostoyevsky, Fyodor, 1821–1881—Family.
   | Authors, Russian—19th century—Biography. | Dostoyevsky,
   Fyodor, 1821–1881—Correspondence.
Classification: LCC PG3328 .M38 2016 (print) | LCC PG3328
   (ebook) | DDC 891.73/3—dc23
LC record available at http://lccn.loc.gov/2016008325

Contents

Preface	vii
Introduction	1
Part One: All in the Family	19
Part Two: To Petersburg	65
Part Three: Darkness before Dawn	133
Conclusion	223
Directory of Prominent Names	227
Notes	237
Source Notes	269
Index	283

Preface

More than a century after his death in 1881, Fyodor Dostoevsky continues to fascinate readers and reviewers. In the past several years alone, there have appeared over a dozen studies in which scholars examine the writer's religious realism, his dialogues and dialectics, even the transposition of his novels into opera, drama, and film.

Biographies of Dostoevsky also abound. In America, studies on the writer's life include Avrahm Yarmolinsky's *Dostoevsky: His Life and Art* (1957), David Magarshack's *Dostoevsky* (1962), Ronald Hingley's *Dostoevsky: His Life and Work* (1978), Richard Freeborn's *Dostoevsky* (2003), and Robert Bird's *Fyodor Dostoevsky* (2012). In the former Soviet Union, works on Dostoevsky's existence feature Leonid Grossman's *Dostoevskii* (1962), which was translated into English in 1975. Finally, in France, there is Konstantin Mochulsky's *Dostoevskii: Life and Work* (1947), which was rendered into English in 1967, and which remains a classic on the writer today.

Regrettably, though, these and other biographies on Dostoevsky show a key flaw. They give short shrift to his formative years, the interval between his birth in 1821 and the publication of his first work, *Poor Folk*, in 1845. Scholars so rushed to what they saw as the more dramatic and illustrative moments in Dostoevsky's life that they committed a grievous error against the writer: they not only overlooked many of the early but bypassed seminal people, places, and events that influenced Dostoevsky's childhood, adolescence, and youth; they also bypassed the corresponding images and ideas of his early years that fed directly into his thought and art.

The grand exception to the lack of studies on Dostoevsky's formative period has been Joseph Frank's *Dostoevsky: The Seeds of Revolt, 1821–1849*, published in 1976, which, as the initial volume of a five-tome work on the writer, was the first study to focus on the writer's early life in a scholarly and systematic way, in a macro-approach to the subject. Frank considered the young Dostoevsky not only against the broad sweep of history and culture in both Russia and the West but also against the detailed and long overdue analyses of his early works.

Of necessity, therefore, Frank's *Dostoevsky: The Seeds of Revolt* relegated to the sidelines many of the lesser but no less important people, places, and events that, like a many-pieced puzzle, came together to form a complete and integral picture of Dostoevsky's early life. Still open for scholarly investigation are the Morsonian prosaics of his formative years—for example, the details and dynamics of his family, his schooling, his early years in St. Petersburg, and most importantly, the diverse stimuli—physical, social, and cultural—that influenced Dostoevsky and his writing in the first twenty-four years of his life.

Fyodor Dostoevsky: In the Beginning (1821–1845); A Life in Letters, Memoirs, and Criticism, the first of what will be a multivolume work on the writer, seeks not only to complement Frank's *Dostoevsky: The Seeds of Revolt* but also to put forth a portrait of the writer in a new and seminal way. As in my three-volume study of the Russian writer Ivan Bunin,[1] I seek a diary-portrait of Dostoevsky drawn from the letters, memoirs, and criticism of the writer, as well as from the witness and testimony of family and friends, readers and reviewers, observers and participants as he stepped forward into existence.

In *Fyodor Dostoevsky: In the Beginning*, I note several things. First, I have sought as complete a picture as possible of the young Dostoevsky via an exhaustive study-search of all published materials on the writer. Second, I have arranged excerpts chronologically, interpolating the voices of both the young and the mature Dostoevsky with those of individuals who were part of his life, or who were on the scene during that time. Third, I have given equal emphasis to all the speakers in the work. Some appear often; others, only once. Each one, though, weaves a strand in the tapestry. To these speakers, also, I have given maximum freedom. Anything and everything they have said about Dostoevsky—the truths and lies; the good, bad, and ugly; even the laughable and ludicrous—I have included in my work, in endnotes, counterarguments, and/or pertinent information. Fourth, I have resisted the admittedly great temptation to draw parallels between the people and events of the young Dostoevsky's life and the characters and happenings of his early and mature fiction. Any references to the writer's works are the province of the speakers alone.

As has been the case with my studies of Ivan Bunin, Leo Tolstoy,[2] Anton Chekhov,[3] and Nikolai Nekrasov and the Russian physiologists,[4] it is my hope that *Fyodor Dostoevsky: In the Beginning* will shed light on the many dark and unexplored corners of the young writer's life. My purpose is not only to render a clear and cohesive picture of the early years of one of the world's greatest authors but also to stimulate interest in the many people, places, and events that served as catalyst-seedbeds for his images and ideas. On one hand, the young Dostoevsky had an almost embarrassingly conventional childhood, adolescence, and youth. He moved in lockstep from a stable family, through excellent schools, and if he had wanted, to a promising career in service to the state. On the other hand, the young Dostoevsky was host to disturbing—often bizarre and painful—people, places, and events that etched acid-like into his mind, heart, and soul and that, equally important, demanded expression in both his early and his mature writing.

It was the young Dostoevsky's lot to live in lulls before storms. Thunder and lightning—physical and metaphysical—loomed in the distance. Gusts and gales—physical and metaphysical—threw him off course and threatened to drown him in waves of transition and change. Some of these disturbances were momentary; others, enduring, if not lifelong. Indeed, the tempests that often rained on Dostoevsky's parade led him not only to cast aside familial values but also to see existence as nasty, brutish, and short: a dog-eat-dog world peopled by lice and lords, mice and men, and ruled by a God who, if existing at all, cared little for creation.

With apologies to Luigi Pirandello, the young Dostoevsky was (at least) six characters in search of an author. In the beginning, he was like Alyosha Karamazov, sweetness and light: a model son, sibling, and student. Later, he was akin to other characters in Dostoevsky's final novel. Like Fyodor, he liked the ladies. Like Dmitri, he chose heart over head. Like Ivan, he thought too much. Like Smerdyakov, he wished he had never been born. To the mix were also added doubles, other figures from his writing. The young Dostoevsky saw himself as both an extraordinary and an underground man. At dawn, he was Golyadkin Senior, at war with society; at night, he was Golyadkin Junior, at peace with it. With lightning speed, he moved between oppressor and oppressed, a Svidrigailov and Marmeladov rolled into one. As did Stepan Verkhovensky, the young Dostoevsky babbled about everyone and everything; as did Stavrogin, he held his tongue about his sins until he burst forth in self-serving apologia and false confessions. Indeed, if readers were startled, even shocked by the cast of characters in Dostoevsky's writing, it was in part because he had spent the first twenty-four years of his life wearing the same masks, playing the same roles, and suffering the same trials-and-errors, crimes-and-punishments that informed the young men (and women) of his writing.

Throughout it all, one certainty was the young Dostoevsky's salvation: his wish to be a writer. Somehow, some way, sometime, he knew he was destined for greatness. Literally from the day he was born, consciously and unconsciously, the young Dostoevsky looked to his surroundings for people, places, and things, as well as for images, ideas, and ideals for his works. Dostoevsky did not write *Poor Folk* overnight. Progress, personal and aesthetic, was again prosaic: small, incremental, one step forward, two steps back. In this, he was Everyman (and -woman): filled with dreams and doubts, surviving on wisdom and wit, and clawing his way to greatness. Indeed, it is my final hope that readers of *Fyodor Dostoevsky: In the Beginning* will identify with the early triumphs and tragedies of the man, and that they will see the highs and lows, the peaks and valleys of his childhood, adolescence, and youth—physical and mental, individual and social, aesthetic and spiritual—as the formative stages not only for a great writer, but also for themselves.

Fyodor Dostoevsky: In the Beginning consists of a preface, an introduction, three parts, a conclusion, endnotes, a directory of names, and notes on sources. The first part, "All in the Family," focuses on Dostoevsky's early formation and schooling—his time in city and country, and his ties to his family, particularly his parents. The second part, "To Petersburg," features Dostoevsky's early days in Russia's imperial city, his years at the Main Engineering Academy, and the death of his father. The third part, "Darkness before Dawn," deals with the writer's youthful struggles and strivings, culminating in the success of his work *Poor Folk*.

Further, each section is introduced by a brief article on select people and places in the young Dostoevsky's life. The preface to "All in the Family" is a piece on Dostoevsky's father, Mikhail Andreevich Dostoevsky; a sketch on Dostoevsky's brother, Mikhail Fyodorovich Dostoevsky, heads "To Petersburg"; and an essay, "St. Petersburg, 1845," introduces "Darkness before Dawn."

For their assistance in *Fyodor Dostoevsky: In the Beginning*, I wish to thank, first and foremost, Irwin Weil of Northwestern University, Yuri Corrigan of Boston University, Jeffrey Brooks of Johns Hopkins University, and Douglas Smith, author of *Former People: The Final Days of the Russian Aristocracy* and of an upcoming book on Grigori Rasputin, for their generous and helpful comments and suggestions. Also, I note my gratitude to Joseph Lenkart, Jan Adamczyk, and the members of the Slavic Reference Service at the University of Illinois, who, with exceptional diligence, inexhaustible patience, and admirable good cheer, found answers to the myriad, complicated, and often outrageous questions I asked regarding the young Dostoevsky; and who, as always has been the case in my forty-year tie with the group, ended their responses with offers of further assistance.

Here at Notre Dame, I wish to thank Thomas Merluzzi, Director of the Institute of Scholarship for the Liberal Arts, for his continued financial support; Laura Sills, Therese Bauters, and the staff of Interlibrary Loan and Document Delivery for supplying materials for research; and Cheryl Reed, who transformed my chaotic files into a professional document. I also acknowledge my research assistants—Kaitlin Spillane, David Brosnan, Spencer Andrews, Paul Phelan, Katie Harris, Joshua O'Brien, and Ruslan Lucero—whom I drove to the brink (and beyond) with endless queries on pages and dates; obscure questions on people, places, and events; and tortuous searches through newspapers, journals, books, and cyberspace for citations and claims. Truly, *Fyodor Dostoevsky: In the Beginnning* would not have come into being without their loyalty and support.

I am also indebted to Amy Farranto and Nathan Holmes of Northern Illinois University Press for their enthusiastic reception of *Fyodor Dostoevsky*, as well for their professionalism and efficiency in preparing my work for publication. I also wish to thank the copyeditor of my study, Candace McNulty, for her meticulous attention to my work.

Last but not least, I thank my wife, Gloria Gibbs Marullo, for thirty-six years of unstinting encouragement and love; my cats, Bernadette Marie (now 18 1/2), Bridget Josephine, Benedict Joseph, Francis Xavier, and Agnes Mary, the latest stray on my doorstep, for unconditional warmth and love; and Sister Mary Colleen Dillon, S.N.D., and the sisters of Lourdes Hall of the Sisters of Notre Dame of Covington Kentucky, for their unceasing prayers on my behalf.

May you all know happiness, health, and peace.

—TGM

Introduction

However surprising it may seem, the first years of the young Dostoevsky could not have had a more normal, even idyllic beginning. Indeed, if in both his early and mature writing he flirted with ideas of utopia and eden, it was in part because he had experienced both entities in his childhood, adolescence, and youth.

The young Dostoevsky's parents were exemplary. His father, Mikhail Andreevich, was a well-respected physician, a self-made man; his mother, Maria Fyodorovna, a loving and talented homemaker. Unlike the parents in *Netochka Nezvanova*, *Crime and Punishment*, *Demons*, and *The Brothers Karamazov*, Mikhail and Maria were grounded in life. In truth, they had little choice. Although Mikhail was a nobleman, family circumstances were extremely modest. Nowhere in the formation of the young Dostoevsky was there a trace of the privilege and wealth that graced the early years of his illustrious counterpart, Leo Tolstoy, his junior by seven years. Mikhail and Maria, together with their six children and servants—a coachman, a lackey-janitor, a cook, a housemaid, a laundress, and a nurse—lived on the first floor in a three-storied annex of the Mariinsky Hospital for the Poor, a stately Doric-columned structure built by Empress Maria Fyodorovna, the second wife of Paul I, between 1803 and 1806. (The Mariinsky Hospital exists to this day as the Institute for Tuberculosis.) The ancestral home consisted of a long, dark passage, flanked by a drawing room and a parlor, both of which were lit by tallow candles, not lamps. "Father did not like them," brother Andrei recalls. A windowless partition in the back served to close off the nursery where young Fyodor and his brother Mikhail slept on chests until they entered boarding school. (The place is now a museum.)

Even more unspectacular was the summer home in the village of Darovoe (near Tula, roughly ninety miles south of Moscow). There the family lived in a tiny thatched one-story cottage of three small rooms, with walls made of wattle and smeared with clay. The terrain and soil were poor, but the place bordered on a small field, ravines, scrub, a shady copse of linden trees, and a dark birchwood forest named Brykovo.

What the Dostoevskys lacked in financial wealth, they made up for in intellectual and emotional largesse. Like the doubled-headed eagle that symbolized their homeland, Mikhail and Maria looked to the past and the future to define the present. Rooted deeply in patriarchal Russia, they schooled their children in indigenous history and faith. Daily readings on Russia-gone-by—Karamzin's multivolume *History of the Russian State* was a key example—were as hallowed as frequent visits to the Kremlin. Mikhail and Maria believed not only in God, his Holy Mother, the angels, and the saints, but also, despite frequent and grave evidence to the contrary, that celestial powers shielded them from adversity in this life and in the next. Such trust was solid and sober, pragmatic and everyday; nothing could shake their beliefs. When Mikhail and Maria learned that Darovoe had been destroyed by fire in April 1832, they did not curse God or fate. Rather, seeing the disaster as punishment for (undisclosed) sins, they fell before the family icons, before spending hours in prayer at the Iberian Chapel just outside of Red Square.

Such virtues and values Mikhail and Maria passed on to young Fyodor. His religious formation was extraordinary. From early childhood, the boy attended masses and liturgies and visited churches and monasteries. He learned from deacons, was blessed by priests, and prayed publicly and privately for patronage and protection. Even before the young Dostoevsky could read, he knew the Old and New Testaments—the Book of Job affected him strongly—as well as the lives of the saints, pulp-popular religious stories, and texts from church and biblical history. Even his shenanigans had a religious cast, young Fyodor once taking icons from a wooden chapel at Darovoe and processing with them about a field, singing hymns and verse.

Mikhail and Maria also had a steady hand on the future. Progressive and forward-looking, they stressed education as the way, truth, and life. As a four-year-old, the young Dostoevsky was seated behind a book and made to study. Along with brother Mikhail, he attended the best schools in Moscow. Under the aegis first of Nikolai Drashusov-Sushard and then of Leonti Chermak, the young Fyodor received a superb education in both the sciences and the liberal arts. Particularly with Chermak, the lad claimed as teachers Dmitri Perevoshikov, a distinguished mathematician, physicist, and astronomer and later dean and rector of Moscow University; Ivan Davydov, a linguist, aesthete, philosopher and well-known follower and proponent of Schiller and Schelling; and Alexei Kubaryov, a specialist in Latin literature and author of *The Theory of Russian Versification*, published in Moscow in 1837.

The bonds that Dostoevsky enjoyed with his family he also had with his instructors. Unlike other schools at the time, with their accepted if not vaunted traditions of corporal hardship and discipline, the hallowed halls in which the young Fyodor received his first formal instruction were warm, intimate, and ordered. To his last days, his time with Chermak was among the fondest memories of his childhood, and with good reason. Chermak treated his students as family. He dined with them, attended to their needs, and most importantly, perhaps, continued the morality and ethics that the young Dostoevsky had received at home.

From both his parents and teachers, the young Dostoevsky came to know Western thought and culture not only as intimately as he did his own but without the searing splits that later fissured him, his characters, and his country. French, along with Russian, was spoken in the home. German and English the young Dostoevsky learned in school; Latin, from his father.

Confident in past and future, Mikhail and Maria fashioned a present that was safe and secure. The Dostoevskys functioned as a closed unit, a warm and loving world onto themselves. Ventures from home were rare; visits by family and friends were few. If young Fyodor had friends at school, they stayed there. Further, whatever was going on outside, law and order reigned inside. Unlike the chaotic households of the writer's fiction, Mikhail, Maria, and children adhered to an almost ritualistic table of hours. Days were filled with reading, study, and play; night with music, literature, and games. Rules and regulations insured a nononsense atmosphere. Young Fyodor was consistently on a tight leash. He was exhorted to make his way in the world, to be diligent, independent, and judicious. He was restricted as to his choice of playmates and friends. He did not play balls and with sticks; he lacked pocket money; beyond going to school, he was forbidden to walk about Moscow alone.

Unlike other children of the era, though, the young Dostoevsky was encouraged to be seen and heard. Particularly during meals, he and brother Mikhail were urged by their parents to talk at length about courses, teachers, and grades. Their faces and tongues were open books; everything, even literary spoofs and the hijinks of their fellow students, were fair game, even if they incurred their father's displeasure.[1]

The love and attention that the young Fyodor received from his parents and teacher he also received from a colorful cast of relatives, servants, and others. Along with brother Mikhail, there were his brothers Andrei and Nikolai; and his sisters, Varvara, Vera, and Alexandra.[2] (He was particularly close to Varvara; Vera's twin sister died in childbirth.) There was Maria's sister, Alexandra Kumanina, who served as a second mother. There was his great-uncle, Vasili Kotelnitsky, a professor at Moscow university, who took him to circus and fairs. Last but certainly not least was his nurse, Alyona Kryukova, who, as a self-styled bride of Christ, dueled with house-sprites and regaled her charge with homespun wisdom, theology, and tales. Mention must also be made of the peasant Marko Efremov (Marey in Dostoevsky's famed story), as well as the other serfs who loved the child as their own.

From his earliest years, the young Dostoevsky showed a split personality. On one hand, he engaged the world with open arms. By his own admission, the young Fyodor was lively, inquisitive, and intelligent. Claims by memoirists as to early gloom and doom are not true. The young Fyodor was oftentimes so fiery, passionate, and intense that Mikhail worried, prophetically, that his son would land in jail. Also as a sign of things to come, testing and crossing borders were a way of life. The young Dostoevsky bent and broke rules; he pulled pranks and fast ones; he cheated at cards and other games (and, a lesson to Raskolnikov and Dmitri Karamazov, was always caught). Forever on the move, physically and mentally, young Fyodor loved to roam the park about the Mariinsky Hospital, as well as the groves and ravines at Darovoe. (The estate there held a lifelong claim on his heart.) On trips, he sat in the coachman's seat and investigated every stop along the way. He adored horses and dogs (one appropriately named Zhuchka, like the famed dog in *The Brothers Karamazov*), if not all living things. Rambunctious to the extreme, the young Fyodor vaunted his agility and strength and imitated anyone and anything that caught his fancy—a runner, one moment; the next, a monkey. Considering how in both literature and life the adult Dostoevsky walked a fine line between myriad dualities, it comes as little surprise that as a lad, he once mimicked a tightrope walker. Only snakes and dark rooms claimed his fear.

The young Fyodor engaged groups with similar verve. In activities that showed a predilection for unspoiled worlds, he was the chief among Indians, the Robinson among Fridays. Equally important, perhaps, he was fascinated by people of all ranks and stations. Although the young Dostoevsky's parents wished him to associate with the best in society, he often sought out the worst. In truth, the boy could not help but do so, since just beyond the confines of his home were the first exemplars of the humiliated and injured who would people his fiction. The Sushchevskaya district in which the young Fyodor lived was among the most squalid localities in Moscow. Home to tramps, suicides, criminals, and their unidentified victims, it was known by locals as "the poorhouse." Also, just beyond the Mariinsky Hospital was a lunatic asylum, a home for abandoned infants, and still another portent of the future, a station for prisoners on their way to Siberia. In an ironic flourish that would have made Ivan Karamazov smile, one street bore the name "God's home" (*Bozhedomka*). The environs about Darovoe were hardly better. The peasants in the village there eked out an existence amid poverty, sickness, and thievery, all the time watching, in fascination and envy, the lives of their masters.

To the poor and downtrodden, Dostoevsky was caring and concerned. Risking Mikhail's displeasure, he sought out ailing children and adults in the hospital garden. He was even more solicitous with the peasants at Darovoe. Always at their beck and call, and sensitive to suffering children in a way that would shame Ivan Karamazov, the young Dostoevsky once ran several miles to fetch water for a peasant babe. Such solicitude extended outside the home. At Chermak's school, the young Fyodor befriended beginners, protecting them from bullies, helping them with their studies, and amusing them with stories. True, there were incidents of "loathsome lordliness"—games of "horsies," in which young Fyodor and company raced troikas made up of peasant boys and girls—but like any irregularities in the Dostoevsky household, such activities were the exception, not the rule. Indeed, in no way would Mikhail or Maria sanction genuine cruelty or debasement.

As if to herald the doppelgänger of both his early and mature fiction, though, the young Dostoevsky could also withdraw from people, places, and things. Although popular at Chermak's school, he immersed himself in books, rarely taking part in games and other activities and having little to do with anyone other than several upperclassmen there. A sensitivity to seaminess held sway. Again like the third Karamazov son, the young Fyodor cared little for vulgar jokes and pranks. Still another indication of trouble to come was that for all his vigor and verve, the young Fyodor was prone to mysterious bouts of illness. An early, if unsubstantiated, claim of epilepsy—"the falling sickness," as it was known then—appears. Also, at age sixteen, Fyodor fell victim to an unidentified illness of the throat that caused him first to lose his voice, then to speak only in whispers, and for the rest of his life to converse in a hoarse, muffled voice.

The young Dostoevsky was also no stranger to psychosocial breakdown and cruelty. His protective parents held sway only for so long. An urban playmate bleeding to death from rape and a village idiot abused by her family and mourning her dead child were first instances of violated innocence. A peasant boy who wrung the necks of sparrows for fun and a courier beating a coachman before a roaring crowd were early catalysts not only for ruinous rebellions against God but also for salvific shoulderings of society. Even at an early age, the young Fyodor was wary of his fellow Russians, if not humankind. At this point in his life, though, the dark side of national existence affected the boy but little. Nothing, it seemed, upset his youthful applecart.

In these early years, also, no one saw young Fedyushka [Fyodor] as a prodigy. A literary Mozart he was not. With hindsight, though, it seemed almost axiomatic that the lad would become a writer. His three-year-old self was already composing fairy tales—"earnest, terrible, but with a touch of humor." At home, the young Dostoevsky heard native tales about the Firebird and Alyosha Popovich, and foreign ones about Aladdin, Sinbad, and Bluebeard. Stories of East and West he knew also from Russian literature. The works of Derzhavin, Karamzin, Zhukovsky, Zagoskin, Lazhechnikov, Veltman, Narezhny, and Dal were standard fare. Alexander Pushkin claimed a special allegiance. It was a sign of the young Fyodor's aesthetic acumen that over the objections of his parents (and teachers of fiction of that time) he chose Pushkin over Zhukovsky.

The young lad was even more taken with a wide array of Western writers. Family and private readings of Cervantes, Shakespeare, Dickens, Scott, Hoffman, and Radcliffe brought him to dreams and raves. Defoe's *Robinson Crusoe* styled him as castaway. Schiller's *The Robbers* triggered a lifelong association with the writer. Voltaire's *The Henriade* was his choice in a declaiming contest with brother Mikhail. (He won.)

Fyodor's early schooling solidified the allure. Chermak and company not only excelled in languages and literatures; they also hosted an extensive library of periodicals and books. As a student, the young Fyodor owned books published by *The Library of Reading*, a conservative monthly of literature, science, the arts, industry, news, and fashion. Into his literary purview also came such native writers as Baratynsky, Vyazemsky, Voekov, Odoevsky, Lermontov, Krylov, and Gogol; and such foreign ones as Balzac, Hugo, and Scribe. George Sand had a particular tug on his mind and heart. There was this drawback, though. Much as the young Dostoevsky profited from such writers, he was prone to take their tales too seriously. As he admitted later in life, the fiction that consumed his early years filled his mind, heart, and soul with torrid sentiment. Duality again claimed his being. Sometimes, the young Fyodor rose to the heights, to "new life, dreaming terribly about anything and everything that was 'splendid and sublime.'" Other times, he wallowed in more earthly fallows, yielding to images and ideas that were "seductive, passionate, and corrupting, and with which [he] struggled in [his] soul." Precisely what these items were, the young Dostoevsky declined to say; but like Alyosha Karamazov, he was not the perfect child that everyone, including himself, deemed himself to be. Plausibly, the lad awakened sexually at a very early age. Even more tantalizing, perhaps, and also akin to so many of his fictional characters, the young Dostoevsky was spellbound by sentimental worldviews in which lust overruled love, and in which white knights, black villains, and distressed damsels simplified the world in dark and dangerous ways.

The halcyon existence of Fyodor's early childhood came to an abrupt halt with the death of the thirty-seven-year-old Maria on February 27, 1837, from tuberculosis and, plausibly, numerous pregnancies. (It is a measure of the impact of literature in the Dostoevsky home that the children declaimed to Maria her favorite verse in the final months of her life.) Fyodor so adored his mother that her passing left him with an enduring, almost existential void. Suddenly, life became dismal and lonely. Even here, though, his love for literature prevailed. Together with his brother Mikhail, he chose a citation from Karamzin to mark his mother's grave. Even more revealing, perhaps, he told one and all that if his family had not been wearing mourning for Maria, he would have asked his father to wear black for the passing of Pushkin also at this time.

If a door had closed on the young Dostoevsky, a window soon opened for him. No sooner had Maria died than Mikhail planned for both Fyodor and Mikhail to attend the Main Engineering Academy in St. Petersburg and to pursue careers as officer-engineers.

Upon first glance, the decision was an intelligent one. Initially, things went well. The kindness and solicitude that Fyodor and Mikhail knew with Chermak they now enjoyed with Koronad Kostamarov, who, as head of one of the best preparatory schools in the imperial capital, prepared the brothers for the entrance examinations into the Main Engineering Academy. Like Chermak, Kostamarov saw the lads as family. Indeed, the love and attention he gave to the two was often so encompassing that they seemed his only concern.

At Kostamarov's school, both Fyodor and Mikhail lived up to and even exceeded their father's expectations. Letters from sons to father were replete with progress in studies, confidence in the Almighty, interest in siblings, concern for Mikhail's health, and gratitude for all that he was doing on their behalf. Both boys took pains to convince Mikhail that they were running a tight ship, academically and financially. Regularly, they informed the man of time in classes and study, and accounted to him for expenditures on clothes and necessities.

The calm was only surface deep, though—the problem being that both Fyodor and Mikhail heard different drummers. Their dreams—"splendid and sublime"—were to be not officer-engineers but artist-writers. A month before they left for St. Petersburg, Fyodor was composing a novel on Venetian life and hankering for visits to Constantinople and the East. Mikhail was writing three poems daily. The first thing that the two wished to do upon their arrival in the northern capital was to visit Pushkin's apartment and the site of his fatal duel. Complicating matters was the fact that Fyodor and Mikhail fell under the sway of one Ivan Shidlovsky, whom father and sons had met at a hotel on their first day in St. Petersburg, and who, having graduated from the Juridical Faculty in Kharkov at an early age, was serving in the Ministry of Finance.

Ostensibly, Shidlovsky had it all: a poet-idealist-*intelligent* who was tall and handsome, intelligent and upbeat, eloquent and loquacious, passionate and cultured. He was loved by everyone. Officers relished his racy verse; monks revered him as a theologian. Women called him "our Chrysostom"; peasants saw him as a prophet. Although Shidlovsky was only five years older than Fyodor and Mikhail, he became their mentor and guide. (Revealingly, father Mikhail approved of the relationship.) Shidlovsky influenced both boys both positively and negatively. Positively, he eased the first steps of the lads into adulthood. For them he made a home away from home. He acquainted Fyodor and Mikhail with life in St. Petersburg, traveling with them throughout the length and breadth of the city. He engaged the two in conversations that catered to their interests and strengths, particularly religion and literature. (Revealingly, Shidlovsky was the first to predict a great future for Dostoevsky as a writer.)

In truth, though, Shidlovsky caused Fyodor and Mikhail more harm than good. He was a prototype for the would-be/wanna-be men-gods that would people the writer's mature fiction. To his newfound friends, Shidlovsky styled deific nobility and brilliance: an exalted, almost mythic sense of self. He was a vulcan who pitched lightning and fire; a sailor who sought the Almighty in stormy seas; an anchorite who walked and talked with God. To his taste, Shidlovsky was also a red-hot lover. He burned in embraces, tore kisses from his chest, and relished raptures that transcended heaven and earth. Not unlike Goethe's Werther, he even attempted suicide over an unhappy love. For all the hoopla, though, Shidlovsky was a failure-fraud who, if he had remained with Fyodor and Mikhail for any length of time, would have taken them down the same twisted paths that he followed in life. Colorful and contradictory, Shidlovsky was saint and sinner, a being who showed "spiritual beauty . . . [and] physical decline." He was as much an atheist as he was a believer, as much taken by life as he was "enthralled by dreams of self-destruction."[3]

Drinking and carousing one moment, Shidlovsky was a pilgrim-monk and "pure priest of poetry" the next, his romantic escapades being more fiction than fact. Prone to philosophical, religious, and aesthetic ravings, as well as to what he termed "literary miscarriages," Shidlovsky never completed anything, be it an intellectual project like a history of the church, or a professional one like journalism, or a religious one like taking final vows. In short, Shidlovsky exemplified the duality that young Dostoevsky himself experienced in life. He showed that pro-and-contra—physical, and philosophical, social and spiritual—were not peculiar to him alone, but endemic to all humankind. It was perhaps for that reason that Shidlovsky remained etched in Dostoevsky's consciousness throughout his life. Whatever his strengths and weaknesses, he was for the writer "extraordinary."

A more pressing problem for father and sons was that Mikhail was not permitted to sit for the entrance examinations for the Main Engineering Academy. Nearsightedness and alleged early signs of consumption were one reason; the difficulties of enrolling both boys at the same institution at state expense was a second (and more valid) one. Misfortune set its sights also on Fyodor. Although the lad had passed the entrance examinations with distinction, he learned that publicly funded positions at the Main Engineering Academy had suddenly become unavailable. Only the financial intervention of Aunt Alexandra Kumanina allowed him to realize his father's dreams for both his sons. The victory was Pyrrhic. For whatever reason, Mikhail was sent to a branch of the Main Engineering Academy in Revel (now Tallinn). At age seventeen, young Fyodor was alone for the first time in his life. Insult added to injury when the boy learned that immediately after he and Mikhail had been rejected for funded positions at the Main Engineering Academy, four wealthy students were admitted to the institution at state expense.

Fyodor's first years at the Main Engineering Academy proceeded smoothly. Like other schools the young Dostoevsky had attended, the school was considered one of the best institutions of its kind; but assessments of the place, often by the same individual, are frequently so contradictory as to obscure life there. Founded by Grand Duke Nikolai Pavlovich in 1804 and housed at the Mikhailovsky Castle since 1819, the Main Engineering Academy hosted 120 or so students (called "conductors"), between fourteen and eighteen years old, and divided equally among Poles, Baltic-Germans, and Russians. Regarding strengths, the students at the Main Engineering Academy lived a privileged existence. Their room, board, and uniforms well exceeded the norms of the day. Also unusual for the time was the fact that the conductors at the Main Engineering Academy received stipends and could buy vodka, beer, and tobacco. They were also exempt from the corporal abuse that marked such schools in Russia and elsewhere. Punishment for infractions was relatively humane and seen as beneficial, as making boys into men. The students at the Main Engineering Academy functioned as model citizens. They championed honesty, impartiality, and respect for individuals. Courses in science, drawing, and fortifications, together with summer camp and military maneuvers, fulfilled their oath of loyalty to the tsar and prepared them for service to the state. Daily drills, demanding classes, and professional pride instilled in themselves and their institution leveled national and social differences and made for a cohesive group. Seniors mentored juniors. Ties were lifelong.

Or so it seemed. Regarding weaknesses, the students at the Main Engineering Academy were isolated from the outside world, often for weeks at a time. They did not receive newspapers or periodicals. They also lived by unspoken codes of behavior. Without the knowledge of the authorities (or more likely with their tacit approval), older students reined in younger ones for deceit, boasting, and (unspecified) immorality with insults, pranks, and bullying. First-year students or "hazel hens" had to lick ink off paper, or to crawl under tables at one end, and at the other, to be whipped with twisted braids. Shades of Alyosha Karamazov: perceived mama's boys were forced to say dirty words. Violence was commonplace. Resistors and incorrigibles were beaten so mercilessly that they were hospitalized, admitting only to unspecified accidents for their injuries. Concern for externals, fear of higher-ups, and bouts of suspicion and spite frayed further ties between and among authorities, teachers, and students. The result was that the students at the Main Engineering Academy looked at life with distrust, even cynicism. Quickly, they learned the difference between truth and lie, ideal and reality; equally important, they internalized the rules for survival and success.

At the Main Engineering Academy, the young Dostoevsky fulfilled duties and obligations faithfully, but he was not happy. The rough-and tumble camaraderie, as well as the *comme il faut* extracurriculars of wine, women, and song, were not for him. Academics claimed neither mind nor heart; lessons in drawing and drill, mathematics, and fortifications were particular bugbears. The young Fyodor was also revolted by the collective chase for rank, privilege, money, and marriage; such items were for him a life of *stushevat'sia*, "to sink gradually into nothingness." Even little things the lad could not do right. To the mortification of everyone present, he saluted Grand Duke Mikhail Pavlovich, the brother of Nicholas I, as "Your Excellency" instead of "Your Imperial Highness" (and was called an idiot by the man in response).

No, the young Dostoevsky had other ideas and plans. Like his father, he too sought to make his own way, physically and mentally. Revealingly, the lad did not rebel openly, the rambunctiousness of his childhood a thing of the past. The rites and rituals of student life—these the young Dostoevsky viewed with indifference. When not in classes and drills, he was off on his own, out of sight and mind of others. From his situation, though, he found relief. Lectures on history and literature made up for lessons on integral calculus. The lad also knew solace and support conversing with select friends about religion, music, and literature; or perched behind a book in a remote corner of a corridor, room, or tent. The young Dostoevsky was often so consumed by this reading that he noticed neither people nor time. Indeed, his favorite hours were late at night, when he could work unimpeded, a practice that would remain with him for the rest of his life.

At the Main Engineering Academy, the young Fyodor impressed one and all as sad, sickly, sleepy, and strange, as someone who was best left to his own devices, in peace. Visible, though, was the halo over his head. He was modest and sincere, gentle and kind. His adherence to Orthodoxy, his love for the Gospels and other religious works, and his admiration of teacher-priests styled him as an idealist-mystic. His excellence in studies, his anger at injustice, and his unwillingness to kowtow to higher-ups classed him as a model-paragon. He kept peace among groups, to protect hazel hens, servants, and teachers (!) from bullies, and cared for poor village children. His prolonged conversations with a priest-teacher earned him the nickname of Photius the Monk. The passions aroused by Walter Scott had also cooled considerably. Nowhere is there evidence of the amorous adventures typical of Russian youth at this time.

At the Main Engineering Academy, though, the young Dostoevsky was often his own worst enemy: an Underground Man come to life. Sometimes the lad was melancholic and morose, "floating in some kind of cold, polar atmosphere which not a single ray of light crept through." Other times he was heedless of life; and lacerated with such "injured pride . . . [that he felt] like smashing the world in a single stroke." Almost with delight, he confessed to a new and strange pleasure—torturing himself.

In his mind at least, he had ample cause for his angst. The young Fyodor was chronically short of money. If he was not spending every ruble he had on himself, friends, and anyone who needed help, he was allowing himself to be robbed by servants, hucksters, and cardsharps. The rare letters to his father, his brother, and relatives were rife with dire laments on his poverty, as well as with crass (and obsequious) requests for things he needed or wanted, often to keep up appearances. (Responses of gratitude were notoriously slow in coming.) The young Dostoevsky also ran afoul of superiors. Although the lad did well on examinations, he had to repeat a year because of an (undisclosed) run-in with a teacher. Small wonder that the young Fyodor complained of a cold heart and a dead soul. Small wonder that he looked to his past as a dreamer, his present as a zombie, and his future as a failure-freak. Small wonder, also, that he bemoaned the loss of a talent he was not sure he possessed.

In 1841, the young Fyodor was promoted from student to field engineer–officer; but his final years at the Main Engineering Academy had become unbearable. He no longer concealed his misery. Indeed, he seemingly went out of his way to antagonize his superiors, to be even more divorced from his surroundings. His drawing and plans were done hastily, with little effort. For young Fyodor, also, the wolf was not at the door but had come crashing through. Brother Andrei, along with Mikhail, received pleas for funds. The physical and mental stress took new tolls on the boy's health. His face became earthen-colored; his voice, sharp and hoarse; his chin and glands, swollen. Tormented by a dry cough, rheumatism, and even abscesses and boils, the young Fyodor feared that he would die in his sleep. Even more distressing, perhaps, was his mental distress—for example, complaints that someone was snoring alongside him at night. Such afflictions, moreover, the lad bore stoically and in private, appealing to doctors only when the suffering had become intolerable.

If the young Fyodor wanted anything from this period in his life, it was out of his present situation. Mercifully, "the freedom, the wharf" that he could not find physically, he found aesthetically. His love for literature was his rock of ages. The young Fyodor astounded his friends with his knowledge of authors and works, demanding that they read old favorites like Shakespeare, Scott, Hoffman, and Schiller; and new ones like Homer, Racine, Corneille, Balzac, Hugo, Lamartine, Maturin, Cooper, Soulié, and Heine. Into his pantheon he also admitted a Russian writer: Gogol. It is again indicative of the young Fyodor's aesthetic sense that while others damned Gogol as vulgar and base, he proclaimed the writer's gifts, particularly the "invisible tears through visible laughter" of his 1842 *The Overcoat*.

Even more prophetically, perhaps, he attracted audiences to his stories. Speaking quietly and slowly, in a way that was graceful and direct, the young Fyodor regaled listeners with recollections from childhood and episodes from history. It was in such a spotlight that the lad morphed into his earlier self: cheerful, witty, "the soul of society." Whatever doubt and derision his schoolmates had for the boy, were forgotten in scenes when, late at night, the young Fyodor "leapt from behind the door . . . and spoke with special nervous inspiration." In such moments, it became apparent that with the lad, still waters ran deep, and that just beneath the calm seethed sound and fury. When he took center stage, the young Dostoevsky gestured wildly, cried out, even spat. His voice was penetrating and loud, his lips bedecked with foam. Sometimes to spectators, the possession was not artistic but demonic.

There were other pleasures: plays, ballets, operas, and concerts (Liszt was a particular favorite). There were also such joys as literary readings and gatherings; studies in history and philosophy; and the company of select friends—Dmitri Grigorovich was one—who, often gregarious and carefree, were quite unlike himself.

Most importantly, perhaps, the young Dostoevsky was putting pen to paper in drama and prose. (Poetry he found too restrictive.) For once in his time at the Main Engineering Academy, fate smiled upon him. Now a fourth-year student at the school, the young Fyodor had an apartment (the first of many). Even with one or more roommates, including his brother Andrei, he now had a place to call his own. Mornings the young Dostoevsky continued to attend classes, but afternoons and evenings, he locked himself away with sketches and drafts that would culminate in his 1845 work, *Poor Folk*. His desk and floors covered with scraps of paper, the young Fyodor dreamed of being the next Pushkin or Gogol. Realizing that there was more to life than the one he was living, he looked for trouble and the troubled in basements, attics, and everywhere in between. For the "humiliated and injured" of his fiction, he hosted spongers, losers, and hangers-on.

Like any beginning writer, the young Dostoevsky saw that the reality he wished to capture had, ironically, seized him with demands for food, clothing, and shelter. His 1843 entry into the drafting department of the St. Petersburg Engineering Corps showed him even more of what mundane life had to offer. Daily the lad cursed his fate, despising his superiors and dreaming of early retirement. In his position, he did the minimum, barely enough to get by. If the characters in his early fiction curried favor with their bosses, he did not. The story goes that his work was so substandard that the young Dostoevsky was again called an idiot—this time by Nicholas I—for drawing a fortress without gates. In the office, the young Fyodor was revolted by toadies. In the field, he was repulsed by peasants in chains and soldiers with whips.

Unsurprisingly, the young Dostoevsky lasted in state service for little more than a year; but his trials had just begun. Again, he was his own worst enemy. Beyond his salary, the lad received money from translations; handouts from Aunt Alexandra; and, after rancorous negotiations, funds from Pyotr Karepin, husband of Fyodor's sister, Varvara, and guardian-manager of the family estate. As was the case with his time at the Main Engineering Academy, though, he was often penniless, thanks to attendance at concerts and plays; visits to coffeehouses and restaurants; losses to billiard-players and cardsharps; dealings with moneylenders

INTRODUCTION   13

and pawnbrokers; and bills from salespeople, laundresses, tailors, barbers, and shoemakers. Also continuing apace were handouts to beggars, freeloaders, and ne'er-do-wells; as well as thefts by servants and others—often with young Fyodor's knowledge, and even approval. (The only group he disliked were foreigners, particularly Germans.) Revealingly, the young Fyodor's encounters with the "poor folk" of the capital touched him but little, if at all. Neither in his letters nor in the memoirs of family and friends is there the concern for unfortunates that he showed for the peasants of his childhood. He was also markedly apolitical. Nowhere is there any anger over the Russia of Nicholas I, particularly the institution of serfdom. Nowhere also is there any interest in the debates that raged between Westerners and Slavophiles over the future of their land. At this point in the young Dostoevsky's life, it was all about him.

One could argue that he had no choice. Often the lad survived only on bread and milk, bought on credit. He was writing fast and furiously, but as yet he had nothing to show the public. Dustups with Karepin over money were almost daily occurrences. Indeed, his brother-in-law became the lightning rod for the lad's frustration and unhappiness; and with good reason. In this period, Karepin was the first and only individual to challenge, even mock Dostoevsky's dreams of becoming a writer. Father Mikhail may have bristled at his son's aspirations, but he had held his tongue. Not so Karepin. Almost with glee, he took the young Fyodor to task not only for his literary aspirations, but also for what he saw as personal and social ills.

In truth, Karepin had good reason for his censure. He had been provoked to fury not only by the young Dostoevsky's repeated requests for money but also by his equally enduring demands that he be granted his inheritance, even it meant injustice and hardship for his siblings. Often Karpenin went on the defensive. Stony silence greeted the young Fyodor's cloying sweetness, as well as his faux-affirmations of respect, loyalty, and love. Financial pittances answered the lad's philosophical panderings, his dramatic protestations of need, his convoluted schemes for his birthright, and his empty threats of legal action. Equally as often, Karepin went on the offensive. A self-made man of the world, he fired broadsides at young Fyodor's waywardness. The lad was a disgrace to his parents' memory; he was arrogant and egotistical, coarse and immature; he needed time, experience, and the wisdom of elders (Karepin being first in line). Young Fyodor's request for his inheritance Karepin challenged as unfeasible, unjust, immoral, even illegal. The lad's profligate spending, his rebuff of societal rules, and, with pointed reference to his writing, his relish for the "abstract laziness and languor of Shakespearean dreams," Karepin derided as the stuff of scoundrels and madmen. For Karepin the solution for young Fyodor's ills was clear. The lad, he insisted, should return to service. He should seek a more "genuine poetry . . . [in] the successful completion of duty ... [in] the joy ... of notice by superiors ... [and in] the reward ... from labor in a direct and noble path."

Young Fyodor responded in kind. Akin to the tortured ties between the "masters" and "men" in both his early and mature fiction, he welcomed Karepin's financial rescues; but he also decried what he saw as the man's condescension, interference, and, most outrageously, his scorn for the lad's dreams as "Shakespearean soap bubbles." To his brother-in-law, young Fyodor acknowledged his mistakes; but he asserted his freedom and independence. Stung particularly by the charge that he was a scalawag-son, the youth shot back that his parents, particularly his father, had so wanted his happiness that living or dead, they would bless whatever path he chose in life. The die was cast. The young Dostoevsky would rather rot in prison than return to service.

The stand against Karepin was not without its costs. More than ever, young Fyodor cracked under the physical and emotional stress. His poverty, together with a careless diet, sleepless nights, and an irregular lifestyle, exacerbated old ills and triggered new ones. The young Fyodor was also at odds with other kith and kin. Over matters of inheritance and other sundries, Aunt Alexandra saw him as a brat; his sister Varvara, as a monster; and his siblings, as a spendthrift, a lazybones, and most interestingly, a womanizer. Depression, bipolarism, and fears of strokes and fits consumed young Fyodor's being. Even darker demons haunted him. The sight of a funeral procession triggered such an attack of nerves that he lost consciousness. Worse yet, perhaps, was his alleged confession of the rape of a ten-year-old child.

In truth, the trials and travails of young Fyodor were disguised blessings in that they steeled him in what he himself acknowledged as his idée fixe to become a writer. Terrified of failure, of starvation and cold, and of the beckoning Neva, the river that sliced St. Petersburg in two, he assumed a stance of do-or-die. Once again, if windows closed, he opened doors. The lad read voraciously. He enlisted brother Mikhail and his wife, Emilia, for assistance and support. He saw artistic blessings as material boons. Greedily, the lad embraced fortune and fame: the literary commercialism of Russian literature in the late 1830s and early 1840s. With hanging tongue, he, too, would be a Pushkin who commanded ten rubles for a line of poetry, a Gogol who demanded a thousand rubles for a page of prose. Immediately, instinctively, the young Fyodor became an entrepreneur. He studied competitors, contacted editors and publishers, and approached booksellers and censors. His letters to Mikhail were model business plans, replete with projected profits and "can't-fail" bottom lines. Unlike so many of his heroes, early and mature, he harnessed ideas to action. The young Fyodor translated Balzac's *Eugénie Grandet*. He proposed Russian-language editions of Sue's *Mathilde*, Sand's *The Last Dandini*, and all of Schiller's plays. Most importantly, perhaps, he was delighting in his first novel, *Poor Folk*. From all accounts, the writing came easily. Unlike the difficulties of his later works, the young Fyodor did not complain of writer's block or that his characters were fighting him along the way. There were harried moments, true; but his misery loved the company he believed he kept. If Pushkin and Gogol revised their works umpteen times, so could he.

Understandably, the young Fyodor brooded over the shortcomings of his first work, as well as the reception of *Poor Folk* among readers and reviewers. He also had little idea about how to bring the work to the public, but he need not have worried. The stars aligned again. If the young Dostoevsky was happy over *Poor Folk*, others were ecstatic. An enthusiastic Grigorovich took the work to Nikolai Nekrasov, a poet-publisher in his own right who had recently electrified the Russian literary world with *The Physiology of Petersburg*, a collection of prose and verse on everyday people. Nekrasov, realizing that he had a hit on his hands, demanded that he and Grigorovich congratulate the author immediately. For once, a legend of Russian culture is true. At four in the morning, a sleepy and stunned young Dostoevsky was awakened by two men—one his roommate, the other a complete stranger—who embraced him in rapture and tears.

The fun was only beginning. It was to be Dostoevsky's lot in life that, good or bad, when it rained, it poured. On the following day, Nekrasov took *Poor Folk* to the great critic Vissarion Belinsky, proclaiming—again now famously—that a new Gogol had arisen. Belinsky's skepticism—"You find Gogols springing up like mushrooms" was his now equally well-known reply—soon dissipated. The young Dostoevsky, the great critic believed, was exactly what the national literary expression needed if Russia was going to break from its centuries-old backwardness and to be a Western liberal-democratic state. It did not matter that like its equally famed counterpart, Gogol's *Overcoat*, Dostoevsky's *Poor Folk* was misunderstood by Belinsky as a sociopolitical exposé of people at the mercy of fate. Indeed, more than a century would pass before readers and reviewers, with a more accurate understanding of the writer and his fiction, would see that in *Poor Folk* he was doing precisely the opposite. His first hero and heroine are not the butts of life's jokes; rather, they have no one but themselves to blame for their unhappiness. Posing as "humiliated and injured," they engage in struggles of dominance and control, hurting themselves and others in the process. However faulty his reception of *Poor Folk*, though, Belinsky believed he had what he needed. For him, the maker-breaker of Russian writers, a star, even a savior, was born.

The young Fyodor became an overnight sensation. Everyone in the Russian literary world wanted to meet the new wunderkind, to attend readings of *Poor Folk* at literary soirées, and to read the work in Nekrasov's *Petersburg Miscellany*, his second successful anthology of Russian and Western poetry and prose. The kudos over *Poor Folk* and its writer were often so lavish that the young Fyodor began to believe the hype. He was an "extraordinary man" in literature and life. As he saw it, everyone loved him. They hung on his every word; they applauded his every thought; they marveled at his every deed. They chased after him with projects; they threw money at his feet. Even women were a viable, if belated, option, the new star-stud enjoying a flirtation with Avdotya Panaeva, vivacious hostess of the Russian literary world, on one hand; and on the other, with a host of costly "Minushkas, Klarushkas, Mariannas" for more adult fare.

Like all the self-styled supermen (and women) of his major fiction, the young Fyodor paid a high cost for his success. He was lonely at the top. The heir apparent to the Russian literary throne also brooded over sustained momentum, worrying whether he could write another work as successful as the first. Initial attempts at *The Double*, his second work, seemed less than promising. His difficulties with the piece brought him to see himself as Golyadkin, the tortured hero of the piece, a schizophrenic loser-fraud who finds peace only in an asylum. Only five months after his discovery in the Russian literary world, the young Dostoevsky was bordering on self-parody. Further, in his growing duality—his belief that in art as well as in life, he was both lord and louse—the young Dostoevsky was sowing the seeds for his own destruction; he was alienating readers and reviewers, as well as setting the stage for catastrophe, a decade-long stay in exile in Siberia.

There were other problems. Belinsky, seeking to be a father-mentor to the boy, overstepped boundaries. In well-meaning but overarching enthusiasm, he sought not only to instill in the young Fyodor his own views on literature and life but also to manage the lad's personal and professional affairs, complete with censures of his disorderly existence. Nekrasov cooled quickly to the young Fyodor because of mutual mistrust as well as the youth's demands for profits. Censors threatened to cut *Poor Folk* to ribbons, even to cancel its publication altogether. Most seriously, perhaps, and as a further omen of trouble to come, Russian litterati were less than taken with the young Fyodor in person. If, like the messiah-obsessed characters of Dostoevsky's mature writing, they were expecting a savior-god, they were shocked to encounter someone far less. The young Fyodor, small and sickly, sensitive and shy, with darting eyes and chewed lips, could not have made a worse first impression. Even more damaging were moments when the lad became arrogant and argumentative, convinced of his greatness and superiority, particularly with writers his own age.

Like any man-god and his disciples, the young Fyodor was given a long leash. Initially he was greeted with bemused tolerance, with good-natured teasing and jibes. In still another sign of storms on the horizon, though, the lad came to annoy, even anger local litterati by his unwillingness to join them personally and professionally. As was the case throughout his early years, he preferred to be alone, to think his own thoughts, to go his own way. The lad held even Belinsky at arm's length. Rumors—fact and fiction—about the "little idol" started to fly, including a false claim, enduring to Dosteovsky's final days, that he was demanding that Nekrasov, in the *Petersburg Miscellany*, distinguish *Poor Folk* from the other selections in the work with a special font and a black or gold border.

The young Dostoevsky, though, did not lose his deific status. That would come later. For readers and reviewers in 1845, Russian literature was too fragile and precious a commodity to doubt an individual who, they hoped, would follow the path forged by Pushkin, Lermontov, and Gogol. It is one of the greatest ironies in the national written expression that the fans of young Fyodor would not be deceived in their expectations; but that they would have to wait almost twenty years before the apple of their literary eye would take root, grow, and flower-tower in both Russian and world fiction. Indeed, what they were seeing in the young Fyodor was only the beginning of a life and literature that would have momentous consequences not only for their time but for years to come. Anything else was beyond their and their idol's wildest imagination.

PART ONE

All in the Family

MIKHAIL ANDREEVICH DOSTOEVSKY

One of the most controversial aspects of Dostoevsky's early years is his father, Mikhail Andreevich Dostoevsky. Courtesy of Dostoevsky's daughter, Lyubov; his first biographer, Orest Miller; Dostoevskian scholars Konstantin Mochulsky and Joseph Frank; and most notably (and notoriously) Sigmund Freud, Mikhail Andreevich has long been seen as Fyodor Karamazov come to life: a dark and evil figure whom the young Dostoevsky, supposedly from oedipal motives, wanted out of his life, if not dead.[1] Although such a portrait of Mikhail Andreevich has been discounted by most scholars, suspicions and misgivings about the man remain. For his famous son, father Mikhail is still deemed a bane, not a boon.

The evidence is that Mikhail Andreevich was not a saint but also that he was not a sinner. Indeed, he was quite unlike the steady stream of failed fathers and other sadomasochistic losers, dreamers, and perverts that people Dostoevsky's early and mature fiction. Rather, Mikhail Andreevich was a loving husband and devoted father who, though beleaguered and eventually defeated by life, did everything he could to ensure that his children would have a better existence than he.

From his earliest years, Mikhail Andreevich made his own way in the world. Energetic and determined, he triumphed over all obstacles. Resisting familial pressures to enter the priesthood, the fifteen-year-old Mikhail left Kamenets-Podolsk in western Ukraine for Moscow. Six years later, in 1809, he entered the medical school there. During Napoleon's invasion of Russia, Mikhail served as a staff physician in the military, working in a field hospital at the Battle of Borodino, the largest and bloodiest single-day action in the French assault on the homeland. (Of the 250,000 troops in the struggle, at least 70,000 became casualties.) Two days before Napoleon entered Moscow, Mikhail moved more than 30,000 wounded men to safety. Later, he helped to stem a typhoid epidemic in the provinces.

Steadily, Mikhail climbed the ladder of success. In 1813, he gained official status as a doctor. Five years later, he became the chief medical director of the Military Hospital in Moscow; and in 1821, he was named junior house surgeon at the already noted Mariinsky Hospital for the Poor.

On January 14, 1819, Mikhail Dostoevsky married Maria Nechaeva, the daughter of a well-to-do Muscovite merchant-manufacturer who had lost most of his fortune in the 1812 evacuation of Moscow. (The story goes that the family, fleeing the city, lost all their money in a river crossing.) Mikhail was thirty years old; she was nineteen. Most likely, the union was a matter of convenience, Maria being married off to the first available suitor.

Unlike the tortured marriages in Dostoevsky's fiction, the union between Mikhail and Maria was founded on enduring love and respect. He was the model husband; she, the dutiful wife. In Maria, Mikhail found what the writer could not achieve in his heroines—a woman whose head may have been in the clouds but whose feet were planted firmly on earth. From Maria, Mikhail knew unconditional love, staunch applause, and enduring patience and forgiveness. From her, Mikhail also had the comforting knowledge that whatever the challenge or obstacle, she and God (in that order) would see him through.

He responded in kind. Letters between the two read like an impassioned romance. They are filled with concerns over health, wishes to know even trifles, and most importantly, affirmations of love to the grave and beyond.

With Maria at his side, Mikhail moved higher in life. On April 2, 1825, he was named holder of the order of St. Anne of the third rank. Other honors followed. In January 1829, Mikhail was granted the order of St. Vladimir of the fourth rank; and on April 21, 1832, the order of St. Anne of the second rank. Most importantly, on April 7, 1827, Mikhail became a Collegiate Assessor, thereby investing him and his offspring with noble status. Finally, on April 18, 1837, Mikhail was inducted into the ranks of senior external councilors.

The high expectations Mikhail had for himself he extended to his family, relatives, peasants, and everyone else in his purview. Under his watchful eye, everyone toed the line. Infractions met immediate responses. Mikhail once slapped Maria's brother in the face for rudeness to the women in a confrontation over the man's affair with a maid.

The goodwill and cheer Mikhail enjoyed from Maria he also encountered with his children. Young Fyodor was a case in point. From his earliest years to his final days, the lad had only love and respect for the man. The collective wish of Dmitri, Ivan, and Alexei Karamazov for the death of father Fyodor, be it in oedipal competition or socially engineered anger at evil, was for the writer the stuff of fiction. Untrue also are claims by memoirists that Maria, Alyona Kryukova, and others shielded the young Fyodor and his siblings from Mikhail's wrath. Rather, alone or with others, privately in letters or publicly in gatherings, the young Fyodor honored Mikhail as the paterfamilias; wished him happiness and health; grieved over his sorrows; and thanked him for his care and concern, sacrifice and support. True, the kudos and gratitude were often template-like: formal, routine, cloying, and as Frank notes, "somewhat *exalté*."[2] Beyond a doubt, though, *fils* was quite comfortable with *père*. Indeed, son was sufficiently open and trusting with father to pour forth ramblings about life, to vent anger at obstacles, injustices, and crises, and, most poignantly, to beat his breast for dashing the man's hopes for him. Any breakdowns between the two rested with young Fyodor alone, son being too busy or preoccupied to write to father; or when he did, filling his missives to the man with endless requests for money and sundries, as well as describing the deprivations he suffered from lack thereof. Adding to the gap between the two was what young Fyodor pinpointed as Mikhail's key weakness: his inability or unwillingness to move with the times, to remain in "blissful ignorance" of everything about him.

With Maria and his children, Mikhail gave as good as he got. He was always teaching his children. Cracked pavements were lessons in geometry. Long walks and talks were common, if not everyday, occurrences. Just as Maria insisted that Mikhail tell her the trivia of his life, so did he demand that his brood tell him theirs. Mikhail also put his money where his mouth was. Claims by memoirists that Mikhail was miserly with his family are false. For Maria and his children, he did whatever he could to keep his family safe and sound.

Periodically, most often when he was alone, Mikhail did go off the deep end. He could be "gloomy, nervous, and suspicious." Things, major and minor, general and specific, real and imagined, lacerated his soul with anger, frustration, and fear. Periodic depression and premonitions of disaster rose to the fore in the alleged injustice of God, as well as in loneliness, finances, bad weather, the indifference of colleagues, the success of others, even the inability of Fyodor and Mikhail to learn Latin. Such lumps and bumps caused the man to curse his life, to upbraid his household, to withdraw into his shell, even, unjustly, to accuse his pregnant wife of hiding money and of having an affair. (He was forgiven on both counts.)

By and large, though, Mikhail's distress was not unlike that of any man worrying about family and future amid mounting bills, growing children, and other challenges and vicissitudes of life. Further, outbursts were frequent but fleeting, ending in renewed avowals of loyalty and love.[3]

The loss of Maria in their twentieth year of marriage dealt the forty-eight-year-old Mikhail a blow from which he never recovered. Initially, he sought refuge in work. Soon, though, he abandoned the strict discipline he had set for himself and others. Less than four months after Maria's death, Mikhail retired from state service and withdrew into the home at Darovoe. There he moaned, groaned, and even beat his head against the wall. Like Svidrigailov and Marfa Petrovna in *Crime and Punishment*, he even conversed with the dead Maria. Even more seriously, perhaps, Mikhail began to abuse alcohol and took up with a sixteen-year-old servant named Katerina, possibly even giving her a son.

The grief and suffering that consumed Mikhail after Maria's death he did not inflict upon his sons. Indeed, it was the strongest measure not only of the man's belief in education but also of his determination that Fyodor and Mikhail find their path in life that he did not keep the two at home. Although Mikhail knew that he was signing his death warrant, he took his sons to St. Petersburg to continue their schooling there. (He never saw them again.) As already noted, his choice of vocation for his two boys could not have been more misguided. On one hand, it can be argued that the father did not know his sons well. In no way could or would Fyodor and Mikhail become officers or engineers. On the other hand, Mikhail knew that the two, whatever their aesthetic or romantic bents, had to live in a cold and cruel world, and that service to the state offered a stable and secure existence. Fyodor and Mikhail would not be like him, a doctor merely getting by; rather, they would become the gentlemen he himself had so wanted to be.

Again, Mikhail opened his pockets. Uncomplainingly, he paid the tuition, fees, and sundries for Fyodor and Mikhail to attend the school of Koronad Kostamarov, as well as for advanced study in St. Petersburg and Tallinn. Although Mikhail was himself often short of funds, he never denied Fyodor and Mikhail in their requests. The tie was just not material. As he had done with the two under his roof, Mikhail insisted on knowing everything about Fyodor and Mikhail away from home— their studies, their teachers, their friends, "even the most trifling things." Like any good parent, Mikhail was delighted when he heard from his boys and panicked when he did not. He, too, worried if his boys would finish school on time, if at all.

Even more revealing, perhaps: the tight leash on the boys when they were under his wing Mikhail loosened considerably once they had left the nest. Rarely did Mikhail intervene in Fyodor's and Mikhail's lives other than to offer counsel and support. He did for them whatever he could; beyond that, he consigned them to the Almighty. With pounding heart, he read about their unhappiness with school, self, and humankind. With gritted teeth he read about their love for literature and the arts, their own desires and hopes. Again, though, his stance was laissez-faire. After all, Mikhail knew he had no one to blame for the predicament. He was the one who had introduced to his sons the very things they wished to pursue. "How can I thank you for the formation you gave me!" Mikhail wrote to his father, "How sweet and joyful it is to become lost in thought over Shakespeare, Schiller, and Goethe!"

If the past augurs the future, it would seem unlikely that Mikhail, if he had lived, would have engaged in, as Frank asserts, a "terrible and heartbreaking clash of wills"[4] with young Fyodor over his wish to be a writer. For one thing, neither father nor son was violent emotionally. For another, Mikhail would have done what he always did with his two oldest children: he would have objected politely but then relented, consigning his boy to divine providence, believing that eventually young Fyodor would return to his senses and service.

Mikhail's shortcomings after Maria's death, though, were hardly cause for what still remains as another lingering trope of his vita: his alleged murder by his peasants. Although family and friends attest to the violent end of the man, evidence for their claims is again lacking. The very people who charge foul play—brother Andrei is a key example—also note the warm and close ties between Mikhail and his serfs. The driver David Saviliev, one of the alleged conspirators in the murder, was a personal favorite. The same financial generosity that Mikhail showed his sons he extended to his peasants. When the Dostoevskys lost their estate to fire in 1832, Mikhail loaned money to the locals to rebuild their homes, but forwent reimbursement. (Earlier, Maria had also planned a series of canals to bring water for their livestock.) Letters by Maria note that the peasants at Darovoe were alive and well, that they welcomed arrivals of the family in joyful and tender ways, and that when Mikhail was in Moscow, they sent to him kind wishes and regards. Incidents of master against man—Mikhail wishing to scold a housemaid or flog a serf as examples to others—were rare. Nowhere also is there evidence for Frank's claim as to the unbearable exactions and severity of Dr. Dostoevsky, that he made the hapless peasants pay dearly for his own grief and desolation.[5] Also, in the years immediately prior to his death, Mikhail had been in poor health. Rheumatism, poor vision, and tremors in his hands had forced his retirement six months after Maria's death. Often confined to his bed, Mikhail was so weak that he dictated letters to his daughter. Old demons also reclaimed him, mounting debts, deprivations, and bad harvests driving him to the brink.

It should also be noted that accounts of the alleged murder of Mikhail Dostoevsky were the stuff not only of Soviet researchers in the 1920s who, with Marxist sentiment, stressed class struggles of rich and poor; but also by peasants who, not without relish, related events as they supposedly occurred nearly a century later. Facts yielded to fiction. Lurid accounts of Mikhail's cruelties to the serfs (and to Maria who interceded on their behalf) made for great press but fail to find resonance with anyone who knew the man personally. Even more open to question are the events of the alleged murder: a gang-up of serfs who rushed to kill the master after he had voiced anger over their work. Contradictions abound. Some peasants say the slaying was spur of the moment; others that it was the result of a long-standing plan. They also disagree on the number of peasants involved, from a select few to as many as twenty; the place of the incident, on the estate or on a road between Darovoe and another family estate, Cheremoshnya; and the method for the murder—did the assailants beat Mikhail to death, or exert pressure on his bladder, or suffocate the man with a pillow or by pouring spirits down his throat?

Even the reason for homicide remains unclear: an unspecified act of revenge for Mikhail's alleged tryst with the daughter of one of the group has also been claimed as a motive for the crime. It is also doubtful that, whatever their feelings for Mikhail and even if they had wished for their master's demise, peasants would have risked exile in Siberia not only for themselves but for all the other males in the village as well. Also countering charges of murder were the reports by investigators into the crime. Claims by the family and others of a cover-up are lacking. Most certainly, Mikhail's supposed attackers lacked the funds to bribe doctors and officials. Nor, given the times, could they hope to keep a code of silence over the alleged deed. After an exhaustive inquiry, also, medical and judicial officials found no evidence of foul play. Given Mikhail's failing health, their conclusion that the man had died of a stroke was the only plausible explanation for his passing.

With Mikhail's death, though, there is this disturbing fact. Nowhere is there any evidence of young Fyodor's reaction to the passing of his father. If he experienced, as Frank asserts, a "shock of guilt and remorse," a "frenzy of self-accusation," and with a nod to Freud, a "burden of parricidal guilt"[6] over Mikhail's death, he kept it to himself.[7] His letters to his brother and others show a distressing business-as-usual tone, as if Mikhail had not died at all.

Throughout his life, though, and as already noted, the great writer recalled his father with reverence and respect, if not love. For him, Mikhail represented the best of his generation. For him also, his father was the wellspring of the faith, morals, and values that sustained the young Fyodor in his early years, and that would gush forth to replenish his parched soul later in literature and life.

1803

1803 and after.
Andrei Dostoevsky, from his memoirs.[8]

> My grandfather wanted his son and my father to follow in his footsteps, i.e., to become a priest.[9] But Father did not feel called to such a profession. So with the blessing of his mother . . . he left for Moscow, where he enrolled at the Moscow Medical-Surgical Academy.[10]

1803 and after.
Lyubov Dostoevskaya, from her memoirs.

> My grandfather, Mikhail Andreevich Dostoevsky, was his own man. . . . He never spoke about his family and never answered questions about his origins.[11]

At age fifty, my grandfather was seemingly conscious-stricken for having abandoned his home. In a newspaper he published an advertisement requesting that his father and brothers furnish information about themselves. But no one answered. Probably, his parents were already dead.[12] The Dostoevskys do not live very long lives.

[Imagine] the remarkable energy of this fifteen-year-old boy who came to a strange city, and who, without money or patronage, attained an advanced education, acquired a good position in Moscow, put seven children on their feet, furnished three daughters with dowries, and gave a thorough education to his four sons. Rightfully proud, my grandfather set himself up as an example to his children.

1812

Circa 1812 and after.
Lyubov Dostoevskaya, from her memoirs.

> My grandfather Mikhail entered military service as a staff physician and took part in the campaign of 1812.[13] . . . Soon thereafter he was named chief doctor of a large state hospital in Moscow. By that time he had married Maria Nechaeva, a young woman from Moscow. She brought a small inheritance to her husband.

1820

After 1820.
Fyodor Dostoevsky, from an 1876 letter to Andrei Dostoevsky.

> Despite their faults and failings, both our father and mother believed in . . . indispensable and noble striving to be *better people* (in the literal, most *elevated* sense of this word).

After 1820.
Fyodor Dostoevsky, from *A Writer's Diary*.

> As far back as I can recall, I remember the love shown to me by my parents.

After 1820.
Andrei Dostoevsky, from his memoirs.

> Toward the end of the 1870s . . . I was talking with my brother Fyodor . . . and mentioned Father. Suddenly, he came alive, grabbed me by the hand . . . such was

his habit when he spoke from the soul . . . and said passionately: "Yes, brother, you know what remarkable people our parents were . . . and how at this moment, they would be so forward-looking. . . . Such family people, such a father . . . you could not find anyone like them!"

After 1820.
Andrei Dostoevsky, from his memoirs.

Our parents, especially Mama, were very religious. Without fail, we went to Mass every Sunday and major holiday, and, on evenings before, to vespers and matins. Such visits were quite agreeable since our church was very large and good.

After 1820.
Lyubov Dostoevskaya, from her memoirs.

My grandfather's faith had little in common with the religion of Russian intellectuals: mystical and hysterical, lamenting and lachrymose.

After 1820.
Orest Miller, from his biography of Dostoevsky.

According to relatives, Mikhail Andreevich was gloomy, nervous, and suspicious.

After 1820.
Andrei Dostoevsky, from his memoirs.

I am convinced fully that whoever reads my father's letters would not call him *gloomy, nervous, and suspicious* as claimed by O. F. Miller . . . allegedly from relatives. Our father had his faults, but he was not gloomy or suspicious, *a misanthrope*. Just the opposite, with his family, he was always cordial and sometimes merry.

After 1820.
Andrei Andreevich Dostoevsky, from a 1924 letter.

[Dostoevsky's mother] was a woman in the highest sense: kind, religious, but practical in running a home. She was also gifted musically (the guitar).

After 1820.
Andrei Dostoevsky, from his memoirs.

Auntie Aleksandra Fyodorovna Kumanina . . . was only four years older than Mama but . . . Mama saw her as a mother more than a sister. She loved and respected Auntie to an extreme, a devotion that she instilled in all of us. Auntie Alexandra was godmother to all us children.

As a child I loved this woman in an unconscious way, and . . . when I became older, I worshiped her. I marveled at her truly great and practical mind. I respected and loved her like a mother![14]

1821

October 30, 1821.
From the records of the Spiritual Consistory of Moscow.

In the home . . . of the staff physician Mikhail Andreevich Dostoevsky . . . has been born a child—a son, Fyodor.[15]

After October 1821.
Lyubov Dostoevskaya, from her memoirs.

My father had brown and genuinely Ukrainian eyes from his father, and a kind smile from his mother.[16]

1822

Circa 1822 and after.
Andrei Dostoevsky, from his memoirs.

Our domestic staff included . . . the driver David Saveliev . . . father's personal servant. Beyond his four horses, David knew nothing else and had no other tasks. But with so many trips, he had enough work to do. David had been a serf even before father's marriage and lived with us until the day papa died. . . . Papa especially loved and respected David over all the other household serfs.[17]

Circa 1822 and after.
Andrei Dostoevsky, from his memoirs.

The laundress Vasilisa . . . went into hiding or, more simply, ran away. My parents were sensitive to such flights . . . since they underscored the meager existence of our peasants who saw our life as good. . . . Such escapes were common when peasants were acquired without land, and were explained as people who missed their homes.

December 1822 and after.
Andrei Dostoevsky, from his memoirs.

> Our nurse, Alyona Frolovna [Kryukova] ... [was] a truly remarkable individual ... [whom] my parents respected ... and saw a member of the family.[18] Alyona Frolovna was ... a petty-bourgeois woman from Moscow who was very proud of her background. ... At the time, she was about fifty years old. She was rather tall and very fat: her stomach fell almost to her knees. She ate a great deal, but only twice a day.
>
> Alyona Frolovna ... managed the pantry. ... We all called her Nanny and addressed her with the familiar "you."[19] ... Father and Mother called her Alyona Frolovna, and she ... addressed them as Mikhail Andreevich and Maria Fyodorovna. (All the other serfs called them "Master" and "Mistress.") ...
>
> A spinster, Alyona Frolovna called herself "a bride of Christ." ... She often complained that [in the household] she heard conversations which, as an old maid, she found indecent to hear. My parents smiled when they heard such laments, but they were also very pleased to learn about such matters. ...
>
> Alyona Frolovna did not keep strict fasts ... saying that God would not judge her. She also thought it a great sin to eat something without bread. ... "First take a bite of bread," she often said, "and then put the other food into your mouth ... that's how God ordered such things!" ...
>
> Alyona Frolovna also used snuff ... which she bought weekly ... from a very unattractive and slovenly individual ... whom Papa jokingly called "Frolovna's fiancé."
>
> "Phooey! God forgive us!" she replied indignantly. "My fiancé is Christ, the heavenly king, not some tobacco-man!"

December 1822 and after.
Fyodor Dostoevsky, from *A Writer's Diary*.

> [Alyona Frolovna] raised us children. She was ... a bright and merry character who told us the most wonderful stories!

December 1822 and after.
Andrei Dostoevsky, from his memoirs.

> From time to time ... our nurse [Alyona Fyodorovna] cried out in her sleep ... in a kind of frenzied wail. My father had ... to bring her back to consciousness by force.
>
> On the next day he asked: "What happened to you, Frolovna?"
>
> She replied: "Oh, Mikhail Andreevich, a house-sprite—so terrible-looking, with horns—was choking me." ...

"You should eat less at dinner," papa said.

"I try to follow your advice, kind sir," she replied, "but then I dream about gypsies."

December 1822 and after.
Anna Dostoevskaya, from her memoirs.

> Gratefully, Dostoevsky often recalled his nurse, Alyona Frolovna, and talked about her to his children.

December 1822 and after.
Anna Dostoevskaya, from her notebook.

> It was the nurse, Alyona Frolovna, who, in her love for the children, concealed their wrongdoing from their father and defended them from his outbursts.

1823

1823.
Anna Dostoevskaya, from her memoirs.

> Fyodor Mikhailovich recalled that when he was two years old, he was taken by his mother to receive communion at the village church, and that a dove flew in one window and out the other.[20]

1824

Circa 1824.
Fyodor Dostoevsky, from his autobiography.

> [As a child] I was quick, lively, and sharp. I was also curious, persistently inquisitive, but also quite tiresome—and gifted. About the age of three, I took it in my head to make up fairy tales which were earnest and terrible, but with a touch of humor. I remember them to this day.

Circa 1824.
Orest Miller, from his biography of Dostoevsky.

> When Fyodor Mikhailovich . . . was about three years old, his nurse brought him out to guests in the living room, forced him on his knees before the icons, and,

as always was the case before bedtime, made him recite this prayer: "Oh Lord, all my hopes I place on you. Mother of God, save and protect me." Such a display the guests enjoyed very much . . . remarking: "Oh, what an intelligent little boy he is!"

Fyodor Mikhailovich said this prayer throughout his life, and repeated it to his children at their bedtime.

Mid-late 1820s.
Fyodor Dostoevky, from *A Writer's Diary*.

In my childhood, I listened to stories long before I learned to read. . . . I loved tales about robbers and pirates.

Mid-late 1820s.
Andrei Dostoevsky, from his memoirs.

Alyona Frolovna often informed mother: "The wet-nurse Lukeria has come." We children rushed into the living room, almost clapping our hands in joy. . . . When twilight came . . . we waited in the dark unlit hall. The wet-nurse entered, sat us on chairs . . . and began to tell stories. Our delight lasted for some three or four hours, the stories being told in a whisper so as not to disturb our parents. Indeed, the stillness was such that we could hear the scratching of father's pen.

And what stories did we hear! . . . There were tales about the Firebird, Alyosha Popovich, Bluebeard, and many others.[21] . . . Some were terrible to listen to.

Mid-late 1820s.
Orest Miller, from his biography of Dostoevsky.

The stories that Fyodor Mikhailovich heard as a child included ones taken from *One Thousand and One Nights*.[22] . . .

But that these stories were often told in a dark room explains why, as a child, Dostoevsky was afraid of the dark (as he himself said).

Mid-late 1820s.
Andrei Dostoevsky, from his memoirs.

Every Easter . . . My brothers and I visited our great-uncle . . . Vasili Mikhailovich Kotelnitsky.[23] . . . He was childless, with his own home. . . . During holidays and Shrovetide, we all came to his house for the entire day. Since all the *balagany*[24] were near his home, he took us to all the shows there. . . . We saw clowns, actors, weight lifters, and Petrushkas.²⁵ . . . For a long time, we imitated the actors and staged our own comedies.

Mid-late 1820s.
Andrei Dostoevsky, from his memoirs.

> In summer we went to the Troitsky Lavra²⁶ . . . [where] for two days, we attended all the services and bought toys for children.

Mid-late 1820s.
Fyodor Dostoevsky, from an 1870 letter to Apollon Maikov.

> I am an expert in this world. I have known the Russian monastery since childhood.

1825

1825.
Orest Miller, from his biography of Dostoevsky.

> Even as a four-year-old youth, he was seated behind a book and told: "Study!" But outside . . . the huge and shady garden at the hospital beckoned so sweetly. He told me that when his father went out on visits, his mother allowed him and his siblings to run about freely.

1826

Circa 1826 and after.
Andrei Dostoevsky, from his memoirs.

> Attached to the hospital was a large and beautiful garden . . . [that] was our haven in summertime. There, in well-ordered fashion, we took walks with our nurse, sitting on benches and spending entire hours there. . . . We were allowed to play only on hobbyhorses; but it was strictly forbidden to play ball, especially with sticks . . . since such activities were seen as dangerous and unseemly.
>   Around the hospital . . . were no children our own age. . . . We had to be satisfied with the games among ourselves, something we found very boring.
>   One time we saw a runner . . . who ran for money . . . and in his mouth a handkerchief, soaked in some alcoholic substance. . . . For a long time after that, my

brother Fyodor . . . ran endlessly through the garden walkways, also with a handkerchief in his mouth.

Also in the hospital garden were patients dressed in coarse camel-brown robes. . . . On the sly, my brother Fyodor loved to talk with these individuals, especially if there were boys among them; but such activities were monitored severely. Father became extremely displeased if he heard about what my brother was doing.

Circa 1826 and after.
Anna Dostoevskaya, from her memoirs.

Fyodor Mikhailovich recalled his happy, serene childhood in a willing way. He always spoke of his mother with ardent affection. He especially loved his older brother Misha and his older sister Varenka. His younger brothers and sisters did not make a strong impression on him.

Circa 1826 and after.
Anna Dostoevskaya, from her notebook.

Mikhail and Fyodor had such a dark room . . . that they studied in a hall. . . . But as soon as father went out on visits, they put down their books and went to see their mother . . . in the living room. There the three of them gathered around a round table. The two read something aloud while their mother worked.

Circa 1826 and after.
Stepan Yanovsky, from an 1884 letter to Anna Dostoevskaya.

It was precisely in childhood that something gloomy and burdensome seized hold of Fyodor Mikhailovich.

1828

Circa 1828.
Andrei Dostoevsky, from his memoirs.

At that time Misha [Mikhail] was eight and brother Fyodor was seven.[27] . . . They were extremely close. . . . In conversations, my older brother Mikhail was less sharp, energetic, and passionate than my brother Fyodor who . . . was like genuine fire, as my parents used to say.

February 1, 1828, and after.
Andrei Dostoevsky, from his memoirs.

> One time we saw a play, titled *Jocko, or the Monkey of Brazil*.[28] I do not recall the content of the piece, but I do remember that the artist who played the monkey, was also an expert tightrope-walker. For a long time my brother Fyodor raved about him and tried to imitate him.

June 28, 1828.
Lyubov Dostoevskaya, from her memoirs.

> Several years after the birth of his sons, my grandfather Mikhail enrolled together with them in the books of the Moscow Hereditary Gentry.

After June 1828.
Andrei Dostoevsky, from his memoirs.

> [Our family] belonged to a very ancient noble Lithuanian lineage that existed before 1600 . . . [but my father] registered himself as a nobleman . . . only after he obtained the rank of Collegiate Assessor (which conferred the status of hereditary nobleman).
>
> Whenever anyone asked my father why he never tried to prove legally his ancient noble origins, he replied with a smile that he did not belong to the race of geese who had saved Rome.[29] But he also had not done so because of the expense.

1829

Before 1829.
Fyodor Dostoevsky, from *Winter Notes on Summer Impressions*.

> During the long winter nights, and still unable to read, I opened my mouth in ecstasy and horror when, before bedtime, my parents read the novels of Radcliffe, after which I wandered off as if in a feverish dream.[30]

Circa 1829.
Fyodor Dostoevsky, from an 1879 letter to Anna Dostoevskaya.

> I was laughed at in my childhood because I lagged behind my brother in reading.

1829.
Fyodor Dostoevsky, from an 1861 letter to Yakov Polonsky.

> From earliest childhood I dreamed of going to Italy. Already with the novels of Radcliffe, which I read already at eight years of age, all kinds of Alfonsas, Katarinas, and Lucias entered into my head. I still rave over all those Don Pedros and Doña Claras.[31]

1829.
Anna Dostoevskaya, from her memoirs.

> [When Dostoevsky wrote in *The Brothers Karamazov*]: "The first time something spiritual entered into me was when I was eight years old," he was talking from personal memory.

1830

Circa 1830 and after.
Lyubov Dostoevskaya, from her memoirs.

> My grandfather had a European view of formation . . . [and had] a passion for French. He often talked to his wife in French and taught his children to converse in this tongue. . . .
>
> His eldest sons . . . sought to please their father by memorizing French poems and declaiming them in front of the family. . . . Sometimes there were competitions in which my father and his brother also recited Russian poems, and my parents decided who was the better orator.

Circa 1830 and after.
Andrei Dostoevsky, from his memoirs.

> Whenever Uncle [Mikhail Fyodorovich Nechaev] visited our home, there was always a small domestic concert. After dinner, Mama and Uncle played their guitars . . . first serious things, next mournful melodies, and finally, happy songs to which Uncle sometimes sang. . . . It was always delightful.
>
> Papa was always very cordial to Uncle, but he also got angry with him, especially in later years when Uncle began to carouse and drank heavily, about which Papa often cautioned him.[32]

Circa 1830 and after.
Andrei Dostoevsky, from his memoirs.

> Visitors appeared at our house rarely. . . . On the rare occasions when my parents went out at night, our games at home became noisier and more varied. . . . But they were usually home by nine or ten.

Circa 1830 and after.
Andrei Dostoevsky, from his memoirs.

> We got up very early in the morning, at six o'clock. At eight o'clock Father went to the hospital or the wards. . . . The rooms were tidied, the stoves heated. . . . At nine o'clock Father came home but drove off at once for rounds. He had quite a large private practice. . . . He returned at twelve o'clock, and we had dinner . . . after which Father . . . lay on the couch in his robe for a nap. . . . During this time . . . people spoke little and in whispers. . . . This was the most boring time of the day . . . but it was also pleasant, since the entire family, excepting Papa, gathered in one room. . . .
>
> In the summertime . . . when Papa was resting . . . I had to get a branch from a linden tree . . . to chase away the flies. . . . Such an activity was a torment . . . since I was alone and had to sit motionless in one spot. And God forbid . . . if a fly bit the sleeper.
>
> At four o'clock we had tea, after which Father went to the hospital for a second time. Evenings we spent in the sitting room lit by two tallow candles. . . . We did not have lamps; Papa did not like them.
>
> If Father were not busy, he read aloud to us.
>
> During holidays, especially at Christmas, sometimes we all played cards. . . . My brother Fyodor, being intelligent and quick, always tried to pull fast ones and was caught many times.
>
> Punctually at nine o'clock the table was laid for supper, and after we had eaten, we knelt before the icon and, having said our prayers and bid our parents good night, we went to bed.

1831

Circa 1831.
Fyodor Dostoevsky, from *A Writer's Diary*.

> In our family, we knew the Gospels almost from early childhood.

Circa 1831.
Fyodor Dostoevsky, from *A Writer's Diary*.

> Who has not read the *Monthly Readings*?[33] ... When I was child, I heard these narratives even before I learned to read.

Circa 1831.
Fyodor Dostoevsky, from an 1875 letter to Anna Dostoevskaya.

> The Book of Job was one of the first works to make an impression on me. I was still almost a child at the time!

Circa 1831.
Andrei Dostoevsky, from his memoirs.

> The first book from which we learned to read ... was *Four Hundred Sacred Stories from the Old and New Testament*.[34] It had several rather poorly done lithographs: "The Creation of the World," "Adam and Eve in Paradise," and "The Flood." I remember that sometime in the 1870s, Fyodor Mikhailovich was talking about our childhood and mentioned that book. With delight, he told me that he had come across a copy of *Four Hundred Sacred Stories* and that he now regards it as a sacred object.

Circa 1831.
Fyodor Dostoevsky, from *A Writer's Diary*.

> I was hardly ten years old, but I already knew almost all the key episodes of Russian history from Karamzin,[35] which my father read to us aloud in the evening. Every visit to the Kremlin and the cathedrals in Moscow was a solemn occasion.

Circa 1831.
Fyodor Dostoevsky, from an 1870 letter to Nikolai Strakhov.

> I grew up on Karamzin. ... My mind and taste developed from his writings. I am indebted to him for the awakening of my soul, my first and noble intellectual delights.

Circa 1831.
Vladimir Kachenovsky, from his memoirs.[36]

> [In the hospital garden] where we played ... were two light-haired boys. ... They always led the games, their authority being readily apparent. ... They were Mikhail and Fyodor Dostoevsky.

Circa 1831.
Zinaida Trubetskaya, from a 1991 conversation with Sergei Belov.

> At a gathering . . . a guest suddenly posed this question: What was the greatest sin on earth? Some said patricide; others, murder for profit. . . .
> Dostoevsky who, silent and gloomy, was sitting in the corner. He paused . . . but suddenly, his face became transformed, his eyes glowed like coals. . . .
> "The most horrible sin," he said, "is to rape a child. . . . To take a life, that is a terrible crime, but to take away faith in the beauty of love, that is one even more terrible." . . .
> He then told a story from his childhood.
> "When I was a child, I lived . . . next to a hospital for poor people where my father was a doctor. There I played with a young girl . . . the daughter of a coachman or a cook. She was a fragile, graceful child about nine years old. Whenever she came across a flower . . . she always said: 'Come here and look. What a pretty, sweet flower!'"
> "A drunken scoundrel, though, raped this girl and she died, oozing forth blood. . . . I sent for my father who . . . came running, but it was too late. Throughout my life this memory has haunted me as the most terrible sin, one for which there is and can be no forgiveness . . . and because of this very crime, I executed Stavrogin in *Devils*."[37]

Circa August 1831 and after.
Fyodor Dostoevsky, from an 1861 article.

> We were raised on Schiller's works, he became part of us and affected our development in many ways.

Circa August 1831.
Fyodor Dostoevsky, from an 1880 letter to Nikolai Ozmidov.

> When I was about ten years old, I saw a production of Schiller's *The Robbers*[38] . . . and I assure you that the very strong impression that I took away from that work influenced my spiritual side in a very productive way.

August 1831.
Fyodor Dostoevsky, from *A Writer's Diary*.

> I was only nine years old. . . .
> It was one August at our home [at Darovoe].[39] . . . Summer was ending, and soon I would have to return to Moscow to spend the entire winter over boring French lessons. I was so sorry to leave the country. . . .

Some thirty paces away, a lone peasant was plowing in the clearing....

I knew almost all our peasants, but I did not know this one. I really did not care, since I was absorbed completely in my own affairs. I was busy, breaking off a branch from a walnut tree to hit some frogs . . . and to collect beetles and bugs, some of which were very stately. I loved lizards, small, quick, red-and-yellow, with their little black spots. I was afraid of snakes, but I met snakes far less often than lizards. . . . I also liked nothing better than the forest, with its mushrooms and wild berries, its insects and birds, its hedgehogs and squirrels. I also loved the damp aroma of rotting leaves. Even now, as I write this, I smell our birches in the country: such impressions stay with you for life.

Suddenly, amid the deep silence, I heard a clear and distinct shout: "There's a wolf!" I screamed, and beside myself with fear, crying at the top of my voice, I ran out into the field, straight into the plowing peasant.

It was our peasant Marey. . . . He was a man of about fifty, heavy-set, rather tall, with heavy streaks of gray in his bushy, dark-brown beard. I knew who he was, but up until now I never had had the chance to speak to him. Marey had stopped his little filly when he heard my cry, and when I, having rushed up to him, seized his plow with one hand and his sleeve with the other, he saw how terrified I was.

"A wolf is running about!" I cried, completely out of breath.

Instinctively, Marey jerked his head to look around, for an instant almost believing me.

"What wolf?"

"I heard a shout. . . . Someone just shouted 'Wolf!'" I babbled.

"What do you mean, lad? What wolf? You're just imagining things. Go on, what kind of wolf can there be around here!" he muttered, reassuring me.

But I still trembled and clung to his coat even more tightly; I must also have been very pale. He looked at me with an uneasy smile, evidently alarmed for me.

"You've had a real fright, you did!" he said, shaking his head. "Enough of that, my dear. And you, such a fine lad at that!"

He stretched out his hand and stroked my cheek suddenly.

"Enough of that, there's nothing to be afraid of, nothing at all. Christ be with you. Cross yourself, lad."

But I could not cross myself. The corners of my mouth were still trembling, and seemingly struck him in a particular way. Quietly, he stretched out a thick, earth-soiled finger with a black nail and touched it gently to my lips.

"Now, now," he smiled at me with a broad, almost maternal smile. "Lord, why such a fuss, there's nothing to be frightened about!"

At last I realized that there was no wolf and that I must have imagined someone crying "Wolf." Still, there had been such a clear and distinct shout. . . .

"Well, I'm off now," I said in an inquisitive way, looking at Marey shyly.

"Well, then get a move on, I will keep an eye on you. Can't let the wolf get you!" he added, still with a maternal smile. "Well, Christ be with you, off you go." He made the sign of the cross over me, and then over himself. I set off, looking over my shoulder almost every ten steps. Marey continued to stand with his little filly, looking after me and nodding every time I looked around. . . .

I had to confess that I was a bit ashamed at being so frightened, but I kept walking, still very much afraid of the wolf, until I had gone up the slope of the gully to the threshing barn. . . . Suddenly our dog Volchok came dashing out to meet me. With Volchok I felt assured totally, and I turned toward Marey for the last time. I could no longer make out his face, but I felt that he was still smiling kindly at me and nodding his head. I waved to him, and he returned my wave. . . .

"Giddy-up," came his distant shout once more, and his little filly once more started drawing the wooden plow. . . .

When I came home, I told no one of my "adventure." And what kind of adventure was it anyway? Very quickly I also forgot about Marey. On the rare occasions when I met him later, I never even struck up a conversation with him, either about the wolf or anything else. . . .

I recall the tender, maternal smile of the poor serf, the way he crossed me and shook his head when he said: "Well, you've had quite a scare, young man!" I especially remember his thick finger, soiled with dirt that he touched, quietly and with such tenderness, to my trembling lips. . . . If I had been his own son, he could not have looked at me with such love. Who had prompted him to do that? He was our serf, and I was his master's little boy. No one would have found out and rewarded his kindness toward me. Did he, perhaps, love children greatly? There are people like that. Our encounter had been solitary, in an empty field, and only God, perhaps, looking down, had seen what profound and noble feeling and what delicate, almost feminine tenderness could fill the heart of an otherwise coarse, bestially ignorant Russian serf who at the time did not expect or dream of his freedom.

August 1831 and after.
Andrei Dostoevsky, from his memoirs.

Marey . . . actually existed in life.[40] He was a handsome peasant, middle-aged, dark-haired with a solid black beard, streaked with grey. . . . He was also an expert on cattle. . . .

One time at a fair . . . Mama and Marey were looking at cows to buy. I was also there. Mama liked one cow very much for its beauty but unfortunately it had a small tail. Mother looked at it for a long time, but Marey . . . knew that it was unsuitable. When Mama wanted to buy the cow, Marey answered: "You can't be serious, mother of mine, Maria Fyodorovna. What kind of cow is that? Why, she ain't got nothin' to swat flies with!"

1832

April 12, 1832.
Fyodor Dostoevsky, from *A Writer's Diary*.

I was only nine years old[41] when I recall, on the third day of Easter week... our entire family... was sitting at our round table having tea.... Suddenly there appeared our house serf, Grigori Vasiliev, from the country....

"What's wrong?" my father cried out in alarm. "What is it?"

"The estate has burned down," Grigori Vasiliev announced in a deep voice.[42]

My father and mother were... not wealthy, and this was the present they had received for Easter! Everything had burned to the ground: the huts of the peasants, the granary, the barn—even the seed for the spring sowing, along with some cattle and one peasant, Arkhip [Saveliev].

At first, we imagined total ruin. We fell on our knees and began to pray; my mother wept. Suddenly our nurse, Alyona Frolovna, stepped forward.... For many years she had not drawn her salary from us. "I don't need it," she often said.... She whispered to Mama: "If you need some money, take what I have. I got no use for it."[43]

April 12, 1832.
Fyodor Dostoevsky, from his notes for *A Writer's Diary*.

Genuine saints—are they individual cases (the nurse Alyona Frolovna) or a general feature of the people?

April 12, 1832.
Andrei Dostoevsky, from his memoirs.

[At Darovoe] on Good Friday a peasant named Arkhip [Saveliev] took it into his head to roast a boar outside. The wind was terrible. His house caught fire and with it the entire estate.[44] ...

My parents understood that [the fire at Darovoe] was not a great misfortune, since our entire estate was rather ramshackle, and that it would have to be rebuilt sooner or later. Grigori returned home with a promise from our parents that they would share their last shirt with the peasants. I recall that several times papa told Grigori what to give to the people there.

Late April 1832.
Andrei Dostoevsky, from his memoirs.

> [When we arrived at Darovoe] we saw several charred columns ... and ancient linden trees ... also blackened by the fire.... Our old dog Zhuchka greeted us with loud wails, waving his tail.[45] ...
>
> Within the week, work [to rebuild the estate] gathered steam, and all the peasants rejoiced. To each head of a family, Mama gave 50 rubles. Such a sum was a lot of money at the time.

Late April 1832 and after.
Andrei Dostoevsky, from his memoirs.

> Every spring we moved to the village for the entire summer.[46] Because of work, father remained in Moscow, and came only for a few days, in the middle of the season....
>
> During our travels [to Darovoe] my brother Fyodor ... always chose to sit on the coachman's seat. There was not a single stop along the way when he did not jump down from the carriage and run about the surroundings.

Late April 1832 and after.
Lyubov Dostoevskaya, from her memoirs.

> The yearly pilgrimages to the family estate of Darovoe[47] ... sent my father into ecstasy because ... he loved horses greatly.

Late April 1832 and after.
Andrei Dostoevsky, from his memoirs.

> In the village ... was a large and shady grove of linden trees ... riddled with ravines ... and bordered by very thick birches.... My brother Fedya [Fyodor] so loved this place that everyone in the family called it Fedya's grove.[48] ... Unwillingly, Mother allowed us to play there, despite rumors that snakes and even wolves ran about there....
>
> It was my brother Fedya who, already an avid reader, acquainted us with the life of savages. Indeed, "playing savages" was our favorite game. After we had found a thick spot in the grove of linden trees, we built a hut from branches and straw ... and covered it with brush and leaves. Our hut was home to all kinds of wild tribes. We stripped naked and painted our bodies with tattoos. About our waists and heads were decorations made from leaves and dyed goose quills. With homemade bows and arrows, we pretended that we were attacking our surroundings ... taking as captives local peasant boys and girls and holding them for handsome ransoms in our hut.... My brother Fedya was always the leader of these tribes....

My brother Mikhail took part rarely in such games since they were not in keeping with his character; but at the time, he was beginning to draw . . . so he became our costumer and daubed us with colors.

Especially important to us was that no adults observed us as savages. . . .

Once, during an exceptionally dry summer, Mama, wishing to prolong our pleasure and play, decided not to call us to dinner, but ordered that our meals be brought to us . . . and put under a bush. Delighted with this arrangement, we ate without knives and forks . . . like the savages we thought we were. . . .

Another activity that my brother Fedya invented was a game called "Robinson."[49] . . . Of course, my brother was Robinson and I was Friday. In our grove of linden trees, we tried mightily to reproduce all the deprivations that Robinson had suffered on his uninhabited island. . . .

I also recall . . . an unforgivable prank . . . a procession. Beyond the grove of linden trees was a cemetery and a ramshackle wooden chapel with icons on the shelves. The door to the place was never locked. . . . One time my brother Fedya and I walked in and, without thinking, took the icons. Singing various church hymns and verse, we began to make our way around the field.[50] . . . When we were at the village . . . we spent entire days watching the workers in the field. All the peasants, especially the women, loved us dearly . . . especially brother Fyodor. With his lively character, he did all kinds of things, asking to lead a horse with a harrow or to chase after one with a plough. He also loved to talk to the peasants who responded willingly. He loved to fulfill any errand or to do any favor, to be useful in any way he could. One time a peasant girl, having spilled a jug of water, had nothing to give her child to drink. Immediately, my brother Fedya ran the two or three miles to home and brought her back some water.

Late April 1832 and after.
Andrei Dostoevsky, from his memoirs.

The idiot Agrafena [Lavrentieva] . . . did not have any family, but spent all her time running through the fields. Only at the height of winter was she taken by force and given a hut. At that time, Agrafena was about twenty or twenty-five years old. She spoke little, unwillingly, in an incomprehensible and disconnected way. She made herself understood only when she recalled her child who was buried in the cemetery. Whenever I read the story of Lizaveta Smerdyashchaya in *The Brothers Karamazov*, I instinctively recall our idiot Agrafena.[51]

Late April 1832 and after.
Vera Nechaeva, from notes from a 1926 visit to Darovoe.

Dostoevsky again saw Agrafena [Lavrentieva] when he visited Darovoe in 1877. To the end of her life, she went about dressed only in a shirt, having left her home because of the abuse of her family. Often in winter she was found in the cemetery, covered with frost, with tangled grey hair and bare feet. Agrafena could not talk, except for several indistinct words.

Late April 1832 and after.
Andrei Dostoevsky, from his memoirs.

[At Darovoe] everyone had an "aide-de-camp" . . . a serf boy, who had to dig up worms and thread them on the hook. . . . In a word, "there was the most loathsome lordliness!"[52]

Late April 1832 and after.
Andrei Dostoevsky, from his memoirs.

[At Darovoe] we also played "horsies" . . . teams of peasant boys and girls. . . . They were our pride and joy; so much so that we fed them as well and as much as possible, bringing to our "horsies" large portions of what we had left behind at dinner. We drove these teams . . . along the road from our village to Cheremoshnya. Very often we had races with prizes for the winning team.

Also, having watched the sale of horses at Zaraisk[53] . . . we organized the same kind of exchange for our horses. . . . Like horse dealers, we looked at the horses' teeth, lifted their legs, examined their hoofs, etc.

June 29, 1832.
Maria Dostoevskaya, from a letter to Mikhail Dostoevsky *père*.

I thank you, my dearest friend, for your letter. Having received your missive, I have revived completely, and I thank God a hundred times that He has deigned to hear my prayer and brought you safely to Moscow. Do not be angry with God, my friend, and do not worry about me. You know that we have been punished by Him,[54] but that we have also known his mercy. With full firmness and faith, place yourself under His sacred providence. He will not abandon us with His kindness.

June 29, 1832.
Fyodor, Mikhail, and Andrei Dostoevsky, from a letter to Mikhail Dostoevsky *père*.

We call witness to our deepest respect for you and we kiss your hands, dearest Papa.[55]

Late summer 1832.
Andrei Dostoevsky, from his memoirs.

[By the end of the summer] the village [of Darovoe] was rebuilt like new. There was not a trace of the fire. . . . Mama told the peasants that the money she had given to them was a loan, and that they should pay it back when they could. But of course, these were only words. No one ever asked the peasants for the money.

Early fall 1832.
Andrei Dostoevsky, from his memoirs.

For a year or more, two teachers came to our home.[56] The first was a deacon who taught religion. . . . He had a special gift for speaking. Seated at a card table before us four children . . . with Mother off to the side . . . he told us stories . . . from the sacred scriptures . . . the Flood and the adventures of Joseph. About the birth of Christ he spoke so exceptionally well that Mama left off her work and began not only to listen, but also to gaze upon the inspired teacher. I can say without hesitation that his lessons and stories touched our childlike hearts. I very much regret that I do not recall his name; we simply called him Father Deacon.

He also demanded that we memorize . . . from a text, titled *Principles*[57] . . . which began: "There is One God, worshiped in the Holy Trinity, Who is eternal, Who is without beginning and end, and Who always was, is, and will be."

November 8, 1832, and after.
Andrei Dostoevsky, from his memoirs.

The days of family holidays, especially father's name-day, November 8th,[58] were for us always special occasions. . . . These greetings were always in French, rewritten many times in a painstaking way on letter paper, and placed inside a tube. They were given to father and repeated by heart. . . . One selection was from *The Henriade*.[59] (God knows why.) Father was touched, and he kissed his greeters fervently. On this day, there were also many guests, especially at dinner. . . . Once or twice there was an evening reception with dancing; but . . . none of us boys danced willingly.

1833

Circa 1833.
Fyodor Dostoevsky, from *A Writer's Diary*.

I knew a certain young peasant lad . . . who loved to torture animals. He particularly liked to slaughter chickens. . . . He also climbed on the straw roof of the barn for sparrows in nests; and when he found one, he began to wring their necks.

But this torturer was also quite afraid of the mother hen when she . . . stood before him, defending her chicks; when that happened, the torturer hid behind me.

January 1833–fall 1834.
Lyubov Dostoevskaya, from her memoirs.

My grandfather was very thrifty, even miserly,[60] but when it came to educating his sons, he spared no cost.[61] Initially, he placed his sons—Mikhail and Fyodor—in the French boarding school of [Drashusov]-Sushard.

January 1833 and after.
Andrei Dostoevsky, from his memoirs.

My father was extremely attentive as to the moral formation of his children, particularly Mikhail and Fedya [Fyodor]. . . . I do not recall a single instance when they, as youths, were allowed to go anywhere alone. Indeed, such a thing my father considered to be highly improper. . . . Although our parents were in no way stingy . . . they, as was then customary, saw it as unacceptable that their children had pocket money. . . .

My father . . . also kept repeating that he was a poor man and that his children had to make their own way through life, or otherwise, with his death, they would become beggars and the like.

January 1833 and after.
Andrei Dostoevsky, from his memoirs.

At our hospital was a priest, Father Ioann Barshev . . . who had two sons . . . who became well-known lawyers and professors.[62] . . . My father often said: "If only I could live enough to know that my sons would turn out as well as the Barshevs, I would die peacefully!"

January 1833 and after.
Lyubov Dostoevskaya, from her memoirs.

My grandfather affirmed constantly that his sons had to work incessantly. . . . "You must rely only on your own powers," he said. "You must work a great deal, be careful in your behavior, and weigh your thoughts and words."

Summer 1833 and after.
Fyodor Dostoevsky, from an 1880 letter to Nikolai Ozmidov.

> When I was about twelve years old . . . I read all of Walter Scott. . . . I seized upon . . . many splendid and noble impressions . . . which were seductive, passionate, and corrupting, and with which I struggled in my soul.

Summer 1833 and after.
Anna Dostoevskaya, from her notebook.

> [As a child] Dostoevsky loved Walter Scott's *The Edinburgh Dungeon* and *Rob Roy*,[63] Dickens's *Oliver Twist, Nicholas Nickleby*, and *The Old Curiosity Shop*.[64] He did not like Thackeray.

Summer 1833 and after.
Lyubov Dostoevskaya, from her memoirs.

> My father could not remember his wife's maiden name . . . but he could recall all the names of all the heroes . . . of Walter Scott who had made such an impression in his youth and whom he talked about as if they were his closest friends.

July 9, 1833.
Mikhail Dostoevsky *père*, from a letter to Maria Dostoevskaya.

> First of all, I wish to inform you, my dear friend, that, give glory to the Creator, we are all healthy. Our affairs here are very quiet. . . . No one is sick, but we are in need, and my old age is boring.[65] But God has always been merciful to me, so we will endure.
>
> More than anything, the rain oppresses me. Here in Moscow it has been pouring nonstop; and if you are having the same weather at Darovoe, we will have a disaster on our hands. The rye will die, and the hay . . . will also rot since no one listened to me and stored it in the barn. . . .
>
> I await your letters with impatience. I regret, my friend, that [on my last visit to the country] I did not spend time with you in the way I wanted. Everything got in the way. I had no fun with you, and I also was not kind to your singers.[66] Give them my regards and thank them for me.
>
> You will not believe me when I tell you that my time with you now seems to me as if in a dream. In Moscow I meet only frustration and fuss. I sit . . . and am sad. There is nowhere for me to lay my head, no one to share my grief.

Everyone is foreign and looks at me with indifference. But God will judge them for my distress....

I'm so downcast in my soul that I no longer wish to write. Farewell, the dearest hope of my life. Do not forget me in the lacerated condition of my soul, a feeling I have never experienced in my life....

Don't worry about me.... Everything will take care of itself. You yourself have asked that I hide nothing from you. Farewell, my sincere one, be healthy and happy as much as possible. Take care of your own peace of mind and happiness. I kiss you passionately. Kiss our children for me, and tell the older boys that they should study and not cause you any problems.... Farewell, my friends, and do not forget the one who loves you with all his soul and being.

August 6, 1833.
Mikhail Dostoevsky *père*, from a letter to Maria Dostoevskaya.

[The head doctor at the Mariinsky Hospital] got the order of St. Stanislav, second class with a star, while I, of course, got nothing.... But this is how it always was and always will be: The sheep graze, but it is the shepherd who feeds them, shears them, and makes a profit.

August 23, 1833.
Mikhail Dostoevsky *père*, from a letter to Maria Dostovskaya.

I hear that Kharlashka is a lazy good-for-nothing.[67] I will have to watch him more carefully, and if need be, to flog him.

August 23, 1833.
Fyodor Dostoevsky, from a letter to Maria Dostoevskaya.

We have arrived at Papa's in good health. Papa and Nikolinka are also in good health.[68] God grant that you be well, too.... Respectfully I kiss your hands and remain your obedient son.

August 23, 1833.
Fyodor Dostoevsky, from a letter to Maria Dostoevskaya.

We have ... baby rabbits and squirrels. The squirrels kept Papa up all night because they scraped, jumped, and ran about. Also be so kind, dearest Mama ... as to bring my little knife when you come.

1834

1834–1836.
Andrei Dostoevsky, from his memoirs.

> Readings as a family took place in the living room, and invariably, were led by Father or Mother. . . . My elder brothers, even before they had entered school, also read aloud. . . . Karamzin's *History of the Russian State* . . . particularly the last volumes. . . . The names of Godunov and the Pretender still remain etched in my memory.[69] . . . [We also read] the biography of Mikhailo Vasilievich Lomonosov by Ksefont Polevoi.[70] . . . Derzhavin (especially his ode "God"),[71] Zhukovsky . . . Karamzin (*Letters of a Russian Pilgrim*, *Poor Liza*, and *Marfa, the Boyar's Daughter*)[72] . . . and Pushkin, primarily his prose . . . *Yury Miloslavsky, The Ice House, Streltsy*, and the sentimental novel *The Kholmsky Family*.[73] We also read the tales of the Cossack [Dal]-Lugansky. . . .
>
> My brother Fyodor loved the stories of Narezhnyi, especially his *Seminarian*, which he read constantly.[74] . . . He also raved over Veltman's novel *Heart and Pillow*;[75] and Karamzin's *History* was for him a reference book, which he read when nothing new was around. . . .
>
> Both he and my brother Mikhail also knew by heart almost everything by Pushkin that fell into their hands. . . . Pushkin was still alive at the time. Teachers spoke about him as a contemporary poet, but they did not go on about him at length . . . or demand that their students know his verse by heart. In fact, when authorities on art, teachers of literature, and even our parents chose Zhukovsky over Pushkin, they provoked passionate outbursts from my brothers, particularly Fedya. Once . . . when my elder brother recited by heart "The Count from Hapsburg,"[76] and Fedya "The Death of Oleg,"[77] my parents chose the former over the latter . . . because at the time, Zhukovsky was seen as a better poet.[78]

April–May 1834.
Fyodor Dostoevsky, from a letter to Maria Dostoevskaya.

> When you left, dear Mama, I became so sad that . . . even now I cannot drive away my sorrow. . . . I cannot wait for that joyful moment [when we will be together again]. Every time I think of you, I pray to God for your health.

Late 1834.
Andrei Dostoevsky, from his memoirs.

> Uncle Mikhail Fydorovich (my mother's brother)[79] was always our dear guest. But . . . then Uncle stopped visiting us altogether.

We had a maid named Vera . . . a very pretty young girl . . . who was having an affair with Uncle Mikhail. Mama, suspecting something amiss, saw Uncle pass a note to Vera. She tore the note from the girl's hand: Uncle Mikhail had set up a rendez-vous. . . .

My parents summoned Uncle Mikhail . . . Mama told her brother that he had caused a scandal under her roof. . . . For a long time, Uncle did not say anything; but then he called Mama a fool. . . . Outraged, my father hit Uncle in the face. . . . Uncle, flushed and upset, left our home and never returned.

Early September 1834–spring 1837.
Andrei Dostoevsky, from his memoirs.

My brothers entered the boarding school of Leonti Ivanovich Chermak . . . one of the oldest private academic institutions in Moscow.[80]

Early September 1834–spring 1837.
Lyubov Dostoevskaya, from her memoirs.

Chermak's school was very expensive,[81] its pupils being sons of the Muscovite intelligentsia.[82] . . . Chermak treated the students kindly, as if they were his own sons. He also hired the best teachers in Moscow and demanded that they teach in a serious way.

Early September 1834–spring 1837.
Andrei Dostoevsky, from his memoirs.

Leonti Ivanovich [Chermak] and the male members of his family often ate with the students. On holidays, the entire female contingent of his family also ate with whatever few students were there.

Early September 1834–spring 1837.
Andrei Dostoevsky, from his memoirs.

A man of advanced years, Leonti Ivanovich was himself a little or completely uneducated individual; but he [surpassed] directors of state-run institutions of learning. At the beginning of each lesson, he visited all the classes. . . . If he found students without an instructor, he remained there until the delinquent individual appeared. Chermak greeted the offender with the kindest smile, extending one hand, but with the other, pulling out his watch to check the time. . . .

Chermak . . . also attended to the slightest needs of all his students, particularly those who did not have parents or relatives in Moscow. . . . He invited good students into his study for a small piece of candy. Even older students accepted such rewards gratefully. If someone became ill, Chermak sent him immediately to his wife ... who took care of the boy before she sent for the doctor.[83]

Early September 1834–spring 1837.
Andrei Dostoevsky, from his memoirs.

> Chermak's students ... also received a fundamental moral formation, making them visible figures in society.

Early September 1834–spring 1837.
Dmitri Grigorovich, from his memoirs.

> I often met graduates from Chermak's boarding school.... All of them were remarkable for their superb literary preparation and erudition.

Early September 1834–spring 1837.
Leonti Chermak, from his course plan for his school.

> A. Sciences: Theology, Logic, Rhetoric, Arithmetic, Algebra, Geometry, Geography, History, and Physics.
> B. Languages: Russian, Greek, Latin, German, English, and French.
> C. Arts: Penmanship, Drawing, and Dancing.[84]

Early September 1834–spring 1837.
John Sherwood, from an 1843 report to the Grand Prince Mikhail Pavlovich.

> At that time there existed academic institutions, for instance, Chermak's school in Moscow, that prepared youth only to be enemies of the fatherland.[85]

Early September 1834–spring 1837.
Fyodor Dostoevsky, from an 1880 letter to Vladimir Kachenovsky.

> Whenever I am in Moscow, I always pass Chermak's school ... in an agitated way.[86]

Early September 1834–spring 1837.
Vladimir Kachenovsky, from his memoirs.

> On my first day at school ... I gave way to bouts of childish despair....

Suddenly I heard a familiar voice.... It was Fyodor Mikhailovich Dostoevsky who, ... chasing away the bullies and pranksters, began to comfort me by telling me how happy he was here.... Fyodor Mikhailovich was always very solicitous and kind. He met me after class, helped me with my studies ... and lifted my spirits with the most wonderful stories....

Fyodor Mikhailovich was a serious and thoughtful individual with a pale face and light-colored hair. He took part in games only rarely.... He almost never left his books; and, whatever free time he had, he spent talking to several of the older students at the school.[87]

Early September 1834–spring 1837.
Andrei Dostoevsky, from his memoirs.

When my brothers were at Chermak's school, they came home only on weekends.... Barely had they managed to say hello when everyone moved to the dining-room.... They related everything that had happened during the week ... their grades ... their teachers ... and the childish and sometimes improper pranks of their schoolmates. Dinners often lasted for quite a long time. My parents were content to listen, giving the floor to the new arrivals....

My brothers hid nothing from their parents.... My father never lectured them about the pranks.... He only said: "What scoundrels, scamps, and rascals they are! ... Mind you don't act like that!" And he meant what he said!

Fall–winter 1834.
Andrei Dostoevsky, from his memoirs.

In [Chermak's] modest institution no one taught Latin,[88] so it was my father who instructed my brothers in this subject. One morning ... he brought a copy of Bantyshev's Latin grammar[89]....

With father, my brothers ... stood like statues, declining *mensa, mensae, mensae* ... or conjugating *amo, amas, amat*. My brothers feared these lessons greatly. My father, for all his kindness, was extremely demanding, impatient, and hot-tempered.... The slightest slip-up caused him to burst into anger and to call my brothers "lazybones," "dimwits," and the like. In extreme cases, he stopped the lesson altogether which, for my brothers, was worse than any kind of punishment.

My father, though, always treated his children in a humane way.... We were never punished physically. I also do not recall a single instance when my brothers were made to kneel or stand in the corner.

1835

Circa 1835 and after.
Andrei Dostoevsky, from his memoirs.

None of my brother's friends ever came to the house. . . . One time, though, they were allowed to have someone visit, but the friendship ended quickly. This individual studied at the *gimnaziia* and was several years older than they. He had managed to get a copy of Voekov's satire "The Insane Asylum"[90] (before it had been published) and had committed it to memory. From him my brothers learned several lines of this satire and recited them in my father's presence. My father became very displeased and said that the work was the idle doings of *gimnazisty*. When he was assured that it was a piece by Voekov, my father added that it was still not nice to poke fun at highly placed individuals and well-known writers, particularly Zhukovsky.

Circa 1835 and after.
Orest Miller, from his biography of Dostoevsky.

The reason none of Dostoevsky's friends ever visited his home was the exacting fastidiousness and caution of his parents, especially his father, over his choice of friends. Fyodor Mikhailovich himself often said that he tried to have friends, but that his extreme sensitivity to offense prevented him from doing so. His delicate heart could not tolerate the coarse jokes and pranks of others.

1835 and after.
Andrei Dostoevsky, from his memoirs.

In our home there were also small books published by *The Library for Reading*.[91] . . . These were the exclusive property of my brothers. My parents did not read them.

1835 and after.
Mikhail Dostoevsky, from an article.

When we were still very young . . . with what impatience we awaited each of the small books of *The Library for Reading*, and how we were enraptured by the poetry in them.

1835 and after.
Andrei Dostoevsky, from his memoirs.

My brother Fedya [Fyodor] was an extremely passionate individual who asserted his views with conviction and sharpness.... More than once my father said to him: "Calm down, Fedya ... or you'll wear a red cap!"[92]

April 26, 1835.
Maria Dostoevskaya, from a letter to Mikhail Dostoevsky *père*.

I am writing to inform you, my dearest, that we have arrived safely at Darovoe ... and that as usual, were met by the servants and serfs in a joyful and tender way. Everything in our villages is in order; all our peasants are alive and well....

Oh, my friend, if only I knew that you were at peace, I would not worry or think about anything. Write, my friend, write the entire truth. I look forward to hearing news from you....

Farewell, my dearest. I send to you a sincere kiss. I kiss the children in your absence and I will be always faithful and sincere to you until the grave.

April 29, 1835.
Mikhail Dostoevsky *père*, from a letter to Maria Dostoevskaya.

With all my heart, my angel, I rejoice that you have arrived [safely] ... especially in your current condition, [when] you complain about pain in your sides and back. Even though money is tight ... please get some balsam and spread it on your sore spots. Also, for God's sake, if your cough has not gotten better, tell me right away. I will send you a prescription immediately....

You, my dear friend, worry that I am alone ... but what is to be done, my dear ... I do suffer from a sadness beyond words, but I will endure, and perhaps circumstances will improve.... Farewell, my very dearest ... I will pray to the Creator that He keep all of you, my dear ones, under His holy protection.... Farewell, my inestimable treasure ... and do not forget that I love you more than my life itself.

May 1, 1835.
Maria Dostoevskaya, from a letter to Mikhail Dostoevsky *père*.

Do not worry about sending money ... so far I do not need anything, and if I do, I can sell the oats.

May 3, 1835.
Maria Dostoevskaya, from a letter to Mikhail Dostoevsky *père*.

My sides have healed and there is no trace of my cough left. In vain do you trouble yourself with such thoughts. Truly, when you are apart from loved ones, you make up all kinds of things. I know you well....

My dear children... believe me when I tell you that any and all lines you write to me in our time apart comfort me in words that I cannot express.

May 9, 1835.
Mikhail Dostoevsky *père*, from a letter to Maria Dostoevskaya.

I cannot recall such cold, snow, and hail... My head has suffered a great deal, but thank God, that has passed....

Write about the smallest trifles; from you such things are for me quite pleasant.... Do not fret about us being alone. I will be your eternal faithful friend who will always adore you.

May 16, 1835.
Mikhail Dostoevsky *père*, from a letter to Maria Dostoevskaya.

This week I have been very sad and I do not know where to turn.... But do not worry about me, I am healthy; and as I even have some money coming in and bet with confidence that I am richer than you....

[The servant] Vasilisa sometimes acts suspiciously. So now I keep a close eye on her.... Write, my friend, how many bottles of fruit liqueur we have in the storeroom.

May 19, 1835.
Mikhail Dostoevsky *père*, from a letter to Maria Dostoevskaya.

I find it particularly unpleasant that you... have not been able to go out walking. So I beg you... rest from all your activities, in particular your lace-frame, since, in your condition, to sit in a hunched position is very harmful....

Tell me how many dresses, dickies, caps, and so on you have in the storage room here.... I fear that the laundress has been stealing.

Circa mid-May 1835.
Andrei Dostoevsky, from his memoirs.

Our walks [with papa] always took place in extremely orderly fashion, since, even in Maria's Grove, we were not allowed to run about and to have a good time....

During our walks, my father always . . . [instructed us] on the rudiments of geometry, on the sharp, straight, and obtuse angles, and on the curved and broken lines that . . . one encountered on the blocks in Moscow.

Circa mid-May 1835.
Andrei Dostoevsky, from his memoirs.

Papa spoke enthusiastically about Petersburg and his time there: his travels, the paved wooden bridges, the visits to Tsarskoe Selo by train, the building of St. Isaac's Cathedral, and many other impressions.[93]

Before May 23, 1835.
Andrei Dostoevsky, from his memoirs.

One evening at home my parents were talking about something in a very serious way. Mama said something to father and he became surprised and withdrawn. Then Mama burst into hysterical crying, and Papa could barely calm her.[94]

May 23, 1835.
Mikhail Dostoevsky *père*, from a letter to Maria Dostoevskaya.

God knows why you have heartburn now, since you did not have it with your other pregnancies. I advise you . . . to get some magnesium. . . .

My angst is deadly. . . . I go about as if in a dream, and God knows what is crawling about in my head. . . .

Although I do not have much money, there is enough for domestic expenses so that I can do a thing or two for the children in summer. . . .

P.S. Regarding the household . . . I am convinced completely that anything you do will be fine.

May 24, 1835.
Maria Dostoevskaya, from a letter to Mikhail Dostoevsky *père*.

Do not worry about the storage room. Only trash is in there, and anything valuable is locked away in a trunk. . . .

Do not brag, my friend, that you are richer than I. I, too, have now grown rich. People have settled their accounts with me and I still have not sold the oats.

May 26, 1835.
Mikhail Dostoevsky *père*, from a letter to Maria Dostoevskaya.

> I am very surprised that you are so rich. Surely you have had money you did not tell me about. . . .
>
> You write that a cow did not calve successfully. . . . If the cow-maid was guilty, you acted wrongly if you scolded her lightly and did not punish her as an example to the others. . . .
>
> Right now I am so disturbed in my soul that I cannot write more. Farewell, my dearest hope, and do not forget me in the lacerated condition of my soul, the likes of which I have never experienced in my entire life.

May 29, 1835.
Maria Dostoevskaya, from a letter to Mikhail Dostoevsky *père*.

> Tell me, my friend, the reason for your angst. . . . My heart dies when I imagine you in such a state. I implore you, my angel, my divine, consider my love for you, and know that . . . I pray for you and love you, my one and only friend, more than life itself.
>
> Our children love us and make us happy. What need have we of greater riches when they are our sole treasure? So, my dear friend, I implore you, rid yourself of all sad thoughts. God is merciful and will not abandon us with His kindness. Believe me when I say that when you are happy, I am happy, and that when you are sad, I cry from grief.

May 31, 1835.
Maria Dostoevskaya, from a letter to Mikhail Dostoevsky *père*.

> Your answers to my letters have been so fleeting and cold that I do not know the reasons for the change . . . but your last letter crushed me completely.
>
> [My largesse] has been the result of my thriftiness. . . . I'm keeping accounts of expenses and the next time we are together, you can see them. . . . I've never kept hidden any of our money from you, not even a kopeck.
>
> You also reproached me for my heartburn. . . . Are you not tormenting yourself, my friend, with suspicions, both unjust and ruinous for both of us, as to my faithfulness to you? . . . I swear to you, my friend, by God, the sky, and the earth, on my children, on all my happiness, and on my life itself, that I have never betrayed, nor will I ever betray that heartfelt vow I gave to you, my friend, my one and only, before that sacred altar on the day of our marriage.
>
> I also swear to you that my current pregnancy is the seventh and strongest bond of our mutual love—from my side, a love that is pure, sacred, passionate, unspoiled

and unchanging.... Is it enough for you to hear this vow, which I have never told you before because, first, I am ashamed to degrade it in my faithfulness now in the sixteenth year of our union; and because, second, you, in your suspicion, are little inclined to hear me out, much less believe in our promises to each other....

I affirm that my vow [to you] is even more genuine, for what woman in her pregnancy would be so bold as to swear before God when with every hour, she might stand before His terrible and just judgment. It is up to you, my dearest, to believe my vow or not, but I will remain forever in that sweet hope for God's providence which has always been my support and which has strengthened me in my mournful suffering. Sooner or later, God in His mercy will hear my tearful prayers and comfort me in my sorrow, having illumined you with His sacred truth, and opening to you all the purity of my soul.

Farewell, my friend, I cannot write more as I cannot collect my thoughts in my head. Forgive me, my friend, that I did not hide the torment of my soul ... but take care of yourself if only for my love for you. As for me, do not order me about, but know that I am sacrificing not only my peace, also my life for you....

For the same Creator I ask you, my friend, don't be sad. Perhaps you're ill, my friend. Is that why you are tormenting me so? Good God, Merciful Defender, Heavenly Queen, may she preserve and have mercy on you, my dear!... Don't worry about me, I'm completely well, only I'm sad ... weak and sad.

June 2, 1835.
Mikhail Dostoevsky *père*, from a letter to Maria Dostoevskaya.

Don't worry about me, my dear, I am calmer now. In truth I don't hide from you that sometimes ... I become angry at the Creator for the short days He has given me as my part of life ... but it will pass.... My poverty disturbs me greatly, but I've grown used to it as the air I breathe. I pray only to the Creator that He gives me spiritual peace.... Don't forget me, a poor and homeless one. Invariably and always, I worship you to the end of my days.

June 8–10, 1835.
Maria Dostoevskaya, from a letter to Mikhail Dostoevsky *père*.

Forgive me, my dear friend, my very dearest, that I have caused you so much sadness with my own grief; but ... it is intolerably bitter to see you in such a false and unjust sorrow as you have now.... God knows why such a thing occurred to you....

My friend, I have, perhaps, reread your letter about fifty times.... For three days I went about life like a crazed woman.... I'm looked at with lowly suspicion especially now when I breathe my love for you.

> Meanwhile, the years go by; the face becomes wrinkled and jaundiced; and innate joy turns to sad melancholy. This is my lot, my recompense for my enduring, passionate love for you. . . .
>
> Forgive me that I'm writing the sharp truth of my feelings. I do not curse, I do not hate, but I love, I worship you, and I share with you, my one and only friend, everything that I have in my heart. . . . Do not be sad or distressed over me. I've long ago submitted to my fate and have becomes accustomed to my life. I kiss you endlessly.

June 23, 1835.
Mikhail Dostoevsky *père*, from a letter to Maria Dostoevskaya.

> Do not be angry with me for telling you the truth brought about by my pure, sincere, enduring, and tormented love [for you]. Don't worry about me. I'm healthy and as always, I'm looking after the happiness of my family, the moral formation of my children, and now more than ever before, I am laboring each day for their daily bread.

August 19, 1835.
Mikhail Dostoevsky *père*, from a letter to Maria Dostoevskaya.

> How good it would be if you could harvest the oats before it rains, but I'm calmer now and assured firmly that you'll not let anything slip by. . . .
>
> I'm sending you a coat. . . . I regret that given my inadequacies, I cannot send you more. Would you believe, my friend, that I'm in such need, the likes of which I've never encountered before. . . . Not a single copeck is coming in.

1836

Circa 1836.
Andrei Dostoevsky, from his memoirs.

> In the last years [at Chermak's school] . . . my brothers, with particular enthusiasm, talked about their teacher of Russian language. He was for them their idol, since they recalled every step he took. Most likely, he was an outstanding teacher. . . . My brothers spoke of him . . . also as a gentleman.[95]

1836 and after.
Anna Dostoevskaya, from her memoirs.

> Fyodor Mikhailovich always recalled [his brother] Mikhail Mikhailovich with the most tender feeling. He loved him more than anyone else of his family.

1836 and after.
Fyodor Dostoevsky, from his memoirs.

> My brother was rather weak and could not refuse requests. . . . He always behaved like a gentleman.

1836 and after.
Fyodor Dostoevsky, from his memoirs.

> Mikhail Mikhailovich was a persistent and energetic individual. He belonged to that rare group of people who not only think up and begin an idea or plan, but who, despite the obstacles, also carry it through to the end.
> Unfortunately, though, my brother . . . was accepting and impressionable. He kept . . . his thoughts deep inside himself . . . especially his unhappiness and lack of success. When he suffered, he suffered alone. . . . He loved to share joy and success with his family and close ones. In such moments, he did not want to be alone.

Early fall 1836 and after.
Andrei Dostoevsky, from his memoirs.

> Mother became seriously ill. As a doctor, my father knew what was wrong, but he comforted himself with the thought that he could keep the sick woman alive. She began to decline very quickly, so much so that in a relatively short time, she could not comb her long and thick hair. The medical procedures began to tire her greatly.

Early fall 1836 and after.
Lyubov Dostoevskaya, from her memoirs.

> My grandmother was a meek, beautiful women who devoted herself entirely to her husband and family. She was also in poor health, exhausted by numerous childbirths.

1837

1837 and after.
Fyodor Dostoevsky, from *A Writer's Diary*.

> George Sand appeared in our literature when I was in my early youth. . . .
> At that time [in Russia] people were allowed to talk only about novels. Everything else, including almost every new idea, especially from France, was forbidden strictly.

Oh, of course, quite often the [powers that be] overlooked such "ideas." How could they catch everything? . . . Some "terrible things" slipped through (all of Belinsky, for example). . . . But by the end of the decade . . . we were left only with blank pages.

But novels were still permitted. . . . And it was specifically with George Sand that the public's guardians made a huge blunder. . . .

Ever since the eighteenth century . . . Russians, from our intelligentsia to the masses, became immediately aware of every intellectual movement in Europe. . . .

This was precisely what happened with the European movement of the 1830s. . . . We knew the names of newly appeared orators, historians, publicists, and professors. We even came to know, albeit incompletely and superficially, the . . . novel and above all, [the works of] George Sand.

Senkovsky and Bulgarin had warned the public about George Sand even before her novels appeared in Russian. They said . . . that she wore trousers . . . and that she was depraved.[96] Senkovsky, who had himself been planning to translate George Sand for his *Library for Reading*, called her Mrs. Yegor Sand in print,[97] seemingly very pleased with his witticism.[98] . . . Bulgarin wrote in *Northern Bee* that [Sand] indulged in daily drinking bouts . . . and participated in "Athenian evenings"[99] . . . but no one believed him. But . . . no one believed him.[100]

Sand appeared in Russian translation . . . in the mid-thirties;[101] but most surprising was the impression [her writings] made. Along with everyone else, my youthful self was struck by the sublime, chaste purity of her characters and ideals, as well as by the modest charm and the severe, restrained tone of her narrative.[102] . . .

I was sixteen, I think, when I first read her tale *Uscoque*[103]—one of the most charming of her early works. I remember that afterward, I had a fever all night long. I think that I am not wrong in saying . . . that George Sand held roughly first place in the entire pleiad of new writers who thundered . . . across Europe.[104] Even Dickens, who appeared in Russia at virtually the same time,[105] was perhaps not as popular as she was. I am not including Balzac, who arrived [in Russia] before her,[106] but who wrote such works as *Eugénie Grandet* and *Père Goriot*[107] . . . (and to whom Belinsky was so unfair when he overlooked completely Balzac's significance in French literature.)[108] . . .

From novels, Russian readers could extract everything that the powers that be tried to keep from them. At least in the mid-forties, most readers knew, if only incompletely, that George Sand was one of the brightest, most upright, and most consistent representatives of the Western "new people" of the time, individuals who . . . began to refute directly those "positive" achievements that marked the end of the bloody French (or rather, European) revolution at the end of the preceding century. . . .

People who had met George Sand in Europe said that she was preaching a new status for women and that she was predicting the "rights of the free wife" (this is what

Senkovsky said about her).[109] But that was not quite correct.... George Sand ... was not about women's rights alone....

At the age of sixteen, I was amazed by the strange contradiction between what people wrote and said about her, and what I myself could see. Many, or at least some, of her heroines put forth such a sublime moral purity that could not come about without a thorough moral scrutiny of the poet's own soul ... an understanding and recognition of the most exalted beauty, mercy, patience, and justice. ... [and] a sense of the most chaste impossibility of compromise with falsity and vice ... [but also with] universal forgiveness, mercy ... and enormous responsibility, voluntarily assumed.

Sand's heroines sought sacrifices and noble deeds. I particularly liked ... her Venetian tales (including *Usoque* and *Aldini*),[110] as well as the female characters that culminated in her novel, *Jeanne*,[111] a brilliant work which presents an enlightened and, perhaps, final solution to the historical question of Joan of Arc.

In a contemporary peasant girl, George Sand resurrects the historical Joan of Arc and in a graphic way.... No one could carry within her soul so pristine an ideal of an innocent girl, chaste and so powerful in its purity.[112] ... [In *Jeanne*] is the upright, honest, but inexperienced character of the young womanly being, of that proud chastity which fears nothing and which cannot be defiled by vice, even in some den of iniquity. The demand for some splendid sacrifice (which supposedly awaits her alone) strikes the heart of the young girl, and, suddenly, without ever pausing to think or to spare herself, she—fearlessly, selflessly, and self-sacrificingly—takes a most perilous and fateful step. The things she sees and encounters do not trouble or frighten her in the least; just the opposite. Courage at once rises up in her young heart, a heart which only now, for the first time, becomes aware of all its power—the power of innocence, honesty, and purity. Courage doubles her energy and shows new paths and horizons to a mind that, until now, still has not known itself fully but is vigorous, fresh, and undefiled by life's compromises....

George Sand loved to end her poems ... with the triumph of innocence, sincerity, and young, fearless simplicity. Could such images disturb society and arouse doubts and fears? On the contrary, the strictest fathers and mothers began permitting their families to read George Sand; they could only wonder, "Why is everyone saying such things about her?" But then voices of protest began to be heard: "In this very pride of a woman's quest, in this clash of chastity and vice, in this refusal to surrender to all kinds of perdition, in this fearlessness with which innocence rises up to struggle and to look straight into the eyes of the offender—in all this there is a poison, the future poison of women's protest, of women's emancipation." So what? Perhaps they were right about the poison; a poison which was coming to the fore, but what it sought to destroy, and what it was to save—these were questions which were not resolved for a long time.

January 1837.
Andrei Dostoevsky, from his memoirs.

> In early 1837, Mother got worse. She almost never got up from her bed, and by February, she was completely bedridden.[113]

January 1837.
Lyubov Dostoevskaya, from her memoirs.

> For days on end our grandmother did not leave her bed and loved when her children declaimed her favorite poems.

Late February 1837.
Andrei Dostoevsky, from his memoirs.

> Every minute of the day we prepared to lose Mother. . . . At the end of February the doctors told Father that their efforts were in vain and that the end was near. He was crushed.

February 26–27, 1837.
Andrei Dostoevsky, from his memoirs.

> Immediately before her death agony, Mother became conscious. Asking for the icon of the Savior, she first blessed all her children, adding barely audible blessings and exhortations. Then she did the same thing with father. The scene was heartbreaking and we were all sobbing. Soon after, Mother slipped from consciousness, and at 7 a.m. . . . she passed from this earth in the thirty-seventh year of her life.[114]

After February 27, 1837.
Anna Dostoevskaya, from her memoirs.

> Dostoevsky told me about his dismal, lonely youth after the death of his tenderly beloved mother.[115]

After February 27, 1837.
Alexei Suvorin, from an 1881 article.

> Something terrible, enduring, and torturous happened to Dostoevsky in childhood, the result of which would be falling illness.[116]

After February 27, 1837.
Andrei Dostoevsky, from an 1881 letter to Alexei Suvorin.

> What precisely is the "something terrible, enduring, and torturous" [that happened to my brother], I do not understand.

March 1837 and after.
Anna Dostoevskaya, from her memoirs.

> One bright morning Fyodor Mikhailovich took me to the Lazarevskoe Cemetery, the resting place of his mother, for whose memory he retained a heartfelt tenderness.[117] We were very pleased to find that the priest was still in the church and could recite a memorial prayer at her grave.

March 1837 and after.
Andrei Dostoevsky, from his memoirs.

> The time after mother's death was for my father a period of great activity. At work, he forgot his unhappiness, or at least endured it in a normal type of way.... The harvests and his time in the village also kept him very much engaged. But then there were the fall and winter months when the field work came to an end....
>
> Father became a widower at a relatively young age.[118] ... After mother's death, he locked himself up in two or three rooms of his home.... According to Alyona Frolovna, father talked aloud alone, claiming that he was engaging his deceased wife in everyday conversations.... He was not far from madness.... Little by little, he also began to abuse alcohol ... and even drew close to a girl named Katerina who had been a servant when the family lived in Moscow. But given his age and situation, who could condemn him for such a thing?[119]

March 1837 and after.
Akulina Isaeva, from her memoirs.[120]

> Alone after the death of his wife, Mikhail Andreevich grieved terribly.... He moaned and groaned, ran about the room; he even beat his head against the wall.

March 1837.
Andrei Dostoevsky, from his memoirs.

> My brothers went crazy when they heard about the death of Pushkin and wanted to know all the details of his passing.[121] My brother Fyodor ... kept repeating that if

the family were not wearing mourning for the death of Mother, he would have asked father if he could wear black for the passing of Pushkin.

March 1837.
Andrei Dostoevsky, from his memoirs.

My father let my brothers determine the inscription for my mother's gravestone. They decided that on it would be only her first and last names and the dates of her birth and death. For the other side of the marker, they chose a citation from Karamzin: "Rest in peace, dear ashes, until the joyful morning."[122] So it was done.

PART TWO

To Petersburg

Mikhail Fyodorovich Dostoevsky

If Fyodor had one friend in his years as a child, adolescence, and youth, it was his brother Mikhail. Despite their strong tie, the two could not have been more different—Dostoevskian doubles in real life. If the young Fyodor blazed forth with fire and light, Mikhail was a simmering, steady flame: quieter, shyer, and more studious, sensitive, and stable than his flamboyant brother. If Fyodor was the roughneck, Mikhail was the gentleman. If Fyodor kept a stiff upper lip, Mikhail was prone to tears. If Fyodor needed friends, Mikhail wanted a family. If Fyodor confided everything to everybody, Mikhail kept things close to the vest. Fyodor was rooted firmly in reality, but Mikhail hovered in the clouds. Fyodor lunged forward, but Mikhail held back. Fyodor spent lavishly, but Mikhail counted his pennies. Fyodor was determined to be a writer, but Mikhail drifted from job to job, never finding his place in life. About life, liberty, and the pursuit of happiness, he was more agonized than his brother.

Such a stance, though, did not mean that Mikhail did not pursue his own ideas or plans. Like his brother, he too was a "man of action." With a face that was intelligent and handsome, eyes that were fiery and expressive, and a lips that were mocking and pressed, Mikhail crusaded for a perfect world. More than anyone else in his family, he believed that God was on his side and that the world cried out for (his idea of) justice. Outraged that applicants had bribed their way into the Main Engineering Academy, Mikhail vowed that he and Fyodor would succeed on merit. He was also a model of resilience.

He likewise was the good son. More than Fyodor, Mikhail pleased-appeased his father. *Fils* strove to fulfill *père*'s wishes for civil and military success. He affirmed his love for the man, chided him about his health, informed him of events, and detailed expenses and needs. The son also knew what his father wanted to hear, true or otherwise. It was Mikhail *fils* "who called [Mikhail *père*] to life." It was Mikhail *fils* who wrote to Mikhail *père* not as a "father, but a friend."

Still, and as his father had done, Mikhail sought to carve his own way through life. He was not shy about his likes and dislikes. Life in St. Petersburg, Mikhail wrote to his father, was idiotic, and his schoolmates idiots. Associates in Tallinn were "pygmies" who, chasing after money and rank, had souls "like fatty pieces of beef." Mikhail was also not afraid to tell his father that he heard a different drummer. Poetry, he confessed, was his life, a path assigned by God and fate. Verse filled his soul with the sky, his heart with divinity, and his chest with ecstasy and tears. It moved calamity to growth; suffering to joy; and solitude to enlightenment and peace. In his own mind at least, Mikhail kept great company. Cadets and engineers be damned, the lad intoned. He moved among "hapless and homeless wanderers with a knapsack of grief on their shoulders and a staff of firmness in their hands." He walked with the "same artist crowned by God with a crown of thorns, a lawgiver for all times and peoples, a moral king on earth who is recognized only in heaven." He could be stripped of everything, *fils* continued to *père*, but give him Schiller and he would be content.

Whatever his strengths and weaknesses, Mikhail was also the one double (fictional or real) whom young Fyodor cherished. He was the kinder, gentler Dostoevsky to whom, after Maria, young Fyodor looked for solace and support. In these early years, it was only Mikhail to whom young Fyodor showed vulnerability, happiness, and hurt. It was only Mikhail from whom he feared a loss of friendship and affection. And, it was also brother Mikhail with whom young Fyodor shared a sense of family, loyalty, and love. His brightest moments were the times he stayed with Mikhail and his family; his darkest, when he left them to live life alone. Even with the success of *Poor Folk*, young Fyodor envied his brother for his home and hearth.

Like many individuals in Dostoevsky's early years, Mikhail gave unstintingly. Notwithstanding his own lackluster life, he never minded being second to his younger brother. From his sibling, also, he endured a great deal. Letters from young Fyodor were few and far between. The missives he did receive were often pedantic and condescending—prolix ramblings by Fyodor as to what he saw as Mikhail's errors in philosophy and art, his misreadings of Corneille and Racine, and his shortcomings as a person and a writer. (In a case of the pot calling the kettle black, Fyodor found Mikhail's alleged laziness and egoism to be particular bones of contention.) Indeed, the abuse was unending. Fyodor demanded forgiveness from Mikhail for anger at his own silence and neglect. After his father's passing, and with faux-Christian sentiment, he volunteered his brother as the guardian for his siblings. And, himself now parentless, it was to his brother Mikhail to whom the young Fyodor appealed for money and sundries. Equally painful, perhaps, Mikhail was a singularly captive audience to his brother's anxiety and angst. If

Fyodor was articulating in his letters to Mikhail, as critics including Frank have asserted, his "sense of his mission as a writer,"[1] he was driving his brother to the brink as to precisely what his mission was.

Still, Mikhail was glad for a place in his brother's life. Persistent and energetic, he was often the one behind the scenes, bringing ideas and plans to fruition. Together with his wife, Emilia, Mikhail also brought law and order into his brother's chaotic life. Money, clothes, apartments, even roommates were all part of the bill. Like his father, Mikhail never refused his often wayward sibling, no matter how bizarre or outrageous the request. He also did not care that the charity was one-way. If, on the rare occasion, Fyodor sent Mikhail one ruble, Mikhail responded with a hundred.

Further, against the tides of doubt and derision that welled up in his younger brother, Mikhail not only was the first to proclaim Fyodor's talent but also did everything in his power to ensure its flowering and growth. What he told his brother-in-law, Pyotr Karepin, he told others: Brother Fyodor would be a star.

To be sure, Mikhail profited from the brotherly concern. With a family to care for, he was grateful and glad to be included in young Fyodor's proposed translations and projects. Indeed, whatever his alleged shortcomings, Mikhail was esteemed by his brother for his industry and giftedness, particularly his expertise in translation. Indeed, just as Mikhail urged young Fyodor with fiction, so was he was exhorted by his brother to make the most of his talents. To be sure, the symbiosis was lasting and successful. Indeed, it can be argued that throughout their early years, Fyodor and Mikhail were not only brothers but also the only friends the two had in life.

1837

April 1837.
Andrei Dostoevsky, from his memoirs.

> Not long after mother's death, my father began to think seriously about a trip to Petersburg (which, up to this point, he still had not visited) to take his two oldest sons to enroll at the [Main] Engineering Academy.

April 1837.
Lyubov Dostoevskaya, from her memoirs.

> My grandfather never intended that his sons become doctors; rather, he wanted to see them in the military where at the time, an educated individual could attain a

great deal. Being a practical person, my grandfather chose a military-engineering institution because, upon graduation, one could have a brilliant career as an officer in the Imperial Regiment of the Guards, or become an engineer and make a fortune.

Early May 1837.
Andrei Dostoevsky, from his memoirs.

Every year, as was her custom, Auntie Alexandra Fyodorovna [Kumanina] traveled to Troitsky Lavra; but this year, she begged Papa to allow his two sons to worship at the sacred place.... I often heard from Auntie how, on the way there and back, both brothers delighted her by declaiming poems, a great many of which they knew by heart.

Early May 1837.
Andrei Dostoevsky, from his memoirs.

The trip to St. Petersburg was almost delayed because my brother Fyodor became sick suddenly.... He came down with a disease of the throat and lost his voice. With great effort, he spoke only in a whisper, making if difficult to hear him. The affliction resisted all treatment....

My father, himself a strictly conventional doctor, took the advice of others and tried homeopathy. My brother Fyodor was separated almost completely from the family. He even had to eat at a separate table.... Brother first became better, then worse. Other doctors assumed that travel might help . . . [and] advised father to travel [to St. Petersburg]....

My brother Fyodor carried the traces of this disease for the rest of his life.... His voice never sounded completely natural and was more hoarse than it should have been.

Mid-May 1837.
Andrei Dostoevsky, from his memoirs.

On the day before the departure, Father Ioann Barshev celebrated the farewell service.

Mid-May 1837.
Fyodor Dostoevsky, from *A Writer's Diary*.

My brother and I were striving for a new life, dreaming terribly about anything and everything that was "splendid and sublime." . . . We dreamed only of poetry and poets. Even on the road, my brother wrote verses—three pieces a day—and in my mind I was continually composing a novel on Venetian life. Only two months earlier Pushkin had died.... My brother and I agreed that when we arrived in Petersburg, we would visit the scene of his duel immediately, as well as his former apartment, in which Pushkin had yielded up his spirit.

Mid-May 1837.
Fyodor Dostoevsky, from *A Writer's Diary*.

I once decided on a project—if only to run off to Venice, the Venice of which I had read my fill in the stories of Hoffman and George Sand.[2]

Mid-May 1837.
Fyodor Dostoevsky, from *A Writer's Diary*.

My older brother and I were traveling with our late father to St. Petersburg to enroll in the Main Engineering Academy. . . .

One time, before evening, we stopped at an inn by a posting station. . . . Suddenly a courier's troika came flying up to the station entrance and a government courier leapt out . . . a tall, extremely stout, and strong fellow with a purplish face. He ran into the station, and . . . downed a glass of vodka there. . . . Our driver said that such couriers drank a glass of vodka at every station, without which they could not withstand the "punishment" [of their travels].

Meanwhile a new troika of fresh, spirited horses rolled up to the station and the coachman, a young lad of twenty or so . . . jumped into the seat. Immediately the courier flew out of the inn . . . and got into the carriage. Before the coachman could even start the horses, the courier stood up and, silently, without any words whatsoever, raised his huge right fist and dealt a painful blow right on the back of the coachman's head.

The coachman jolted forward, raised his whip, and lashed the shaft horse with all his might. The horses started off with a rush, but the courier was not satisfied. He was not angry; he was just acting according to the way he did things, from something that had been preconceived and tested through many years of experience. The terrible fist was raised again, and it struck the back of the coachman's neck again and again; and so it continued until the troika disappeared from sight.

The coachman, who could barely hold on because of the blows, kept lashing the horses like one gone mad; and . . . the horses flew off as if possessed. Our coachman told me that all government couriers travel this way and that this one was known to everyone. Once he had had his vodka and jumped into the carriage, he began beating "always in his same way," for no reason at all. He did so in a measured way, raising and lowering his fist, and "kept on like that for nearly a mile." Then he stopped. . . .

Whenever the courier got within about a mile of the station, though, he commenced beating [the coachman] again, his fist going up and down. . . . The coachman's neck hurt for a month. . . . People laughed at him: "Didn't that courier whack you on the neck!" they said. Perhaps, on that very same day, the lad beat his young wife. "I'll take it out on you!" he likely said.³

Mid-May 1837.
Fyodor Dostoevsky, from the notebooks for *Crime and Punishment*.

My first personal insult, the horse, the courier.

Mid-May 1837.
Mikhail Dostoevsky *père*, from a draft of a petition to the emperor.

In January of this year . . . I made bold to trouble Your Imperial Highness⁴ with a petition regarding my large family and my poor financial state. [I asked] that although only one son [per family] can be admitted to Main Engineering Academy at state expense, you place both my oldest boys, Mikhail (16) and Fyodor (15) [there]. This present petition is for his most merciful Imperial Highness to decide: does the placement of both my boys [at the Academy] depend on their passing the entrance examination, for which I have been ordered to bring them to St. Petersburg.

Early June 1837.
Mikhail Dostoevsky, to the authorities.

Because of extreme poor vision, the chronic attacks of rheumatism . . . and the tremors in my right hand, and notwithstanding the increase in salary, I cannot accept the post you have offered to me.⁵ . . . Also, since these afflictions, together with the shock of my wife's death, . . . make it impossible for me to continue in my present position . . . I respectfully ask to be relieved of all duties.⁶

July 1837 and after.
Andrei Dostoevsky, from his memoirs.

After he returned from St. Petersburg, my father intended to settle down once and for all in the village (he had already retired).⁷

July 1837 and after.
Lyubov Dostoevskaya, from her memoirs.

My grandfather Mikhail was not loved by his children. . . . He was addicted to drink, and when drunk, he was mistrustful and mean. When his wife was alive, she . . . was a go-between for her husband and her children. She . . . controlled the amount he drank. But after her death, he began to drink, was unable to work, and retired.

July 3, 1837.
Fyodor and Mikhail Dostoevsky, from a letter to Mikhail Dostoevsky *père*.

We received your letter. How rare such a missive is, and for that reason, it is so dear to us. . . . Thank God you are well! If only He would allow that your affairs be put in order. But He will. He will grant His mercy to us, too. Up until now, God seems to have given us refuge. He will continue to do so in all our undertakings. Let us rely on His Providence, and everything will turn out as it should. . . .

Things are going well. . . . First we study algebra and geometry; then, we draw plans for fortifications—redoubts, bastions, and the like. Koronad Filippovich [Kostomarov][8] is very pleased with our progress and treats us in an especially kind way. He bought for us excellent instruments for 30 rubles and paints for 12 rubles. It was absolutely impossible to do without such things, because plans are always drawn with paints and our present comrades are too stingy to lend us any of their own. Except for paper for writing and plans, we have no outside expenses. . . . We are working very much. . . .

We hope that tomorrow . . . Shidlovsky will come to see us, and we will wander around Petersburg and see the sights. . . .

We think that you are now hustling and bustling about, all on account of us! How can we ever thank you for that!

July 23, 1837.
Fyodor and Mikhail Dostoevsky, from a letter to Mikhail Dostoevsky *père*.

Koronad Filippovich [Kostamarov] is counting on us more than all the eight other students who are studying with him.

Soon we will begin studying military formation . . . so that we can gain favor with His Royal Highness Mikhail Pavlovich.[9] He loves order to the extreme. . . .

In the country now you are probably harvesting wheat, which we know is your favorite activity. . . .

What are our brothers and sisters doing in the country? They all must be strolling, running about, stuffing themselves, and sunbathing to their heart's content. We imagine that Sasha [Alexandra] has grown a great deal; the fresh air is good for her. Most likely, Varenka is doing needlework and surely is not forgetting to study her lessons and reading Karamzin's *Russian History*. She promised us to do that.

As for Andryusha [Andrei] . . . he, too, surely is not forgetting history, which he . . . does not know well. In the fall you will most likely take him to Chermak's school. . . . So still for a long time will you have to concern yourself with the education of your children; you have so many of us [to take care of]. Just judge how we must pray to God for the preservation of your precious health.

August 1837 and after.
Lyubov Dostoevskaya, from her memoirs.

> Having situated his youngest sons—Andrei and Nikolai[10]—in Chermak's school and having given his elder daughter off in marriage to a Muscovite,[11] my grandfather . . . devoted himself to the estate. His two youngest daughters—Vera and Alexandra—he took with him and subjected them to a burdensome life. . . . The education they received was not broad: French, German, a bit of piano, and graceful needlework. . . .
>
> My grandfather Mikhail never allowed his daughters to go out alone; on those rare occasions when they visited the neighbors, he was always in tow. The zealous supervision of their father grated on the delicate emotions of my aunts. With indignation they recalled how in the evenings their father looked under their beds to see if lovers were hiding under there. At that time my aunts were still genuine children—innocent and pure.

August 1837.
Andrei Dostoevsky, from his memoirs.

> [At Chermak's School]. . . . But several upperclassmen, former friends of my brothers, often stopped me to ask: "Hey, you, Dostoevsky, how are your brothers doing? What news do you have about them?" I told them what I knew; and these questions comforted me because . . . there were people who knew and liked my brothers.[12]

August 20, 1837.
Fyodor and Mikhail Dostoevsky, from a letter to Mikhail Dostoevsky *père*.

> Oh, Papa, if only you knew what a worthy young man this Shidlovsky is! We do not know how to thank him for all he has done for us. He loves us so, as if we were family. Every Sunday he visits us; and if the weather is good, we go with him to church, after which we drop in at his place for lunch before we return home.
>
> [Kostomarov] has also been very kind to us. He is with us constantly. You should see how we are preparing for our examination now. For entire days on end we stand at the blackboard and Koronad Filipovich tests us on almost everything. . . .
>
> About us, be at peace completely. We are doing our best to please you. Believe that if God has seemingly protected us to date, He will not abandon us now.

We do not know, dear Papa, where you got the idea that we were writing to you about money. We still have enough! . . . We have bought everything we need. . . . We also do not at all need anything new because where else do we go besides to school?

September 2, 1837.
The authorities of the Main Engineering Academy, from an administrative order.

M. M. Dostoevsky [*fils*] . . . because of weak health (and . . . because he wears glasses for extreme nearsightedness . . . which is "strictly forbidden" by the rules) . . . is not permitted to take the entrance examinations into the school.

September 6, 1837.
Fyodor and Mikhail Dostoevsky, from a letter to Mikhail Dostoevsky.

We were introduced by Koronad Filippovich [Kostomarov] . . . to the Inspector . . . and the Director-in-Chief of the Main Engineering Academy. The Director treated everyone kindly . . . [but] *it was all so boring!* . . .

We can hardly wait for the examination. . . . We are so happy that there are so few candidates. . . . Everyone is afraid of *Kostomarov's* students in the extreme.

September 27, 1837.
Mikhail Dostoevsky *fils*, from a letter to Mikhail Dostoevsky *père*.

Even before the exam, at the doctor's examination, they said that my health was poor; but that is just absolute nonsense.[13] . . .

The main reason [for their claim of my presumed poor health] . . . is that, first, both of us are trying to enroll in the same year; and that, second, we are trying to do so at public expense.[14] I cannot think of anything else. [The doctors] also believe that I cannot endure all the hardships of military service and drill; but my health allows me to be absolutely certain that I could bear even more. Such a claim cost me a lot of tears. . . . I had hoped that I could smooth things over somehow.

Koronad Filippovich [Kostomarov] kept trying to reassure me. The Director . . . is ready to accept me, if a doctor will agree. . . . Who can do this better than Mikhail Antonovich *Markus*?[15] He carries great weight in Petersburg. . . . His word alone could change everything. . . .

My brother [Fyodor] passed the examination with distinction. We assumed that surely he would be among the first, since hardly anyone had more points than he. In geometry, history, French, and theology, he received tens.[16] . . . In everything else, he earned nines. Nonetheless, he came in twelfth.[17] Almost all who came in first were young and had given money—that is, gifts. Such an injustice angers Brother to no end. We have nothing to give; and even if we did, we surely would not have done so, since such a thing is unprincipled.... We serve the Emperor, not money.

But it is all the same, because position will never eclipse merit... and Brother can be first at the Academy.

The main problem now is that the Director has announced that there is not a single [state]-subsidized vacancy. As a result, despite the permission of the Emperor, they cannot accept brother at public expense. What a mess. Where are we going to get hold of 950 rubles? Does this mean we will have to give away every last thing we own? You have already given us everything you have. My God! My God! What will happen to us! But He will not abandon us! Our only hope is with Him.... He does not abandon poor orphans! His mercy is great!

October 8, 1837.
Mikhail and Fyodor Dostoevsky, from a letter to Mikhail Dostoevsky *père*.

Brother has been granted full acceptance [to the Main Engineering Academy] and now goes for lessons in military formation. Today all the new students were presented to Grand Duke Mikhail Pavlovich... and the review, which everyone feared, ended in a very successful way....

From Auntie[18] we have received a letter—an answer to ours, which we sent to her together with a letter to you. She and her husband pity us greatly; and with your permission, they wish to send 950 rubles for each of us right away [for our schooling]. We were greatly surprised by their offer, all the more so since in our letter to them we never alluded to our situation and did not ask them for anything. Allow them to do what they wish to do on our behalf.... It will cost them nothing, but it will influence our fate greatly. Besides, up until now they have not done anything [for us]; so, in this instance, which one may call critical, let them lend the money to just Brother and me. Without it, it will be absolutely impossible for Brother to enter the school, because he has already signed to pay the funds; if he had not done so, he would have lost his right to enroll, and his place would have been taken by someone else. Perhaps our sinful prayers have reached God, and our situation is somewhat taking a turn for the better....

Konorad Filippovich [Kostomarov] and others are advising me to enroll directly in the so-called Engineering Cadets, which will cost us almost nothing at all. Such a designation is certainly no worse than that of the Engineering Academy. In two years or perhaps in a year or year and a half, I can, *at the very least*, be an officer.... The Engineering Cadets also live at the Engineering Castle... and at public expense.

Their job consists of drafting plans and, in the summer, of presiding at construction sites. They study on their own. . . .

Only one thing we beg of you, dear Papa! Do not distress yourself over all such things; but believe that God is arranging these, too, for our happiness.

October 17, 1837.
Mikhail Dostoevsky *père*, from a letter to Mikhail *fils* and Fyodor Dostoevsky.

You will be quite distressed—of this I have no doubt—when you receive my letter. [In my previous missive] I wrote to you in a very coarse way,[19] but I did so when I was not myself, having suffered so much grief and pain that it almost led me to the grave. But now, thank God, the bloodletting has saved me and I am your same father as before. . . .

Write to me in detail about what you are studying . . . especially since I have already sent you 300 rubles more than the agreed-upon sum for these subjects. . . . Also give me the name of the doctor who examined you. Write to me in detail about the most trifling things.

November 6, 1837.
Mikhail Dostoevsky *père*, from a letter to Mikhail Dostoevsky *fils*.

I congratulate you, Mishinka [Mikhail], on the coming Day of your Angel. . . . May the Heavenly Creator bless you, and may your angel, your protector, preserve you from all misfortune and disaster. What a pity that because of my current poverty, I cannot send you something. . . .

Now I ask and order you . . . to find out from Kostamarov what your situation is, and if there is any hope for you to remain in Petersburg . . . for given our poor circumstances, you cannot remain there without a purpose. . . . Also [I] asked him why he has requested 300 rubles from me and whether he has received them and what he intends to do with them.[20]

November 8, 1837.
Mikhail Dostoevsky *père*, from a letter to Koronad Kostomarov.

For your comforting letter . . . I thank you with all my soul. . . . Being assured in letters from my children of your eternal care, I do not doubt that you are taking care of everything they need.

In my last letter to you, I, having no information about my children, was tortured by doubts and despair. I ask you to forgive me that I burden you with my correspondence so often. But I am writing also to a father.

76   PART TWO

December 3, 1837.
Fyodor and Mikhail Dostoevsky, from a letter to Mikhail Dostoevsky *père*.

> We received your letter today, together with the 40 rubles, money washed with the sweat of your labors and personal deprivations. Oh, how expensive things are now! We thank you from the bottom of our hearts which feel so fully everything you are doing for us. . . .
>
> Koronad Filippovich [Kostomarov] assures me that I will be accepted [into the Main Engineering Academy]. I asked him, though, that he inform you about everything himself. He promised to do that. . . . He also told me that I should write to you not to worry about money . . . and that he will not trouble you any more about funds if I happen to stay at his place for the first few days of January. . . . But under this *noble* pretext, is he somehow thinking to ignore the 300 rubles on our part? The Lord only knows! . . .
>
> Be well and as happy as possible. God hears prayer from your children.
>
> P.S. We have enough money for now. So you can rest easy. Ivan Nikolaevich Shidlovsky sends you his regards. On Sundays he visits us or invites us to his place where we spend an entire morning.

Late December 1837–early January 1838.
Fyodor and Mikhail Dostoevsky *fils*, from a letter to Mikhail Dostoevsky *père*.

> Oh Papa, how bitter it sometimes is to be among these people, not knowing whom to turn to with a request, to see the absolute impossibility of enrolling [in the Main Engineering Academy] and to wait for God only knows how long [for an answer]. But do not worry! I have gotten used to these people and will be able to manage them. The main thing is that one should be too *tactful*.

1838

January 1838–June 1843.
Marquis Astolphe de Custine, from his memoirs.

> Russians now pass by the old Mikhailovsky Castle, not daring even to glance at it.[21] In schools and everywhere else, it is forbidden to talk about the death of Paul I there.[22] The very event [of his passing] is never mentioned by anyone.
>
> I am surprised that up until now the Mikhailovsky Castle with its mournful memories has not been torn down. Tourists, though, are very happy to see this historical building with its ancient exterior outlined so sharply against a city in which

despotism ... levels everything and creates anew, forever wiping away the traces of the past. In truth, this restless striving is the reason why the Mikhailovsky Castle is still standing ... its massive four-cornered structure, its unusual height seemingly pressing down upon the other buildings in the city; its deep canals, its tragic history, its secret staircases and doors so amenable to crime ... give to the ancient castle a special majesty which one rarely meets in Petersburg.[23]

January 1838–June 1843.
Anna Dostoevskaya, from her memoirs.

The historical topography [of the Main Engineering Academy] was sharply imprinted on Fyodor Mikhailovich's memory. He very much loved the place for its architecture.

January 1838–June 1843.
Nikolai Leskov, from his 1882, "The Ghost in the Engineering Castle (From the Memories of Cadets)."

Almost from the very building of the [Main Engineering Castle] ... people noticed ... its mysterious phenomena ... spirits and ghosts. ... Peter the Great was supposed to have left his grave to warn Emperor Paul that his days were coming to an end. ...

First-year students [at the Main Engineering Academy] were so scared by the seniors ... that they became shy and superstitious to the extreme. They were particularly unnerved ... by the bedroom of [the deceased] Emperor Paul ... who, the seniors insisted, still lived in this room and, every night, left it to survey his beloved castle.

January 1838–June 1843.
Alexander Saveliev, from his memoirs.

[In the Mikhailovsky Castle] was an oval room ... with a hook on which hung a dove, which belonged to the Khlysts[24] ... with their "ecstasies" and the like.

January 1838–June 1843.
Filipp Vigel, from his memoirs.

One Sunday [in 1822], I visited two old maids ... named Labat-de-Vivance ... zealous ... if not rabid Catholics, who, by the kindness of the Tsar for services their father had rendered to the state, were given an apartment on the top floor of the Mikhailovsky Castle. After a friendly discussion, there was a momentary silence, during which I heard strange singing. "What's going on?" I asked. "Ah, *c'est le sabbat*," they exclaimed, pouring forth tears....

Looking down a hall . . . I saw figures in stretched shrouds and pointed white caps who, with incredible swiftness, appeared and disappeared, whirling about like lightning. The Labat ladies also suggested that I enter . . . the open conduit to hear their singing. To a voice that said: "Beyond the valleys, beyond the mountains," I made out only the words: "God gave us a maiden."

January 1838–June 1843.
Fyodor Dostoevsky, from *A Writer's Diary*.

Tradition has it that in her home in the Mikhailovsky Castle in the 1820s, Mme. Tatarinova,[25] together with her servants and guests (including a government minister), twirled and spoke prophesies.

January 1838–June 1843.
Alexander Saveliev, from his memoirs.

The conductors [students] among which F. M. Dostoevsky found himself[26] . . . were a very special group of young men . . . with their own customs, traditions, and rules. . . . Most of them had had a proper domestic upbringing; several even had a university education. Externally, everyone observed the etiquette of good society. They loved the school and were proud of their calling as students there—so much so that several of them crossed the borders of modesty and sense.

In this small world, the young men [of the Main Engineering Academy] vaunted honesty, impartiality, respect for the individual . . . [as well as] their own moral duties and obligations.

January 1838–June 1843.
Alexander Saveliev, from his memoirs.

In the [Main] Engineering Academy . . . punishments . . . were rather severe . . . and the same for conductors and officers. . . . If a conductor or an officer let his hair grow long, he was put "under the razor." . . . If he were found smoking, he was placed under detention or set to work. People were punished even more strictly for inattention to dress. . . .

The small family of conductors were isolated for weeks at a time. They did not receive newspapers; they were almost ignorant of the outside world. . . . Although the regulations, customs, and laws . . . were sometimes worse than draconian, they also accomplished a great deal of good . . . countering the foolish or harmful aspects of their upbringing at home. The closeness among friends at the [Main] Engineering Academy was lifelong; happy or sad circumstances could not break the tie. . . .

Older students punished younger ones for violating customs and rules, or for deceit, boasting, and immoral behavior. . . . Incorrigible individuals were urged to leave the school. All this was done in private. None of the authorities knew what was going on. . . .

Beginning students, or "hazel hens" as they were called, were subject to all kinds of pranks, insults, and beatings.

January 1838–June 1843.
Alexander Saveliev, from his memoirs.

The exclusive nature of the military, the grievous relations between the older and younger students, as well as between the administrators and subordinates, not to mention the lack of collective coordination to assess the strengths and weaknesses of the pupils—these incurred the secret suspicions, mistrustfulness, and sometimes maliciousness and spite . . . that destroyed ties among the people there. . . .

Students [at the Main Engineering Academy] soon learned to tell the difference between truth and deception. They could not be bought off by popularity or sweet-talking. Rather, they developed a spirit of skepticism; they little trusted claims by the administration. . . . The slightest weakness of one at the expense of the others, especially in the final year . . . could affect the future service, and even the fate, of a young person. Such a situation sowed deep moral wounds in the souls there.

January 1838–June 1843.
Alexander Saveliev, from his memoirs.

"Hazel-hens" had to fulfill the orders of older students without question; [otherwise] . . . they were subject to the customary punishments. . . . There were also students who did not enjoy the attention or good-will of the group . . . since either by accident or on purpose, they had broken with tradition.

Members of the senior class were accorded special honor and respect, being beyond anyone's control and even more important than the administrators and patrons. To their credit . . . these individuals displayed excellent traits and, more than the higher-ups, participated actively in preserving order and influence among their younger colleagues.

The primacy of older students over younger ones aroused mutual antipathies . . . and not without . . . arguments, factions, and the like. . . .

As a first-year student, F. M. Dostoevsky was undoubtedly subjected to such unpleasantries. There were no exceptions.[27]

January 1838–June 1843.
Dmitri Grigorovich, from his memoirs.

My first year at the [Main] Engineering Academy was an absolute torment.[28] ... It was not the severity of the authorities to the students, the marching and rifle practice, or the difficulty of the studies, so much as it was my new schoolmates with whom I had to live amid the same walls, to sleep in the same rooms.... Here were customs that are possible only in the most savage society. The higher-ups could not help but know what was going on ... but they looked upon such things as inevitable. They were concerned only with correct externals and satisfied superiors....

A first-year student would be standing somewhere, not daring to bat an eyelid. An upperclassmen would say to him in a quarrelsome voice:

"Hey you, hazel-hen, you over there, it seems you've been out carousing?"

"Have mercy ... I ... nothing."

"So now it's nothing.... Look at what I've got for you!"

There followed a punch in the nose or a shove on the shoulder for no reason at all.

"Hey you, hazel-hen, what's going on with you?" another would say. "Go into the third room. Next to my bunk is my notebook. Bring it here and step lively, or you'll get it but good!"

It was also considered fun to pour water into a novice's bed, or to put ice down his collar, to force him to lick ink off of paper, or to make him say dirty words if he was a Mama's boy who was embarrassed easily.... First-year students also had to crawl under a table at one end ... and be whipped with twisted braids when they came out at the other.

God forbid if the individual should cry or defend himself. The son of Dr. K ... was ready to strike back with his fists, when suddenly a gang of students beat him up so badly that he had to be taken to the infirmary. Fortunately, the victim had been taught to say that he had had an accident on the stairway, because if he had said what really had happened, he would have paid for it dearly....

A sword of Damocles hung over the head of each student.... The most innocent infraction—an unfastened collar or button—meant that the offender was sent to detention or made to stand for hours on end with a knapsack on his back and a gun on his shoulder.

January 1838–June 1843.
Roster of Classes for the Main Engineering Academy (1825–1863).

The first cadet class: theology, Russian literature,[29] French,[30] drawing of situations, civic architecture, history, topography, analytic geometry, descriptive geometry, physics, artillery, and fortifications.

The junior officer class: differential and integral calculus, statistics, descriptive geometry, physics, tactics, architecture, construction, and fortifications.

The senior officer class: law, theoretical mechanics, applied mechanics, chemistry, geology, military construction, and fortifications.

January 1838–June 1843.
Alexander Saveliev, from his memoirs.

At the Main Engineering Academy was a teacher by the name of Mr. Tol . . . [who] taught Russian language and literature. . . . None of the students could say what philosophical system or whom among the educated socialists Tol supported. For them it was enough that he spoke about such subjects as the nature of genuine, truthful religion, as well as about Buddhism, Taoism, Communism, and equality . . . topics that never occurred to us to read or listen to. In his presence, students could sit wherever they wanted, with shirts open at the collar, and . . . to smoke. Someone in the class, or even the teacher himself looked through the keyhole for higher-ups who might enter unexpectedly.[31]

January 1838–June 1843.
Fyodor Dostoevsky, from an 1869 letter to Sofia Ivanova.

[My time at the Main Engineering Academy] was a mistake and ruined my future.[32]

January 1838–June 1843.
Fyodor Dostoevsky, from an 1858 letter to Ivan Zhdan-Pushkin.

[At the Main Engineering Academy] I saw boys . . . who had already calculated their life away: what rank they wanted to attain; . . . how they would rake in the dough; and how, as soon as possible, they would get to a well-to-do and independent position in life.

January 1838–June 1843.
Fyodor Dostoevsky, from *A Writer's Diary*.

The verb *stushevat'sia* means to disappear, to perish, to descend *to nothingness* . . . but not immediately, to be wiped off the face of the earth with thunder and crashing . . . but to sink gradually . . . like a shadow in a drawing, done in shaded lines, that moves from black into white until it disappears completely. . . .

Although I was the first one to use the verb *stushevat'sia* . . . I was certainly not the one who invented it. It was thought up by my classmates when I was at the Main

School of Military Engineering.... We had to draw ... fortifications, structures, and military buildings ... and [if] you drew poorly ... you were deprived of such advantages as promotion to a higher rank. So, everyone tried hard to draw well.

All plans were drawn in India ink ... and everyone tried to learn how to shade a given surface well, from dark to light to white—to nothingness; a good shading gave to the drawing a stylish look.

Suddenly, people began to ask: "Where's so-and-so?" "Ah, he's disappeared [*stushevalsia*] somewhere." Or, one friend would tell another that he had get to work: "Well, now you'd better disappear [*stushuisia*]." Or, a senior student would say to a beginning student, "I called you; where did you manage to disappear to [*stushevat'sia*]?" ...

Some three years later I remembered the verb *stushevat'sia* and used it in my tale.[33]

January 1838–June 1843.
Lyubov Dostoevskaya, from her memoirs.

Most of my father's classmates [at the Main Engineering Academy] were the sons of provincial colonels and generals.... [They were for him] energetic animals ... who loved to laugh, run, and play. They poked fun not only at the serious views of their Muscovite classmate but also at his passion for reading. Dostoevsky, in his turn, despised their ignorance. For him they belonged to another world.

January 1838–June 1843.
Lyubov Dostoevskaya, from her memoirs.

The young puritans [Mikhail and Fyodor] dared to talk about women only in poetry. One can imagine how such modesty amused their classmates in the [Main] Engineering Academy, since typically, Russian youth began their amorous adventures at an extremely early age. Most likely, Dostoevsky suffered greatly from his cynical schoolmates. When my father wrote in *The Brothers Karamazov* that when Alyosha hears dirty words from his classmates, he put his hands over his ears—he was conceivably talking about himself.

January 1838–June 1843.
Alexander Saveliev, from his memoirs.

At the [Main] Engineering Academy, Dostoevsky ... was so original and independent that he aroused curiosity and bewilderment: strange, unnatural, and enigmatic.... But, after a while, administrators and schoolmates stopped paying attention to him.[34]

Fyodor Mikhailovich was a modest individual who discharged his academic and military responsibilities in an impeccable way. He was also a very religious man, fulfilling the obligations of his Orthodox faith with passion. One always saw him with the Gospels, Zschokke's *Hours of Devotion for the Advancement of Genuine Christianity and Familial DivineWorship*,[35] and other religious works. . . . After lectures in theology . . . Fyodor Mikhailovich often stayed behind to talk with the priest for long periods of time. Such a thing so impressed his schoolmates that they nicknamed him Photius the Monk.[36]

January 1838–June 1843.
Alexander Saveliev, from his memoirs.

[At the Main Engineering Academy] Fyodor Mikhailovich sought to reconcile groups. He kept his friends from playing jokes and pranks . . . but there were times when his authority was to no avail, especially when his schoolmates tyrannized "hazel-hens" or treated the servants in a coarse way. . . .

To his friends, also, he was so honest and agreeable . . . that he maintained ties with them . . . like Freemasons, complete with oaths and vows for life.

Fyodor Mikhailovich was also an enemy of anyone who sought to ingratiate himself . . . with higher-ups. . . . His calm and serene face hinted at . . . an inherently sorrowful disposition of the soul; but, when he was asked about what was troubling him, he answered in the words of Montesquieu: "Never speak the truth at the expense of your virtue."[37]

January 1838–June 1843.
Alexander Saveliev, from his memoirs.

With a sense of noble honesty and profound indignation, Fyodor Mikhailovich told me about several authorities [at the Main Engineering Academy] . . . who stole . . . [and] were rewarded . . . because of their families and ties to powerful people . . . or who supported and found positions for students who paid him or gave them presents.

January 1838–June 1843.
Alexander Saveliev, from his memoirs.

To several of his friends, F. M. Dostoevsky seemed to be an idealist and a mystic. . . . Such individuals do not submit to any pressures, but their stubbornness costs them dearly.

January 1838–June 1843.
Alexander Saveliev, from his memoirs.

[At the Main Engineering Academy] F. M. Dostoevsky was not valued adequately for his diligence, success in studies, and moral qualities and behavior. . . . [Such indifference] weighed heavily on the soul of the extremely impressionable youth who looked for mercy and justice in people. . . .

Dostoevsky, though, loved to recall the school, his classmates . . . and the subjects he had taken.

January 1838–June 1843.
Alexander Saveliev, from his memoirs.

Days at the [Main] Engineering Academy followed a well-known established order. Classes were held twice a day, from 8:00 to 12:00 and from 3:00 to 6:00. From 7:00 to 8:00 conductors attended review sessions, and from 8:00 to 9:00 they engaged in gymnastics, fencing or dancing.

Fyodor Mikhailovich took part in these later activities; otherwise, he was not to be seen. During those times when his colleague-conductors were sitting at their desks, preparing for the next day, Fyodor Mikhailovich was strolling through the recreation hall with one of his friends (Berezhetsky[38] or Grigorovich),[39] or talking with the officer on duty. To Shidlovsky[40] and others, he was explaining some formula or drawing from descriptive geometry items which for them were as clear as Chinese grammar. Most often, Fyodor Mikhailovich was helping a friend with a composition on a given theme.

January 1838–June 1843.
Alexander Saveliev, from his memoirs.

Fyodor Mikhailovich . . . studied at his small table . . . or at his favorite place . . . the embrasure of a window in the corner . . . in the bedroom of the troupe which looked out onto the Fontanka.[41]

Often Fyodor Mikhailovich did not notice anything going on about him. . . . Only when the drummer came through the bedrooms beating evening reveille would he pack up his notebooks and books. . . . Deep into the night, Fyodor Mikhailovich worked at his table. Having thrown a blanket over his underwear, he did not notice the strong wind that was blowing from the window where he sat. . . . When I said that it would be better to study earlier with clothes on, Fyodor Mikhailovich agreed kindly, but also insisted that the nighttime quiet, the semi-darkness of the bedroom . . . was conducive to peaceful work. He gathered up his notebooks and seemingly went to bed. After a little while, though, he was again in the same dress, at the same table. Working at night was a habit that remained with Fyodor Mikhailovich for the rest of his life. . . .

No other conversation . . . [at the Main Engineering Academy] left me with such profound impressions and sad emotions as my exchanges with Dostoevsky. He always spoke quietly, slowly, with pauses—a particular makeup of his chest and lungs . . . but always in a way that was rhetorical, graceful and assertive. The simplest recollection of his childhood, an unimportant historical episode he portrayed slowly, but splendidly with particular inspiration. Because he himself was aware of the impression that his stories were making on his listeners, he loved to talk about everything with enthusiasm . . . but with a certain biliousness.

January 1838–June 1843.
Dmitri Grigorovich, from his memoirs.

My friendship with Dostoevsky began almost from the first day he entered the school.[42] . . . Of all the boys there, there was no one with whom I became such good friends so quickly as with Dostoevsky. Although Fyodor Mikhailovich was not an open or expansive individual . . . he was always happy me to treat me as a friend. . . .

I fell completely under Fyodor Mikhailovich's spell. It was for me a most beneficial time. In all respects, Dostoevsky was far more advanced than I. His erudition astounded me. Whatever he said about the works of writers, about names I had never heard of, was for me a discovery. Before I met Dostoevsky, I and most of my classmates had read only specialized textbooks and materials, not only because we were forbidden to bring "outside" reading into school, but also because . . . we were indifferent to literature.

Pushkin's death in 1837 was a special event for all of us, but I am sure that Dostoevsky was the only one who had read his works . . . even as schools sought to conceal news of the poet's passing and to order that the less spoken about Pushkin the better. . . .

The first things that I read in Russian were dictated to me by Dostoevsky. There were translations of Hoffmann's *Tom-Cat Murr*[43] and of Maturin's *The Confession of an English Opium Eater* (an extremely gloomy work, which Dostoevsky esteemed greatly).[44] Walter Scott's *The Astrologer*[45] and especially Cooper's *Lake Ontario*[46] instilled in me a passion for reading. . . . Dostoevsky was also a huge fan of the novels of F. Soulié . . . especially his *Notes of a Devil*.[47]

January 1838–June 1843.
Alexander Saveliev, from his memoirs.

What especially angered Grigorovich—the beating of the drums, the drying of socks on marches, or that standing like a crane on one leg until ordered to stop—Dostoevsky regarded with indifference. He hung out his socks to dry zealously, he learned to be a batman, even though he knew that . . . by his sickly nature and pale face, he was not cut out to be the typical handsome engineering student.

Whereas Grigorovich was angered by such phrases as "march as if your nose counted on it" . . . "keep your left ear cocked more sharply" . . . "throw away your third rib," and "give it all you got" . . . Dostoevsky saw such expressions as curiously original.

January 1838–June 1843.
Alexander Saveliev, from his memoirs.

Dostoevsky attended lectures on history and literature by Plaksin and Turunov more often than classes in integral calculus. . . . He was also the editor of a lithographed newspaper at the school titled *The Revel Smelt*.[48]

January 1838–June 1843.
Alexander Saveliev, from his memoirs.

Like Dostoevsky, I. Berezhetsky was a talented and modest youth who liked quiet and solitude. He was also a reserved individual . . . an *homme isolé* . . . . Dostoevsky and Bererzhetsky were together constantly reading items from *The Northern Bee*,[49] or works by Zhukovsky, Pushkin, and Vyazemsky. . . . While their classmates were taking dance lessons, playing games, or marching on the parade ground . . . the two, under the pretext of illness, either read in a room or walked together through the halls. The same can be said when both of them were at Peterhof[50] during the summer. . . . At a time when colleagues, in the company of their officers, were strolling through the gardens or going off swimming, they were never anywhere to be found. Similarly, in mock games of storming the Samson Fountain,[51] they were missing. . . .

Dostoevsky and Berezhetsky shared outstanding spiritual strengths; e.g., they empathized with the poor, weak, and defenseless. . . . They took every opportunity to stop the customary violence senior students meted out to beginners, servants, and the like. Dostoevsky and Berezhetsky were angered by the jokes and pranks which the students played on the teachers of foreign languages, especially the Germans. Respected by their classmates, they stopped such shenanigans as they were happening or nipped them in the bud. Further, when someone played a joke on a teacher that neither Dostoevsky and Berezhetsky could stop immediately—for instance, when a student came out into the hall riding the back of the teacher who taught German—the two boys did not let such an outrage go unpunished. Their verdict was that the guilty party was to be beaten by the older students of the school.

January 1838–June 1843.
Konstantin Khlebnikov, from his memoirs.

I recall how F. M. Dostoevsky and Berezhetsky got carried away by their readings . . . of Schiller. . . . They read and read . . . and suddenly started to argue. They ran through all our cells and bedrooms . . . each refusing to hear the objections of the other. . . . Berezhetsky starting a sentence and Dostoevsky finishing it. . . .

F. M. Dostoevsky won our attention with his inspired stories. Late into the night . . . he leapt from behind the door, stood [before us], and spoke with a special nervous inspiration. The muffled and completely husky sound of his voice was riveting, electrifying.

January 1838–June 1843.
Alexander Saveliev, from his memoirs.

Berezhetsky loved to vaunt his wealth (he wore watches and diamond rings) . . . and his enlightened education. . . . F. M. Dostoevsky was the son of a poor staff-doctor, a youth with a solid education, a firm character, and a sense of personal worth.

January 1838–June 1843.
Alexander Saveliev, from his memoirs.

The old clerk Igumnov . . . was an extremely kind individual who was loved by the students. He was a great lover of literature and gifted with a splendid memory. He also had a great moral influence on the youth there. His historical stories from Russia's past were extremely interesting, particularly those about the Engineering Castle, about life there in the twenties and about the sects of "God's people" and their curious religious rites (their dances, twirling, and songs). . . .

In winter evenings, most often on the invitation of F. M. Dostoevsky, Igumnov entered the recreational hall and stood in the middle of the room. Students filled the place quickly, benches and stools appeared, and complete silence reigned. With his fine memory, Igumnov delivered entire ballads by Zhukovsky, poems by Pushkin, stories by Gogol and others. Those present were in ecstasy over Igumnov's performance. They did not limit themselves to applause, but each time, collected for him a sizeable financial reward.

1838.
From the Church Registry of the Descent of the Holy Spirit.

Katerina's son, Simeon, illegitimate, three months old.[52]

January 19, 1838.
Mikhail Dostoevsky *fils*, from a letter to Mikhail Dostoevsky *père*.

Brother has already entered the [Main Engineering] Academy, as you can see from the fact that I am writing in my name alone. On Sunday I hope to see him in full uniform. I do not know how he will get along with his colleagues.

Late January 1838.
Mikhail Dostoevsky *fils*, from a letter to Mikhail Dostoevsky *père*.

Thank God! Thank God! You do not have to worry or be upset anymore! Oh, how can I thank God! He alone has the power to do the impossible! I have been accepted [into school]![53] . . .

On Saturday and Sunday I saw brother! Oh, Papa! What a dashing figure he cut in his new uniform! I also hope, if not this week, then next, that I, too, can also put on such dress. . . .

How bitter to think that you, our most kind and dear Papa, are worried and distressed when you should rejoice! Brother has bought everything he needs; and a thousand times, he asks your forgiveness for not writing to you.

January 29, 1838.
Mikhail Dostoevsky *fils*, from a letter to Mikhail Dostoevsky *père*.

I saw brother today! . . . The students have been so kind to him. . . . The only thing is that he finds boring is to stand at attention before every officer. . . .

What a pity that for a few months we will be deprived of our dear kind poet Ivan Nikolaevich Shidlovsky! He is going to Kharkov to take a break from the *idiotic* life of Petersburg as you yourself called it!

February 4, 1838.
Fyodor Dostoevsky, from a letter to Mikhail Dostoevsky *père*.

Finally I have enrolled in the Main Academy of Engineering. Finally I have donned a full-dress uniform and have entered fully into the service of the Tsar. I have just now barely managed to squeeze out a free moment from classes, studies, and service—a precious moment, dearest Papa, in which I can talk with you at least in writing. It has been so long since I last wrote to you; and after hearing, at my last meeting with my brother, that you had reproached me [for my silence], I very much wanted to correct my shortcoming, however involuntary it was....

Thank God, little by little, I am getting used to life here. About my comrades, though, I cannot say anything good. The administrators here, I hope, have a very good opinion of me....

I received the 50 rubles [you sent me].... I really need the money now and I hasten to acquire everything I do not have. I do not go anywhere on Sundays or other holidays because relatives have to sign out for anyone they are taking to their homes....

I have also just found out that... the Director-in-Chief has arranged to have four new candidates enrolled [at the Main Engineering Academy] at public expense, in addition to the candidate who was a student at Kostomarov's and who won my place there. What baseness! I'm in a complete state of shock! We, who have to struggle for every last ruble, must pay, whereas others—the children of wealthy fathers—are accepted for free. God be with them!

February 12, 1838.
Mikhail Dostoevsky *père*, from a letter to Mikhail Dostoevsky *fils*.

How great are God's mercies. How we, undeserving ones, are grateful to the all-merciful God, for his ineffable goodness to us! How unjust are we when we murmur when others serve as an edifying example, when for all our entire lives, the Almighty has sent us short-termed suffering for our benefit and well-being. I do not have words to express His heaven-sent ineffable kindness. Truly I, together with you, proclaim glory to the Almighty on heaven and earth.

I thank you, my beloved, for your joyous news. Would you believe that you alone have called me to life and have resurrected home in our poor family....

If you have actually entered the Cadets, write to me honestly as to whether you are satisfied with your situation, since it always seems to me that you are sacrificing yourself only to put us at ease.... Write to me openly and honestly not as your father, but as your friend.

You write to me that Fyodor is bored when he has to stand at attention before officers. Tell him not to be so, since such a thing is an invariable part of military service. Also tell Fyodor that the best thing he can do is to become an officer himself, since he will find it pleasant when people of lesser rank pay him homage. Also tell him that he who cannot obey will never rule.

February 17, 1838.
Mikhail Dostoevsky *fils*, from a letter to Mikhail Dostoevsky *père*.

> Well, Papa! I am now in genuine service! I serve the Tsar-Our-Sovereign....
>
> As usual, my friends are very kind, but also as usual, they are stupid.... But having been at Kostomarov's [school], I should be used to such a thing....
>
> [I am also studying] Italian and Polish. In a year I will be reading in the original: Dante, Bocaccio, Tasso, Aristo, Petrarch, Mickiewicz, and [Kvitka]-Osnovyanenko.... I also have read Racine, Molière, V. Hugo, Goethe, and Schiller.

February 28, 1838.
Mikhail Dostoevsky *fils*, from a letter to Mikhail Dostoevsky *père*.

> Brother is also very satisfied with his School. They have the most wonderful teachers.

March 1838.
Report Card from the Main Engineering Academy.

> With a score of 10 for the highest grade: Berezhetsky—7.1; Dostoevsky—7.0; Grigorovich—6.9.

April 15, 1838.
Mikhail Dostoevsky *fils*, from a letter to Mikhail Dostoevsky *père*.

> Well, Papa, I am not staying in Petersburg ... but [am being sent] to Revel....
>
> I am even glad ... because my trip there will make my life more varied and diverse. It is sad to live without impressions, it is sad not to rouse the heart with their upheavals. A cold life and a calculating century also try to put a heart to sleep!...
>
> There I will live as a hermit.... With friends I will not utter a word, but will speak constantly with my lessons and books.

April 15, 1838, and after.
Lyubov Dostoevskaya, from her memoirs.

> When my father learned of the impending separation from his brother, his grief knew no bounds. He ... was completely alone, without relatives or friends. Also, since my father did not know anyone in Petersburg, he had to spend all his vacations at the school.

May 8, 1838.
Mikhail Dostoevsky *fils*, from a letter to Mikhail Dostoevsky *père*.

> Thank you very, very much for everything—for the money, for your letter, and especially for the news (however sparse) about brother Fyodor! More than six months have passed, and I still don't know anything about him.[54] Such a thing distresses me greatly. Like you, Papa, I have begun to make up God knows what for the reasons for his silence. . . . I've even begun to read various orders, thinking to find his name on lists of the living and the dead. . . .
>
> You can imagine how I wish I could assure you that he is healthy and the like. . . . For the love of God, tell me what has been and continues to be the reason that has forced him to smash the pen to write us? That is the mystery! . . .
>
> I am being called . . . to a fate assigned by God—a road which I must follow until death—a road that is straight, not one of those village paths that others travel down! Since from childhood my heart has striven for Literature, would I not be in my rights to think that for me the road is open to the literary field? In poetry is my happiness. This will never change! . . .
>
> Be at peace, Papinka! Your son will not be lost in life. He will bring honor to his name . . . I am also sending you my poem that I wrote in the new year.

May 26, 1838.
Mikhail Dostoevsky *fils*, from a letter to Mikhail Dostoevsky *père*.

> You are distressed, my incomparable parent, over my posting [to Revel], but such a thing gladdens me to the extreme. From the bottom of my heart . . . I am grateful . . . that I am being sent away from here. . . . I'll hear less of the stupidities, the male witticisms that, like evil jackasses, spring from the mouths of my former friends, those beehives of innate ignorance who grate on my ear so mercilessly. . . .
>
> My happiness? . . . But where is that happiness about which people spin dreams on the morning dawn of our days, and which we forget sweetly under this lullaby, under the reed-pipe of our imagination, our heart? . . . No! There is no happiness in this world! . . . It has been carried off long ago into the sky, from the time when people forgot the laws of nature. Must happiness be in honor, ranks, crosses, and money? No! Let such happiness be the province of pygmies whose souls . . . like a fatty piece of beef, melt away in the steelyards of shallow calculation. . . .
>
> Papa! Papa! Were you ever happy? . . . Here are splendid poetic lines by Shidlovsky:
>
> Only the strong soul knows grief
> Knows such a thing with care.

The heart and the mountain Master
Kiss with a mournful tear
Heaven and earth come together
In a sigh so dear.

That is genuine poetry! That is comfort to all the hapless and homeless wanderers in this world, with a knapsack of grief on their shoulders and a staff of firmness in their hands! But here is still more powerful comfort: *Come to me, you who labor and are overburdened, and I will give you rest!*[55]

Can it really be that working as a field engineer can make me happy? Oh, I would be so very base if my happiness were so shallow! No! For me there is in life another goal for which I have sacrificed everything—my future, my views! Good God! Can I, dare I call a *goal* that which ties my soul to the Sky and that fills my heart with the sweet pre-sensation of the divine being! The entire sky enters into my chest in a powerful way, and my chest takes root into the sky and begs only for tears and ecstasies—yes, ecstasies! My goal, my hope, my *everything is poetry*! Good God! Can it be that my dream is deceiving me, as it has deceived others? No! Surely, the voice that is inviting me to the sky is not the voice of the sky itself? Can it be that it has roused my heart in vain, and carried my soul off into a world of fantasies, and dreams? Can it also be in vain that since the age of nine, it has called me to write poetry, even be it with rhythms and stops? No! his is not a deception! Do not take from me my joy, my delight! The heart is a soothsayer! It would tell me!

Why does the artist dedicate his entire life to his art? Why does he not worry about anything else other than his art? Surely is he not the same artist crowned by God with a crown of thorns, a lawgiver for all times and peoples, a moral king on earth who is recognized only in heaven! . . .

P.S. Papa! How can I thank you for the formation you gave me! How sweet and joyful it is to become lost in thought over Shakespeare, Schiller, and Goethe! How can one place a value on these moments!

P.P.S. I still have not received any letters from Brother. . . . But I lent money to him. For books. And for skates! This always happens! He has to have money to spend on trifles.

May 27, 1838.
Mikhail Dostoevsky *père*, from a letter to Fyodor Dostoevsky.

Several times in letters I have scolded [your brother] that . . . he has written about you in an unenlightening way. . . . I am also angry at him that he is wasting his time on trivialities, on poetic scribblings.

Circa June 1838.
Alexander Rizenkampf, from his memoirs.

At age sixteen,[56] Mikhail Mikhailovich Dostoevsky looked like what he would be throughout his life: thin, small, with a sunken chest. His face was very handsome: intelligent, oblong-shaped, slightly dusky, and framed with long, chestnut-colored hair. Despite his enduring paleness, his color was healthy. His eyes were dark-blue, open, extremely expressive and often fiery; his nose was also oblong-shaped and slightly crooked; his lips were thin, lively, and often pressed in a mocking way. Upon a first meeting, especially with strangers, Mikhail was cautious and reserved; but as soon as someone had roused his empathy or had touched . . . upon one of his favorite subjects—literature or music, for example—he became more informative and, in the end, even inspired. No one could declaim like he could. . . .

I never saw Mikhail Mikhailovich angry. Whenever he was displeased, he let out some precise and often acid gibe. He was a man of society, gentle and restrained, but also often . . . courteous and optimistic, the consequence of his innate kindness to one and all.

June 1838.
Alexander Rizenkampf, from his memoirs.

Mikhail Dostoevsky invited me into this room . . . and read one of his poems:

"A Mother"
Always a heavenly smile on her lips
Her eyes never with a tear
Always a bright glance on her face
Her voice never with a fear.
Oh shadow so dear to me, how many tears did I shed
When I, grieving, was parted from you
When I carried your open coffin into the church
And for the last time, my friend, bid you adieu.
When all around, people sang: "Rest with the saints!"
When I threw the earth into the ditch, Mother dear,
And bowing to the earth, all headed for home
To talk about things with those who were there.[57]

June–September 1838.
Alexander Rizenkampf, from his memoirs.

Mikhail Mikhailovich's time in [state] service afforded him sufficient free time to write poetry. All his verse, written in a precise and legible way (a handsome style that was remarkably like that of Fyodor Mikhailovich) on smooth and precisely torn paper, lay open on his work table. Mikhail Mikhailovich believed in his poetic gifts and often repeated these lines by Goethe:

> Do not know what I would be without the poetic gift
> But in horror do I recall that thousands are without it.

The hours that I spent in the company of Mikhail Mikhailovich Dostoevsky will always remain among the most pleasant recollections of my life.

June 1838 and after.
Ekaterina Dostoevskaya, from her memoirs.

> Unlike his brother Fyodor, my father [Mikhail] . . . never lost control of himself. Although a passionate lover of music, he did not play an instrument. He was a splendid painter with water-colors. In him one noticed a certain absent-mindedness. . . . He also suffered from twitching muscles of his mouth.

June 1838 and after.
Lyubov Dostoevskaya, from her memoirs.

> The stinginess of my grandfather grew with his increasing passion for drink. He sent his sons so little money [when they were at the Main Engineering Academy] that they were in need of everything. My father could not allow himself even a cup of tea when he returned from classes . . . under a driving rain. He did not have a change of boots . . . or money to pay orderlies. . . .
>
> My father was often indignant over my grandfather's stinginess . . . but the rift did not last long.[58]

June 1838 and after.
Lyubov Dostoevskaya, from her memoirs.

> To everyone my father was kind and tender . . . trusting and naive. . . . For fear that he would succumb to the miserliness of his father, he never refused anyone who asked for money and gave whatever he could.

June 5, 1838.
Fyodor Dostoevsky, from a letter to Mikhail Dostoevsky *père*.

> Good Lord! How long has it been since I last wrote to you! How long has it been since I have tasted those minutes of truly heartfelt bliss, splendid, noble, and pure . . .

a bliss which is felt only by those who have someone to share the hours of both delights and disasters, and in whom one can confide everything that is going on in their souls. Oh, how greedily do I now revel in this bliss....

Our trimester examinations... lasted for at least a month. We had to work day and night; drafting especially did us in.... As you know, I'm not good at drawing. Only in drafting fortifications do I do reasonably well, but what can I do with that?[59] That hurts me greatly... because I'm in the middle of the class... and drawing is considered more important than mathematics. Such a thing disturbs me a great deal.

In all my other subjects, I have perfect scores....

The second reason for my long silence is my drills in formation.... Five reviews by the Grand Duke and the Tsar have worn us out.[60] ... We performed ceremonial marches, did maneuvers, and before every review, were tormented with instruction.... All these reviews heralded a huge, lavish, and brilliant *May Parade*, at which the royal family and 140,000 troops were present.... In the coming months, we are heading for camp. Because of my height,[61] I ended up in the company of skirmishers who must undergo a double instruction: training for the battalions and skirmishing....

Who would have thought or assumed that Brother would be ordered somewhere else?... That is what God wants. What is His will cannot be changed by any force. Fate usually plays with the world like a toy. It assigns roles to humankind... but it is blind. But God is the path along which one can escape any misfortune. But brother is not in any misfortune. Of course, it is bitter and painful to see the grief of a father like yourself.... But be at peace, dearest Papa, my brother's service and position also have their advantages.... The main thing is practical experience. That he is getting now. He can go to school anytime anywhere.... Recently I received a letter from Brother... and I think that his life is enviable....

My present financial situation is somewhat poor.... The May parade demanded many repairs and additions to my dress coats and accouterments. All my new comrades had new shakos; but the one I had from the Academy was so bad that it could have caught the Tsar's attention. So I had to buy a new one, which cost 25 rubles. The rest of the money I used to repair my instruments and to buy brushes and paints. All necessities! By the time camp rolls around, I will be in terrible shape because to be without money there will be a catastrophe. So, if it is possible, dear Papa, send me the least little bit.

Summer 1838 and after.
Andrei Dostoevsky, from his memoirs.

During what was to be my last stay in the village... I did not notice anything abnormal in my father's life.

June–July 1838.
Alexander Saveliev, from his memoirs.

When Fyodor Mikhailovich went to camp at Peterhof and spent the night in the village, he saw . . . the most horrible poverty, the absence of business and trade, the poor clay-like soil, the lack of work . . . the wretched huts . . . the masses of children and young people. . . .

For these individuals, Dostoevsky, Berezhetsky, and many of their friends . . . collected and distributed money.

August 9, 1838.
Fyodor Dostoevsky, to Mikhail Dostoevsky *fils*.

True, I am lazy, very lazy. But what can be done when only one thing remains for me in the world: to be endlessly idle! I do not know if my melancholic ideas will ever subside. Only one condition has been given to the lot of humankind. The atmosphere of the soul consists of a merging of heaven and earth. What an unlawful child is man. The law of spiritual nature has been broken. . . .

It seems to me that our world is a purgatory of heavenly beings, darkened by sinful thought. It is also my view that our world has taken on a negative meaning, and that satire has emerged from elegant, refined spirituality. . . .

But to see only the cruel covering under which the universe languishes, to know that a single burst of will is sufficient to smash it and to merge it with eternity, to know and to be like the last creation on earth . . . how terrible are such thoughts! How fainthearted is man! Hamlet, Hamlet![62] When I recall those wild savage speeches, when I hear the groaning of a numb world, neither sadness, nor grumbling, nor reproach grips my breast. . . . My soul is so overwhelmed by grief that it fears to understand it, lest it be torn to pieces.

Pascal said that he who protests against philosophy is himself a philosopher.[63] A pitiful philosophy! Well, Brother, it seems as if I have gotten carried away by my chatter. . . .

You complain of your poverty. But what can I say? I'm not rich either. Would you believe that during our march from camp, I did not have a single copeck to my name; that . . . I got sick from hunger and a cold (it poured rain all day and we were out in the open); and that I did not have a penny to soothe my throat with even a swallow of tea. I recovered, but my lot was most distressing until I received money from Papa. I immediately paid off my debts and spent the rest.

But the description of your situation exceeds everything. Is it really possible not to have 5 copecks, *to feed onself* on God knows what, and with a fond gaze to sense the sweetness of those marvelous berries of which you are so fond! How sorry I feel for you! . . .

You boast that you have reread a great many things . . . but please do not imagine that I envy you. At Peterhof I myself have read at least as much as you. All of Hoffman in Russian and German[64] (i.e., his untranslated *Tom-Cat Murr*),[65] almost all of Balzac (Balzac is great! His characters are the products of a mind of the universe! It is not the spirit of the time, but an entire millennium that, in struggle, has prepared such a culmination in the soul of man). Goethe's *Faust* and his short poems.[66] Polevoi's *History* and *Ugolino*,[67] [Zhukovsky's] *Undina*,[68] (about *Ugolino* I will write you a few things later). Also Victor Hugo, except *Cromwell* and *Hernani*.[69] . . . Write and comfort me as often as possible. . . . Write or you will torment me with worry.

P.S. I have a project: to become insane. Let people rant and rave, let them be treated, let them be made intelligent. If you have read all of Hoffman, you surely remember the character Alban.[70] How do you like him? It is terrible to see an individual who has the inscrutable in his power, a person who does not know what he should do, and who plays with a toy that is—God!

Early October 1838.
Mikhail Dostoevsky *fils*, from a letter to Mikhail Dostoevsky *père*.

From your letter one can see that you are doing things beyond your strength. But what is the point of all your strivings, all your cares and concerns, if they cost you your health! . . . I so fear for you, dear Papa, that truly, if it were possible, I myself would begin to help you and share your efforts and pains!

Do not worry about brother Fedya [Fyodor]. He has written the same things to me, but these are only conjectures on his part. Things depend more on his examinations than on his drawings. Even if he has to repeat a year, that would not be the worst thing. In fact, it might even be for the better. . . . As for his being dismissed, I, in truth, do not know anything except only to swear to you that such a thing could never happen. Only individuals who behave badly or who sit in the same class for 4 or 5 years in a row are expelled! . . . Do you really imagine that Fedya is the only one there who draws poorly? Believe me when I say that more than half of the students there not only draw poorly, but also do not know how to study at all! . . .

Shidlovsky writes to me often, and the most huge and intelligent letters, to boot! He continues to love me so very much! He is an incomparable individual!

The list I sent to you contains the books necessary to prepare for the examination. . . . Some of them cost over a hundred rubles! . . . Can you send me some money?

October 29, 1838.
Mikhail Dostoevsky *fils*, from a letter to Mikhail Dostoevsky *père*.

Brother has not written anything for a long time. He has exams now.

October 30, 1838.
Fyodor Dostoevsky, from a letter to Mikhail Dostoevsky *père*.

For God's sake, dearest, Papa, do not be angry at me for my silence.... My exams have come to an end.... I did *excellently* on them. But ... I'm being held back in class for another year.... Oh, how many tears has this [situation] cost me. How ill I became when I heard the news. Promoted into the next class were people who did a hundred times worse than I (but who had the patronage and protection of others).... Obviously, one cannot forge his own way through life....

I was out of favor with several of the teachers here and those with the loudest voices to boot.... I even had run-ins with two of them. One word from them, and I was kept back....

Out of a possible perfect score of 10 (15 for algebra and fortifications), I received:

an 11 in algebra (the teacher in this class definitely wanted to keep me back; he is angrier at me more than anyone else); and,

a 12 in fortifications, an 8 in artillery, a 10 in geometry, a 10 in history, a 10 in geography, a 10 in Russian, a 10 in French, a 10 in German, and a 10 in theology....

What do I care? ... But I've lost an entire year! Don't be angry with me, Papa! ... Have mercy on yourself. Look at our poor family, at our poor little brothers and sisters who live only through your life and who look only to you for support. Why should you get upset, not take care of yourself, and surrender to despair? You love us all so much that in our fate, you do not wish to see a single failure. But who has not experienced such a thing?

You are now tormenting yourself with the groundless thought that if I am kept back, I will be expelled from school. But am I really devoid of such talent that the people here will do such a thing? Or maybe I do not know how this institution is run, its rules and regulations? ... What baseness!

Believe that my entire life will have a single goal: to love and please you. What can be done? Such is the will of God.

P.S. I will be more punctual in my letters now.... Oh, when will the time come when I will embrace you with love and joy! But now yet another year of this worthless, insignificant petty-officer service!

You have ordered me, dearest father, to be open about my needs. Yes, I am truly poor now. I have even borrowed to send you this letter and have nothing to repay the person. Send me something right away. You will get me out of this hell.

October 31, 1838.
Fyodor Dostoevsky, from a letter to Mikhail Dostoevsky *fils*.

Oh, how long, how long has it been since I have written to you, my dear Brother.... I've not been promoted! Oh horror! Still another year, an entire extra year! I would not be so furious if I did not know that it was baseness, and baseness alone that deposed me. I would not regret such a thing if the tears of our poor father did not burn my soul. Until now, I did not know what people meant by injured pride. I would have blushed if I had let that feeling possess me.... But you know what? I feel like smashing the entire world in a single stroke.

Before the examination, I lost, I killed so many days. I got sick and lost weight. But on the examination, I did superbly in the full force and volume of that word—still I was left back. Such was the wish of one teacher (of algebra) whom I had been rude to during the year, and who today had the audacity to remind me of my misbehavior, citing it as the reason why I am being kept behind.[71] ... But to hell with it all. If that's the way things are, so be it....

My friend! You philosophize like a poet. But just as the soul receives an ounce of inspiration in an uneven way, so is your philosophy uneven and false. [You say] in order to *know* more, one has to *feel* less; but when one thinks of the reverse, one comes up with a rule that is hasty and rash, the ravings of the heart. What do you mean by the word, *know*? To know nature, the soul, God, love.... Those things are the province of the heart, not the mind. If we were spirits, we would live and hover in the sphere of thought over which our soul lives when it wishes to decipher an idea or the like. But we are dust, people who must decipher a thought they cannot embrace readily. The mind is the conductor of thought through a perishable external shell into the composition of the soul. The mind is a material capability ... but the spirit or the soul lives on the thought which the heart whispers to it.... Thought arises in the soul. The mind is the instrument, a machine moved by the fire of the soul.... Moreover, the mind of the individual, when attracted to the realm of knowledge, operates independently of *feeling* and, consequently, of the *heart*. But if the goal of knowledge is nature and love, a clear field will open up for the *heart*....

One should not assume that philosophy is a simple mathematical problem with nature as the unknown variable.... Note that the poet, in a moment of inspiration, tries to solve the mystery of God. In so doing, he also fulfills the purpose of philosophy. It also follows that the ecstasy of poetry is the ecstasy of philosophy ... and that philosophy is that same poetry, only in the highest degree! ...

It is strange that you think in the spirit of today's philosophy.... How many muddleheaded systems have been born in fiery intelligent minds. To come up with the correct result from this diverse heap, one needs a mathematical formula. These are the rules of today's philosophy....

Brother, it is sad to live without hope.... I look ahead and the future terrifies me.... I float in some kind of cold, polar atmosphere which not a single ray of light has crept through.... For a long time now, I have not felt any bursts of inspiration.... I am often in the same situation that the prisoner of Chillon[72] undergoes after the death of his brothers in the prison.... The heavenly bird of poetry does not fly to me or warm my chilled soul.... Even my previous dreams have left me, and the wondrous arabesques I once created have lost their splendor. The thoughts that used to scorch my heart and soul with their rays are now devoid of flame and warmth. Either my heart has grown hard or... I am terrified to continue on.... It is terrible for me to say that all the past was one golden dream, ornate musings....

Brother, I've read your poem.... It brought forth several tears from my soul and for a while lulled it with the cordial whispering of remembrances. You say that you have an idea for a drama.... I'm glad to hear that.... Write it.... Oh, if you would be deprived of even the last crumbs from a heavenly feast, what would there be left for you to do....

Listen, brother! As I see it, fame also facilitates a poet's inspiration. Byron was an egoist: his thoughts about glory were insignificant and vain.... But the idea that sometime after you follow your former rapture, a pure, nobly splendid soul will rush forth from the ashes; and the thought that inspiration, like a heavenly mystery, will illuminate pages over which you have cried and future generations will weep—I do not think that such a musing does not steal into the poet's soul even at the very moments of creation. The empty cry of the crowd is insignificant. Ah! I just recalled two lines by Pushkin in which he describes the poet and the mob:

And spits (the crowd) at the altar, where your fire burns,
And in childish playfulness rocks the tripod on which you sit![73]...

Truly, is not that charming?

P.S. Write me the main thought of Chateaubriand's *The Genius of Christianity*.[74] Not long ago, I read in *Son of the Fatherland*[75] an article by the critic Nisard on Victor Hugo.[76] Oh, how low he stands in the opinion of the French. How insignificant does Nisard claim Hugo's novels and dramas to be. People treat Hugo unjustly; and although Nisard is an intelligent person,[77] what he writes about Hugo is ravings. One more thing: write me the main idea of your drama. I am sure that it is splendid, although ten years is too short a span to develop dramatic characters. At least that is what I think.

Oh, brother, how sorry I am that you are short of money! Tears rush down my cheeks. When did this happen to us?...

In your poem, "A Vision of Mother," I do not understand the strange shape with which you clothe the deceased woman's soul. The character from beyond the grave is incomplete. The verses are good, though, though in one place, there is a blunder. Don't be angry with me for my comments.

Very soon I'll read through all of Ivan Nikolaevich [Shidlovsky's] new verse.[78] How much poetry is in them! How many brilliant ideas! . . .

I feel sorry for poor Papa! What a strange character he is! Oh, how many misfortunes has he to endure! It is bitter to the point of tears that there is nothing to comfort him. And you know what? Papa does not know the world at all. He has lived in it for fifty years and has the same opinion of people he had of them thirty years ago. What blissful ignorance. But he is very disillusioned. That seems to be our common lot.

Late October 1838.
Dmitri Grigorovich, from his memoirs.

> Dostoevsky . . . was a mediocre student. He forced himself to do just enough so that he could be promoted . . . and would not be held back from graduation. His strategy was not always successful, though. In one of his classes, he failed the final examination and had to spend an additional year in school. Such a reversal Dostoevsky took in an extremely hard way. He even became sick over his setback and had to spend time in the infirmary.

Circa November 1838 and after.
Vsevelod Soloviev, from his memoirs.

> Dostoevsky told me: "In your article about Shidlovsky, mention without fail that although . . . no one knows him . . . he was for me a great man whose name should not be forgotten. . . . For God's sake, dear one, say that. . . ."
>
> According to what Dostoevsky told me, Shidlovsky was an individual who reconciled an abyss of contradictions. Although he possessed immense intelligence and talent, he never wrote a word or developed his gifts. Rather, he surrendered to drunkenness and carousing—and vows in a monastery. . . . He also spent time in hard labor in Siberia.[79] When he finished his sentence there, he had a ring made from the irons of his fetters. He always wore this ring, and when he died, he swallowed it.

Circa November 1838 and after.
Nikolai Reshetov, from his memoirs.

> Ivan Nikolaevich Shidlovsky was an extremely remarkable individual, quite apart from ordinary beings. . . . He was a very tall and handsome man with splendidly

expressive eyes. He was also highly confident . . . the result of his fine mind, good education, and overall approach to the world.

What attracted people to Shidlovsky was his superb way of speaking. An idealist, his conversations centered primarily on abstract subjects. Shidlovsky was also a poet who wrote verse as freely and easily as if he were speaking.

The impression Shidlovsky made on his listeners was truly fascinating, something that even I, as a twenty-year-old youth, also experienced. No matter what the group or gathering, Shidlovsky was always there, everywhere, as a welcome guest. Everyone, young and old, listened to his inspiring stories with pleasure. Women went wild over him, calling him . . . "our Chrysostom." Shidlovsky possessed a wonderful memory. He also declaimed poetry in an excellent way, and was a passionate fan of Pushkin, many of whose poems he knew by heart. He often said that one of the key reasons why he set out to work in Petersburg was his ardent desire to see Pushkin face-to-face. To his great sorrow, though, Shidlovsky confessed that he had not found the writer among the living; but that on the day of his arrival to the city, he saw Pushkin in his coffin.[80] . . .

When Ivan Nikolaevich met with military officers, the conversation was not about elevated things alone. Puns and witticisms were the order of the day; his verse ceded nothing to Barkov's muse.[81] He never refused to engage in drinking bouts; indeed, they eventually became for him a necessity.

To the grief of his mother, Ivan Nikolaevich avoided the affairs of the estate completely. He often dressed in strange clothes and left home to visit monasteries. Knowing well both theology and sacred scripture, he enchanted the monks with his spiritual discussions and in meetings which usually ended in lavish drinking. For a while, Ivan Nikolaevich lived in one of the monasteries around Voronezh.[82] The monks, lacking a superior and unhappy about the restrictions over drink, took advantage of his presence to abuse the alcohol that was there. When the bishop of the Voronezh got wind of the goings-on, he blamed Shidlovsky, and forbade him from engaging in any of the activities in all the monasteries of the region.

The last time I encountered Ivan Nikolaevich was . . . an early morning one spring . . . I saw a tall individual in strange clothes and standing in the middle of a crowd of peasants. . . . Men were standing with bared heads; many of the women were crying. Ivan Nikolaevich . . . always knew that he could always find listeners among the folk alongside a local tavern. In fact, this was not the first time he had been to such a place. Having finished his sermon, Ivan Nikolaevich turned to the people . . . and said: "Orthodox Ones, let us praise the Lord God!" In response, the entire crowd moved closer to him. . . . I cannot say that the choir was the best-looking group, all the more so since on the night before, they had been celebrating a wedding. But there was something charming in this picture, i.e, simple people singing a common prayer in an emotional way.

Shidlovsky was surprised that I was meeting him in such circumstances and with such a group. But solemnly, he responded: "To teach the Word of God to our younger brothers is my truthful calling! Look at how sincere and content these good people are!" At that very moment, as if to affirm what Shidlovsky had just said, a peasant approached Ivan Nikolaevich to thank him for his sermon and to bid him to have "one for the road" before everyone left for their homes. He then brought Shidlovsky a glass of vodka. Despite the fact that it was early morning, Ivan Nikolaevich did not refuse the offer.

From Shidlovsky, I heard stories about Mikhail and Fyodor Dostoevsky who, at that time, were still young officers. . . . He particularly spoke a great deal about Fyodor Mikhailovich, for whom he predicted a great future as a writer.

Circa November 1838 and after.
L. Shidlovskaya, from her memoirs.

I. N. Shidlovsky engaged in a large work . . . a history of the Russian Church. Such scholarly activity, though, did not take up all his spiritual activity. An inner discord, a dissatisfaction with his surroundings—these were hypothetically the reasons that, in the fifties, aroused in him a desire to enter the Valuisky Monastery.[83] Apparently not finding satisfaction and moral peace there, he undertook a pilgrimage to Kiev, where he appealed to a spiritual elder who advised him to return home to the village, where he lived until his death, never shedding his clothes as a novice-monk.

Shidlovsky had an outstanding mind and a brilliant wit. He brought together a vast education and profound scholarly knowledge. His life, strange and rife with all kinds of falsities, testified to his strong passions and stormy nature. To his followers, he came across as an unusual person. His influence on society and his personal conversation were beyond words. The deep moral feeling of Ivan Nikolaevich stood out in marked contrast to his other strange deeds: a sincere faith and religiosity united with temporary skepticism and negation. It was this aspect in his character that was noted so rightly by F. M. Dostoevsky.[84]

Circa November 1838.
Ivan Shidlovsky, from his poetry.

> I am a Vulcan!
> My element is fire!
> In love can you, will you reject
> All other amusement and desire?

> I can feel in no other way
> My being I cannot surrender or rest
> Like lightning will I burn in your embrace
> With a kiss will I tear my heart from my chest. . . .
> But love me now and always
> Do not think where such heavenly feeling will lead.
> We are here for all time, together
> What are life and death? What in them do we need?

November 1838 and after.
Alexander Rizenkampf, from his memoirs.

> At the [Main] Engineering Academy, Fyodor Mikhailovich told me of his love for Pushkin's *Egyptian Nights*,[85] Zhukovsky's "The Smalgolsky Barin,"[86] and other verse. . . . Having told me of his own literary attempts, he confessed that the only thing he regretted at the school was that the strict regimen of the place did not permit his absence from classes and drills. . . .
>
> Fyodor Mikhailovich was a rather roundish and stocky fair-skinned blond with a circular face and a slightly snub nose. He was not as tall as his brother. His light chestnut-colored hair was, for the most part, cut short. He had a high forehead, sparse eyebrows, and small, deep grey eyes. He also had pale, freckled cheeks, and somewhat thick lips. The color of his face was always earthen and sickly looking. . . . His teeth, ruined from constant smoking, caused him grief. . . .
>
> No less than his brother, Fyodor Mikhailovich was courteous and kind, but when he was not in a good mood, he often looked at everything through dark glasses. When flushed with wine, he forgot propriety and sometimes got carried away to the point of swearing and forgetting himself. . . .
>
> Fyodor Mikhailovich . . . loved poetry passionately, but he wrote only prose since he lacked the patience for rhythms and the like. Seizing upon some subject, he became so enlivened by it that his entire body boiled and seethed. Thoughts came to him like splashes in whirlpools. Whenever that happened, he descended into a kind of frenzy. His way of declamation, splendid and innate, moved beyond artistic self-possession. His voice, hoarse by nature, became penetrating and loud, foam gathered about his lips; he gestured, cried out, and spat all around him.

November 1838 and after.
Lyubov Dostoevskaya, from her memoirs.

> My father did not like wine and, like all nervous people, he tolerated it poorly.

November 19, 1838.
Mikhail Dostoevsky *père*, from a letter to Varvara Dostoevskaya.

> I thank you that you did not forget November 8th, i.e., the day of my angel, during which, as you know, I set aside all the cares of life, and dedicate the day first to God—my single comforter in this woeful existence—and second to myself. But there was no cause for joy.
>
> Day by day, my ill health has grown worse and in the end has confined me to bed completely. As you know, given my years, and all the more because of the unpleasantries of life, I am used to having blood drawn, but as there is no good medical assistant in Zaraisk, and fearing that my hands would be harmed, I delayed [bloodletting] for a long time, and made my illness worse.
>
> Unfortunately, I have also received a letter from Fedinka [Fyodor] ... who informs me that at an examination he quarreled with two teachers, an act which was taken for coarseness, and so will remain in the same class until May of next year. In my sickly condition, such a thing so distressed me that it led to complete exhaustion. My left side began to grow numb, and my head began to spin. I called on God for help, and also summoned the medical assistant who so tortured me with four cuttings that I fainted four times.... I recall only in a dream Sashinka the mourner, and that [I] your father had died. But I am alive ... but my life is forged in a crucible of misfortunes.

November 28, 1838.
Mikhail Dostoevsky *fils*, from a letter to Mikhail Dostoevsky *père*.

> Papa! Dear Papa! Why do you grieve so much over brother? I've already written to you that such a matter is not worth such distress.... He passed the examination in splendid fashion. In almost all his subjects he received perfect grades. A single argument with his teacher in algebra was the cause.
>
> Papa! Who in his lifetime has not suffered injustice and affliction? I think that you yourself can serve as an example of such things! It seems to me that in this world, misfortune and the blows of fate can always be considered as signs of God's favor. But all these *physical* joys and all this dirty unhappiness in which the heart and mind lie swaddled in pitiful sleep, these are the stuff of only the mocking of fate, which, from pity and suspicion, does people out of their share of things, since it considers them unworthy for battle with themselves! ... In misfortune, an individual becomes more of a person and approaches the divine ideal! Self-consciousness suffuses from the features of his face; his stance and demeanor become prouder because he feels himself to be worthy of life, because he feels he has the right to say: "I have lived, I have known grief!" One example that calamities produce greater people than good fortune is enough to comfort any sufferer!

But what about spirituality? Faith? Religion? They help people who are more unfortunate than fortunate! . . . Who would not want to be the poorest being on earth, but also to be a *person*, rather than a happy and unfeeling beast! Oh, Papa! For the sufferers there are joys! Oh, and what joys they are! Let them take everything from me, let them leave me naked, but let them give me Schiller and I will forget the entire world! What are all these external things to me, when my spirit is hungry! He who believes in the splendid is already happy! I often cry from joy, more often than from grief, and I look forward to the visit of these minutes! That is joy! A joy that is spiritual, not physical!

You have sent me money, dear Father, but I am afraid that you have deprived yourself of necessities if only to share what you have with me! I always keep thinking that you are without things. So I do not know how to thank you. . . .

Papa! Should I confess something to you?! I have kept the money [you sent me]! I cry about such a thing, tormented by the thought that it was sent for books, but that I kept it for myself: But what was I to do? I was without a copeck! It was with difficulty that I got hold of the fifty copecks to send you a letter for your name-day. Now winter is approaching and it is getting very cold, but I have nothing warm to wear. At work, I must sometimes stand outside . . . without a full-dress uniform but in a single cold and thin overcoat! My boots are also in poor shape. I have no gloves . . . and I also have to eat. . . . Oh, if you only knew how I am economizing. I'm eating no more than one meal a day. Oh, if only you would not be angry with me! A thousand times I ask for your forgiveness! . . .

P.S. Well, Papa! Rejoice with me! It seems that I am not without poetic talent! I have already written a great many small poems, and sent off several to Shidlovsky. He praises them to the extreme! I myself am beginning to believe that there is poetry in them. Now I have begun to write a *drama*. Already I have managed to come up with a first act! If you're really not angry at me, I will send you something! . . . Poetry makes up all my current existence, all my sensations, sorrow and joy. . . .

P.P.S. If you will be able to send me some underwear, I will be very grateful. I particularly have very few . . . pillowcases, handkerchiefs, and towels.

December 16, 1838.
Mikhail Dostoevsky *fils*, from a letter to Mikhail Dostoevsky *père*.

Already there is a festive spirit outside. How quickly does our time fly by! But let it do so, if such a flight does not tear the last surfing boards from the hands of poor swimmers! Truly, one can compare the passage of time to the Russian sprite who, according to legend, assumes the shape and form of anything it passes! It only has to take an object into its hands and pour itself completely into whatever it likes to take on all kinds of forms. . . .

In spite of all my protests, Brother has been quiet for so long that I myself have stopped writing to him. Most likely, he does not feel sadness when he does not receive letters from anywhere! How sad I sometimes become with the single thought that I am here alone, that there is not a single soul here with whom I could share my sensations! . . . I am better, I find it easier when I sit alone in my room surrounded by books and swamped by papers! Everyone is surprised that I do not die from boredom without friends and staying at home all the time. But . . . I am bored with such people. I have become convinced that solitude, and only solitude is my genuine element! Truly if I could break off all ties with the world and the chains imposed about my being by the pleasantries of society, if I could lock myself up in only my soul alone so that I would be happy! Then, perhaps, I could fulfill my purpose in life!

Good God! How many thoughts, how many feelings sometimes perish because I do not have time for such things! . . . I have laid down a rule for myself to study firmly and without fail history, English, and Italian! . . . How many riches of the human mind are hidden from me solely because of my lack of knowledge in these areas! Oh, but I still must study other things to get somewhere in life! Now I study mathematics and fortifications diligently. . . .

How are you getting along, dear Papa? The other day I had such a terrible dream that worried me a great deal as if something unpleasant had happened to you. For God's sake, write to me as quickly as possible! . . .

Yes! Already the holidays will soon be here. . . . Let the grey time,[87] having, like a snake, shed its skin, and now in new garb, begin to shine forth more brightly before your eyes!

1839

Circa 1839.
Alexander Saveliev, from his memoirs.

> Fyodor Mikhailovich was little inclined toward military service. . . . One time . . . when he was presented to Grand Duke Mikhail Pavlovich . . . he became flustered, and said "Your Excellency" [instead of "Your Imperial Highness"]. That was enough for the authorities and Dostoevsky to catch hell.

Early 1839.
Dmitri Grigorovich, from his memoirs.

> [At the Main Engineering Academy] Dostoevsky prevailed upon . . . Beketov, Vitkovsky, and Berezhetsky [and myself]—to take up reading. As a result there came

to be a literary circle, which kept to itself and which came together whenever its members had a free moment.... We read indiscriminately, anything and everything that fell into our hands or was carried into school in secret.

January 3, 1839.
An order from the Military Engineering Academy.

As certified by the commander colonel of the company of the guards, the following students have shown weakness in their behavior and knowledge of service....
Dostoevsky, Fyodor ...
And should be put under special command and given daily study.[88]

January 17, 1839.
Ivan Shidlovsky, from a letter to Mikhail Dostoevsky *fils*.

The graceful elegance of your verse returns me to my youth, to that pure simplicity that is devoid of contemporary vanity and frenzied Byronic egoism, and without which one cannot enter into the Heavenly Kingdom. Yes, an individual is more powerful than any noble manifestation of the Creator if he preserves the reflection, the expression of the eternal in an inextinguishable and endless faith, as well as in an unconscious, but clear and all-embracing instinct. We must believe that God is good, for otherwise he is not God; and that the Universe is the visible, tangible beauty of this goodness, as well as the substantial, necessary unity of this and other truths. Only then can our spirit recognize everything in itself; only then will it throw a web of sympathy around the boundaries of its being; and only then in the center of this web will it embrace God Himself. This is the only true sign of the great poet, who is man at his highest peak. Splatter him with dirt, cover him with dust, slander him, oppress him, torture him, his soul will stand firm, true to itself. The Angel of inspiration will guide him safely out of the dungeon of life into the world of immortality and into the lodge of all-pervading glory.

Polevoi said it well when, in my presence, he asserted that one should look at the individual as a pathway to emerging greatness in humanity, but also that the body is like a clay pitcher that will break sooner or later, and that past virtues and occasional vices will disappear.[89] The Almighty has granted you a powerful and wondrous contemplation, an active imagination, and a creative will. Do not let go of all these things. Stand firm against all petty temptations! I see you with the wreath of one who has been chosen.

Do you know that I myself have changed internally? The abacus now does not concern me. My will asks from Heaven a feat that is difficult but bright. The salvific shield of proud contempt toward everything has concealed it. From the very moment of my return from home, my heart began to warm more and more with the fervor of humility and faith. Now, long ago, on Christmas Eve, it ceded to a determination to break the chains of being, to abandon this captivity. The river bottom, the bottom of my dear Fontanka, beckoned to me passionately, like the marital bed of a betrothed one.[90] Such a thing had to happen so that returning across the ice from vespers, which served as a final confession of my clouded soul, I fell into an ice hole. The water was already up to my ears when a soldier and a dumb old woman dragged me out, after which, despite even the moralizing of my frightened Vasili,[91] my thoughts still were not at peace. Through the very holiday nature of vespers, though, some kind of wondrous enlightenment fell on my eyes. Tears splattered hotly—and I came to believe, I recognized that my life is an unbreakable link of divine favors, that He is the All, that He extends His mercy at every moment, and that He fills new instants with all the fulness of His generosity. Consequently, to cut short my days means to turn away from certain Divine mercies. A boldness that transforms itself into a worthy undertaking is possible only when it is realized in an essence that has experienced its tie with life, in an essence that fate has refused, rendering it as an expiated sacrifice to all the torments of people. So it was with Werther[92] and Chatterton.[93] They rejected the conditions of life, and life no longer remained for them. But I still have the darkness of duties to life: poetic hours, beef, and wine. Perhaps even a laurel wreath will come my way. After all, not everyone can pick from the tree of glory as a fortunate individual like yourself! So I remain patiently not to spin, but to wear to rags the threads of existence. Up until now my thought has never needed people less than now. I am ready to become a thief, a desperado for the fulfillment of life's necessities, for the continuation of my days with this goal—to bear all the horrors of the soul and to give birth to them in the light.

Do not think that all this is the result of the praises which you, as a good friend, showered upon me, or from the manly force of your verse, wondrous in its images, as well as of other people who empathize strongly with my wish to write, and who find my lines very dear and the like!

I know that my literary miscarriages surpass anything written by Timofeev, but that they are nothing more than the most superficial gloss of harmony; all the rest, even the image of expression, remains to the side. In any case, I forgive your contradictions . . . from an excessive, if somewhat blind (assessment), and attachment to me. I am happy over an attachment more than the highest assessment. I am writing this only because I cannot help but to do so. But now truly I do not envy anyone's flight, anyone's success.

There exist people for whom the appearance of my name in print—if one can understood what this means—only adds to my deformed growth. . . . People demand poetry.... [One female acquaintance] ... is on the lookout for hymns. She wishes that the world read my verse. She sees me as genuflecting before her so that she may appear as another idol for my poetry, which she understands as noble and worthy because it is good, miraculously good—and enticing, wondrously enticing! But she will not pluck the chords from my many-stringed lute, made spell-bound with the fragrance of an occasional flower.

But why not sometimes fall into reverie, squeezing the tender hands of a splendid woman, even if you do not love her, covering these hands with your kisses, feeling her very warm, velvet lips against your cheeks! I never had anything against such things, and I hope that God will forgive me for them! ...

How fortunate to be a contemporary of such strivings forward! Someone will be the Genius-Master who will forge its link! God grant that He show you the way! ...

You were surprised about my wish to be a Journalist since you thought that such an occupation was worse than service in a Department; but truly you do not want to penetrate into that invisible, magic force with which a Journalist forms minds, creates social opinion, sheds light on views already in existence, and in the forest, in the darkness of misunderstandings, looks for new growth amid the dead wood and points to geniuses—directly or indirectly, positively or negatively. He also serves as an argument for the Judgment of posterity....

I would like to enter the sphere of a Journalist, but I have neither the talent, nor the necessary capacity for ceaseless hard work....

I love you to the extreme—very, very much. I love you first of all as a hiding place in which my soul, freely and fearlessly, has taken shape and continues to do so; and second as a Poet with a clear view of the world. Be steadfast, dearest friend, not only in this current year, but when time will end for me, which I cannot help but hope for soon, seeing my goalless insignificance. Do not carouse anywhere with anybody, but be joyful alone. What should be done? What should I engage in? I go to Church as often as possible, but my soul is not always capable of getting carried away by prayer.

Late January 1839.
Mikhail Dostoevsky *fils*, from a letter to Mikhail Dostoevsky *père*.

You have expressed a wish, dear Papa, to read my attempts at poetry! And so, I offer you a sparse plate from my poetic kitchen. I know, though, that the content of my verse is to your liking.

I cannot recall deceased Mama without powerful spiritual trepidation! This summer I saw her in a dream, as if she had descended purposely from heaven only to bless me. Such was the impetus for my verse.[94] ... You write that I should send you everything that I have written right away. But would it not be better if I would wait and send you an entire package of my verse?

Oh, Papa, I myself am beginning to have talent, or perhaps I will be able to leave something behind after me. But is it really my fate to have it perish in the triflings of life? You have written to me that poetry be my rest and relaxation! Papa! But is it a toy which I can play with when I want to? Can one play with something which feeds my entire life, and without which my existence would be nothing? Play with something that I love more than my life? No! No earthly endeavors will tear from my heart my attempts for art! . . .

How little time there is! . . . Only now have I become convinced that a person should devote himself only to one thing. I have dedicated myself to art, and if not that, then to someone else who is higher than us!

I have begun to write a drama in three acts, but my schoolwork tears me away from it. The heat of my inspiration grows cold and I am forced to set it on fire. But my play again tortures me. My destroyed characters are again entering into my head. But if only I had the time, the time! I would write it!

How I want to study English! . . . I do not have enough education. I feel such a thing, but with time, with time.

February 2, 1839.
Mikhail Dostoevsky *fils*, from a letter to Mikhail Dostoevsky *père*.

Your letter and package I received the other day. . . . The underwear is marvelous! And the handkerchiefs and the shirts! They are so fine and white! I love good underwear to an extreme. . . .

You note, papa, that I am spending a lot of money; but up until now, I could not but do otherwise, since I kept providing myself with everything and also have been paying off debts which I incurred upon my arrival to Revel. . . . Ah, Papa, Papa! Do we really demand money from you? Do we ourselves not enter into your situation? We ask your help only in extreme circumstances, ones which are almost completely unknown to us. We do so also with childlike obedience, not thinking to cause you any irritation! He who loves is one who wants to be understood, that all his love be known, and thus, Papa, I wish you would rest. Be assured of my love for you! . . .

Would it not be better if you could begin to send me a little money every month? Thus I would not . . . rush from one extreme to the other, from poverty to contentment. Second, I would manage and in such a way make ends meet. This would be for me 1,000 times better . . . because without you noticing it, you would be enriching me. Can you forgive me for writing these lines? Goodbye, dear Papa!

February 24, 1839.
Mikhail Dostoevsky *fils*, from a letter to Mikhail Dostoevsky *père*.

At the beginning of this week I received your letter with the 60 paper rubles in it. I also wish to thank you for your parcel. . . .

Why conceal it? . . . I am completely indifferent to the calling [of engineering], especially when I see the field officers about me, individuals whose heads are as empty as the paper upon which I am writing to you. . . . You never find them with a book, on their foreheads you never notice even a trace of a thought. You speak to them about something a bit real or practical—and they are bored. Can they really be so happy racing about visiting from morning to night? Truly, throughout the entire day they do not learn anything; they do not think up anything. At night, they sleep, themselves not knowing that they are not worthy of such rest! I do not understand, I absolutely do not understand how they can live with their minds and hearts in such peace. Their hearts are decidedly asleep; they wake up only when their owners observe rank or when the bat-boy lets the tea grow cold. . . . That is why the most tender feelings, feelings that ennoble a person and bring one to the divine, assume a coarse cover. One of these officers is a groom who is marrying, for love, an intelligent, sweet girl, but for all that, he has in no way given himself over to the first plan of life's picture. He has the same trifling desires as before! His emotions are beyond all sense! His judgments also. What is the point of being such an individual? From a hundred fresh nuts there fall two or three that are rotten, no more; but from a hundred people you can reckon that half will not be worthy of such a designation! That is the entire difference between nuts and people! The advantage is nonetheless with the former, not the latter. . . .

I study, read, and write—these are my occupations. . . . The penchant for a life that is more intellectual than physical forces me to forget about boredom completely. . . . I sometimes become sad, but never bored. Sadness and boredom are two completely different things! The first is the inclination of the heart to dreaminess, the second is the consequence of intellectual hunger or idleness. . . .

Whenever I manage to have a spare ruble, obtained from rations that I have sold, I always go to some splendid opera. Not long ago I saw *Fenella*,[95] which I have been wanting to see for a long time. So I reward myself fully for my monastic existence with the sounds of Auber, Rossini, and Bellini.

German literature, by its noble character, forces me instinctively to become its patron. With every page of Schiller, Goethe, and Klopstock, one becomes more intelligent; understanding grows with every volume; taste becomes noticeably purer; and with each passing day, critical views become more truthful. The other day I somehow took it into my head to compare me now with the way I was a year ago, and without boasting I can say that I myself marveled at the change! But I still don't do anything, or, at the very least, very little. From English literature, I know only Shakespeare, which I have read in Schlegel's translation.[96] But that is more than sufficient. In his dramas there is an entire world.

March 23, 1839.
Fyodor Dostoevsky, from a letter to Mikhail Dostoevsky *père*.

> Good God! Must I always be the reason for your despair? Everything that I so feared has happened—that I feared would happen has come to be. I am despair, complete despair! . . .
>
> [I know that] you are also despondent over the fate of your son. At your feet I beg your pardon for all the unintentional grief I have caused you.
>
> Although I have been left back a year, I have not lost time. I have been studying military science and have accomplished a great deal. I have followed the courses of the highest class and intend to test out of a class and move into the next one. But I have spent a great deal of money (on books and other things) and I have kept borrowing [from others]. I owe everyone around, and large sums at that. . . . Good God! Will I continue to take your last copecks forever? But your help is essential, otherwise I will perish. The deadline to pay back my debtors has long since passed. Save me. Send me 60 rubles (50 rubles for debts, 10 for pre-camp expenses). Soon I will be in camp and I will need things again. My God! I know that we are poor. But as God is my witness, I am not asking for anything superfluous. So I beg you to help me as soon as possible. Time is passing. I'm all out of paper. Yours to the grave forever and to the end of time.
>
> P.S. Best wishes for Easter, dearest Papa. From the bottom of my heart, I wish you happiness. I have just now received communion. I borrowed money for the priest. For a long time now I have not had a copeck to my name. . . .
>
> If you can send me 100 rubles, I can sit for the examination. If not, it will be another year. I am doing this for you, dearest Papa; it is all the same to me.

May 5, 1839.
Fyodor Dostoevsky, from a letter to Mikhail Dostoevsky *père*.

> I imagine that even now you are worried, since you did not receive an immediate response from me. Dearest papa! I hasten to calm you and to justify my present silence as much as possible. Examinations are here already. We need to study . . . and we use our free time for formation drill. Soon the May parade will be here. . . . I'm very glad that I finally found some free time to talk to you. Oh, how I reproach myself for having been the cause for your grief! Now I will try to make up for it as much as possible. I have received your letter and from the bottom of my heart, I

thank you for the package. You write, dearest Papa, that you yourself do not have any money and that you are not in a condition to send me even a little bit for my time at camp. Children who understand their parents' situation must themselves share all their elders' pride and joys. Children, too, must share fully their parents' need. I will not ask much of you.

If I do not have tea to drink, I will not die of hunger. I will get along somehow! But I beg you to send me at least something for boots for camp. . . . My examinations are going very well. . . . Many of the teachers who disliked me last year are now inclined more favorably toward me than ever. . . . I cannot complain about the people in charge. I remember my responsibilities and am treated justly. But when will I be finished with all this?

You write, dearest Father, that I must not forget my responsibilities. I repeat: I remember them well, and I am already bound to serve by virtue of the oath that I took upon enrolling in the Academy. I have not received any letters from Brother for a long time. But not long ago I received from him a wad of paper covered with writing in which he attacks me like never before for my imaginary silence to you. I confess that he wounded me to the depths of my soul, making me in his eyes a most repulsive creature. . . . I consider myself to be much better person than that. . . .

P.S. Belated wishes for the holiday of Resurrection of the Lord. With what sadness do I recall spending the day with the family! But now? The only thing I want is to get out of the Academy as fast as I can. . . .

Having passed into the highest class, I find it *absolutely essential* to subscribe to the French reading library here. How many great works by geniuses in mathematics and in military affairs there are in French! I see the necessity of reading such things, because I am a passionate fan of military science, even though I cannot stand mathematics. What a strange science! What stupidity to study such a thing. As far as I am concerned, I need only enough as required of an engineer or a little more.

Why would I ever become a Pascal or an Ostrogradsky? Mathematics without an application is a pure "zero"; it is as useful as a soap bubble. I also must tell you that I am sorry to have given up Latin. What a marvelous language it is! I am reading Julius Caesar now, and even after being away from the language for two years, I understand absolutely everything.[97]

May 10, 1839.
Fyodor Dostoevsky, from a letter to Mikhail Dostoevsky *père*.

It is a strange thing: The stupid circumstances of my present life deprive me of many things. . . .

My kind, dear parent! Do you really think that when your son asks financial help of you, he is asking for anything that is nonessential? God is my witness that I do not seek to cause us even the slightest deprivation, not only out of personal gain, but also even out of necessity. How bitter is the service which burdens my loved ones. I have a head, I have hands. If I were free, at liberty, responsible only for myself, I would not ask even a copeck from you. I would be at home with iron need. I would be ashamed even to hint about need. Now, though, I am expressing myself with certain promises for the future; but that future is not far, and in time, you will see me in it.

But now, dearest Papa, recall that I am *serving* in the full sense of the world. Whether I like it or not, I have to conform fully to the rules and regulations of my present society. Why should I make an exception of myself? Sometimes such exceptions undergo horrible unpleasantness. That you yourself understand, dear Papa. You have lived with people. Camp life for every student . . . now demands at least 40 rubles. (I am writing to you about all this because I am speaking to my father.) In this sum, I am not including such needs as, for example, tea, sugar, and so on. Such things are essential no matter what; but they also are so not just because of decency, but because of need. When you get soaked through in raw and rainy weather . . . and are tired and chilled . . . you can fall ill without tea. Such a thing happened to me in March of last year. Nonetheless, as I respect your need, I will not drink tea. I am asking only for what is essential: two pairs of plain boots—16 rubles. My things—books, boots, pens, paper and the like—also must be stored somewhere. For that I must have a trunk. . . . Our beds are heaps of straw, covered with a sheet. . . . Where am I going to put all my things if I do not have a trunk? You should know that the people at the treasury office could care less as to whether I need a place . . . or a trunk. . . . They take care of my clothes . . . but three pairs of state-issued boots will not last six months even in town. There is also no official place for me to keep a trunk. . . . So I will have to arrange to keep something (as everyone does) with one of our soldiers, our servants. . . . But you also have to pay for that. So [I will also need] a silver ruble to purchase a trunk. . . .

(For sending letters, for pens, papers, and so on) I have saved 15 rubles from what you sent me. You can see, dear Papa, that I absolutely need at least an additional 35 rubles. In the first days of June, we will be off to the camps. So send me the money by June 1, if you wish to help your son in his horrible need. I do not dare to demand, and I am not demanding anything excessive. But my gratitude will be limitless.

May 27, 1839.
Mikhail Dostoevsky *père*, from a letter to Fyodor Dostoevsky.

You write . . . that for camp soon you will need the most basic items . . . and that you are upset with your family . . . since, as you see it, they have forgotten you completely.

How unjust you are to me in this regard! . . . I have already sent you . . . what I thought would be enough money . . . and now you are asking me for more. My dear boy, to grumble at your father for sending to you what he can is reprehensible and even sinful.... You will recall that I wrote to tell you that for the third year in a row the harvest was poor.... Now I'm telling you that we have hit rock bottom.... Our current disaster is beyond comparison. Since early spring we have not had a drop of rain or dew! Terrible wind and heat have destroyed everything.... In a word, we are being threatened not only with ruin, but also with starvation![98]

I do not have a copeck to my name . . . but I am sending you an additional 356 paper rubles....

In several letters I have scolded your brother that he . . . writes so little about you other than to say that you are healthy and doing well, but I myself do not have the slightest information about you. I am also angry at him because he wastes his time on triflings, on poetry.... Andryusha [Andrei] is also seemingly doing well, but I have not heard anything from him either. I see that your orderlies are robbing you blind. See if you can get some advice from someone as to how to organize your affairs in the camp a bit more to your advantage. Farewell, my dear friend, may the Lord God bless you with everything your father wishes for you so tenderly.[99]

Before June 1839.
Olga Ivanova, from her memoirs.

Shortly before his death, Mikhail Dostoevsky intended to marry his neighbor, Alexandra Dmitievna Lagvenova, who was very beautiful. The friendship between the descendants of Lagvenova and of Mikhail Dostoevsky continues to this day, across the span of three generations.

Before June 1839.
Stepan Yanovsky, from his memoirs.

Fyodor Mikhailovich told me many things about the burdensome and joyless circumstances of his childhood, although he always spoke reverently about his mother, and his brother, Mikhail Mikhailovich. But he did not like to talk about his father and asked me not to pose any questions about him. About his brother Andrei Mikhailovich he also spoke little.[100]

Before June 1839.
Family members, from their memoirs.

Andrei Dostoevsky was punctual and exacting to the highest degree. He was very hot-tempered but did not bear grudges. He was passionate in conversations, especially in principled arguments. He was a most kind individual, a disinterested person, an idealist. He also had a powerfully developed sense of duty.

Before June 1839.
Andrei Andreevich Dostoevsky, from his memoirs.

My father [Andrei] was distinguished by his exactitude and thoroughness; so much so that I consider all the facts put forth in his memoirs to be unconditionally accurate.

Before June 1839.
Varvara Dostoevskaya-Savostyanova, from her memoirs.

The exactingness of Andrei Mikhailovich was especially apparent in his love for women's needlework. He loved knitting, but he did it not in the way as knitters usually do. Before he went about putting needles together, he wrote down entire list of columns of figures, calculating the stitches and colors in various configurations.

Before June 1839.
Lyubov Dostoevskaya, from her memoirs.

The members of the Dostoevsky family were very proud of their genius-brother, but they also hated him for his superiority. My uncle Andrei was very delighted with the literary talent of his older brother, but he lived in the provinces and rarely came to Petersburg.

Before June 1839.
Fyodor Dostoevsky, from an 1857 letter to Alexander Vrangel.

What disturbs me more than anything else, my friend, is your relationship with your father. From experience, I know extremely well that such bouts of unpleasantness are unbearable, all the more so since I also know that you both love each other. This is a special kind of misunderstanding which the longer it goes on, the more things get confused. Characteristic . . . is the terrible mix of suspicion, the most gloomy and sickly sensitivity, as well as generosity. I do not know your father personally, but in my life, I have known two instances when the relationship with my father was exactly the same as yours. It is necessary to forgive him.

Before June 1839.
Avdotya Spiridonova, from a 1925 interview.

Makhal [Mikhail] Andreevich wanted to punish his peasants, but she [his wife], good soul that she was, began to cry and grieve, praying to Christ-god and saying:

"Do not hurt them." For that Makhal locked her in a shed. "Do not go against my wishes," he said.

But the mistress had such a good heart . . . that the Lord sent her such a son—Fyodor. They tell me that he is quite famous.

Before June 1839.
Danila Makarov and Andrei Savushkin, from a 1925 interview.

The master was a severe, bad man . . . but the mistress was cordial and understanding. He lived with her in a poor way and beat her.[101]

Before June 1839.
Andrei Drozdov, from his memoirs.

Having lost his wife, Mikhail Andreevich became a shattered soul. In his grief, he was extremely cruel to his serfs.

Before June 1839.
Maria Ivanova, from her memoirs.

Toward the end of his life Mikhail Andreevich Dostoevsky was extremely captious and fault-finding, one could say he was half-mad.

Before June 1839.
Danila Makarov and Andrei Savushkin, from a 1925 interview.[102]

Danila Makarov, a peasant from Darovoe, who, he said, has crossed into his eightieth year—"or even more, who knows"—smoked quietly and said:

"I, sir," Makarov said, "don't remember the old master—I wasn't around at the time. My deceased father told me about Mikhail Dostoevsky. He was a beast of a man. His soul was dark! . . . One time he was walking in the garden. . . . The master said —'Here I am! Here I am!'—but Fedot was behind some trees and did not see him. So the master sent for the village elder . . . and ordered, 'Send me Fedot.'

"Fedot, a merry peasant, responded: 'I should comb my beard, the master is calling . . .' When the master asked him: 'Why didn't you acknowledge me?'—Fedot answered, 'There was no way I saw you.' The master countered: 'Off with you to the horse barn for a flogging, so you will see me next time!' And of course, that is what happened. Fedot was flogged!

"There was also Ivan Semyonovich Shirokov, a peasant who kept to himself. . . . Ivan also did not see the master. . . . The master was walking behind the cart—how could one see him? . . . Taking off his hat, our master said: 'Hello there, Ivan! You yourself see. . . . I had to acknowledge you first . . . so . . . off to the horse barn with you!' . . . And of course. . . . Ivan was also flogged!

"In the winter, the peasants didn't know what to do. . . . If you didn't acknowledge the master, he started screaming, but if you took off your hat in the open air, you would catch cold and could not work. . . . So you didn't, and there would be hell to pay. . . .

"They tell me that the *barin*'s son, Fyodor Mikhailovich, became a great writer. I do not believe such a thing. No way could he be one—not with a father like his. I do not believe it."

June 6, 1839.
Andrei Dostoevsky, from his memoirs.

The passion of Mikhail Andreevich Dostoevsky for drink apparently increased and he was almost constantly in an abnormal condition. Spring came, promising little that was good. . . . Affairs in farming were very poor as the result of a bad harvest and hunger threatened. . . . It was at this time in the village of Cheremoshnya, in the field, in a clearing of the forest, there worked a group of peasants, about ten or fifteen men. Beside himself over some unsuccessful actions of the peasants, or, perhaps, so it seemed to him, father flew into a rage and began to shout at them. One of them, bolder than the rest, answered his cry with powerful abuse, and later, fearing the consequences of his action, cried out: "Lads, get 'im!" and with these exclamations, all the peasants rushed to father and in one moment, of course, did away with him.[103]

June 6, 1839.
Danila Makarov and Andrei Savushkin, from a 1925 interview.

The peasants from Cheremoshnya came up with a plan to do away with the master. They agreed among themselves—Efimov,[104] Mikhailov, Isaev,[105] and Vasili Nikitin. All of them are now gone, having died long ago. It was during Petrovka[106] and the peasants were hauling manure. The sun already stood high in the sky. The master asked if everyone had gone to work. He was told that in Cheremoshnya four peasants were still at home, having said that they were sick. "I'll cure what ails them," the master said, and ordered the droshky to be harnessed. And what a club he had with him! When he arrived at Cheremoshnya, the peasants were out on the street. "Why haven't you gone to work?" the master asked. "We're too weak to work," they replied. So with his club, he hit first one, then another. The four ran off into the yard, and he after them. Then Vasili Nikitin—he was a strapping, tall one—grabbed the master from behind, but others stood there, frightened. Vasili cried out: "Why are you standing there? Didn't we agree on this?" The peasants rushed to the master and plugged up this mouth so that there would be no marks on his body. They carried him off to the appointed place . . . and on the road between Darovoe and Cheremoshnya, they dumped his body in a field. The coachman David[107] was the one appointed to do it. He left the master and went to Monogarovo for a priest, but he did not stop at Darovoe. The priest came; the master was breathing, but he was unconscious. The priest heard the master's silent confession. He knew what had happened, but he kept the details to himself and did not turn the peasants in.

June 6, 1839.
Danila Makarov, from his memoirs.

The peasants prepared a bottle of spirits, the entire contents of which they poured down his throat. Then they plugged his mouth with a handkerchief. So the master suffocated.

June 6, 1839.
Lyubov Dostoevskaya, from her memoirs.

My grandfather was found suffocated by a pillow from his carriage, halfway between Darovoe and Cheremoshnya. The driver disappeared with the horses. Several peasants from the village also vanished.

June 6, 1839.
Maria Ivanova, from her memoirs.

From an old neighboring gentry woman, I learned that the death [of Mikhail Dostoevsky] was from pressure on his bladder.

June 6, 1839.
Andrei Dostoevsky, from his memoirs.

The nurse Alyona Fyodorovna lived with Papa in the village and was almost an eyewitness to the tragedy—that is, she saw father's dead body.[108]

After June 6, 1839.
Andrei Dostoevsky, from his memoirs.

They covered up [the crime]. Why did the authorities do such a thing? . . . Why did they not start [proceedings]? So the murders went unpunished." So said our nurse Arina.

June 6–8, 1839.
Andrei Dostoevsky, from his memoirs.

> Like a flock of birds, the local police came to investigate. Of course, the first thing they wanted to know was how the peasants could conceal what they had done. I do not know how much money the police agreed upon, or where the peasants suddenly got hold of what must have been a large sum. I only know that the police were satisfied; and that, after an autopsy, it was certified that my father had died of apoplexy.

June 6–8, 1839.
Danila Makarov and Andrei Savushkin, from a 1925 interview.

> Investigators came from Kashira.[109] They questioned everyone, trying to find out what had happened; but they came up with nothing.

June 6–8, 1839.
Lyubov Dostoevskaya, from her memoirs.

> At the time of the judicial investigation, several of my grandfather's serfs asserted that the murder had been an act of revenge.

After June 6–8, 1839.
Ivan Melikhov, from a 1925 interview.

> The seventy-year-old peasant Ivan Vasilievich Melikhov rejected decisively the murder of Mikhail Dostoevsky. . . . [He said that] the master had been going from Darovoe to Cheremoshnya when he had a stroke. The driver left him in the field and rushed to Monogarovo for a priest. . . . He seemed to have died of a fit. He had had such fits before.[110]

After June 8, 1839.
Andrei Dostoevsky, from his memoirs.

> Father was buried in the church graveyard. On his grave lay a stone without any marking . . . surrounded by a rickety wooden fence. I will have to get a new one.

After June 8, 1839.
Andrei Drozdov, from his memoirs.

> The body of Mikhail Andreevich . . . was buried in the neglected cemetery at Monogarovo. The stone marker was torn from his grave, the gate was broken. The path was so covered with grass that one's legs became tangled. Life had forgotten about him.

After June 10, 1839.
Lyubov Dostoevskaya, from her memoirs.

My father was not at home during the time of his father's terrible death. He no longer went to Darovoe because all the students at the [Main] Engineering Academy had to remain in camp. . . . The crime, committed by his beloved peasants, made a deep impression him.[111] He remembered it all his life, pondering the reasons for this terrible death. It is remarkable that although my grandfather's entire family judged his violent demise an outrage, they never spoke of it. They also did not allow Dostoevsky's literary friends . . . to note it in their recollections of my father. . . .

It always seemed to me that when Dostoevsky created the character of old man Karamazov, he was thinking about his father. Of course, such a statement is not entirely accurate. Fyodor Karamazov comes off as a laughingstock, but throughout my life, my grandfather always kept his dignity. Karamazov was a libertine; but Mikhail Dostoevsky loved his wife sincerely and remained faithful to her. Old man Karamazov threw his sons to the will of fate; but my grandfather raised his offspring with morals and values.

Still, the two shared similarities. When Dostoevsky came up with the image of Fyodor Karamazov, he most likely recalled the miserliness of his father who had forced his sons, as students, to suffer such privation and suffering, and who had distressed them so greatly with his drunkenness and physical repugnance.[112]

When Dostoevsky wrote that Alyosha . . . pitied his father, he was, quite possibly, recalling the moments of empathy he had felt for Mikhail. Perhaps the great psychologist understood that his father was a sick and unhappy man. . . .

I must also note that the similarity between my grandfather and old man Karamazov is exclusively my opinion . . . without any evidence. Most likely, it is incorrect. Perhaps, though, it was not mere chance that Dostoevsky named as Cheremoshnya the village where old man Karamazov sends his son Ivan on the eve of his death. . . .

Even more remarkable is that Dostoevsky had Smerdyakov tell Ivan: "You, of all the children, are the most like Fyodor Pavlovich." Most likely, Dostoevsky lived under the bloody shadow of his father throughout his life; with morbid attention, he lived in constant fear of the vices he could have inherited from his father. But Dostoevsky was another type altogether.

After June 10, 1839.
Lyubov Dostoevskaya, from her memoirs.

My father's family asserted that his first attack [of epilepsy] occurred when he first learned of the tragic death of my grandfather Mikhail. Apparently, then, he suffered from the disease from the age of eighteen on.[113]

After June 10, 1839.
Andrei Dostoevsky, from his memoirs.

> At first people shielded me from the cause of father's death, saying that he had died instantly, from a stroke and the like.[114] But from the conversations that followed after and of which I myself heard, I became convinced quickly that such reports were false. I began to ask first my sister and then my aunt (A. F. Kumanina) to tell me the truth. As a result, I learned . . . that my father had been murdered by his peasants. Later I heard other details of his demise from my sister, Vera Mikhailovna . . . a girl named Arisha . . . and Alyona Frolovna.

After June 10, 1839.
Danila Makarov and Andrei Savushkin, from a 1925 interview.

> The master got along poorly with his oldest daughter, Varvara. . . . When she found out that the peasants had killed her father, she only said: "He died like the dog he was."[115]

After June 10, 1839.
Andrei Dostoevsky, from his memoirs.

> Causes for Father's passing: his powerful love for Mother, his fondness for the bottle, his liaison with Katka [Katerina], his continual state of stress.

Circa June 13, 1839.
Andrei Dostoevsky, from his memoirs.

> No less than a week after my father was buried . . . my grandmother, Olga Yakovlevna, learned from the Khotyaintsevs . . . the truth regarding my father's death.[116] She was advised by them, though, not to pursue the matter for several reasons. It would not return the father to his children; it would be difficult to prove what the police had done; and, most likely, a second autopsy would lead to the same false conclusions. Most important, my aunt was told that if the details of my father's murder were disclosed fully, the result would the complete ruin of his family, since almost all of the male population of the village would have been sent into exile.[117]

After June 13, 1839.
Andrei Dostoevsky, from his memoirs.

> Alexander Andreevich [Kumanin] rendered many kindnesses to our family; and after Papa's death, he sheltered us five orphans (my two older brothers were already

in Petersburg).[118] Truly, he became our benefactor, particularly to my three sisters who, when they married, received from him a huge dowry.[119]

June 16, 1839.
Report from the Kashira Court to the Official Governor.

On this sixth of June the external councillor Mikhail Andreevich Dostoevsky, age 54,[120] and manager of the estate of his deceased wife in the Kashirsky district in the village of Darovoe, was in the field looking after peasants carrying manure and died suddenly.... According to the investigation of the court, the idea that Mikhail Dostoevsky suffered a violent end is beyond suspicion and doubt. The local staff-physician ... affirms an attack of apoplexy, the result of severe hemorrhoidal tension.[121]

June 30, 1839.
Mikhail Dostoevsky,[122] from a letter to Alexandra and Alexander Kumanin.

This week I received from brother Fyodor a letter in which he informed me of the unhappiness that has affected our family.[123] Apparently, Providence finds it necessary to test the firmness of our souls and to force us to drink to the dregs the cup of sorrow. We are absolute orphans without a mother or a father. I am not talking so much about myself or Fyodor. Thank God, we are grown up [but I worry] about the poor children who are left behind.... My God, my God! What have they done to you?

From the village I have received no news at all, and Brother writes in a very unclear way all that has happened. That is why I do not know almost anything in detail. I have heard only that you have taken the children to your place; and for that I have shed tears of gratitude! God will bless you for your kind heart. Uncle! Aunt! Take the place of their parents. Do not let my siblings feel the terrible burden of being orphans. Force the sky to be glad and the angels to rejoice because of your kind deed! Poor Kolya [Nikolai], poor Sashenka [Alexandra]!

I do not know who will be our guardian. If I did not know completely all your good deeds, all that you have done for us, I would not ask you to expand upon them with a still new and kind course of action.... But feeling and understanding all the empathy of your kind heart, I ask you in the name of our entire family, and as the oldest son of the deceased, to take my brother and sisters under your guardianship. Who else other than you could assume such a position, Uncle?

I do not know how to ask forgiveness from you for my long silence, but I dare to assure you that it was not laziness or sadness from my part, but from the endless hustle and bustle of service. Classes and study are the cause. To the deceased I was writing only once a month, and sometimes even more rarely than that. But how could I forget you? ...

You will be surprised at the forebodings of my soul. On the night of the eighth, I saw my deceased Papinka in a dream. I saw him as if he were sitting at the desk, completely white as snow, without a single black hair on his head. I looked at him for a long time; and, I became sad, so sad that I burst out crying. I then went up to him and kissed him on the shoulder. Papinka did not respond, though. I woke up, thinking that something bad was about to happen. I became quite upset, since I had received from Papinka neither a letter, nor money, of which I now find myself extremely in need. . . . If I can, I will come home on leave. I think that the villages have remained with supervision. Good God! Good God! What a terrible death Papinka has had! Two days in the field. . . . Perhaps rain and dust quarreled over his mortal remains. Perhaps in his final moments, he called out to us, and we could not come to him to close his eyes. What did he do to deserve such an end! Let the tears of his sons comfort him in the next life.

Farewell, dear Uncle and Aunt. Tears prevent me from writing further. . . .

P.S. I kiss my brother and sisters. Poor Varenka! You have lost a best friend and most tender father! If you need something, write to me.

June–July 1839.
Pyotr Semyonov-Tyan-Shansky, from his memoirs.

I lived with Dostoevsky in the camp, in a linen tent, not far from the one in which he was (at the time, we did not know each other) . . . [and like him] did without *my own* tea . . . my own boots . . . and a trunk for books. . . . Such things were not absolute necessities, but simply items that one had to have so as not to lag behind comrades who had their own tea, boots, and trunks. In our rather wealthy, aristocratic institution, my comrades spent an average of three hundred rubles for camp, and there were those whose expenses were as much as three thousand rubles. But what I was sent, and not very often at that, was ten rubles for camp; and [like Dostoevsky] I was also oppressed by my lack of money.

July 1839.
Fyodor Dostoevsky, from an 1871 letter to Anna Dostoevskaya.

Today at night I saw *Father*, but he was such a terrible sight. Only twice have I ever seen him like that in life, warning of some terrible disaster.

July 6, 1839.
From the minutes of the meeting of Tula Medical Board.

On July 6 in the Kashirsky district court there appeared a local landowner, a cavalry captain by the name of A. I. Leibrecht, "who, for the death of Dostoevsky, imputed suspicion onto his peasants." "Written evidence" was demanded for such assertions. Leibrecht wrote: "I heard from Mr. V. F. Khotyaintsev [a relative of Dostoevsky's neighbor, P.P. Khotyaintsev] that regarding the death . . . of Dostoevsky . . . a servant-girl heard a cry but was forbidden by her brother to tell anyone. Also, Dostoevsky's family was so distressed by the murder that when they washed the body, they beat their hands on the heels of the corpse and did not want to carry it to church."

July 6, 1839.
The District Police Officer, in response to A. Leibrecht's charge.

The testimony of Leibrecht finds no substantiation given all the painstaking investigations of the death of M. A. Dostoevsky. No one has any doubt as to what happened except him.

July 26, 1839.
From materials into the investigation of the death of M. A. Dostoevsky.

The committee asked V. F. Khotyaintsev to substantiate the claims of Leibrecht. But he rejected everything Leibrecht had said. The differing testimonies demanded a face-to-face confrontation between the two men.

August 9–16, 1839.
Alexander Rizenkampf, from his memoirs.

Fyodor Mikhailovich came to visit me often and together we raved over news not only about literature, but also music. Quite a few fans of both joined our sessions.

August 16, 1839.
Fyodor Dostoevsky, from a letter to Mikhail Dostoevsky.

Yes, my dear Brother, it is always like that with us. We make promises without knowing if we can keep them. It is a good thing that I never promise rashly. . . . What do you say about my silence? That I am lazy . . . that I forget about you and so forth and so on. No! The entire problem was not a single copeck for money. Now I have some, and I am indescribably glad to have it, this long absent guest. . . .

My dear Brother! I have shed many tears over father's passing, but now our situation has gotten still worse. I am not talking about myself but about our family. . . . God grant that you be in Moscow; then I will be calmer about things. . . .

But tell me please, is there anyone in the world more unfortunate than our poor brothers and sisters? The thought that they will be raised by others is killing me. That is why I think your idea of going to live in the country after you receive the rank of officer is a splendid one. There, dear Brother, you can take up their education. Indeed, they would be most fortunate to have that kind of formation. The harmonious organization of the soul amid one's own family; the development of all strivings from a Christian foundation; the pride of family virtues; the fear of vice and shame—these are the consequences of such an upbringing. Only then will the bones of our parents rest quietly in the damp earth. But, dear friend, you will have to endure a great deal. You will have to break off with our relatives or to make peace with them. For you to break off with them would be fatal. Our sisters would perish. For you to make peace with our relatives, though, you will have to court them.[124] Your disdain for government service they will call indolence. But, dear Brother, endure all this. Spit on those miserable little souls and be a benefactor to our brothers. You alone can save them. . . . I know that you have learned to endure. Fulfill my request. It is an excellent one. God grant you the strength for it! I promise that I will agree with you in everything from now on. . . .

What are you doing now? . . . Your job is hellish. . . . Quit as soon as possible.

It has been a long time since I have spoken to you candidly. I do not know whether even now I am in the mood to talk to you about things. I do not know, but now I more often look at the world around me with complete indifference. Moments of awakening occur more forcefully, however. My one goal is to be free. For such freedom, I am sacrificing everything. But I often, often wonder what such freedom will bring to me. . . . Will I be alone in a crowd of strangers? I will be able to break free from all that. But I confess that to live on my present hopes, I need a strong faith in the future and a solid sense of self. But so what? It is all the same if they come true or not. I will do what I want to do. I bless the moments when I am reconciled to the present (such instances have begun to visit me more often now). At such times, I recognize my situation more clearly and am certain that my sacred hopes will be realized in life.

Now the spirit is not calm; but in this struggle of the spirit strong characters usually mature. The clouded gaze becomes clear, and faith in life receives an inspiration that is more elevated and pure. My soul is not open to the stormy impulses of the past. Everything in it is quiet, like in the heart of a person who has concealed a deep secret. As regards a study of the "meaning of the person and life," I am progressing nicely. I can also study characters from writers with whom the best part of my life flows joyously and freely. More than that I cannot say about my life; but I am confident in myself. The individual is a mystery that needs to be solved. And if one spends his entire life doing such a thing, people cannot say that he has wasted his life. I am studying this mystery of the individual because I want to be a human being.

P.S. With my minute-by-minute favorite ideas . . . dreams and thoughts, life becomes more unnoticeable. . . . I can love and be a friend. . . . How many great, sacred and pure [things] there are in this world. . . .

Love, love! You say that you are plucking its flowers. As I see it, there is no more pure and self-sacrificing individual than a poet. How can one share one's delight on paper? The soul always conceals more than it can express in words, colors, or sounds. That is why it is so difficult to fulfill the idea of creativity.

September 1, 1839.
Mikhail Dostoevsky, from a letter to Varvara Dostoevsksaya.

Forgive me, my dear Sister, that for so long I have forced you to wonder at my silence. . . . I now find myself in complete ignorance about our circumstances. What is happening in our village? Have guardians been chosen for us? Are there any obstacles in doing so? I know nothing at all. If I myself came to the village, I probably would take care of everything—or at the very least, get myself out of this tormenting situation of not knowing what happened. Time goes by. This is already the fourth month since Papinka has died—and still nothing has been taken care of. I think that with us things are in terrible disorder. The [village] elder does not know whom to turn to with family affairs. Everything has been sealed. Grigori writes to me that he is even not being allowed to beat father's fur coats and he is afraid that moths will settle in them. The servants are just strolling about. They could be let out on passport and bring in some money. In our current situation that would be a big help to us. Further, who will be our guardian? Someone outside the family? Would this individual care about us? I am afraid, Sister, that the crumbs, collected by our deceased father, will not vanish with his end.

Everyone keeps advising me to go [to the village]. I myself know I should do so, but how and on what? Where will I get the money for such a trip? By the way, I have received a letter from the court in Kashira; the people there are summoning me to the village. Good God, I do not know what to do. Brother also writes to me that I should come quickly! Oh, Varenka, you would not believe how much need he is enduring right now. For two months he has not written a word to me, not having enough money for postage. . . . Our situation is terrible! . . . We do not know to whom we should address our questions, to whom we should turn with our requests. If Uncle[125] were not there to help us, I myself would not know what to do! At the very least I've paid off my debts and now rest easy, although I myself am enduring need. . . . Oh Papinka, Papinka! How much we have lost with your passing!

September 12, 1839.
From the materials of the investigatory commission into the death of Mikhail Dostoevsky.

> Both Leibrecht and V. F. Khotyaintsev appeared in court. Leibrecht repeated everything he had said earlier ("all these rumors," as was said in the document) and exposed Khotyaintsev. His evidence was a retelling of everything that was heard at Khotyaintsev's home. But Khotyaintsev once again denied it all, and added that Leibrecht was "denouncing" him "out of spite." But Leibrecht came up with new evidence in which he disclosed that V. F. had asked Leibrecht directly to tell the land-captain: "Mr. Khotyaintsev, Pavel Petrovich was waiting for him right away to tell him of the entire affair."[126]

September 29, 1839.
Mikhail Dostoevsky, from a letter to Varvara Dostoevsky.

> I have known Elagin for a long time, since our litigation from Khotyaintsev. Always out for himself, he apparently tried to do us harm.... Throughout the entire district of Kashira there are very unflattering rumors about him. When I was in the village, everyone claimed that he was a cardsharp and uttered all kinds of nonsensical things.

October 1839.
Investigators into the murder of Dostoevsky's father, from their report.

> P. P. Khotyaintsev, who proclaimed the "guilt" of Dostoevsky's peasants, is no longer noted in the documents. The court also considered it necessary to "affirm to Leibrecht that from now on he be more judicious in his statements."

October 6, 1839, and after.
Konstantin Trutovsky, from his memoirs.

> Since I could draw better than others ... I was often ordered to do pictures and the like for the senior students.... One time Fyodor Mikhailovich asked me to do a picture for him, and when I did so, he became interested in my talent as an artist, and protected me from the coarse masters of the upper classes.
> At that time Fyodor Mikhailovich was very thin. His face was pale and always somewhat grey; his hair, light and sparse.... He was very well-built and thickset. His gait was somewhat jerky.... His eyes were sunken but with a stare that was penetrating and deep.

There was no student less capable of military bearing than F. M. Dostoevsky. His movements were angular and fitful. His uniform looked clumsy on him; his knapsack, shako, and rifle seemed like chains . . . weighing him down.

Dostoevsky always had a very serious look about him. I never saw him laugh or be very happy among friends. . . .

The reason for our friendship was that I drew so well . . . and how tenderly he talked to me, and advised me to draw more and to read everything that had to do with art.

November 16, 1839.
From the notes of the Kashira District Court.

The cause of death [of Mikhail Dostoevsky] . . . was the will of God, since no one could be found who was guilty for what had happened.

December 25, 1839.
Fyodor Dostoevsky, from a letter to Alexander and Alexandra Kumanin.

My silence—enduring, unjustifiable, and inexcusable—may have seemed to you, dearest Uncle and Aunt, to be a rudeness that is strange, incomprehensible, and unforgivable: black ingratitude at its best. If I take up my pen, it is not to justify myself. No! I know that my guilt, and whatever circumstances might excuse it, are far beneath justifications. Besides, even if I made such justifications, could I hope that you would accept them?

I will say only this: If my sincere and candid confession, my attempt to explain my misconduct before you, is worthy of but slight attention from your part, I will consider myself to be fortunate. I will have regained what I had no hope of regaining—the least small notice and favorable disposition from you.

Having entered the [Main] Engineering Academy, I was so carried away by everything, by the novelty and diversity of a new type of life . . . that my conscience reproaches me grievously for forgetting my responsibilities, for my silence and terrible misconduct toward you. . . . There is no way I can explain or justify my behavior other than perhaps my strange absentmindedness.

I know that this confession of absentmindedness lowers me greatly in your eyes. But I must and will bear my well-deserved shame. The reminders and directives of my deceased parent to break my strange silence with those relatives who have showered us with their favors so often,[127] forced me to examine my behavior thoroughly and, with regard to you, dearest Uncle and Aunt, to see myself in a most unfavorable light. In addition to my grievous fault—my absentmindedness, I saw that my misconduct would assume an even more gloomier appearance, as rudeness and ingratitude. . . . Such a thought has both confused and embarrassed me. . . .

It goes without saying that my embarrassment should not continue for long. To correct my shortcoming was my first order of business, my first thought. But the mere idea that I had violated my primary responsibilities, that I had not fulfilled an obligation imposed upon me by nature itself, devastated me. I do not rely on the conventions of others who affirm that paper does not blush and that two or three vulgar excuses (lack of time and the like) are enough to make amends. Even without you here, I blushed, grew annoyed with myself, and did not how what, how, and with what stance I would write to you. I would first pick up my pen but then throw it down without finishing my letter to you. I beg and implore you, dearest Uncle and Aunt, to believe such a thing. Such are the pure outpourings of a repentant heart. My embarrassment and burdensome situation concerning you was the reason for my prolonged silence.

The sad death of my father and the good deeds which you have shown to our family—kindnesses for which I do not even know how to learn to thank you—aroused, to a large extent, all my previous emotions: both the feelings of shame and the torments of repentance. I feel my guilt. I do not dare hope for forgiveness. But it would be the greatest kindness if you would allow me to write to you or, at the very least, to my sister, from whom I could learn about everything that is dear to my heart. The New Year which, dearest Uncle and Aunt, I greet with the wish for your happiness and health, will be witness to a new me.

During the coming year, I will try to deserve your attention by affirming my sincere attachment to you, my gratitude for your kindnesses to our family, and the continual preservation of that sacred feeling of love, respect, and devotion with which I have the honor of being your obedient and devoted nephew.

PART THREE

Darkness before Dawn

ST. PETERSBURG (1845)

In 1845, the imperial capital of St. Petersburg was eight years away from the one hundred fiftieth anniversary of its founding. Like everything else in Russia, it was a place of contrasts and contradictions.

For some, St. Petersburg was a dream come true, a heaven on earth destined by Peter and God (in that order) to bring Russians into the modern world, physically and socially, spiritually and culturally. For others, St. Petersburg was a nightmare in life, a hell on earth deemed by Peter and Satan (in that order) to drive Russians out of the modern world, physically and socially, spiritually and culturally.

For young men in the provinces, St. Petersburg was the former, not the latter. To them the imperial capital beckoned siren-like not only as Russia's window on the West but also as a vista on fame and fortune: a do-or-die alternative to their otherwise stagnant and stultified lives. To the city came the able and the arrogant, the dreamy and the desperate.

There were winners. Opportunity knocked for those who, bold and brave, wanted a life in service to the state. St. Petersburg, the symbol for the breadth and depth of the imperial vision, was the axis upon which Russia turned. Citizens of the city numbered roughly 480,000 (twice as many as in Moscow), of which 70 percent were men. The place was home to a massive bureaucracy that, since 1800, had increased fivefold. For many in St. Petersburg, peace and prosperity reigned supreme. With apologies to Gogol and Dostoevsky, even determined wannabes could participate, if only vicariously, in the glittering life of Russia's imperial capital.

More often, though, there were losers. Like every urban area, St. Petersburg had its share of people who fell through the cracks, or who, like the young Dostoevsky, heard a different drummer. Happiness and hope gave way to disillusionment and despair. Some, like the young Dostoevsky, negotiated lumps and bumps via school and jobs. Others, again like the young Dostoevsky, struggled with piercing cold and darkness; wrenching poverty and shabbiness; cruel bosses and citizens; and hard-knock lessons and events in which talent ceded to patronage and innocence to corruption.

To their further dismay, loser-provincials joined with other denizens from the "depths." Thousands of laborers worked sixteen-hour days on cathedrals and government buildings. Hordes of peasants toiling in the new cotton mills of the city took their place with herds of tailors, shoemakers, servants, artisans, cooks, bakers, carpenters, drivers, waiters, and copyists. Some two thousand prostitutes filled the one hundred fifty government-sanctioned brothels, not to mention the same number or more who plied their trade without the passports that identified their calling. (Scholars assert that the number of such women increased from 400 to 4,626 between 1843 and 1846.)[1]

Particularly galling to loser-provincials (the young Dostoevsky included) was that high and low, rich and poor lived side by side, as the accepted order of things. In 1845, St. Petersburg was home to some fifty thousand aristocrats who lived almost as well as their sovereigns. Residents of spacious palaces stepped out boldly in front; tenants of cramped slums slunk furtively in back, to "corners" defined by blankets or bedspreads. Along fashionable Nevsky Prospekt and the other glittering thoroughfares of the city, noblemen and merchants, ladies and prostitutes, dandies and serfs went their separate ways, without common purpose or goals. For loser-provincials, life became even more monotonous and meaningless than the very backwaters from which they had sought escape. Even more to the point, St. Petersburg seemed to them to be a charade, an illusion, a mirage: shimmering and sumptuous from without but rotten and decaying from within, as unfathomable and impenetrable as the thick mists and fogs that swallowed the city.

Loser-provincials in St. Petersburg also faced a societal consensus: *Tishe edesh', dal'she budesh'*, or "the quieter you are, the farther you will go." No one, it seemed, was ready or willing to rock the boat. True, people were frustrated and angry over the sociopolitical system. Even with citizens with small stakes in the national life, however, the desire was for the status quo. As one observer noted: "Everything went calmly and normally. Society was in an organic period of existence, and no . . . great changes could be anticipated. . . . The entire order seemed as if it would stand for a long time and no dissonances destroyed the general harmony, for there was a conservative, monarchial sentiment in all strata of society, and there seemed to be no possibility of others."[2]

It would be some thirty or forty years before the contradictions and contrasts of St. Petersburg would first fissure and then crack open the political and social order not only of the imperial capital but also of Russia itself. Indeed, denizens of the imperial city would pay a high price for their benign tolerance and neglect, for ignoring the growing divide between high and low, rich and poor. Even more fateful, *Peterburzhtsy* would also learn a painful, if devastating lesson: If winners inherit the earth, losers eat it, until they can no longer stomach the sand and rocks that, metaphorically, are their daily bread.

Another vortex in the swirling maelstrom of St. Petersburg (and beyond) was that Russian literature—the hallmark of national culture—was in crisis. After an embarrassing late start (a Russian literary language came into being only in the 1820s) national writers seem poised to enter into world fiction; but their admission was threatened. Pushkin had died in 1837, Lermontov in 1841, and Krylov in 1844. Gogol, after writing *Dead Souls* in 1842, had left literature. Ivan Turgenev was only coming to public notice; Nekrasov was seen as a *podenshchik* or "day laborer." Herzen had not yet published in its entirety his novel *Who Is To Blame*? Goncharov, Ostrovsky, and Saltykov-Shchedrin still had not lent their voices to native fiction.

Complicating matters was that Russian writers and editors, publishers and booksellers sensed that their readers were no longer aristocrats and intellectuals exclusively; rather, they were becoming as widespread and democratic as their counterparts in the West. In St. Petersburg in 1840s, fully 70 percent of the population were from the middle and lower classes, including 30,000 *raznochintsy*, or "nonaristocratic intellectuals," 54,000 merchants and petit bourgeois, 24,000 tradesmen, 22,000 servants, and 120,000 peasants. Even more salient, perhaps, the movers and shakers of the Russian literary world knew that such individuals had rubles to spend and could dictate their needs and wants in fiction. Literary commercialism had come to the homeland.

In the absence of established *litterati*, conservative and progressive writers in Russia responded to the challenging changes in the national written expression with "physiologies"—collections of poetry and prose, often sizeable, in which authors, obsessed with sociology, science, and a literature of "fact," observed people, places, and things as types, daguerreotypes, and specimens of the national health. In so doing, they opted for a diversity that was as dramatic as it was democratic. As Nevsky Prospekt was in life, so now was it in literature. Ladies and lords, writers and bosses, officers and merchants walked side by side with beggars and wenches, organgrinders and clerks, yardkeepers and hacks.

Surprisingly, in their fictional search, conservative and progressive writers came up with similar results. The conservatives, obsessed with tsarist demands for autocracy, orthodoxy, and nationality, looked no further than surface reality to fashion faceless citizens who were official and Orthodox, pious and patriotic. The progressives scoured attics and basements, closets and corners, but more often than not—the celebrated 1845 anthology *The Physiology of Petersburg* is a typical example—also claimed urbanites who, in carnivalesque harmony, lived and laughed at life. Unsurprisingly, physiologies were seen by both camps as stopgap measures until new writers entered the Russian literary scene.

Given Russian literature in 1845, it is easy to see why *Poor Folk*, Dostoevsky's first attempt as a writer, caused such a sensation. As would be the case with so many works in his career, the tale—a tortured correspondence between a hapless clerk, Makar Devushkin, and a self-styled damsel-in-distress, Varvara Dobroselova—was the right work in the right place at the right time. It was also startlingly new. Never before in Russian literature had "little" people claimed such focus and flair. Never before in the national written expression had characters talked at length about their joys and sorrows, triumphs and tragedies. No doubt about it, readers and reviewers agreed, the young Dostoevsky had saved Russian literature. Providing even greater cause for rejoicing, he promised more to come; sadly, this was a hope that the writer fulfilled not in the late 1840s but much later, with *Notes from the Underground* in 1864, *Crime and Punishment* in 1866, *The Idiot* in 1869, *Demons* in 1872, and *The Brothers Karamazov* in 1880.

At age twenty-four, though, the young Dostoevsky rested content. He had become what he had wanted to be: a writer who probed deeply into sin and suffering not only in his time but also throughout the ages. At this point in his career, the young Dostoevsky did not seek escape from the morass that, he believed, society sought so willingly. That also would come later, after years of personal pain and doubt. Now he was content only to register his observations, not to mention fascination, with all manner of human perversity, an undertaking of which *Poor Folk* was a fitting, if shocking start.

1840

January 1, 1840.
Fyodor Dostoevsky, from a letter to Mikhail Dostoevsky.

> From the bottom of my heart I thank you, my kind brother, for your sweet letter. No! I am not like you. . . .
>
> I have invented a new and very strange kind of pleasure—torturing myself.
>
> I take your letter, turn it over and over in my hands for a few minutes, feel to see if it is heavy or not . . . and admire the sealed envelope to my heart's content. Then I put it in my pocket. . . . You will not believe what a delightful state of soul, feelings, and heart such actions arouse. I wait like that, sometimes for fifteen minutes or so. Finally, I fall on the letter greedily, tear apart the seal, and devour your dear lines. Oh, what does my heart not feel when I read them! How many sensations crowd the soul, pleasant and unpleasant, bitter and sweet. Yes, dear Brother, unpleasant and bitter ones, too. You will not believe how bitter it is when one is not comprehended

or understood, or when everything is put in a completely different light, not at all what you had wanted to say, but in a different and vile form. . . .

Having read your last letter, I was *un enragé* because I was not with you. The best of my heart's dreams, the most sacred of the rules, given to me by experience, by burdensome and arduous experience, were distorted, mutilated, and shown in a most pathetic form. You yourself write: "Write, object, argue with me"—and you seem to find some point in doing so! There is no point at all, dear Brother, absolutely none at all. . . . Only your egoism (which all we sinners have) leads to a *most suitable* conclusion about another person, about his opinions, rules, character, and feeble-mindedness. . . . After all, Brother, this is very offensive behavior on your part! No! A polemic in friendly letters is sweetened poison. What will happen when we see each other? Such a polemic, it seems, will be an enduring pretext for the discord between us. . . . I am leaving that topic now, but can take it up some more on the last pages of this missive. . . .

To the Kumanins I have sent a most decorous letter. Do not worry. I expect good results from it. . . .

I believe that the life of a person has many, many sorrows, much woe, and many joys. I also believe that a poet's life has thorns and roses, and that because he is a verbal creature, lyricism is his constant companion. Your lyric poems are splendid: "The Stroll," "Morning," "Vision of Mother," "The Rose" . . . "The Steeds of Phoebus," and many others—all splendid. What a vivid tale they tell about you, dear friend! . . .

Shidlovsky showed me your poems. . . . Oh, how unjust you are to him. I do not want to defend Shidlovsky's knowledge and rules to anyone who does not know the man; and I will not change your opinion about him. But only if you had seen him last year. He lived the entire year in Petersburg without a job or anything to do. God knows why he lived there. He is not all that well-to-do to live in Petersburg merely for pleasure alone. But it is obvious that it is precisely why he came to the city—he wanted to escape somewhere. If one took a look at him, one could see that he had become a martyr! He was all shriveled up. His cheeks had become sunken; his damp eyes, feverish and dry. The spiritual beauty of his face, though, grew with his physical decline. How he has suffered! How grievously has he suffered! My God, how he loves a girl (some Maria). But she is married to someone else. Without that love, though, he believes that he would not be a priest of poetry—selfless, noble, and pure. . . .

Making my way to his apartment, sometimes on a winter evening (for example, exactly a year ago), I could not help but recall Onegin's sad winter in Petersburg (chapter eight).[3] Only before me there stood not a cold creature, but an unwilling but ardent dreamer . . . a splendid, noble individual, an accurate portrait whom both Shakespeare and Schiller introduced to us in literature.

But even then Shidlovsky was ready to succumb to the gloomy mania of Byron's characters. We often sat for entire evenings, talking about God knows what! Oh, what an open and pure soul Shidlovsky was! My tears flow now when I recall the past. What was I to him? Nonetheless he concealed nothing from me. He needed to talk to someone. Oh, why were you not there with us! How Shidlovsky wanted to see you! He delighted in calling you a personal friend. I remember how his eyes poured forth tears when he read your poems. Why, he knew them by heart! But you would say that he was laughing at you! Oh, what a poor and pitiable creature he was! But also a pure, angelic soul!

But during that difficult winter, Shidlovsky did not forget his love. Indeed, it flared up more and more forcefully. Then spring came and enlivened him. His imagination began to create dramas, and oh, what dramas they were, dear Brother. You would change your opinion of them, if you had read how he reworked *Maria Simonova*.[4] Shidlovsky reworked the play all winter, calling its previous version hideous. . . . Then there were his lyric poems! Oh, if only you knew the poems he wrote last spring. For example, there is one in which Shidlovsky speaks of fame. Oh, if only you had read it, dear Brother!

After I returned from camp, though, we spent little time together. The last time we met, we walked at Ekaterinhof.[5] Oh, how we spent that evening. We recalled our life last winter, when we talked about Homer, Shakespeare, Schiller, and Hoffman—the last one we spoke about just as much as we read him. Shidlovsky and I also talked about ourselves, our past life, the future, and about you, dear Brother. Now he has long since left, and I do not hear a single word from him. I do not even know if he is alive or not. His health was suffering grievously. Oh, write to him if you can!

Last winter I was in an ecstatic mood. My friendship with Shidlovsky afforded me so many hours of a better life; but that was not the reason for my exalted state. You have, perhaps, reproached me and will continue to do so because I have not written to you. Stupid circumstances like my time in camp were the reason. But how can I possibly tell you, Brother? I have never been indifferent to you. I love you for your poems, for the poetry of your life, for your misfortunes—just these, no more than that. Between us, there was neither the love of a brother, nor that of a friend. . . . I once had a friend, a certain being whom I loved![6]

You wrote to me, Brother, that I have not read Schiller. But you are mistaken, dear Brother! I have memorized Schiller. I have quoted him; I have raved about him. In fact, I think that at that period of my life, fate did nothing greater for me than to allow me to come to know this great poet. I could never have gotten to know Schiller as I did then. Reading Schiller *with him*.[7] I measured *against him* the noble, fiery Don Carlos, as well as the Marquis of Posa and Mortimer.[8] This friendship brought me such a great deal of both grief and delight! But now I will be silent about this tie forever! The name of Schiller has become native to me. It is now a kind of enchanted sound that gives rise to so many dreams, ones that are bitter, dear Brother. That is why I have never talked to you about Schiller and about the impressions he evokes. Just to hear the name of Schiller is for me painful.

I wanted to write a lot to you in response to your attacks on me, that you did not understand my words. . . . But this present letter to you has afforded me with so many sweet moments, dreams, and memories that I am absolutely incapable of talking about anything else. On one thing will I excuse myself. I have never categorized great poets, especially when I did not know their works. I never drew parallels as, for instance, between Pushkin and Schiller. I do not know where you ever came up with such a thing about me. . . . I reject such a classification. Perhaps when I spoke to you about something, I put Pushkin and Schiller side by side, but I think that there exists a comma between the two men. Pushkin and Schiller are not alike in the least. Pushkin and Byron, yes. As for Homer and Victor Hugo, it seems that you did not want to understand me on purpose. Here is what I want to say. As I see it, Homer is a legendary individual. Perhaps, he is like Christ—incarnated as God and sent to dwell among us. Perhaps, Homer can be on a parallel only to Christ, not Goethe. Seek out Homer's essence, Brother. Understand *The Iliad*.[9] Read it thoroughly. (Confess—have you even read the thing?) After all, in *The Iliad*, Homer gave to the entire ancient world a plan for both spiritual and earthly life in exactly as much strength as Christ gave it to the new one. Now do you understand me?

As a lyric poet, Victor Hugo has a purely angelic character, with a childlike Christian direction to his poetry. In this, no one can compare to him, neither Byron, nor Pushkin; neither Schiller (no matter how Christian a poet he is), nor the lyrical Shakespeare (whose sonnets I read in French). Only Homer, with this unshakeable assuredness in his calling, only Homer with his childlike faith and service to the god of poetry, resembles Victor Hugo in the direction of the sources of his poetry, but not in the idea—that was something nature gave to him and which he expressed. . . . I think, though, that in lyric poetry, Derzhavin can stand higher than both of them. . . .

P.S. Now I am going to scold you. When you talk about form, you have nearly lost your mind. No joke—I have long suspected that you are slightly unbalanced mentally. You recently said something like that about Pushkin. But not without reason, I let it pass. I will talk about form in my next letter to you, since there is neither time nor space to do it now. But tell me, please, in speaking about form, where did you get the idea that we can like neither Racine or *Corneille* (?!?!), because the form of their works is bad! You are pathetic! Here is a brilliant idea has just come to me: *Do you really think that Racine and Corneille lack poetry in their works?* Racine has no poetry? Racine, the fiery, passionate Racine? Racine, enamored with his own ideals? This Racine has no poetry? How can you even ask about such a thing? Why, have you read *Andromaque*?[10] Well, Brother, have you? Have you read *Iphigénie*?[11]

Surely you must say that it is a marvelous thing? And is not Racine's Achilles[12] really Homer-like? Truth be told, Racine stole from Homer, how he did so. What women does he have in his works! Try to understand him. Racine was not a genius, though. Could he write a drama? He only had to imitate Corneille. And *Phèdre*?[13] Dear Brother! God knows what will happen to you if you do not say that *Phèdre* is clear and elevated nature and poetry. After all, although the statue is made of plaster, not marble, the work still bears a Shakespearean cast.

Now about Corneille? Listen, Brother. I do not know how to talk to you. It seems as if you are like Ivan Nikiforovich: "After having his fill of eating peas."[14] No, I cannot believe you, Brother. You have not read Corneille, and that is why you do miss the point about him completely. Why, do you know that when one considers Corneille's larger-than-life characters and the spirit of his romanticism, he is almost Shakespeare. You poor soul! You rebuff everything in the same way: "classical form" is all you say. You poor dear! Why, don't you know that it was fifty years later that Corneille appeared after the pathetic, untalented poor devil Jodelle with his lampoon, *Cleopatra*;[15] after Tredyakovsky-Ronsard;[16] and after the cold rhymester, Malherbe, who was almost his contemporary. So how could Corneille invent the form of a plan? It is a good thing that he at least borrowed it from Seneca.[17] But have you read Corneille's *Cinna*?[18] . . . *Karl Moor, Fiesco, Tell, Don Carlos*.[19] Such works would bring honor to Shakespeare. You poor soul! If you have not read *Cinna*, then do so, especially August's conversation with Cinna where August forgives Cinna for his treachery (but how he forgives?). . . . You will see that only humiliated angels talk in such a way. Especially where August says: "*Soyons amis, Cinna*."[20] And have you read *Horace*?[21] Perhaps only in Homer can one find such characters. The old Horace is Diomedes. The young Horace is Ajax Telamonides, but with the spirit of Achilles, and Curias is Patrocles[22] and Achilles and everything that the sadness of love and duty can express. How great it all is. Have you read *Le Cid*?[23] Read it, you poor soul, and fall in the dust before Corneille. You have offended him with your remarks. Read him and read him again. What does romanticism ask if its highest ideals are not developed in *Le Cid*? How splendid are the characters of Don Rodrigues, his son, and his mistress! And what an ending to the piece!

But, dear Brother, do not be angry at my offensive remarks. Do not be an Ivan Ivanovich Perepenko.[24]

The present letter has forced me to shed several tears from memories of the past. . . .

The plot of your drama is charming. In it one can see a truthful idea. I especially like your hero who, like Faust, seeks what is limitless and boundless, but who also goes insane just when he comes across such a thing, that is, when he is loved. That is marvelous! I am glad that Shakespeare has taught you something.

January 28, 1840.
Fyodor Dostoevsky, from a letter to Alexander and Alexandra Kumanin.

Never before, dearest Uncle and Aunt, has joyous news made such a pleasant and delightful impression in my soul than what I experienced when I read my sister's letter. Judging by my guilt before you, could I have expected, should I have expected such good will and favor on your part? When I received your letter, the feelings which stirred inside me were beyond all understanding. All the weight of my guilt, all your justified anger at me, dearest Uncle and Aunt, presented themselves to me in such a vivid way!

But how things have changed! Readily do you return me to your favor, with a love for me that I in no way deserve. But I did not know, nor could I tell you, what had been going on in my heart. After I received your letter, I ought to have rejoiced, but I did not know how to do so. After all, nothing in the world could have made me happier than your forgiveness. But shame, annoyance with myself, and your unparalleled indulgence toward me—me who has abused your good will toward me for such a long time—everything weighed heavily and terribly upon my heart. The punishment of one's conscience is the strongest punishment of all; I bear upon myself all the burden of such a thing. . . .

I am indebted to you, dearest Uncle and Aunt, indebted to you beyond anything I can think or do. If the expatiation of my guilt, along with my repentance and attachment to you, has even the slightest merit in your eyes, I will consider myself still to be a fortunate man, because I will ease my conscience considerably.

But what excited me more than anything else, what filled my soul with so many pleasant memories of the past, and what caused my heart to beat more ardently for you, were the lines written in your own hand, dearest Aunt. I could not have expected such indulgence and good will on your part. . . . Those lines are all the more pleasant for me because it has been such a long time, and exclusively because of my own mistakes and guilt, that I have not heard words so sweet to the heart and such expressions of love for me, dearest Aunt, all of which reminded me of my dear departed mother. . . . With what fervor did I kiss those lines; with what ardor I also kiss your hands 1,000 times, dearest Aunt!

But there is no happiness without grief. The letter raked raw the scarcely healed wounds in my heart. Uncle's death[25] has forced me to spill several sincere tears in his memory. Father, Mother, Uncle, and all in two years![26] Terrible years!

I would have started this letter even earlier, if my examinations had not detained me. They are over now, and I am not wasting a moment. But I sense that I am wearying you with this missive. So allow a sincerely loving and respectful nephew to remain humble and obedient to you forever.

February 9, 1840.
Officials of the Tula regional government, from a directive.

> [We request] immediate information . . . from the Muscovite relatives of the deceased Kashira gentryman and civil servant of the seventh class Mikhail Andreevich Dostoevsky . . . [from] his daughter Varvara, her aunt . . . Alexandra Fyodorovna [Kumanina] and her husband, Alexander Alexeevich [Kumanin], and the nurse, the petty bourgeois, Elena Frolovna [Kryukova], if they suspect anyone in the murder of said individual.

February 13, 1840.
Peasants at Darovoe, from their testimony.

> [Statements were taken] "from Mr. Dostoevsky's peasants, Andrei Mironov and others, and testimony arranged by a personal confrontation between the peasant girl, Marfa Isaeva, and the peasant, Alexei Mikhailov, and also obtained from the village elder, Savin Ivanov, and the house-servant, Grigori Vasiliev."[27]

July 19, 1840.
Fyodor Dostoevsky, from a letter to Mikhail Dostoevsky.

> I am again picking up my pen, my dear but implacable Brother, and again I must begin with a request for goodwill, a request that will become more resolute—the more you become stubborn and angry. No, my dear, kind Brother, I will not leave you until you extend your hand to me as you did previously.
>
> I do not know, dear Brother, why you are acting this way! Although there have been exceptions, you have always been fair to me. You have always forgiven me for my long silence; but when I give you a reason, a reason that is beyond reproof, you yourself know that you seem deaf to my words.
>
> Forgive these reproaches to you, my dear friend. I will not hide from you that they issue forth directly from the heart. I love you, my dear Brother, and your indifference is painful for me. If I were in your place, I would have long since forgotten everything so as to forgive my friend as quickly as possible, rather than to force him to beg even longer for forgiveness. At least for my part, I now see myself in decent circumstances, that is, with money—our guardian has already sent me—but not a great amount. I also promise definitely to write to you every week without fail. I am writing in haste to you because I do not dare go on with a long letter. At any moment we are expecting an alarm and maneuvers that will last for three days.
>
> Oh, my dear Brother! For God's sake write me at least something. If only you knew how I worry about your fate, about your intentions and decisions, and about

your examination, my dear Brother, because it is just around the corner. God knows if this letter will find you still in Revel. God also grant you everything else, too, dear friend. Oh, if we continue this discord any longer, this distress in our *steadfast* friendship, I do not know what torture I will experience because of your silence to me.

After all, this stupid but also decisive turning point in your fate is soon approaching, one which I have always awaited with some kind of trepidation. In truth, what hinges on this examination? Think about it. Your life, your leisure, your happiness, my dear Brother—yes, your very happiness. If your fate or you yourself have not changed since you wrote me last with such delight about your hopes, your Emilia,[28] you, of course, can judge for yourself how a successful examination can change your fate.[29] Just think about this one circumstance in your fate, my dear Brother! Do you think that it would not be too cruel on your part to deprive your brother of your confidence when via my friendship, I could share with you either your happiness or misery, my friend. Oh, my dear Brother! God be your judge for leaving me in such uncertainty, in such terrible uncertainty.

But what has happened to you, my Brother! Has something materialized? Perhaps not your dreams, but something akin to what fate flashed before your eyes when it pointed to some bright corner in the dark perspective of your life, i.e., a corner in which the heart promised itself so much happiness and hope. Time shows a great deal. It alone assesses and determines the entire meaning of these periods of our life in a clear way. Forgive me for what I am about to say, my dear Brother, but time can determine whether the activity of the heart and soul was pure and correct, clear and correct, like our natural striving in the full life of the individual; or, whether such doings were incorrect, pointless, and vain, a delusion brought to bear by a lonely heart that does not understand itself. Such a heart is often as senseless as an infant; but it is also ardent, captive, and pure, seeking nourishment from things about itself but also exhausting its being in an unnatural striving for an "ignoble dream."

In fact, as sad as life sometimes is and as burdensome as its moments are, when an individual, recognizing in himself boundless energy but also sensing the delusions of his life, sees how his enthusiasm is wasted in false activity, in unnatural existence, and in things that are unworthy of his nature, he also senses that his spiritual flame has been crushed, that it has been extinguished by God knows what. When the heart has been torn to pieces, and by what? By a life that is worthy of a pygmy, not a giant; of a child, not a man.[30]

Here friendship is again essential because the heart will fetter itself with unbreakable chains. A person will become depressed and droop before circumstances, before his heart's whims, and before the commands of fate.[31] He will dismiss as an insignificant spiderweb those horrible nets from which no one ever breaks free and before which everything wilts. It is then that fate is truly the command of Providence, that is, it acts on us with the irresistible force of our entire nature. . . .

P.S. Oh, dear Brother, if you had any idea of how we live. But come and visit me as soon as possible, my dear Brother. For God's sake, come. If only you knew how essential it is for us to be together, my dear friend! Entire years have passed by since our separation. A scrap of paper that I send from month to month has been our entire tie. Meanwhile time has flown by. It has aimed both storm clouds and buckets of rain down on us. For us everything has passed in sad and burdensome solitude.

Oh, if only you knew how like a savage I have become here, my dear, kind friend! To love you is for me an absolute necessity. I am completely free here; I do not depend on anyone. Our bond, though, is so firm that it seems to me that I am knitted together to someone for life.

How many changes in our age, dreams, hopes, and thoughts have escaped us unnoticed and yet have we preserved in our hearts! Oh, when I see you, I will feel that my existence will be renewed. Now, though, I feel somewhat distressed. The course of my time is so incorrect. . . . I myself do not know what is wrong with me. For God's sakes, my dear, come and visit me. Come and visit me, my dear Brother . . . I am certain that if you have studied anything, you will pass. Many less talented than you have passed. I know many examples of such a thing. . . .

If you only knew how unbearable it now is for us to live.

December 1840.
Dmitri Grigorovich, from his memoirs.

My new acquaintance with Nekrasov and my stories about him were greeted by Dostoevsky with absolute indifference. Most likely, Dostoevsky did not like Nekrasov's poetry,[32] believing that his verse was nothing to get excited about.

December 1840.
Alexander Rizenkampf, from his memoirs.

Mikhail Mikhailovich came to Petersburg for an examination to the rank of ensign in field engineers. . . . Here we often met Fyodor Mikhailovich. . . . Mikhail Mikhailovich read us excepts from his translations of Schiller's *Don Carlos* and *Hermann and Dorothea*.[33] He also read a great deal of his new lyric poetry. The final lines of one of them still remain imprinted in my memory:

Poet! You are were born with riches,
Without help you have made your way!
The world takes of you, foster-child that you are
So as to push from its bosom someday.
To darken your spirit with coldness and suspicion

So that you groan under the weight of hellish pain
The world looks at you with smiling delight
So that you cry and sing in heavenly gain.

1841

1841–early 1842.
Alexander Rizenkampf, from his memoirs.

> Fyodor Mikhailovich spoke with excitement [about the ballet], about the impression made on him by such female dancers as Taglioni, Shlefakht, Smirnova, Andreyanova, and the male dancer, Ioganson. At the time, also, the Alexander Theater[34] became famous. Such actors as the Karatygins, Bryansky, Martynov, the Grigorievs, Mme. Asenkova, Dyur, and others also had a tremendous effect . . . on the passionate and poetic nature of Fyodor Mikhailovich. We also raved over the talents of the French . . . and German theater. . . . The [German] actress who played Mary Stuart impressed Fyodor Mikhailovich so greatly that he decided to rework the subject for the Russian stage, as a translation or an imitation of Schiller,[35] but independently and in line with history.

1841.
Lyubov Dostoevskaya, from her memoirs.

> According to family legend, my father depicted himself in Ivan Karamazov. He often noted that when he was twenty years old, he was like Ivan.

1841.
Lyubov Dostoevskaya, from her memoirs.

> At twenty years old. Dostoevsky lived in a temperate way, as if he were a saint. . . . He was still a shy schoolboy.

February 16, 1841.
Alexander Rizenkampf, from his memoirs.

> Mikhail Mikailovich . . . invited several of his friends and acquaintances to his place for a farewell party.[36] Also there was Fyodor Mikhailovich who, for the first time, read excerpts from his two attempts at dramatic writing: *Maria Stuart* and *Boris Godunov*.

February 27, 1841.
Fyodor Dostoevsky, from a letter to Mikhail Dostoevsky.

So now we are back to writing letters to each other, my dear friend! Was it all that long ago that we thought we would almost never be parted, spending our time any old way, merrily, with a light heart. But then suddenly, in a single instant, you were snatched from me for a very long time. Being all alone, I have grown sad, my dear Brother. There is no one to talk to, and besides, there is no time to do so. Heaven help me, I have never crammed so much for exams as I have been doing now. They are squeezing the life out of us, my dear. I sit and study even on the holidays. Now March is already approaching. Spring is here, the snow is melting, the sun is warmer and brighter, and the wind is blowing from the south. Pure pleasure. What's not to like? . . .

I have a vicious headache right now. . . . Textbooks on fortifications lie before me and bid for my attention. I cannot stand it, dear friend. . . .

Oh Brother, dear Brother! Quickly! To the wharf, to freedom! A calling and freedom are great things. Again, I have been dreaming and fantasizing about the two like never before. Somehow the soul expands to understand the greatness of life. . . .

God grant you happiness in love, enjoyment, and freedom, and in the peaceful and charming circle that is your family.

If things work out for you, you will be freer than I.

Summer 1841.
P. S. Nikolaev, from his memoirs.

In camp[37] . . . Dostoevsky was constantly sleepy, pensive, and pale. He spoke very little and, more often than not, sat alone in a corner.

August 5, 1841.
Nicholas I. From an imperial decree.

By the highest order of His Imperial Majesty, Dostoevsky is promoted from student to field engineer–officer.

After August 9, 1841.
Alexander Rizenkampf, from his memoirs.

After attending officers' classes in the morning, Fyodor Mikhailovich sat locked in his study, engaged in literary activity. The color of his face was earthen; he was tortured by a dry cough which became worse in the morning; his voice was distinguished by a sharp hoarseness; and there was swelling in the glands in his neck. Fyodor Mikhailovich hid all this from everyone.

Fall 1841 and after.
Konstantin Trutovsky, from his memoirs.

> One time, having met me on the street, F. M. Dostoevsky asked me what I was drawing, reading, and so forth He advised me to use my talents, to engage in art in a serious way . . . and to read the great writers. He also invited me to visit him at his place during the holidays. . . .
>
> At that time [Dostoevsky's] apartment was on the second floor and consisted of four rooms: a spacious vestibule, a small living room, and two additional rooms. One of them was occupied by Fyodor Mikhailovich; the others were completely barren. In the somewhat narrow room . . . where Dostoevsky worked and slept, there was a desk, a couch that also served as a bed, and several chairs. On the table, chairs, and floor were books and papers covered with writing.
>
> I went to see Dostoevsky as soon as possible. . . . He received me affectionately; and, with great interest, he asked me about my undertakings. For a long time, he talked about art and literature. He acquainted me with the best work in fiction, pointed out works for me to read, and even furnished me with several of them.
>
> As before, he was interested in my drawings. At that time I drew many caricatures of our teachers, particularly the mathematician Ostrogradsky, and from Dostoevsky they always provoked both smiles and laughter, things that appeared on his face so rarely.
>
> He also talked about Gogol's writings, opening up my eyes to the writer and explaining to me the significance of his works . . . and the depth of his humor.
>
> It is not surprising that as students of the [Main Engineering] Academy, we were ill-prepared to understand Gogol. Our teacher for Russian literature, Professor Plaksin, saw Gogol as an absolutely ungifted writer and his works as absurdly vulgar and base. . . .
>
> For me, the most powerful and decisive impression was when Fyodor Mikhailovich, with indescribable enthusiasm, explained to me all the depth of thought in [Gogol's] "The Overcoat." At once I understood everything, and especially the significance of "invisible tears through visible laughter."
>
> Dostoevsky also advised me to read . . . foreign writers, especially Shakespeare. On his advice, I began to study French in a serious away, and to read and do translations.
>
> Everything that Dostoevsky told me, I accepted with youthful enthusiasm. To him I am obligated deeply for my development. He taught me to understand and value in literature all that is humane and great. At the very least, he gave me a first and forceful push by his conversations and direction.

> At this time also, Fyodor Mikhailovich was writing his *Poor Folk*, but I did not know such a thing since he never spoke about his work nor gave me excerpts to read. But how he could do such a thing . . . after all, I was only fifteen years old at the time!

Fall 1841 and after.
Anna Dostoevskaya, from her memoirs.

> Fyodor Mikhailovich was convinced that because "one thinks compactly in a compact apartment," he was ready to deny himself everything in an apartment except two spacious rooms.

Mid-October 1841.
Andrei Dostoevsky, from his memoirs.

> At that time my brother was living . . . close to his officer classes at the [Main] Engineering Academy.[38] He had rented an apartment with two rooms, a foyer, and a kitchen. He did not live alone but with an individual named Adolf Ivanovich Totleben[39] who occupied the first room off the entranceway, and my brother the second. Each room had two windows that were very low and gloomy. The smoke from tobacco hung in clouds that rose to the ceiling and made the top layers of these rooms seem filled with constant fog.
> This first meeting with my brother Fyodor was not particularly warm.[40] He paid more attention to my elder brother, Mikhail. At first, I felt awkward being there. My brother, though, introduced me to Totleben who was very kind and made me feel welcome. My two brothers, however, locked themselves up in Fyodor's room, leaving me alone with Totleben.
> During the night Fyodor and Mikhail secluded themselves again, and I had to sleep on the Turkish couch in Totleben's room. Such a situation continued throughout Mikhail's visit to Petersburg. After he departed for Revel,[41] I moved into brother Fyodor's room, but again, he did not pay me any special attention. . . .
> Fyodor and Totleben did not live together for long. I do not recall exactly when they parted company; but I only know that when I took sick in December, my brother and I lived alone.

December 5, 1841.
Mikhail Dostoevsky, from a letter to Fyodor Dostoevsky.

> While I am still upset, do not expect any lengthy letters from me, my dear friend and brother. This time I will limit myself to a much smaller, but nonetheless friendly jotting for your injustice, my dear one. I know that you will find such a thing unpleasant and perhaps, and that you will even fly into a rage. But what can I do? Judge my situation

for yourself. With every mailing I wait for a well-known piece of paper from you, and up until now I have not received anything.[42] You know that this request must reach me in Moscow no later than the holidays because it is only then that Pyotr Andreevich [Karepin] can make the time to travel to our village to negotiate with Elagin. After the holidays it will be impossible for him and also useless, because Elagin will be on vacation. And without this paper, Pyotr Andreevich will not be able to go to Kashira.

Brother! Brother! What a chaotic life you lead! After all, we are losing a lot and even, perhaps, money. If you still have not taken care of this request for me, then, for the love of God, hurry up and do it now; or, better still, send me a copy of it, and I will fill it in myself and send it back for your signature. How I regret that I did not think of such a thing when I was in Peterburg! Why did I forget about the draft when I was at your place? I could have taken care of things and the matter would have ended there. Pyotr Andreevich has asked me many times not to delay in mailing this paper. Brother! After all, our relatives will think that we do not have him as a guardian, and he himself will refuse to take the position. But enough about that. Let us talk about something else.

I'm in a terrible state. My heart is not at ease. The trip to Moscow caused me a great deal of harm. A joke has destroyed religion in France: and I have deep doubt in my abilities. It seems that I am doing something stupid in getting married. But when I look at Emilia, I feel, in the eyes of this angel, a childlike joy, and I become happier. The first year of our life will be particularly hard, but what can I do? We will manage somehow. The second year will be easier. From the thousand rubles I have now, there will soon be no more than a hundred. Perhaps, you may be surprised by such a thing, but I swear to God, it is true. And how we economize! I deny myself everything.

Again I must warn you. Your [servant] Egor is a thief, a debauchee, and a drunkard. How many pranks has my servant told me about him! For the love of God, brother, for the love of the Very Creator, chase him from your home and get yourself a batman. If you have already not been driven mad by his tricks, I would have laughed myself sick with the stories Vasili has been telling me! To so turn a blind eye to your servants! He does not spend a single night at your place. Lost in his own thoughts . . . he lost your silk handkerchief. He takes a single letter to the post office. Brother! He is the worst of villains! Get rid of him! He is robbing you blind. . . .

Tell Andryusha [Andrei] not to be lazy in writing to me.[43] And you, brother, try to write to me a bit more often. I will not remain in debt.

December 22, 1841.
Fyodor Dostoevsky, from a letter to Mikhail Dostoevsky.

You write to me, my priceless friend, about the grief and catastrophe that have crushed your heart.[44] You write in despair, my dear, sweet brother. But judge for yourself about my grief, about *my* woe when I learned all this from you. I became very sad; it was unbearable. You are approaching that moment in life when all our hopes and our wishes blossom; when happiness attaches itself to the heart; and when the heart is filled with bliss. But then what happens? Those moments are darkened and defiled by sorrow, work, and cares.

My dear, dear Brother! If only you knew how happy I am that I can at least help you in some way. With what pleasure am I sending you this trifle, which can at least somewhat restore your inner peace. I know that it is not enough. But what can I do if I cannot send you any more? Dear Brother, I swear to you that I cannot! Judge for yourself. If I were alone, I would for you, dear Brother, go without the barest essentials, but I have another brother on my hands.[45] If I write to Moscow soon[46]— God knows what they will think! So I am sending you this trifle. But dear God, how unfair you are to me, my priceless friend, when you write such words as *loan* and *I will repay you*. Aren't you ashamed, aren't such words sinful, and between brothers, to boot! My friend, you really do not know me. There is nothing I would not give up for you! No, you were in a bad mood when you wrote to me, and I forgive you for that.

When is the wedding?! I wish you happiness and expect long letters from you. I, though, cannot write you a decent one even now. Would you believe that I am writing to you at three in the morning, and that last night I did not go to bed at all. The examinations and classes are terrible. They ask everything ... and so you cram "*in a repugnant way*"—but you cram nonetheless.

I feel extraordinarily guilty before your dear fiancé—my sister, and priceless like you; but forgive my incomprehensible character, my good friend. Can she really have so little of a relative's trust in me; or has someone created such a hideous notion of me—impolite, discourteous, hostile, and filled with every vice—so as to have her predisposed against me, not believing in my absolute lack of time, and becoming angry at my silence. But I do not deserve such an image—*on my honor, I do not*. In a most humble way, I beg her pardon; I ask her indulgence, and cursed one that I am, also the complete forgiveness and absolution of my sins. I would be flattered to be called her kind and sincerely loving brother, but what can I do? I always flatter myself and will continue to do so in the hope that I can at last achieve such a distinction.

I am not writing anything about myself in this letter. I cannot, I have no time—I will leave it until the next time. Brother Andryusha [Andrei] is sick, and I am simply beside myself, having to take so much care of him. There is another problem. His studies and his living with me—free, solitary, and independent person as I am— are driving me crazy. I cannot get to my own things or have any fun. You understand how it is. Andryusha is also such a strange and empty individual that he repels everyone he meets. How I regret my stupid plan to shelter him!

P.S. I am sending you 150 rubles.

Late December 1841.
Andrei Dostoevsky, from his memoirs.

> Somewhere I caught a cold which soon turned into a most powerful typhoid fever.... For a long time I lay in bed and finally became unconscious. My brother Fyodor cared for me in an attentive way....
>
> But then something extraordinary happened which frightened my brother greatly.... At that time my brother was also taking something for an illness.... Having awakened and remembered that it was time for my medicine, he, being only half-awake, mixed up the phials and poured me a tablespoon of his own prescription.... I swallowed it but suddenly I let out a powerful cry because the medicine had burned my mouth terribly and was beginning to affect my insides as well....
>
> My brother looked at the label, and, seeing that he had made a mistake, began to pull out his hair and ran for the doctor.... The doctor arrived at our place right away.... He prescribed an antidote, but said that it would slow up my recovery....
>
> Nonetheless, Brother looked after me very attentively, giving me the medicine that the doctor had prescribed, for which he had to go out daily.

1842

1842 and after.
Alexander Rizenkampf, from his memoirs.

> More often than not, though, Fyodor Mikhailovich avoided balls, masquerades, and parties in people's homes....
>
> I never understood why, despite the conservative reserve in his pleasures, Fyodor Mikhailovich always had excessive expenses.

1842 and after.
Alexander Rizenkampf, from his memoirs.

> Fyodor Mikhailovich always seemed indifferent to women; he almost had a kind of antipathy to them.... Perhaps, in this regard, he was hiding something.

1842 and after.
Anna Dostoevskaya, from her memoirs.

> It always seemed strange to me that ... in Fyodor Mikhailovich's youth, there was not a single serious passionate love for some woman. I explain such a thing by the

fact that he began to live an intellectual life extremely early. Creativity swallowed him up completely; his personal life became secondary.

1842 and after.
Lyubov Dostoevskaya, from her memoirs.

> It is surprising that . . . in his early youth . . . my father did not meet a single woman. Neither a bride, not a liaison, nor even a flirtation! This unusual abstinence . . . this late development of his organism is common in northern Russia. . . .
>
> The complete maturity of the Russian male in the north does not take occur until age twenty-five. . . . Sick organisms, e.g., individuals who suffer from epilepsy, will develop even more slowly. It is possible that at this stage, Dostoevsky's emotions still had not come to the fore. He was like a *gimnazist* who is enraptured by women from afar, but who, fearful . . . has no need of them.

1842 and after.
Alexander Rizenkampf, from his memoirs.

> Fyodor Mikhailovich's curiosity [about women] was so unfeigned that one felt awkward about his [later] stories of meeting with prostitutes.[47]

1842.
Andrei Dostoevsky, from an 1881 letter to Alexei Suvorin.

> In 1842 . . . my brother wrote a drama titled *Boris Godunov*. The manuscript often lay on his desk; and sinner that I am, I often peeked into it with youthful delight over what I had read. Not very long ago, it seems it was in 1875, I confessed to my brother that I had read his drama. But to my question: "Did you save this manuscript, brother?"—he answered, waving his hand: "Oh, enough! . . . It was just young foolishness."

1842.
Orest Miller, from his biography of Dostoevsky.

> What became of Dostoevsky's sketches, *Maria Stuart* and *Boris* is unknown.[48]

February–March 1842 and after.
Andrei Dostoevsky, from his memoirs.

> In early 1842 my brother began to look for a new apartment because he found his current one to be uncomfortable. After several long searches, he found . . . a place

that was merry and bright. It consisted of three rooms, a vestibule and a kitchen. The first room was the common room; on one side was my brother's room; on the other, a small, but completely separate room for me.

February–March 1842 and after.
Andrei Dostoevsky, from his memoirs.

> At that time, two individuals often visited us at our apartment:
> 1. K. A. Trutovsky . . . who drew excellently, often with a simple pencil on scraps of paper . . . [who later] entered the Academy of Arts[49] . . . and became an academician of art.[50] . . .
> 2. Dmitri Vasilievich Grigorovich . . . [who] was . . . about twenty-one years old, that is, the same age as my brother.[51] . . . The two visited my brother, they always had a good time together because Grigorovich always told stories from the theatrical world.[52]

February–March 1842 and after.
Andrei Dostoevsky, from his memoirs.

> My brother was quite carried away with cards. Preferans or whist in the beginning and then faro and shtoss.

April–May 1842.
Alexander Rizenkampf, from his memoirs.

> Beginning on April 9, 1842, the genius Lizst gave a series of concerts that continued until the end of May. Despite the unheard-of cost of tickets (between 20 and 25 paper rubles), Fyodor Mikhailovich and I did not miss a single performance. . . . Fyodor Mikhailovich often laughed at his friends who sported gloves, hats, hairstyles, and canes à la Liszt.
> After one concert, shoving crowds tore a tassel from Fyodor Mikhailovich's sword knot. . . . Until his retirement [from service], Fyodor Mikhailovich always kept this tassel with him . . . telling people how he valued it as a memento of Lizst's concerts.

June 20, 1842.
From a questionnaire for officers of the Main Engineering Academy.

> How sincere are you about service?
> Dostoevsky: Very serious.

What are you mental capabilities?
Dostoevsky: Good.
In what areas do you have competence?
Dostoevsky: Theology, Russian, all areas of pure mathematics including differential and integral calculus, descriptive geometry, statistics, geodesics, field and long-term fortification and mining technology, artillery, military-structural art, architecture, physics, tactics, history, geography, drawing.
What foreign languages do you know?
Dostoevsky: French and German.
What kind of moral formation do you have?
Dostoevsky: Good.
How are your personal affairs?
Dostoevsky: Good.[53]

Late July 1842.
An administrator at the Main Engineering Academy, from a report.

> Upon looking at the journals and plans of student officers . . . those by Dostoevsky were done very quickly . . . and showed little effort.

December 1842.
Fyodor Dostoevsky, from a letter to Andrei Dostoevsky.

> My dear Brother! If you have received the money,[54] for God's sake, send me about five rubles or at least a silver one. I have not any firewood for three days now, and I am sitting here without a copeck to my name. Next week for certain I will receive 200 rubles. (I am borrowing them.) I will pay you back everything then.

December 6, 1842.
Ivan Shidlovsky, from a poem.

> While thought is with me
> And the ability to excite
> Possesses all my soul
> While under sacred truth
> I cannot help but sink into reverie.
> While I love
> Still with torment and angst
> I cherish a passionate dream
> While I believe in purity
> Of the soul with deep emotion.

While in me there is alive and clear
The primary supreme idea
Of the Beginning, Creator, and Godhood
For happiness is in me rightful
I live a life Empyrean.
Let the terrible storm from within
Threaten the misfortune of ruin
Among other people and myself
In my spiritual depths
Enough is the anchor of salvation!
Without fail I will endure
The trials and travails of any storm
God, my pilot, will guard my boat
My guiding star
He warms so clearly from the sky.
He does not lead me to Himself
Father, all-powerful Protector
I await the joyous day
And eternity, replacing time
Opens to me my abode.
And there, in the shining doors
To me of the welcoming paradise.
I look with angst into eyes
And with sad smiles into lips
The path of bliss swimming by
And before the novelty of joys
Disturbing my shy soul
I will think to ask to go back
I will be glad for past storms
I will sigh about life with a tear.

1843

1843 and after.
Andrei Dostoevsky, from an 1881 letter to Alexei Suvorin.

From 1843 to April 1849 (the time of his arrest) I, with rare exceptions, visited my brother on a daily basis,[55] but never during our conversations did I hear anything from him about the ailment [of epilepsy]. I should also note that he did not conceal his illnesses from me and often complained about how poorly he felt. True, in this period of time (I do not recall the precise year), he was somewhat irritable and, it seemed, suffered from some kind of nervous illness. I often happened to come across notes left by him . . . saying something like this: "Today I may fall victim to a lethargic sleep but do not bury me for (some) days." But once again I say that he never mentioned a "falling" disease in this period of time.

1843.
Alexander Rizenkampf, from his memoirs.

Dostoevsky's special attention rested on a young man by the name of Kohler, the brother of the pianist-virtuoso.[56] He was a fidgety, obsequious, almost ragged-looking individual—by profession, a broker, but in reality, a sponger and a hanger-on. Having noted the selfless hospitality of Fyodor Mikhailovich, he became a daily visitor—for tea, lunch, and dinner. Patiently did Fyodor Mikhailovich hear out his stories about the proletariat in the capital.

Often Fyodor Mikhailovich wrote down what he had heard . . . a thing or two of Kohler's material entering into such works as *Poor Folk*, *The Double*, and *Netochka Nezvanova*.

January–early February 1843.
Fyodor Dostoevsky, from a letter to Andrei Dostoevsky.

You wrote to me, dear Brother, that you could not get money earlier than Shrovetide. But I just thought: together with this letter I will send you another one in which I ask you for a loan of 50 rubles. You show it to General [Privits][57] and ask him to give you the money right away. . . . Of course, tell him that you have given me your word of honor and that you wish to help me. For God's sake, dearest Brother, please do not refuse my request. Just as soon as I receive a loan from Brother [Mikhail], I will repay you. You will not be without money. Take what you need out of the 50 rubles. Upon my word of honor, at Shrovetide, I will repay everything. . . . You cannot imagine what terrible, horrible need I am in now. Help me, please.

March–April 1843 and after.
Alexander Rizenkampf, from his memoirs.

The health of Fyodor Mikhailovich began to get better. Apparently, his material means also improved. During Lent he again attended concerts by . . . the famous tenor Rubini and the clarinetist Blaes. On April 18, we attended a performance of *Ruslan and Lyudmila*. With his customary enthusiasm, he read to me excerpts from

Gogol's writings and Lamartine's "The Dying Poet."[58] Most of all, though, he was busy reading French novelists . . . especially Soulié's *General Confession*,[59] Balzac's *Two Brown Tales*,[60] Marryat's *Japhet in Search of a Father*, and others.[61]

When Fyodor Mikhailovich had money, he bought recent issues of *Notes of the Fatherland*,[62] *The Library for Reading*, and other journals. He also often subscribed to some library for Russian and French books. . . . Fyodor Mikhailovich was also interested in German poetry . . . Heine's "To France Were Returning Two Grenadiers"[63] and Beck's *Janko, the Hungarian Horse-Herd*.[64]

When Fyodor Mikhailovich did not have money (and that was quite often), he wrote.

March–April 1843 and after.
Fyodor Dostoevsky, from an 1874 article.

It was at this time, namely in the mid-1840s, that the Italian opera could succeed in penetrating the very mass of the Petersburg public. . . . At that time we considered it the height of delight, our eighty-copeck seats in the fifth tier of the gallery. We became intoxicated on the sweet sounds, forgetting the entire world around us. We not only did not envy the people in the pit, but from our eighty-copeck heights, also looked at them with a certain condescension.

March–April 1843 and after.
Alexander Rizenkampf, from his memoirs.

Fyodor Mikhailovich thought little about whether his writing would bring him any benefit. He often said: "Look at what Pushkin came to, for every line he was paid a gold coin. The same thing happened to Gogol; so perhaps, I will be paid something too."

March–April 1843 and after.
Alexander Rizenkampf, from his memoirs.

I tried to introduce Dostoevsky to certain families. First among them was a respected Belgian by the name of Montigny, who was a mechanic in the arsenal. . . . Even as a student, I often spent festive evenings with this splendid family which included such educated foreigners . . . as Maximilan von Heine (brother of the poet). . . .

But not having mastered French completely, Fyodor Mikhailovich often flushed red. He began to sputter and become irate. One evening, he let loose such invectives against foreigners that the stunned porters took him for some *enragé* and asked him to leave. Several days in a row Fyodor Mikhailovich asked me once and for all to forsake any and all attempts on my part to introduce him to foreigners. What good would come, he said, if he were married off to some Frenchwoman, for then he would have to say goodbye to Russian literature forever!

March–April 1843 and after.
Alexander Rizenkampf, from his memoirs.

> Fyodor Mikhailovich had a scrufola-like composition, a hoarse voice and frequent swollen chin and neck glands. Further, the earthen color of his face gave witness to the faulty condition of his blood (to cachexia) as well as to a chronic illness of his breathing passages. . . . Often there were also abscesses and boils. . . . Fyodor Mikhailovich endured all these sufferings in a stoic way; he turned to medical help only in extreme circumstances.
>
> More often, though, Fyodor Mikhailovich was subject to nervous sufferings. Many times he complained to me that at night someone was seemingly snoring next to him, and that he could not sleep or find a comfortable place for himself. When such a thing happened, he got up and either read or wrote. The next day he went to the Engineering Department completely out of sorts. He cursed his fate, complained about the senior officers, and dreamed of retirement from the service as quickly as possible.

June 8, 1843.
Fyodor Dostoevsky, from a report to the authorities of the Main Engineering Academy.

> Suffering from pain in my chest as well as from ongoing rheumatism, I went to the doctor . . . who informed me that bathing in the sea would be of undoubtable value. . . . I humbly implore Your Excellency to obtain for me . . . a twenty-day leave to Revel to use the local baths there.[65]

June 30, 1843.
Orest Miller, from his biography of Dostoevsky.

> At that time Rizenkampf was sitting for his final examination. From overexertion, he had become sick and lay in bed. Without warning, Fyodor Mikhailovich came to visit him, but he was quite unlike his usual self. Happy, with a fresh look, and pleased with fate, he informed Rizenkampf of the successful completion of his examinations; his graduation from school with the rank of second lieutenant (in field engineers);[66] and the receipt from his guardian of such a sum of money that he could settle accounts with his creditors. . . .

> Forcibly, Dostoevsky dragged Rizenkampf from bed, sat him in a droshky, and took him to a restaurant on Nevsky Prospekt. There Dostoevsky demanded a room with a piano, ordered a lavish dinner with wines, and forced the sick man to eat and drink with him. . . . Fyodor Mikhailovich ate a great deal, sat down at the piano, and—became well.[67]

July 1843.
Orest Miller, from his biography of Dostoevsky.

> Mikhail Mikhailovich, with the help of his wife, furnished his brother with a completely new wardrobe of underwear and clothes, both of which were cheap in Revel.[68] . . . They also asked Alexander Rizenkampf to live with Fyodor Mikhailovich in Petersburg and, as much as possible, to serve as an example of German order.[69]

August 12, 1843, and after.
Orest Miller, from his biography of Dostoevsky.

> On August 12, 1843, F. M. Dostoevsky, after having completed the course of study in science for senior offices, was admitted to service . . . in the drafting department of the St. Petersburg Engineering Corps.

After August 1843.
Fyodor Dostoevsky, from a dictated biography.

> He graduated from the military-engineering academy as a second lieutenant-engineer.[70] He worked in Petersburg, but elusive strivings and goals took hold of him. He began to study especially literature, history, and philosophy.

Mid-August 1843 and after.
Lyubov Dostoevskaya, from her memoirs.

> Having graduated from the Engineering Castle, Dostoevsky acquired a position in an engineering department. He retired from there a week later.[71] . . . More than ever, Dostoevsky wanted to be a writer. The young Grigorovich followed in his footsteps. They decided to live together, renting a bachelor apartment and hiring a servant.[72]
>
> Grigorovich received money from his mother in the provinces; my father, from a trustee in Moscow who afforded him ample means for a modest existence.[73] Unfortunately, though, my father always had the most fantastic notions about financial matters. . . .

> Having paid off his debts, Dostoevsky spent his remaining money quickly.... Translations did not provide him with sufficient income. Aunt Kumanina came to the rescue, securing him with funds.... She was the only one in the family who valued him and was already ready to help him whenever she could....
>
> Grigorovich, knowing society better than my father, not only wrote, but also allied himself with acquaintances who could advance him with people. Having entered literary circles, he also presented Dostoevsky.
>
> Grigorovich was handsome, elegant, and full of *joie de vivre*. He was always courting and delighting the ladies. My father, though, was awkward, shy, unsociable, and rather ugly. He spoke little but listened a great deal.

August 1843–October 1844.
Pyotr Semyonov-Tyan-Shansky, from his memoirs.

> Between graduation from the Main Engineering Academy and his retirement [from service] Dostoevsky received 5,000 paper rubles from salary and funds from his guardian.[74]

September 1843 and after.
Orest Miller, from his biography of Dostoevsky.

> Having returned to Petersburg in September 1843, Doctor Rizenkampf... found... Fyodor Mikhailovich without a copeck, living on bread and milk,[75] and in debt. "Fyodor Mikhailovich," he said, "belonged to that type of personalities who lived well, but who were constantly in need. People robbed him mercilessly, but he, trusting and kind, did not wish to investigate the matter and to accuse the servant and parasite-spongers who took advantage of his negligence."
>
> Living with the doctor became for Fyodor Mikhailovich a constant source of new expenses. Every poor person, who came to the doctor for consultation, he was ready to receive as a dear guest. "I do so to describe the everyday life of poor people," he said in justification. "I am glad for the occasion to become acquainted more closely with the proletariat of the capital."
>
> The huge bills at the end of month, though, drew not so much from the hospitality of Fyodor Mikhailovich as from the fact that his servant, Semyon, being on intimate terms with the laundress, was feeding not only her, but also her family and the entire company of her friends at the expense of his master....
>
> Dostoevsky liked Semyon very much. To the warnings as to the man's long hands, he answered in an extremely calm way: "Let him steal. I will not face ruin because of it." In truth, though, Dostoevsky was ruined completely.[76]

September 1843 and after.
Alexander Rizenkampf, from an 1881 letter to Andrei Dostoevsky.

> Fyodor Mikhailovich held fast to this rule: "Reveal yourself only to those who can help you." . . . His close friend Grigorovich knew nothing about his illnesses.

September 1843 and after.
Alexander Rizenkampf, from his memoirs.

> The German society of Revel, with its caste-like traditionalism, its nepotism and hypocrisy, its impatience with military matters, and its love for the fiery sermons of a local young pastor, made a burdensome impression on Dostoevsky. . . . I struggled to convince him that such things were merely local color and peculiar to the people there. . . . But from that moment in, Fyodor Mikhailovich, with his passion for generalization, became prejudiced against all things German.[77]

November 1843.
Alexander Rizenkampf, from his memoirs.

> The extreme poverty of Fyodor Mikhailovich continued for about two months, but in November, he began to pace up and down the room in an unusual way—loudly, self-assured, almost proudly. . . . He had just received a thousand rubles from Moscow. But the next morning . . . he, with his usual quiet and shy gait, entered my bedroom to ask if he could borrow five rubles. Most of the money had gone to pay for interest on loans; the remainder had been lost at billiards, in part stolen by some player whom Fyodor Mikhailovich . . . had invited to his place and had left alone momentarily in his study where there lay an unsealed envelope of 50 rubles.

November 1843.
Lyubov Dostoevskaya, from her memoirs.

> Dostoevsky was so honest that it never occurred to him that someone wanted to deceive him.

December 1843.
Alexander Rizenkampf, as told to Orest Miller.

> In December 1843 Fyodor Mikhailovich had again fallen into great need. He had to borrow money from a retired junior officer . . . a pawnbroker. . . . Instead of three

hundred paper rubles, Fyodor Mikhailovich received only two hundred, the remaining rubles as interest for four months.... Fyodor Mikhailovich was repulsed deeply by the man. Perhaps, also, he came to mind when, many years later, he described the emotions of Raskolnikov the first time he visited a pawnbroker.

Late December 1843.
Fyodor Dostoevsky, from a letter to Pyotr Karepin.

Kind sir and dearest Brother! First of all, allow me to wish you all the best for the New Year. Although today's respected people find the custom of our ancestors to wish new happiness along with the old as both outmoded and trite, I nonetheless shall include in my greeting to you a wish from the bottom of my heart for the continuation of the old happiness, if it accords with your wishes, and also for new happiness as is the worldly custom of wishing for more. Your happiness, of course, is inseparable from that of my sister Varvara and of your dear little ones. May their happiness, too, be assured for the rest of their lives; and may it bring to your family the delightful, radiant harmony of bliss.

Thank you for your package, although it arrived very late. I was already so greatly in debt that I immediately gave away everything inside of it, right down to the last copeck. I myself was left with nothing. I trust completely the way your calculate my allowance for the year; but if, in the next few days, you could send me 150 rubles or so, my circumstances would be secure for a long while. My present request for money from you is tied by needs about which I wrote to you earlier. I also seek to ask your forgiveness for the several careless words to you, which tore from my soul from both necessity and need.

Awaiting your reply, dearest Brother, with the most profound respect and devotion, allow me to remain your loving relative.

Late December 1843.
Fyodor Dostoevsky, from a letter to Varvara Dostoevskaya-Karepina.

I have not written to you in a long time, dearest Sister. I confess my sin to you sincerely; but as you see, I have been spoiled by your kindness and good will toward me. Thus I always rely on your forgiveness. With me you need to be more severe and unforgiving—two qualities which are quite contrary to your kind and loving heart.

I wish you increasing happiness, dear Sister, as well as health and happiness to your little ones. May they grow up to bring you comfort and joy. Accept these sincere wishes, and do not be angry with me for my apparent silence and coldness.

I repent before you! But I know that you will forgive me.

December 31, 1843.
Fyodor Dostoevsky, from a letter to Mikhail Dostoevsky.

We have not written to each other for a long time, dear Brother; and believe me, such a lapse does not do honor to either of us. You are slow to move, my dear friend.... But since the deed is done, the only thing left to do is to seize the future by the tail, and to wish you happiness in the New Year.... If you have a daughter, name her Maria.[78] ...

Now, my dear Brother, let's talk a bit about business. Although Karepin sent me 500 rubles ... I again owe 200 silver rubles. Somehow I need to work myself out of these obligations, and I have a millstone around my neck until I do. But fate has blessed me with an idea, an undertaking, call it what you wish. Since my idea is an incredibly profitable one, I hasten to propose that you also enter into its labor, risks, and profits. Here's what it is. Two years ago, there appeared in Russian a translation of the first part of *Mathilde* (by Eug. Sue),[79] i.e., one-sixteenth of the novel. Since then, though, nothing has been published. But the attention of the public has been aroused: From one province alone, five hundred people have demanded a speedy continuation of the work....

So, Patton, you (if you are interested), and I are combining our labor, money and time ... to publish a translation of *Mathilde* by Easter Week. We are keeping this undertaking in secret, made by us and examined from all sides *irrévocablement*.[80]

Here is how we will go about it.

We divide the translation into three equals parts and get to it right away. We figure that if each of us can translate twenty pages of the small portion of the pocket-sized edition of *Mathilde* that was published in Brussels, we can finish it by February 15. Patton will have his share done by February 15. We need a translation that is strictly straightforward and legible. You have a fine hand; so you will be able to do such a thing. Our translation of *Mathilde* will also be reviewed by the censorship. Patton is acquainted with Nikitenko, the chief censor;[81] so the matter will be taken care of more quickly than usual. To publish *Mathilde* will mean 4,500 paper rubles on our part. We have found out the prices for paper and printing.

The publishers demand one third down; the rest they will give on credit. Copies of the book will serve as collateral.

A printer acquaintance of mine, a Frenchman, told me that if I give him a thousand rubles, he will publish a total of 2,500 copies, and that he will wait for the rest of the money until the book is sold.

We need a minimum of 500 silver rubles. Patton already has 700. I will be sent about 500 in January. (If not, I will ask for an advance on my salary.) On your part, see to it that you have 500 rubles by mid-February even if you have to take it from your salary. With our collective funds, we will print, advertise, and sell copies of our translation of *Mathilde* for four rubles each. (The price is cheap, French.)

Our translation will be a sellout. Even *Nikitenko* predicts its success.... Three hundred copies will cover all the expenses for printing. If we sell the entire novel in eight volumes at a silver ruble apiece, we will make a profit of 7,000 rubles. The booksellers assure me that the book will be sold out in six months. The profits will be split three ways. If we sell the novel for a paper ruble apiece, your initial 500 rubles will be returned to you and the edition will pay for itself.

So that is what we propose. Do you want in or not? The advantages of such an undertaking are obvious. If you want to do this, begin translating "*la cinquième partie.*" Translate as much as you can from it....

Write me immediately. Do you want to do this or not?

1844

Circa 1844.
Sofia Kovalevskaya, from her memoirs.

Suddenly, in the heat of pleasant reveries and experiences, Dostoevsky began to feel awkward—something that embraced both inner pain and external distress, as often happens to people who have long-standing wounds from guns with bullets still in them....

Suddenly, he recalled [something] in a way that was so lively and real . . . with the disgust of his entire being, as if it had happened yesterday, and not twenty years ago.[82] . . .

He confessed that after a wild night and egged on by drunken friends, he had raped a ten-year-old girl.

My mother threw up her hands ... [and said:]

"Fyodor Mikhailovich! Have mercy! There are children here!" she begged in a despairing voice. I did not understand what Dostoevsky had said, only, from Mama's indignation, that it was something terrible.[83]

January–February 1844.
Alexander Rizenkampf, from his memoirs.

Every now and then Fyodor Mikhailovich hired copyists for the drafts of his writings. But he would be beside himself when he saw their mistakes and the money he had wasted. Still, at the age of twenty-three, he had not announced himself [to the literary world] with a single printed piece.

Grigorovich had already staged two successful comedies,[84] Patton was finishing his translation of Smitt's *The History of the Polish Rising*,[85] Mikhail Mikhailovich

[Dostoevsky] was completing his translation of Schiller's *Don Carlos*, and I myself was placing articles in German in L. Elsner's *The Store for German Readers in Russia*.[86] Fyodor Mikhailovich, however, who believed deeply in his literary calling, had prepared hundreds of short stories[87] but still had not managed to complete a single literary work. As a result, his day-to-day financial circumstances fell into disorder. All this distressed his nerves and brought about attacks of depression, forcing him to fear a nervous stroke or, as he himself said, a fit. As a doctor, I had for a long time noted his distress, demanding without fail that he take energetic medical relief, but I also ascribed all of his symptoms to his irregular life-style, sleepless nights, and careless diet.

Fyodor Mikhailovich loved to hide not only physical ailments but also his difficult financial circumstances. Among friends he always seemed happy, talkative, contented, and carefree. But soon after their departure, he fell into deep reflection, locking himself in his lonely study, smoking pipe after pipe, reflecting upon his sad position and seeking oblivion in new literary fantasies in which suffering humanity played a leading role.

Second half of January 1844.
Fyodor Dostoevsky, from a letter to Mikhail Dostoevsky.

Dear Brother, I had the pleasure of your reply, and so I myself hasten to write a few lines to you. You write that you did not know my address. But my dear Brother, after all, you know that I work in the Drafting Room of the Engineering Department. . . .

At least you have not forgotten me completely, dear Brother. I am very glad for your happiness. I wish you a daughter. . . . May it be God's will that I am fated to be a godfather for someone in your family. God grant that both these children know good fortune. I kiss Emilia Fyodorovna's hands and I thank her for remembering me. . . .

This is a business letter. Regarding our translation of *Mathilde*, things are going well to the point of *nec plus ultra*. The task of editing has been entrusted to me, and the translation will be good. Patton is priceless when it comes to profit. After all, you know that in business such colleagues are better than the most selfless friends. Take care to help us and try to do an elegant translation. . . .

For Heaven's sake, do not let us down, dear Brother. Give us a clean copy of the translation. It would also not be a bad idea if you could send us your translation no later than March 1st. We will finish our sections here and then the translation will go to the censors. The censor Nikitenko knows Patton and promised us to do his part in two weeks. On March 15th we will print everything at once, and put it on sale by the middle of April at the very latest.

You will ask where we will get the money for our work. I will scrape together 500 rubles. Patton has 700; and, his mother, 2,000. She is lending it to her son at forty percent interest. That will be enough, the rest is on credit.

We have made the rounds of all the publishers and booksellers, and here is what we have learned.

Chernoglazov, the translator of *Mathilde*, has neither money nor sense. He does have the translation. So we will advertise our translation when it is half printed, and that should be the end of him. Chernoglazov has no one but himself to blame. Why did he let three years pass between the first and second parts? Besides, anyone has the right to publish two or three translations of the same work. The booksellers insist that 1,000 copies of our *Mathilde* will be sold in the provinces. Moreover, they say that they will receive the money from sales immediately and will take only forty copecks per ruble. They have also said that it makes no sense to charge less than six silver rubles for the translation (the price of the French book of the edition that was published in Brussels). So we will get 3,500 silver rubles all at once in May. These same booksellers also assure me that these days, in Petersburg, we can definitely sell 350 copies of our translation of *Mathilde*, with twenty percent [of sales] going to the storekeepers. So, assuming we sell 1,500 copies, we will receive at least 5,000 silver rubles. Since we owe 1,000 rubles, we will clear 4,000 silver rubles as profit. We also have decided to share everything three ways, as if we were brothers; and so, for your share, you will definitely receive 4,000 paper rubles. But finish the translation now. . . .

I also have a slight favor to ask of you, my dear little Brother. I am currently without money. You should know that during the holidays,[88] I translated Balzac's *Eugénie Grandet* (superb! absolutely superb!). My translation is equally marvelous. At the very least, I will get 350 paper rubles for it. I fervidly wish to sell it; but this future millionaire lacks the money—and time—to have it copied. So, for the sake of all the angels in heaven, send me thirty-five paper rubles to cover the cost of copying. I swear by Olympus . . . by my completed drama, *Yankel the Jew*[89] . . . and perhaps, by the moustache that I hope will show up on my face sometime, that half of what I get for *Eugénie* will be yours.[90] *Dixi*.

Early February 1844 and after.
Lyubov Dostoevskaya, from her memoirs.

My father studied the new heroes of Russian literature, seeking out the inhabitants of attics and lofts in small teahouses and taverns of the capital. Talking to them, he wrote in detail their customs and habits. Because Dostoevsky was shy and did not know how to approach such individuals, he offered to play them in billiards. But since he did not know the game, he lost a great deal of money. My father did not regret the loss, though, because he was making remarkable observations and writing down original expressions.... He then began to describe these little people as they existed in life, and to delight readers with his stories.... Dostoevsky's friends recall that he often invited to his home people ... whom he did not know and had met in taverns, and that for the entire day, he talked to them and listened to their stories. My father's friends could not understand the pleasure he received from these conversations with simple people. When they read Dostoevsky's novels, though, they came across the types whom they had met at his place.

Early February 1844.
Orest Miller, from his biography of Dostoevsky.

Fyodor Mikhailovich was again sent 1,000 rubles from Moscow, but by evening he had in his pocket ... only 100 rubles in all.... A gentleman approached him and said: "Here are dominoes, a completely innocent honest game." Fyodor Mikhailovich also wanted to learn that new game, but for this lesson he paid dearly.... His last one hundred rubles went into the pocket of his teacher.

The next day Fyodor Mikhailovich was again without money and acquired new loans at the most barbarous rates for sugar, tea, and the like.

February 14, 1844.
Fyodor Dostoevsky, from a letter to Mikhail Dostoevsky.

You ordered me to inform you about the circumstances of our translation of *Mathilde*. To my extreme regret, my priceless friend, I must tell you that things are not going too well. So I ask you to hold off for a while and do not translate any more until you receive a more specific confirmation from me....

I really have no basis to suspect failure for our efforts. But in any event, it never hurts to be cautious. As for me, I am continuing to translate. But I am still asking you to stop for a while so that just in case, your efforts will not be in vain. Even now, my dear friend, I feel bad that perhaps, you have wasted your time.

The possibility for failure is found neither in the translation itself, nor in its literary success (our undertaking would be brilliant); rather, it is rooted in the strange events that have arisen with the translators. The third translator was Patton who, for an agreed-upon sum, hired Captain Gartong to correct his translation. This Gartong is the very same individual who translated *Plik and Pok*[91] and *The Lame Devil*,[92] and also wrote the story "Requiem" for *The Library for Reading*. Everything was going well. Patton's mother was going to lend us the money for the project; she had even given her word of honor.

But in April Patton is going with his mother to the Caucasus to serve under his father's command. He tells me, though, that he will definitely finish the translation.

He also says that he will entrust me with its printing and sale. But, for some reason, I do not believe that Jews like Patton would want to trust me with up to 3,000 rubles in a matter which, say what you wish, is a risky one. Indeed, it is for them a risk twice over. In spite of that Patton is translating. I know this and have seen it with my own eyes.

All these reasons have forced me to ask you, my friend, to leave off the translation for the time being. In a very short time, I will notify you of the final decision; but I probably doubt that we will go ahead with it. Judge for yourself. How sorry I feel for you, dear friend, how very sorry. Poor thing that I am, dear friend, please forgive me too. After all I am an unlucky Murad.[93]

March 1844.
Orest Miller, from his biography of Dostoevsky.

In March Doctor Rizenkampf had to leave Petersburg, but without having managed to teach Fyodor Mikhailovich the ways of German precision and practicality.

March–April 1844.
Fyodor Dostoevsky, from a letter to Mikhail Dostoevsky.

I am writing just a few lines to you in haste. I assume that as soon as you received my letter, you immediately set down to work. For God's sake, get going on the translation of *Don Carlos*. It will be a wondrous thing. Move on it as soon as possible. A few days ago, an idea flashed through my mind . . . [that] as soon as I receive the translation from you, I will publish *Don Carlos* at my own expense. I will get the money for the project by taking an advance of my salary. (Such a thing I have already done several times.)

Here is the approximate bill for the printing: The best vellum paper for 1,000 copies—about 5,000 sheets; 500 sheets of the best paper cost 10 rubles—so a total of 100 rubles. Printing with small legible type . . . 30 paper rubles a sheet, and at most, there will be 5 sheets in all. . . . A copy costs 1 silver ruble. 100 copies will pay for the edition with a nice profit, to boot. . . .

Think about it, dear Brother. A translation of *Don Carlos* will be a wonderful novelty in literature. Admirers of the piece will buy it; at the very least, we will sell 300 copies. Just think! You are not risking a thing. Do not worry about me. I understand these things and will not get in over my head. I always manage to pay for an edition.

You have a family. Whether you sit, sweat away at work, or watch people lay bricks, few happy thoughts will enter your head. Your pay is little. You will have bread; but you will not have the new frock coat when you absolutely need to have such a thing. Woe in youth is a dangerous feeling. So you need to work. You have a splendid command of verse. A translator who knows French can have bread in Petersburg. And what bread at that! I am testing the waters myself. (I am translating George Sand[94] and charging 25 paper rubles per sheet.)

Why is Strugovshchikov already famous in our literature? Because of translations. Do you translate any worse than he does? Strugovshchikov has made a fortune on what he has done. You could have done the same thing a long time ago. It is just that earlier we did not know how to go about such a thing. I will write the introduction and you do Schiller's verse. We can start printing in June and by July 1st, I will send a copy in a gold wrapper. In literature, the field is clear. A translation of *Don Carlos* will be received by the public with delight. I am sure that you are translating now. For God's sake, write to reassure me that you are doing so. . . .

P.S. I'm getting sick of the service. I'm as sick of it as I am of potatoes. . . . I cannot come and visit you. They are not giving out any leaves, my dear one. But I will come for weeks when I retire from service.

Spring 1844.
Stepan Yanovsky, from a letter to Orest Miller.

[Dostoevsky said:] Having finished the course of study at the [Main] Engineering Academy, I had to . . . present practical work on a given theme. One assignment was reviewed and approved by the Council before it was sent to Emperor Nikolai I. . . . The Emperor only had to look at my drawing to see that my fortress had no gates! The mistake had passed unnoticed by everyone including the director; but it was immediately picked up by the tsar, who wrote on the drawing: "What idiot drew this?" The inscription was presented to me . . . in a hard cover. Right then and there I decided to leave the department for fear that the designation of "idiot" would perhaps follow me for the rest of my life.

Spring 1844.
Stepan Yanovsky, from his memoirs.

When I asked Dostoevsky: "Why did you not continue with engineering? . . . He answered: "I found it sickening to worm myself into people's graces . . . [especially when] the Emperor had given me such a vile nickname . . . one that I will carry to the grave." . . .

[He added:] "I wanted to write and write, and in my writing . . . to defend the humiliated and the injured."

Spring 1844.
Orest Miller, from his biography of Dostoevsky.

> The inscription by Emperor Nikolai Pavlovich on Dostoevsky's drawing—"What idiot drew this?"— ... was [allegedly] preserved in the archive of the Engineering Department. After painstaking searches there, though ... nothing like this was ever found.[95]

Spring 1844.
Stepan Yanovsky, from his memoirs.

> I never doubted that Fyodor Mikhailovich could draw the plan for a fortress but forget a place for the gates.

Spring 1844.
Alexander Saveliev, from his memoirs.

> It disturbed Fyodor Mikhailovich that as an engineering officer ... he was present at both local and judicial punishments. He could not bear to see arrested peasants in chains at work sites ... or the corporal discipline meted out to soldiers who kept watch....
>
> Fyodor Mikhailovich also lost all inclination for technical work. Often his designs (plans and facades of buildings, watchtowers with their platforms, and the like) were ... without scale, and returned to the engineering team with reprimands or sarcasm about their author. I and others tried hard to calm Fyodor Mikhailovich and to reconcile him to such failures; but to no avail. Disturbed greatly by his lack of technological success, he cooled toward the idea of military service. His worsening illness was the final blow, bringing Fyodor Mikhailovich to leave engineering altogether.

Early April 1844 and after.
Anna Dostoevskaya, from her memoirs.

> Only with *Poor Folk* did it fall to Dostoevsky's lot to write a novel unhurriedly, without pressure, taking the time to think his plan through thoroughly and to work out all the details.

Early April 1844 and after.
Anna Dostoevskaya, from her memoirs.

> With rapture did Fyodor Mikhailovich recall those hours when he wrote *Poor Folk*.

July–August 1844.
Fyodor Dostoevsky, from a letter to Mikhail Dostoevsky.

As soon as I received your translation of *The Robbers*, I read it immediately. . . . Here is my opinion. The songs are translated so brilliantly that they alone are worth the price of the book. The rendition of the prose into Russian—its force and accuracy—is also superb. You complain about Schiller's language; but, my dear friend, it cannot be any other way. I did notice, though, that you got carried away by the conversations in the work, and that quite often you sacrificed the correctness of the Russian word for the sake of a natural style. Further, here and there, non-Russian words make their appearance (although the use of such words as *shtudirovat'* for "to study" and *suvernichiki* for "little souvenirs" are the height of art and resourcefulness). Finally, certain phrases in the work are rendered into Russian with great carelessness. Generally speaking, though, your translation of *The Robbers* is amazing in the full sense of this word. I cleaned up a thing or two and got down to business immediately.

I also went to see Pesotsky and Mezhevich. These two rogues are being stingy. They do not want even to think of publishing all of Schiller in their journal.[96] They do not understand a good idea, so much as they "speculate" on it. Fearing the censors, they refuse to print *The Robbers* separately from others of Schiller's works. In truth, Nikitenko cannot and does not want to take responsibility for the work without crossing out an entire third of it. I still gave him the work to censor, though; later, we can take care of the uneven parts. What can we do!

After I heard the decision of Pesotsky and Mezhevich about publishing Schiller in their journal, I did not even let them sniff at our translation of *The Robbers*. But then here is what I have now decided: to publish *Don Carlos* with them. Such a work will interest the public; people will see that the translation is good. In the same edition of the publication, we will announce an edition of all of Schiller's works. Pesotsky and Mezhevich will pay us for *Don Carlos*; and I will insist that they will pay us well. So, for God's sake, please finish the translation as quickly as you can. In the fall, in one fell swoop, we will publish *The Robbers, Fiesco, Don Carlos*, and *Maria Stuart*. For God's sake, please translate *Maria Stuart*. (But you have to do it in verse; that is essential if you wish it to be a success.) There will be money to publish these things. We need a little over a 1,000 rubles. So we need 700 rubles in cash because publishers always give a third on credit. That is what everyone does, and I can always get my hands on 700 rubles. Having priced the edition properly, I expect that sales of 100 copies can not only pay for our expenses, but also even render a slight profit. And 100 copies is only the beginning. The intention is good, and the venture absolutely worthy of undertaking. Write, my friend, and translate. I will vouch for its success with my head, and I will not leave you without money. Just wait! When people see the translations in our hands, they will come flying at us in swarms. We will have plenty of offers from publishers and booksellers. I now know several of them—they are dogs, the whole lot of them.

So hurry with *Don Carlos*. Hurry without fail. Such a thing will give us money and set our edition in motion. We will have the money right away. I imagine that you have not been idle, but have been translating all the time. If you had wanted a lot of money in the beginning, you should have begun the translation not in sequence, but right off with *Don Carlos*. But it is better to do a good job.

Mezhevich asks most humbly that we send to him as soon as possible all of Schiller's prose writings about drama and the dramatic art if they are ready in translation. He is especially interested about *the naive and sentimental*.[97] So I advise you to translate such pieces. There will be money; so translate quickly. (Don't worry. I will not let anything out of my hands until I get the money.)

So work on *Don Carlos* and the prose now. Then do *Fiesco* and *Maria Stuart*. I am counting on you, dear Brother; above all, do not get discouraged by all you have to do. Remember what happened with *Semela* and *Hermann and Dorothea*.[98] Because a publisher rejected *Semela*, you stopped working on it. But recently it appeared in *The Fatherland Notes* in the vilest translation. *Hermann and Dorothea* also just appeared in print, and both pieces were a success. Why, because you got discouraged with these works too early. So for God's sake, please hurry and work. We will make a marvelous profit. You can do *Fiesco* and *Maria* later, at your leisure. As soon as we have money, we will publish them too. We can get the funds, even if we have to squeeze the Muscovites.[99] . . .

Goodbye, my dear friend. Rejoice in our unexpected windfall.

P.S. I am notifying you that Obodovsky has translated *Don Carlos*. So look sharp, brother, and get a move on. Obodovsky has not yet published his translation. Besides, he does not intend to.

I can get hold of 500 rubles for *Don Carlos*.

August 21, 1844.
Fyodor Dostoevsky, from a petition to Nicholas I.

All Very Most Enlightened, Most Imperial, Great Emperor Nikolai Pavlovich, All-Russian Autocrat and Most Merciful Sovereign!

Here asks Fyodor Mikhailovich Dostoevsky, Second Lieutenant and Field Engineer of the Department of Engineering for the following:

Needing to attend to my domestic circumstances and notwithstanding my earnest desire to continue in the service of Your majesty . . . I wish to be relieved of my position . . . relying on my own reserves and without any compensation from the State.

August 31, 1844.
Fyodor Dostoevsky, from a letter to Pyotr Karepin.

I hasten to inform you . . . that as the result of the natural and extremely unpleasant course of my affairs, I have been forced to retire. I submitted my request ten days ago; and the authorities have given their assent. At the very latest, the imperial decree will be issued in two weeks.[100]

Since I had no money for postage, I did not notify you immediately. The reason for this upheaval in my fate was my critical financial situation. Seeing the impossibility of receiving assistance from anywhere, I did not know what else to come up with other than to retire. Life is poor now. Neither from above, nor from below, nor from right, nor from left is there anything good. Like a lost dog, a person can rot and perish. Even if nearby he had brothers born from the same womb, they will not share anything with him . . . they will try to even take away anything that this perishing individual can rightly call his.

Everyone for himself and God for all![101] That is a splendid proverb thought up by people who have managed to live a bit. As far as I am concerned, I am ready to admit all the implementations of such a wise rule. . . .

I was assigned to the Fortress. I owed about 1,200 rubles. I was also supposed to prepare a supply of clothes to live on the road, perhaps on the way to Orenburg or Sevastopol,[102] or somewhere even farther. Yes, finally I was to have the means to get hold of a thing or two right then and there. Since experience persuaded me firmly that I could be assigned even to Kamchatka,[103] and that I could not expect financial assistance from anywhere, I was forced to choose the lesser evil, i.e., I decided to postpone the catastrophe of my existence for at least two months. They could go and drag me off to prison; but legally I would receive that which I have been begging for, for God knows how long.

I am informing you, Pyotr Andreevich, that I need clothes terribly. The winters here in Petersburg are cold, and the falls are quite raw and harmful to one's health. It is more than obvious that one cannot do without clothing unless one wants an early exit to the grave. In this regard, of course, there is an extremely noble saying: *It serves you right*! But such a saying is used only in extreme cases, and I have yet to reach that point. . . . Since I have not paid the rent, I will have to move out of my apartment. . . . I will have to live on the street and sleep under the columns of Kazan Cathedral.[104] That is an unhealthy way to live, so I need to have a new place to live. There exists a half-saying that asserts that, in such cases, one can find *public* housing at government expense, but again, such a course of action is only in extreme cases, and again I have yet to reach that point. Finally, I need *to eat*, because not eating is unhealthy. But since on this point there is neither financial assistance nor a saying, the only thing left to do is to die. Such a thing, though, is possible only in extreme cases; and, thank God, I have also not reached such an extreme.

For three years I have asked, demanded, and implored that I be given that part of the estate which I inherited from my father. No one has responded to me; no one has wanted to respond to me. I was tormented, humiliated, and mocked. I endured everything patiently. I took on debts, went through all the money I had, and suffered shame, grief, illness, hunger, and cold. Now my patience has come to an end; the only thing that remains is for me to use all the means given to me by law and nature to have people hear me, and to do so with both ears.

In almost every letter, I proposed to you, as manager of all our family's affairs, a plan for allotment, deal, contract, concession, or whatever you would have liked, of the part of my estate for a certain sum of money. You have not answered any of my missives. The fact of the matter is that the sum I requested in exchange for my part of the estate was so insignificant that the interests of the family demanded a most detailed examination of my proposal. The entire affair was to be done in a legal way, so there was no reason for fear. . . . Since I have received no reply from you, I now want to use all means to receive an answer.

As I don't want anyone to dare to say that I am ruining our family, I am saying now—for the last time, of my own will, and in accordance with my personal wish to act in a way that will be best for all—*that I renounce my entire allotment of my estate (which brings an income of up to 1,000 rubles) for 1,000 silver rubles.* I also ask that half of this sum be paid at once, and the remainder at a fixed schedule of times. If this request is not heeded, I will have no choice but to use all my efforts to rid myself of my allotment of the estate, even if that means I seek the services of an outsider. Such a move, I believe, would be rather bad for everyone involved. At first glance, the law will not allow what I ask. But the law also recognizes *the obligation to pay off debts with income other than funds obtained from an estate.* So I think that my request is possible legally, but if it is not, we can come up with something else. The smallness of the sum I am asking will not stop me until I get what I want. What else am I to do? I need money. I don't want to end up in disaster. I need to straighten out my affairs. I am not a free man and nothing will stop me.

One more thing. On this account, I ask you, Pyotr Andreevich, to send me whatever you want, even for ten years in advance or the entire amount of the settlement. I also request that you send me as much money as possible. . . . In May I took an advance on my salary. (I needed to eat.) So now I do not have a copeck to my name. I also have no clothes and I still have to pay debts. There is nothing more I desire than to put an end to the above-noted affairs. They are ruining my life.

September 5, 1844.
Pyotr Karepin, from a letter to Fyodor Dostoevsky.

I am sending you fifty silver rubles without comment, and notwithstanding the arrogance and coarseness that fill your letters, I am enclosing two accounts for the last and the current years. . . . They show that the income from your parents' estate amounts to about 4,000 paper rubles (i.e., about 1,000 rubles in silver) and that such a sum depends on the harvest and the prices of produce.

Of this a certain amount has to be paid to the Trustees' Council Bank to repay a loan of 1,000 rubles, so that each of your brothers can receive only between 700 and 800 rubles a year, and only up to 1,000 rubles in a good year. . . . [So you will see] that you have been sent more money than the others. Andrei has received little and Nikolai almost nothing. . . . I am not even mentioning your sisters. . . . [Additional funds] will depend on the harvest and the price of grain. . . .

To sell your part of the inheritance is impossible because you have hardly reached maturity . . . [not to mention] the profound regret over a son who values so little the labors and concerns of his parents . . . that cost them their lives . . . [and] who now wishes to spend money God knows how. . . . It is also impossible now [to sell your inheritance] because the estate is in the trust of Council of Guardians, the Trusteeship of the Nobility, and the Civil Chamber; [because] personal debts are not paid for; and [because] your brothers and sisters are still young. Finally, although, via a lengthy process of applications to the Council of Guardians, the Trusteeship of the Nobility, and the Civil Chamber, it would be possible, to the benefit of your siblings, to give you your part of the estate, there remains this difficulty: There is not enough money to give you right away, and if you received funds in regular payments now, you would receive them in such a way as to disadvantage your brothers, who also must be taken into account. . . . So there are both moral and official obstacles to consider.

You hardly have had time to feel the weight of the epaulets on your shoulders before two words begin to recur in your letters: your inheritance and your debts. I have held my tongue, seeing this all as a youthful fantasy, and also knowing firmly that experience, time, and verification of social and personal relationships will explain things better to you. . . .

I also want you to note that the inheritance is extremely minuscule. To become angry or complain about such a situation, though, is hardly worthwhile. It does not depend on us; many people in the world are in the same situation. Given the size and amount of your expenses, whatever you would receive would hardly last a year. Then what? . . . In no way do I also doubt . . . that you would agree with me [when I say] to exceed the amount of what you would be paid would be to encroach on another's property. It is not our fault that we were not born millionaires; but are we to blame if we do not take advantage of what God and kindly authorities have placed before us? You are not the first, but one of many, very many people who begin their path in life according to the rules—pure, enlightened and joyous—of labor, diligence, and patience, not to mention the capabilities of a God-given mind and the good education that you have received in an excellent institution. [This being so], can you remain in the realm of spoiled sophisms, in the abstract laziness and languor of Shakespearean dreams? What do they have that is substantial and real, other than images that are inflated and inflammatory, exaggerated and bubble-like . . . [especially when] there has been opened and shown to you the path of honesty, respectful labor, and social benefit. . . .

Listen to what I am telling you, dear Brother! Abandon superfluous dreaminess and turn to genuine good, which you avoid, God knows why. Take up service with the conviction that, no matter how great your talents, you will learn through experience, that everything is necessary in the light of a certain submission to societal opinion, especially to the point of view of one's elders. They have lived more and longer than we have; they also have seen and experienced more than we.

For you there is not only no heartfelt blessing from me for you to leave the service, but I am also even convinced that you should seek other official postings in it—the farther, the better. There you will verify human life from all its diverse phases, since then as now, you are familiar with life only in a one-sided way, from the school desk, if not bookish dreams. . . . An officer in a military uniform must not remain with soft feather beds and elegant meals. A mail carriage, a felt coat, a piece of chopped beef prepared by a bat-boy, and money that the tsar pays for a salary can always be found for travel. How many pleasant sensations are there in the successful completion of one's duty; how much joy is there in the notice of one's superiors, in the love and respect of friends, and in the reward that comes about from the labor in your own direct and noble path. Here, Brother, is the genuine poetry of life and the heartfelt wish of all who are devoted to you.

September 7, 1844.
Fyodor Dostoevsky, from a letter to Pyotr Karepin.

In my last letter to my brother Mikhail, I wrote to ask that he vouch for me to our entire family that after I receive a *certain sum* now, I will in no way violate whatever agreement it will be your pleasure to offer me in the name of the other members of my clan. I also promise that in response to requests from me in the future, my brother Mikhail will have to answer me himself, or that finally, in the event that I do not keep my word, he himself will have to pay me from his own part of the estate. Since I am completely assured that my brother Mikhail will fulfill what I asked of him in my letter,[105] I find it necessary to trouble you once more with a missive.

Just as I used to believe a long time ago, my brother, that although it is indeed difficult to divide the estate legally, it is rather easy to do so among family, to observe it without violation in any way, and to finalize the deal with the law later. Of course, it is not for me to suggest such a solution to you; but my brother's idea may somewhat facilitate the course of affairs.

Guessing and always being certain that in response . . . [to the charge that] I am retiring because of my debts and the disorder in my affairs, as well as to cries and accusations . . . that I want to live off my brothers and sisters, I consider it necessary to receive my portion of the estate. . . . As a result . . . I am naming a sum of 1,000 silver rubles which, with the payment of my obligations, public and private, will be quite sufficient . . . and even quite lower than what I should be allotted. . . .

Of this sum of 1,000 silver rubles, I ask that 500 be paid to me immediately, and that the remaining amount be sent to me at the rate of 10 rubles a month. I ask for the 500 rubles at once to take care of the most essential things: 1,500 to repay debts, and 250 to cover present expenses which are actually three times more. Of course, Pyotr Andreevich, I must admit that the agreement and resolution of this matter are now in your hands. You can reject all these proposals on a thousand pretexts. But a few very candid lines on my part, in which I outline the essence of everything that has been said and written up to now on this matter on both our parts, such lines are essential at the present moment. Never having doubted that intelligence, nobility, and sympathy always accompany your every action, I presume that you will forgive the tenor of the following lines. Necessity dictates them, though.

Here they are.

Can it really be the case, Pyotr Andreevich, that after everything that has happened between us on a well-known point, i.e., the conduct of my inexperienced and misguided youth, that after everything that has been written and said from my side, and that after (I am not arguing here, but admit to my failings) several brazen escapades on my part regarding advice, rules, constraints, deprivations, and the like—you still do not wish to use that power (which has not been given to you) to act in accordance upon those motives which alone can guide the decisions of parents, and finally to assume a stance toward me that, at the first moment of irritation, I attributed to you as indecent. Can it really be that even after all of the above, you will oppose my intentions, *for the sake of my own good and out of compassion for the pathetic daydreams and fantasies of errant youth*? If it is not these reasons that will move your heart now and prevent you from helping me in this most horrible period of my life, then can it be your annoyance at several expressions that tore loose from my pen? From your part, it is natural that there can and should be such annoyance; and I regret any distress that I may have caused you. But there also can be *no prolonged rage or wish to harm*. Such emotions I have always assumed—and am firmly convinced—to be against the rules of noble conduct in general, and of yours in particular. But I still do not understand the reason that has forced you, considering your interest in our family affairs, to keep your distance from me and to condemn me to the most unpleasant filth and circumstances that have existed on this earth.

Here are my circumstances. In the middle of August, I resigned from my post because I had a mountain of debts, because an assignment somewhere would not pay enough to take care of them, and because an officer with such a black mark against him would begin his career in a less than auspicious way. Finally, life was no paradise for me. A rich man is forgiven debts that exceed his earnings. Indeed, sometimes such forgiveness is everywhere viewed with respect. But a poor man gets a kick in the pants. It would have been really great to continue in the service, and at the same time to disseminate complaints [about me] to all possible commands. Finally, my retirement was the result of hastiness. I was tormented by debts that I have not been able to pay off for three years. I am similarly distressed by the lack of hope for paying them off in the future. So I retired with the sole goal of paying off what I owe in a well-known way, i.e., by dividing the estate (which, as you remarked justly, is quite and maddeningly minuscule, but suitable for certain purposes). Regarding respect for parental memory, it is precisely because of such of a thing that I want to use parental property for what my father himself would have wanted me to do. That is, for his son's peace of mind, for the means for a new road in life, and for delivery from the label of scoundrel....

Petitions [for retirement] arising from domestic circumstances will be submitted for imperial decision beginning October 1st. The whole process takes about ten days, a little less than two weeks. The middle of the month is close upon us. My request for retirement will be granted, my creditors will attack me mercilessly, so much so that I will not even have any clothes to wear, and will be subjected to the most unpleasant affairs.

However I foresaw my predicament in part, and if my assumptions and premonitions turn out to be justified, I was ready for come what may. Still, you will have to agree that I will not go off to prison singing songs out of stupid bravado. Such a thing even strikes me as funny.

So that is why, Pyotr Andreevich, I am writing to you for the last time. For the last time, I am depicting my extreme need; for the last time, I am asking you to help me as soon as possible, on the proposed conditions—not all at once, but enough to stop a hungry mouth, and to dress myself.

Finally, and for the last time, I am telling you that, completely ignorant of your decision, I would rather rot in prison then enter into service before my affairs have finally been put in order.

September 19, 1844.
Fyodor Dostoevsky, from a letter to Pyotr Karepin.

> I have received your letter of September 5th, filled with advice and ideas, and I hasten to reply.
> In any other circumstances, I would naturally begin my letter with gratitude for your advice and familial, friendly concern. But the tone of your letter is such that only a blockhead could take it as genuine; it does not suit me at all. . . . It does, though, do me the service of relieving me of gratitude to you.
> Let us assume that, as a guardian, you have the right to reproach me for financial greed and for harming my younger brothers, on whose account I have, up to now, spent large sums of money. On that point, after everything I have written to you for the past two years, I consider it superfluous even to answer you. Clearly you could see from my letters that it is not the amount of money (up to a certain point, of course) in which my salvation and the righting of my affairs depend, but on the timing of when I receive it. I have explained the situation to you a thousand times; I am not the guilty party here.
> But how can you possibly say the same things to me now, and with your words, rouse all my family against me? You should have understood my requests. Can it really be the case that the request for 500 silver rubles at once and for the other 500 to be paid, say, over the course of three years—such a wish will be useful not for me alone? As for the difficulties with the Council of Guardians, the Trusteeship of the Nobility, the Civil Chamber and all the other entities you hurl at me and seek to stun me with, I imagine that such problems do not even exist. Do not people sell estates and transfer the debt on them? Will anyone lose out or a lose a great deal if, as before, the estate remains the property of our family? Further, it is a very private affair that someone is paid 500 silver rubles for years on the strength of so many years of income—even ten.
> At the very least, I am retiring from the service. As I remind you, I submitted my petition in the middle of August. It goes without saying that the very same reasons I am retiring prevent me from entering the service again. I must first pay off my debts. One way or another, they have to be paid. You rise up against my egoism and my decision . . . as the frivolousness of youth.
> But none of this is your concern. I see it as strange that you take upon yourself a labor that no one has asked or given you the right to do.
> Be assured that I revere the memory of my parents in no less a way than you do yours. . . . Moreover, the fact that what I ask would bring parental peasants to ruin does not mean that I would dishonor either my father or mother. Besides, finally, everything remains in the family.

You say that you did not answer many of my letters because, in your opinion, they were superficial and the stuff of youthful fantasy.... But if you consider it vulgar and despicable to discuss anything with me, thinking, of course, that "he is still a little boy who has only recently donned his epaulets," you should have not expressed your superiority over me in such a naive way. You also should not have humiliated me so arrogantly with advice and admonitions as a father would his son, and with Shakespearean soap bubbles, to boot.... What did Shakespeare ever do to get such a ribbing from you? Poor Shakespeare!

If you find it suitable to become angry over my words, allow me to remind you of one of your phrases: "To exceed the size of the possible repayment is to encroach on the property of another." But since you yourself know well that a debt of 1,500 rubles is not the full amount of my repayment, how could you write such a thing?... I am giving you only the facts, a sum, and an amount. You are well aware of the story behind my debts. I was not the one who has incurred them. I am also not to blame that the commerce protected by Bentham[106] prospers here in St. Petersburg as nowhere else on earth. In any case, I will and must place your naiveté (which out of respect for your years I cannot take for intentional rudeness and the desire to wound me) in the same category as Shakespearean soap bubbles.

If such comments anger you, please recall the letter you sent to His Excellency Ivan Grigorievich Krivopishin. Have mercy, Pyotr Andreevich, how could you do such a thing? You see, I cannot accept such a deed because I refuse to accept it in the sense that you are writing a letter about me without consulting me, your goal being to harm my intentions and to stop my Shakespearean fantasy.

Listen to me. Who can stop the lawful will of a person who has the very same rights as you?... But what is the point of talking to you about such a thing! So as not to be an Ivan Ivanovich Perepenko,[107] I am even ready, for the above-mentioned reasons, to take that as naiveté.

The fourth page of your letter seems to me to have avoided the overall tone of your missive, and for that I am sincerely grateful. You are absolutely right: genuine good is a great thing. Long ago a certain wise person, namely Goethe, said that a *little* thing, done well, reveals fully the mind of a person and is absolutely worth a great deal.[108] I cite such a line so that you can see how I understand you. That was precisely what you wanted to say when you first dug into me with the hook of your awkward ridicule. As the study of life and people is both my primary goal and pastime, I now have come to be convinced completely in the existence of Famusov, Chichikov, and Falstaff.[109]

In any case, the deed is done. I have resigned from the military, and I do not have a penny to my name for debts and other things I need. If you do not send me something right way, my last letter to you will quite justify itself.

P.S. You know the reason for my retirement—the payment of my debts.[110] Although the two ideas do not tie up well, that is the way it is. By October 1, the retirement will be finalized. So bear that in mind.

You found it pleasing to write several harsh lines about the *minuscule amount of my inheritance*. But poverty is not a vice. It is what God has sent me. Let us assume that the Lord has blessed you, but not me. But even if only in a small way, I still want to help myself as much as possible, without harming others—also as much as possible. Can my requests to you really be so huge? And, as for the word *inheritance*, why can we not call a thing by its proper name?

Fall 1844–August 1845.
Konstantin Trutovsky, from his memoirs.

When I was eighteen years old,[111] I fell in love.... With youthful openness, I shared with Fyodor Mikhailovich all the ups and downs of the affair. With enthusiasm, I described to him my love's beauty, her movements, her words.... I even showed him my verse, written to the *object* of my love. Her name was Anna Lvovna, but at home she was called "Netochka." Dostoevsky liked that name so much that he titled his new story *Netochka Nezvanova*.

Fall 1844.
Dmitri Grigorovich, from his memoirs.

About this time I happened to meet Dostoevsky on the street.... With a joyous shout, I rushed to embrace him. He was also happy to see me, but I noticed a certain reserve about him. For all his warmth, even his passionate heart, Dostoevsky had not changed since our days together at school, in our close, almost childlike circle. He still showed an intensity and a secretiveness that was quite beyond his years. He also continued to dislike loud and expressive outpourings of emotion. My joy at our unexpected meeting was so very great and sincere that it occurred to me that I may have offended his external coldness.

With unrestrained enthusiasm I told Dostoevsky about my literary friendships and attempts at literature. I also begged him to come to my place without delay so that he could read my latest work. Dostoevsky agreed willingly. Dostoevsky apparently liked my work,[112] but he did not go wild over it. He especially disliked one phrase in the piece. Toward the end of the work, I had written that after the organ-grinder stops playing, a petty official drops a five-copeck piece from the window onto the poor man's feet. "No, no," Dostoevsky said in an irritated way, "that's not right at all! Such an image is too dry.... Rather, you should say, 'The five-copeck fell on the sidewalk, *ringing and jumping about*. . . . Such a phrase is more lively and artistic.'" . . . These two words were enough for me to understand the difference between a dry phrase and a lively, artistic, and literary image.

September 25, 1844.
Mikhail Dostoevsky, from a letter to Pyotr Karepin.

It was with extreme surprise that from your letter I learned that brother Fyodor has retired [from service]. Perhaps, it will seem strange to you that I do not know anything about this. But that's the way it is. I will not begin to hide that I knew about his wish to leave the service, but I did not know that he intended to do so in the current year. In my previous letters to him, still in the spring, I asked him to continue for another year or so, until he felt himself to be stronger in his enterprise. And thus you can imagine my surprise when . . . right after your letter, I received from him a missive in which he informed me that it has been already four months now that he has tendered his resignation;[113] but he does not state any reasons why. He has written to you that he was being dispatched elsewhere. [But] he could not abandon Petersburg and break all the ties that in the future promise a wide road of riches and glory. He wishes to give himself entirely over to literature. Until now, he has been working only for money, i.e., translating things for journals (*The Fatherland Notes, Repertoire*), for which he was paid well. . . .

I predict a great deal for him in the future. He is an individual with profound erudition, as well as with a powerful and independent talent. Having myself read almost all the classics of Europe, I can venture an opinion about what is good and bad. With rapture, I have read his dramas. This winter they will appear on the Petersburg stage.[114] A developing talent [like Brother's] must study; he thus cannot leave Petersburg, nor must he do so. Before him now lies a difficult path—to build a road for himself, to win himself a name. To his talent he has sacrificed everything, but this talent—this I know, of this I am certain—will not deceive him. God grant that he not fail, but also that he endure his first steps. . . . Who can know what lies ahead [for him]?

No matter what, my brother *wants* to sell his part [of the inheritance] to us. You yourself will agree that he is ceding it to us for a song. Is it even conscionable to buy it from him at such a price? He is asking simultaneously for 500 silver rubles to be followed by 10 silver rubles a month. But further, you will send him these 500 rubles this year, as it seems that he is selling his capital for his yearly income. You claim that to conclude this matter legally is extremely difficult, but can it not be done in a domestic, family type of way? [My brother] is sending you a note saying that he is refusing his part [of the inheritance]. You will send him the money, and then within one or two or even, to tell the truth, five years, we will bring the entire affair to a successful end. Brother is so honest that you can give him the sum without a receipt. If you wish, I can be a second guardian for him. I will vouch for him.

Think about it, Pyotr Andreevich. It would be much more pleasant for you, once and for all, to be rid of the fuss and bother. Perhaps you can somehow borrow the 500 rubles [that brother wants]. We could begin to settle accounts from earnings of his part [of the inheritance]. Brother needs the money right away. He still has several debts that demand immediate payment. He will despair if you refuse.

September 30, 1844.
Fyodor Dostoevsky, from a letter to Mikhail Dostoevsky.

I have received *Don Carlos* and, since I am short of time, I hasten to reply to you as quickly as possible. . . . The translation is quite good and there are places where it is amazingly well done. Several lines are bad, though, but that is because you translated them in haste. But perhaps, such a shortcoming involves five or six lines in all. I took the liberty to correct a few things and also here and there to make the lines more sonorous and so forth. More annoying, though, are places where you put in foreign words, for example, *complot*. That we cannot have. Also, although I do not have the original in front of me, you use the word "sir." As far as I know, such a word did not exist in Spain, but was used only in Western Europe in countries of Norman origin. But such things are all absolute trifles. The translation is remarkably good and better than what I expected.

I will take it to the idiots at *Repertoire*. Let them drop their mouths in amazement. If, however, and as I fear, they have Obodovsky's translation, I will take it to *Notes of the Fatherland*. Also rest assured that I will not sell it for pennies; but that as soon as do, I will send you the money. As for the edition of Schiller, I agree with you, of course. I myself even wanted to suggest to you that we divide it into three parts. Let's deal first with *The Robbers, Fiesco, Don Carlos, Treachery*,[115] and *Letters about Carlos* and "Naiveté."[116] That will be very good. Regarding publishers for such things, we will have to see. But the reality of the situation is that we would do better to do it ourselves; otherwise, there will be no profit. So you just do the translating and leave the financial matters to me. Do not worry. We will find money for this somehow, one way or the other, just the same. But here is the thing, Brother. We need to finish this business in a month, i.e, we need to decide on a date because an *announcement* cannot be issued later, and without an *announcement*, we are finished. That is why I will order a few words to be printed about our work in *Repertoire*.

The translation will cause a sensation. Even with minimal success, the profit we will receive will be amazing.[117]

Well, Brother, I myself know that I am in hellish circumstances. I will explain:

I retired [from the service] because I retired. I swear to you that I could not serve any longer. When the best time is taken from you for nothing, you hate life. The fact of the matter is that in the final analysis, I never wanted to serve for a long time. After all, why waste one's good years? Finally, there is the main thing: they wanted to send me off on assignment somewhere. So tell me, please, what would I have done without Petersburg? What would I be fit for? Do you understand well what I am saying?

Don't worry about my life. I will soon find a piece of bread. I will work like the devil. Now I am free. But what I am going to do now, at the present moment—that is the question. Just imagine, brother, I owe 800 rubles, of which 525 paper rubles are for my landlord. I wrote home that my debts were 1,500 rubles, knowing full well their habit of sending only a third of what I ask.

No one knows that I am retiring. Now, if I do retire, what will I do next? I do not have even a copeck for clothes. My retirement becomes official by October 14th. If those pigs in Moscow delay, I am done for. Very seriously, I will be dragged off to prison (that is clear). A truly comical situation if I say so myself. You talk about a family division if I receive my part of the inheritance.[118] But don't you know what I am asking? That I be separated from any participation in the estate now, and when circumstances permit, for complete relinquishment and for the concession of my estate to my brothers and sisters from this moment on—I am asking for 500 silver rubles at once and another 500 to be paid at the rate of ten silver rubles a month. That is all. You have to agree that the amount is not much and that I am not hurting anyone. But they refuse even to hear of such a thing. You also have to agree that it's not for me to propose such a thing to them now. They don't *trust* me; they think that somehow I'll trick them. Please vouch for me, my friend. Tell them exactly the following: *you are ready to vouch . . . that I will not ask for anything more* than what I am doing now. If they don't have that much money, then in my situation, 700 or even 600 rubles can be cause for joy. I can still turn things around. . . .

You say that my salvation is a drama. But after all, a production does take time. The same goes for payment. My retirement is right around the corner. (By the way, dear Brother, if I had not already submitted my resignation, I would do so now. I do not regret what I have done.)[119]

I do have this hope, though. I am finishing a *novel* the size of *Eugénie Grandet*.[120] It is a rather original thing. I am already recopying it and by the 14th I will surely receive a reply to it. I will give it to *The Fatherland Notes*. I am satisfied with what I have done. Perhaps I will get 400 or so rubles for it. Such is my hope. I would go on at length about my novel, but now I am short of time. (I will definitely get a drama under way. That is what I am going to live on.)

That pig Karepin is as dumb as an ox.[121] These Muscovites are so inexpressibly vain and stupid, not to mention casuists. In his last letter to me, Karepin, for no reason at all, advised me not to get carried away by Shakespeare. He said that Shakespeare and a soap bubble are the same thing. I wanted you to understand this comical trait of his, the irritation with Shakespeare. But what does Shakespeare have to do with anything? Did I write him a letter in response! In a word, it was a model of polemics. How I gave him a going-over! My letters are a chef d'oeuvre of belles-lettres.

Brother, for God's sake, please write home as soon as possible. I'm not doing well at all. After all, the 14th is the absolute deadline for our work. It has already been one and a half months since I submitted my resignation. For God's sake, ask the people in Moscow to send me some money. The main thing is that I do not have any clothes. Khlestakov is willing to go to prison, but only *in a noble way*.[122] But if I don't have even *pants* to wear, how can I even do that?

Karepin drinks, has rank, and believes in God. I thought that all up myself. . . .

I'm quite delighted with my novel. I cannot get over the fact that I have written such a thing. I will surely get some money from it, and then—Excuse the fact that my letter is devoid of logic.

September–October 1844.
Fyodor Dostoevsky, from a letter to Andrei Dostoevsky.

It's a shame that you left here, Brother! I myself did not have a single copeck. That is why I was in low spirits. I still have not been able to make ends meet. I'm sending you now such a tiny pittance that I am ashamed; but honest to God, there's no way I can send you more.

Circa October 1844.
Andrei Dostoevsky, from his memoirs.

Pyotr Andreevich [Karepin] held many positions and did well everywhere. . . . He was not only simply kind, but biblically so. . . . He hailed from the people, and achieved everything by dint of his industry and intelligence. . . . When he became my sister's fiancé, he was already a nobleman.

Circa October 1844.
Anna Dostoevskaya, from the notes for a biography of Dostoevsky.

[Karepin] was a truly worthless individual.

Circa October 1844.
From the account of the guardianship of the Dostoevsky children for 1844.

Dispersal of Funds for the Dostoevsky Children

To Mikhail Mikhailovich: 700 silver rubles
To Fyodor Mikhailovich: 2,412 silver rubles, 50 copecks
To Andrei Mikhailovich: 150 silver rubles
To Nikolai Mikhailovich: 65 silver rubles 25 copecks
(for clothes and schoolbooks)

October 3, 1844.
Mikhail Dostoevsky, from a letter to Pyotr Karepin.

I have just received from Petersburg a letter from my brother Fyodor that has distressed me to no end. With the missive still in my hand, I hasten to share with you, my Brother, this distress—a fate which is not at all pleasant, but necessary since it concerns our common relative, our dear brother, with whom I, from birth, have been bound with an unbreakable friendship. As you already know, he has entered retirement. Such a thing does not trouble me very much. A person with his gifts will not remain without bread. He has chosen for himself a new and better road, and since one cannot be two things at the same time, he has given himself over fully to that toward which he feels more of an inclination.

You, dear Brother, don't know my brother Fyodor personally. So you probably judge his deed as the rash whim of a child who suddenly, without consulting reason, decides on a course of action that can affect his entire life. I know my brother well; I know him as an individual with rules and experience. For God's sake, don't laugh, it is so. In his deed I'm more than ready to see the unusual force of his character and soul, a great self-sacrifice to his new calling. Has he not seen, surely, what unpleasantries, what deprivations he is surrendering himself to as spoils, at the very least for the first time in his life. Believe me, dear Brother, when I say he has foreseen all these things, that he has prepared himself for everything, and that nonetheless he has taken this step, because he has followed his conviction. Previously, he feared all our demonstrations and declarations, so that even me, his best friend—he told me about all this only after the matter was done and there was no possibility of making amends. But still I repeat to you—this does not bother me. Because even if he will take up only translations for journals, he will have an income of up to 8,000 rubles yearly. Right now he's being paid 25 rubles a page, and half a page he can do in a day very easily. Furthermore, he has finished a splendid novel and two dramas, which, I assure you, are remarkable. All of this will bring him some additional funds, but what is more important, it will make him famous. Believe me, dear Brother Pyotr Andreevich, he will be richer than all of us. We will be proud of him yet.

But one thing does bother me: his current situation. He must have 1,500 paper rubles. It is clear that if, moving into retirement, he does not pay his debts, he'll be put in prison for quite some time. So as to avoid this unpleasant trip, he wants to strike up a deal, to cede his part of the inheritance to us. The conditions are already known to you. Nothing could be more advantageous for us. Five hundred silver rubles is not so great a sum that one can get hold of any time. It can be obtained and always paid out from his part of the inheritance. In such a way his debts can be paid off in large amount in a year and everyone will be satisfied. Any judicial process in the handling of this affair, as you say, is in no way possible. But in a family manner, it always can be done. There's only this complication: whether, having received the money, Brother will nonetheless still have claims to his share [of the inheritance]. *But in this, as you wish, in a written and formal way, I guarantee that this will never be the case.*

My dear Pyotr Andreevich! I ask that you send to Brother almost as much as he asks. His demands are the most moderate. After all, neither you nor anyone else has the right to prohibit such a thing. He has reached maturity; he himself knows what he is doing. If he has taken it into his head to give us his share of the inheritance, to refuse income from it, who in the world has the right to keep him from doing so?

Seeing the inevitable calamity that threatens him, I've taken it upon myself to talk to you once again, dear Brother. There's no other way to help him. He asks from you only what is his. You've no right to refuse him in this request. Furthermore, how will he, having lost patience, give to his creditors his share if only to settle accounts with them? But it is possible to do so. His retirement will begin by October 15. Most likely, his creditors will not want to lose anything and they themselves will begin to raise a fuss about things. By this time, he is certain to be in need of money. How grateful I would be, dear Brother, if you somehow could resolve this matter. I find it terrible to think that he will be sitting in prison.

Brother Fyodor is willing to give an Act, a certificate, or a signature, everything that is proper so that, in a solemn way, he can refuse his share of the inheritance. From my side, I am also ready to do the same thing, whatever I can do to serve as a guarantee to you.

October 19, 1844.
Nicholas I, by executive decree.

> His Imperial Highness . . . deigns to issue the following decree.
> DISCHARGED FROM SERVICE:
> In the Department of Engineering. . . . For domestic reasons. . . .
> Field Engineer–Second Lieutenant, Dostoevsky.

After October 19, 1844.
Dmitri Grigorovich, from his memoirs.

> I began to see Dostoevsky more and more often . . . so much so, in fact, that we decided to live together. At that time, my mother was sending me fifty rubles monthly; and from his relatives in Moscow, Dostoevsky was receiving roughly the same. At that time, such sums were more than enough for two young men . . . but it was usually gone in the first two weeks. The remaining time we lived on rolls and barley coffee. . . . Our apartment consisted of a kitchen and two rooms with three windows; the back room was taken by Dostoevsky, the one closest to the door by me. As we did not have a servant, we ourselves had to set the samovar and buy food. . . .
>
> When I began to live with Dostoevsky, he had just finished his translation of Balzac's novel *Eugénie Grandet*.[123] Balzac was one of our favorite writers. I say "our" because both of us immersed ourselves in his works and considered him to be incomparably greater than all other French writers. . . . I do not recall how or through whom Dostoevsky's translation of Balzac's work appeared in *The Library for Reading*;[124] but I do remember that when we got hold of the issue, he was quite angry that his translation of *Eugénie Grandet* had been cut by almost a third. We later found that such an abridgement was customary with Senkovsky, the editor of the journal. He also did the same thing with original works, but their authors did not object so as to have the happiness of seeing their name and work in print.
>
> I should also mention that when I told Belinsky that it was my roommate who had translated *Eugénie Grandet*, the great critic showered our idol Balzac with the most coarse abuse. He not only called Balzac a petty bourgeois writer, but he also said that if he had a copy of *Eugénie Grandet* in his hands, he could prove to me the vulgarity of the work on each and every page. I was so taken aback that I forgot everything that I was ready to say when I entered Belinsky's home. I lost my head completely and left there as if scalded, angry at myself more than Belinsky. I did not know what he thought of me. (Most likely, he saw me as a child, unable to utter two words to defend my opinion.)
>
> Meanwhile Dostoevsky was spending entire days and also parts of nights behind his desk. He did not say a word about what he was writing; and to my questions he responded in an unwilling and laconic way.[125] Knowing his sense of reserve, I stopped asking. I could see the many pages covered with his distinctive style of writing. The letters poured forth from his pen as if beads, finely hewn. Such a handwriting I saw later only with one other writer: Dumas-père. As soon as Dostoevsky stopped writing, a book quickly appeared in his hands. . . .
>
> Intensive work and prolonged sitting in one place, though, had an extremely harmful effect on Dostoevsky's health. They exacerbated an illness that had appeared several times in his youth and during his time at school. Several times in our walks

together, Dostoevsky had nervous attacks. One time . . . we encountered a funeral procession. Dostoevsky turned away suddenly. He wanted to return home, but before we had taken even a few steps, he suffered an attack so strong that I, with the help of several passers-by, had to carry him to the nearest park bench. Only by force could we bring him back to consciousness. I should also note that after such attacks, Dostoevsky usually suffered a depressed state of mind, a condition that lasted two or three days.

Late October 1844.
Fyodor Dostoevsky, from a letter to Pyotr Karepin.

In my last letter to you, I declared that I was writing for the last time until my circumstances should turn out for the better. I did such a thing because I had nothing else to write. After all, having presented you with all the horror of my situation, I had exhausted all means of persuading you. Now the critical deadline has passed, and I am alone, without help and at the mercy of all the calamities, all the trials and tribulations of my ghastly predicament, i.e., destitution, nakedness, humiliation, and shame. . . . What else is there left for me to do but to begin again? Where to appeal?—judge for yourself.

You should know that at the moment you are reading this letter, I will already have retired (check the newspapers). I have neither clothing nor money nor anything with which to pay my creditors. I also will not have an apartment, because I doubt that the landlord will keep me in my old one.

I started to write so as to shed light on several things that I expressed incorrectly in my last letter to you. I will try to speak as clearly as possible.

From your letters, Pyotr Andreevich, I see that a division of the estate is, as you say, impossible, first because the estate is burdened with public and private debts, and second because over the course of three years, I took more money than was my proper share, the result being that when all the accounting is done, I will have to make up for such a sum by contributing additional money for the others at a loss to myself.

But now my brother Mikhail and I propose a *family division*, which will exist inviolably until the final one. Of course, if there's even the slightest objection on anyone's part in this matter, then such a proposal cannot be realized. The matter we propose is based on the fullest mutual trust of all involved, and if there is any misunderstanding, there can no agreement at all. I presume that you in your capacity as guardian may doubt my fairness and fidelity here . . . so that is why I propose the following. But before getting down to business, you know the amount of the sum I am proposing to you—1,000 silver rubles, of which 500 is to be paid at once and the remaining money to be disbursed over the longest possible period. . . . Why am

I asking such a moderate sum, why do I want, in the words of certain people, *to rid myself* of my father's (minuscule) property—in your own current position. Pyotr Andreevich, these questions are superfluous. The fact of the matter is that in such a request I see my deliverance from troubles and the possibility for arranging things for the better. That, for me, is worth something. Finally, 1,000 silver rubles according to the proposed schedule of payment is that sum that may give rise to assumptions about youthful flightiness and wastefulness. But in the first place, I'm not dealing with profiteers; and, in the second, I'm far from thinking of being a benefactor to anyone. Simply put, in my circumstances, I find it unjust to ask for more; and to eliminate suspicions, I am resolved to do the following.

To give an acknowledgment of debt to be addressed to one of the members of the family, if it cannot be addressed to all of them, or even to you, Pyotr Andreevich. This acknowledgment of debt will be for such a sum as to cover completely both the money to be paid out to me in a lump amount, and my further requests for income until the final division. The acknowledgment of debt will be dated, for example, January 1, 1845. I'll not pay it, of course. You then will have the full right to act according to the laws, and my income will be applied formally in favor of the family right up until the final division of the estate itself. At the time of the division I'll notify you formally that I have received the money in full. The acknowledgment of debt will be torn up, and everything will proceed as it should. If in the last instance there should be any difficulty whatsoever, I could give a promissory note of such a sum so that all my claims at the (real) division of the estate would come to an end.

Such a thing seems to me quite simple and possible, Pyotr Andreevich. I cannot express to you what a beneficial deed that will be for my fate. I'll provide for myself completely now. I'll also extract myself from the vile situation with which I have been struggling for almost two years. I also will be able to continue service. Truly, though, it is in vain that I'm writing all of this to you. I understand that this is not the place to enumerate my hopes. I could also draw for you a picture of my loathsome situation. Such a thing, though, would be comprehensible to you even with the one-hundredth part of my life that I have discussed with you. Since I am without means, with debts, without clothing, and sick to boot (which, however, is beside the point), I'm naturally coming to the decision, one way or another, to straighten out my circumstances. You are a *practical* person, Pyotr Andreevich. With us, too, you function as a *practical* person and in no other way but that. And since you are a *practical* person, you will not have the time to pay attention to my affairs, even though they are trifling, or perhaps because they are so inconsequential. But if these trifling affairs make up one's entire salvation, his well-being, all his hope, you need to excuse this persistence and importunity. That is why I ask you most humbly to help me with all I have written to you. My situation is now decided and definite. All the horrors that are possible in life have fallen onto my head, so that I have decided: what will be, will be!

Since according to your calculations I see that there is no money, I ask you to borrow some if only because the matter is beneficial for the entire family and because you yourself are sufficiently secure financially.

Finally, Pyotr Andreevich, if you again do not respond to my request for even the shortest period of time, I will perish.[126] I thus am forced to ask you to supply a certificate (drawn up in formal style), testifying to the fact that you really are our guardian, and how much income (however minuscule) the estate gives me under all circumstances, even the most remote. I am asking you for such a thing to show my creditors so that, if worse comes to worst, I can repay them. I also ask that you send this certificate to me as soon as possible. I ask your forgiveness, Pyotr Andreevich first, because my requests tear you away from your other activities and second, because I am requesting a certificate from you immediately. I ask you again, in a most earnest way, Pyotr Andreevich, to examine my proposal and to agree with what I am asking. The matter can be concluded just as I have written to you. There should be no difficulties. I myself would have sent to you the acknowledgment of debt, but I have no money. You, however, can entrust the matter to someone in Petersburg. Finally, if things get really bad (thus I ask you to answer me as soon as possible), I will perhaps venture out and earn even more creditors and concede to them everything as a result of acknowledgments of debts and of certain obligations at a rate of ten times more than what I have used. In Petersburg such a thing can be done. How this will all turn out, you yourself be the judge: there will be troubles for everyone. Therefore, for God's sake, I ask you once more, Pyotr Andreevich, to please answer me as soon as you can. Besides all my other calamities, I do not have a copeck to my name for my daily needs. God forbid that you should undergo what I am enduring now. Finally, do not forget about sending the certificate. You have to agree that in my situation, such a thing is absolutely essential.

P.S. I assume that regarding the sending of the certificate, I'll not encounter any difficulties from your side. Such a thing seems clear to me.

November 1844.
Fyodor Dostoevsky, from a letter to Mikhail Dostoevsky.

I should point out to you, dear Brother, that my last letter to the people in Moscow was a little too bilious, even rude. But I had been thrown into every possible calamity. I was suffering in the full sense of the word. I had not the slightest hope. Indeed, it is not surprising that physical and moral torments forced me to write the bilious, harsh truth. . . .

I have gotten into fights with everyone. Most likely, Uncle [Kumanin] considers me an ungrateful brat, and our sister [Varvara] and brother-in-law [Karepin], a monster. Such a thing torments me greatly. But with time I hope to be reconciled with everyone. Of all our relatives, you alone are left to me. All the others, even the children, have been turned against me. They probably have been told that I am a spendthrift, a womanizer, and a lazybones. They probably have been warned: "Don't be like him," "Don't follow his example," and so on. Such a thought I find to be horribly depressing.

God, though, sees me as such a gentle lamb that neither from the side nor from the front do I resemble a brat or a monster of ingratitude.... Now, from the point of view of all things *common*, I have been cut off from all of you. Left are the fetters that are stronger than anything else here on earth, moveable or unmoveable. Whose business is it, anyway, as to what I do with my life? The imprudent risk of changing my situation, my entire life, for a shaky hope, I even consider to be a noble thing. Perhaps I am mistaken. But what if I am not?

So God be with them all! Let them say what they want. Let them wait. I will follow the hard road!

November 28, 1844.
Mikhail Dostoevsky, from a letter to Pyotr Karepin.

You cannot imagine, dear brother Pyotr Andreevich, how I have rejoiced, having learned from your letter[127] that you have finally come to a resolution with brother Fyodor. At the very least, with this sum, he'll satisfy his momentary needs and will live for an entire year—and this means a great deal in his situation. This year, the fate of my brother can change in a significant way. No matter what you say, dear Brother, I have a blind belief in his unusual giftedness; and I'm certain that on this chosen path, sooner or later, he'll make a glorious name for himself. True, I agree with you completely that all might turn differently, not suddenly, but in a more careful and sensible way. But so to speak, this depends on the point of view from which you come to look at an object. From one side, brother can seem so to be a flighty, irrational person . . . this I'll not argue with you. But on the other side, he's an individual with a powerful soul and an energetic character.

Incidentally, dear brother, and in the case that my brother is mistaken [about his talent], he will be accepted again at any time into the corps of engineers. Truly, even if he submitted a request tomorrow, he would not be refused. That is the way it is in the state service—it is of no consequence. There one must look for *positions*, which take a while to find. So let's hope that God will not abandon him and that everything will work out for the best. Brother will remain a lieutenant.

You are angry at him, dear Brother, for his rude letter to you, but believe me when I say that he himself is sorry for what he has done.... He is not an evil person. Rather, he is very, very kind. What a pity that you do not know him personally. You would change your opinion of him. His novel will come out in January. It is a splendid original thing!

From your letter, dear Pyotr Andreevich, I *learned* that the money you sent to Brother was from your own personal funds. For that accept my most profound gratitude.

1845

1845 and after.
Fyodor Dostoevsky, from *A Writer's Diary*.

By the middle of the forties, the fame of George Sand and the faith in the force of her genius stood so high that we, her contemporaries, all expected something incomparably greater from her in the future, some unprecedented new word, even something final and decisive. These hopes were not realized; it turned out that . . . by the end of the forties, she had said everything she was destined to say. . . .

George Sand was not a thinker, but she was one of the most clear-sighted "seers into the future" (if I may be permitted such an ornate term), a happier time awaiting humanity, the realization of ideals which, strongly and splendidly, she believed in throughout her life and which she herself could raise in her very soul. The preservation of this faith to the end is usually the lot of all elevated souls, of all genuine lovers of humanity. George Sand died a deist,[128] believing firmly in God and in her own immortal life, but about her one must say more: Although (as a Catholic) she did not profess Christ in a formal way, she was, perhaps, the most Christian of all her contemporaries, the French writers. Of course, as a Frenchwoman George Sand, like her compatriots, was unable to confess consciously the principal idea of Orthodoxy, that "in all Creation there is no name other than His by which one can be saved."[129] Still, despite this apparent and formal contradiction, George Sand was . . . perhaps one of the most thoroughgoing confessors of Christ, even while unaware of being so. She based her socialism, her convictions, her hopes, and her ideals on the human moral sense, on the spiritual thirst of humanity, on its striving for perfection and purity, not on the "necessity" of the ant heap.[130] Unconditionally (even to the point of her immortality), she believed in the human condition, elevating and expanding the understanding of it throughout her life, in each of her works. She thus merged her thoughts and feelings with one of the most basic ideas of Christianity, that is, the acknowledgment of the human personality and its freedom (and accordingly, its responsibility). Hence her acknowledgment of duty and rigorous moral scrutiny, as well as her complete awareness of human responsibility. Perhaps, there was not a thinker or a writer in France in her time who understood so clearly that "man does not live by bread alone."[131] As far as the pride in her scrutiny and protest are concerned . . . this pride never excluded mercy, the forgiveness of an offense, and even limitless patience rooted in compassion for the offender.

In her works, George Sand was often attracted to the beauty of these truths and often incarnated types of the most sincere forgiveness and love. About her people write that she died as an admirable mother who worked to the end of her life, a friend to the local peasants, loved deeply by her friends. It seems that she was inclined somewhat to value her aristocratic origins (on her mother's side, she descended from the royal house of Saxony),[132] but, of course, one can state firmly that if she valued her position in society, she rooted it only in the perfection of the human soul. She could not help but love the great, she could not reconcile herself with the base and compromise her beliefs; and here, perhaps, she may have shown an excess of pride. It is true that she also did not like to portray humbled people in her novels, to depict the just but pliant, the eccentric and the downtrodden, such as we meet in almost every novel of the great Christian Dickens. On the contrary, she elevated her heroines proudly and placed them as high as queens. This she loved to do, and this trait . . . is rather characteristic of her fiction.

Circa January 1845.
Fyodor Dostoevsky, from 1861 *Petersburg Visions in Poetry and Prose.*

I recall one wintry evening I was hurrying home from the Vyborg side [of the city].[133] At the time I was still very young. Reaching the Neva, I stopped . . . and cast a piercing glance along the river into the smoky, frosty-murky distance, which suddenly had turned crimson with the last purple ray of the setting sun burning out on the misty horizon. Night was falling over the city, and the entire immense expanse of the Neva, swollen with frozen snow, was strewn with myriads of endless sparks of spindly hoarfrost under the last ray of the sun. It had become twenty degrees frost. . . . Frozen steam poured forth from tired horses and rushing passers-by. The tense air trembled at the slightest sound; columns of smoke rose like giants from all the roofs on both embankments and rushed upward through the cold sky, weaving and unweaving along the way, so that new buildings seemed to come from old ones and that a new city was forming in the air. . . .

It seemed that this entire world, with all its inhabitants, strong and weak, with all their dwellings, the shelters of the poor, or the glittering mansions of the rich, in this twilight hour, resembled a fantastic, magical vision, a dream that in turn would vanish instantly and rise up like steam into the dark-blue sky.

Suddenly, some strange thought welled up inside me. I shuddered, and at that moment my heart seemed to be flooded with a warm rush of blood that suddenly had boiled up from the surge of a powerful but up to now unknown sensation. It was as if at that moment I understood something that until now had only been stirring within me, but still had not been understood; it was as if I had caught sight of something new, of a completely new world that was unfamiliar to me and known only from some kind of obscure rumors and unfamiliar signs. . . .

Tell me, ladies and gentlemen, have I not been a fantasist, a mystic since childhood? What was this incident? What had happened there? Nothing, absolutely nothing. It was merely a sensation, and everything else turned out fine.

March 24, 1845.
Fyodor Dostoevsky, from a letter to Mikhail Dostoevsky.

Most likely you are tired of waiting for my letter, dear Brother. But I have been held back by my unstable situation. I cannot do a complete job of anything when before my eyes there is nothing but uncertainty and indecision. But since, regarding my personal circumstances, I still have not done anything good, I am writing all the same because I should have written a long time ago.

From the Muscovites[134] I have received 500 silver rubles. But I had so many debts, both old and new, that there was nothing left for printing. That would have been nothing, though. I could have borrowed from the printer or not paid off all my domestic debts, but the novel[135] was still not ready. I had almost finished it completely in November; but in December I took it into my head to redo it all. I redid it and recopied it, but in February I again began to clean it up anew, ironing it out, and making insertions and deletions. About mid-March I was ready and satisfied. But then the censors need at least a month. It is impossible to get anything approved of earlier. They claim they are swamped with work. I took the manuscript back, undecided as to what to do. In addition to the four weeks for the censors, printing will eat up about three weeks. It would come out by May. That will be too late! Then people left and right began to persuade me to submit my work to *The Fatherland Notes*. But that is nonsense. If I submit it there, I will be sorry. In the first place, they will not read it, and if they do, it will be six months later. They have enough manuscripts here without this one. And if they do print it, they will not give me any money for it. It is some kind of oligarchy. What is glory to me when I am writing for bread?

So I have decided on a desperate leap: to wait, perhaps to enter again into debt, and by September 1st, when everyone will have moved to Petersburg and, like hounds, will be sniffing out something new, to use my last crumbs of which there even might not be enough to publish my novel. To give one's work to a journal means to yoke oneself not only to the main *maître d'hôtel*, but also even to all the sluts and kitchen boys who nestle in the nests from which enlightenment spreads. There is not one dictator, but twenty. To have something published yourself means to make your own way in life. If the work is good, it will not only not perish, but it will also release me from this long cabala of debts, as well as give me something to eat.

Now about food! You know, brother, that in this regard, I'm left to my own resources. But no matter what, I have sworn that even if things head to disaster, I'll remain strong and not write on order. To do so would crush and ruin everything. I want every work of mine to be distinctly good. Look at Pushkin and Gogol. They did not write a good deal, but both are awaiting monuments. Now Gogol charges 1,000 silver rubles per signature page, and, as you yourself know, Pushkin got ten rubles for each line of verse. But their fame, especially Gogol's, was purchased with years of poverty and hunger. The old schools are disappearing. The new ones are daubing in oils, but they are not writing. All talent is leaving in one grand sweep. One sees only a monstrous unworked idea and strength . . . but only a crumb of action. Béranger, speaking about contemporary French feuilletonists, said that they stick a bottle of Chambertin in a bucket of water.[136] People also imitate them in Russia. Raphael would paint for years, reworking and polishing. The result was a miracle; gods were created under his hand. Vernet paints a picture a month. For it exhibition halls of special dimensions are ordered. The perspective is rich, the sketches are on a grand scale; but there is a copeck of anything worthwhile. They are merely decorators!

I'm seriously pleased about my novel.[137] It's an austere and well-constructed work. It has horrible deficiencies, though. Its publication will reward me. Now for the time being I'm empty. I'm now thinking of writing something for a debut or for money, but I don't feel like writing trifles, and for anything worthwhile one needs a great deal of time.

The time is approaching when I promised to visit you, dear friend. But I don't have the means, that is, the money to do so. I've decided to stay in my old apartment. Here I have at least made a contact and you don't know anything at all for six months. The fact is that I want my novel to take care of everything. If this business does not succeed, I, perhaps, will hang myself.

I would like to save at least 300 rubles by August. Even for that sum I could publish my novel. But money crawls like crabs, all in different directions. I have debts of roughly 400 silver rubles (with my expenses and the addition of clothing). At least I will be dressed decently for two years. I will definitely come and visit you, though. Write me as soon as you can about what you think of my apartment. That is a decisive step. But what can I do?

You write that you are horrified by a future without money. But Schiller will redeem everything. In addition, who knows how many copies of my novel will be bought. . . .

P.S. I think of you often. Perhaps you would like to know what I do when I'm not writing. I read. I read a terrible lot, and reading has a strange influence on me. I'll reread something I've read and reread long ago and I seem to acquire new energy, to penetrate into everything, to understand distinctly, and I myself extract the ability to write.

To write dramas—well, brother, for that you need years of peace and hard work. At least I do. It is good to be writing now. Drama now has moved to melodrama. Shakespeare pales in the twilight, and through the fog of myopic dramatists he seems a god, like an apparition of a spirit on the Brocken or the Harz Mountains.[138] But maybe I'll write [one] in the summer. Two or three years and we'll see, but for now let's wait.

Brother, with regard to literature, I'm *not the same person* I was two years ago. Back then there was childishness, nonsense. Two years have both brought and taken away a great deal.

In a feuilleton in *The Invalid*,[139] I just read about German poets who, in a madhouse, died of starvation and cold. There were about 20 of them and what names they had! I am still somewhat terrified even now.[140] One should be a charlatan.

April 5, 1845.
Nikolai I, from a certificate for Dostoevsky's retirement from service.

> By order of his Imperial Sovereign Emperor
> Nikolai I, autocrat of all-Russia
> and so forth, and so forth.

The bearer of this document, having served in the Engineering Department as a field second lieutenant–engineer, *the son Fyodor Mikhailovich Dostoevsky* . . . of the Orthodox faith. Twenty-two years old.[141] From the nobility. He has not served in the elections of the nobility; he has not participated in campaigns. He has not had special orders by the highest commands or his superiors. He has not had rewards, highest favors, letters of praise, or public letters of gratitude from the Sovereign and others. . . . He also has not been subject to complaints. He has not been remiss in the fulfillment of his duties, but he has not been cited for the same by his superiors. He has not allowed disorder or injustice with his subordinates, nor has he been cited for improper behavior.

May 4, 1845.
Fyodor Dostoevsky, from a letter to Mikhail Dostoevsky.

Forgive me for not having written for such a long time. But right up to this very minute, I've been hellishly busy. I cannot untangle myself from my novel. In fact, it has been such hard work that had I known what I was getting into, I would not have started it in the first place. I took it into my head to revise it still one more time and, honest to God, it has been for the better. It is now almost twice as good. But now it is finished, and this revision was the last. I have given my word not to touch it again. The fate of first works is always like that; you revise them to infinity. I do not know if Chateaubriand's *Atala*[142] was his first work, but I recall that he revised it seventeen times. Pushkin made such revisions even with his minor poems. Gogol polishes his marvelous creations for two years. And if you've read Sterne's *A Sentimental Journey*,[143] a tiny little book, then you remember what Walter Scott says in his *Preface* [to the work] about Sterne, citing his authority La Fleur, Sterne's servant.[144] La Fleur said that his master covered nearly a hundred quires of paper, writing about his journey to France. Well, the question arises—where did it go? It all made up a little book that a good scribbler like Plyushkin,[145] for example, would have fit on half a quire. I don't understand how that same Walter Scott could write such a thoroughly finished piece as *Mannering*,[146] for instance, in a few weeks. Perhaps because he was forty years old.[147]

I don't know what is going to happen to me! Unjustly do you say that my situation does not torment me. It does so to the point of sickness, nausea. Because of tormenting thoughts, I don't sleep for entire nights on end. Intelligent people tell me that I'll be lost if I publish my book as a separate entity. They say to me—let's suppose that the book will be good, very good. But you're not a merchant. How will you publicize it? In the newspapers, do you think? You definitely will need a bookseller on your side. But a bookseller is a smart man. He'll not compromise himself with announcements about some unknown writer. He'll lose credit with his clients. Each of the respectable booksellers is the owner of several journals and newspapers. First-rate authors are those who pretend to take part in these publications. If a new book is announced—it is in a journal certified by their signature; and such a thing means a great deal. As a result, a bookseller'll realize that when you come to him with an unpublished ware, he can squeeze you to an impossible degree. That's the way they do it. And a bookseller is a niggardly soul, he'll squeeze me without fail, and I'll wind up in the swamp. That is just where I will be.

So I've decided to appeal to the journals and for next to nothing, to give my novel over to *The Fatherland Notes*, of course. The point is that *The Fatherland Notes* sells 2,500 copies, consequently, at least 100,000 people read it. If I publish it there, my literary future, my life, all is assured. I'll have made my life in the world. I already have access to *The Fatherland Notes*. I always have money and, in addition, let my book come out, let's say in August or September, and in October I'll reprint it at my own expense, by then firmly assured that the novel will be bought out by people who buy such things. Furthermore, announcement will not cost me a copeck. So that is what I am going to do![148]

I cannot come to Revel before taking care of the novel because there is no time to be lost. I need to get moving. I have many new ideas which, if my first novel comes to be, will consolidate my literary renown. So these are my hopes for the future.

As for money—alas! I don't have any. The devil knows where it has disappeared to. But on the other hand I have few debts. As for the apartment, in the first place, I still owe a thing or two; and, in the second I am in an uncertain situation—will I go to Revel or not? Will I place the novel or not? If I go, I will have time then to move; because, no matter what apartment one rents, the expenses and stuff in moving will cost more than staying. I have already calculated it all. An apartment, a novel, Revel—three fixed ideas—My wife and my umbrella.[149] . . .

P.S. If I place my novel, Schiller will find itself a place, or I am not I. The Eternal Jew[150] is not bad. Sue is not too clever, though.

I just don't want to write, Brother; but your situation and Schiller so disturb me that I forget about myself.[151] But things are not easy for me either.

And if I cannot place my novel, then, perhaps I will throw myself into the Neva. What can I do. I have already thought about everything. I will not survive the death of my *idée fixe* . . . .

We're having terrible weather here. The heavens have opened and Providence has sent the Northern Palmyra several thousand head colds, coughs, cases of consumption, fevers, temperatures, and similar gifts. Lord have mercy on us sinners. Did you read Veltman's *Emelia*[152] in the last issue of *The Library for Reading*? What a marvelous thing it is. *Tarantas*[153] is also well written. But what vile illustrations.

Answer soon because I am bored.

Late May 1845.
Dmitri Grigorovich, from his memoirs.

One summer morning, Dostoevsky called me into his room. When I got there, I found him sitting on the couch that also served as his bed. On a small desk before him lay a rather thick notebook filled with large note paper with folded margins and covered with writing.

"Take a seat, Grigorovich," Dostoevsky said with unusual liveliness. "I rewrote the whole thing yesterday. I want to read it to you. Sit down and do not interrupt me."

What he read to me in one sitting and almost without stopping, soon appeared in print under the title, *Poor Folk*.

I always had esteemed Dostoevsky highly. . . . From the very first pages of *Poor Folk*, I realized that what Dostoevsky had written was better than anything I had done to date. . . . My delight knowing no bounds, there were several times when I wanted to throw myself on Dostoevsky's neck from joy. His dislike of noisy and expressive outpourings was the only thing that held me back. I could not sit there quietly, though, and every so often I interrupted Dostoevsky's reading with enthusiastic outbursts.

Late May 1845.
Fyodor Dostoevsky, from *A Writer's Diary*.

Thirty years ago (!) there occurred [between Nekrasov and myself] something that was youthful, fresh, and good. . . . that time, we were some twenty years old.[154] . . . In the beginning of winter [1845] I suddenly began *Poor Folk*. I. . . . Having finished the piece, I did not know if it was any good or whom to give it to. Other than D. V. Grigorovich, I had absolutely no literary acquaintances. . . .

When Grigorovich stopped by to see me, he said "Bring me your manuscript" (he himself had not read it). "Nekrasov wants to publish an anthology next year, and I will show it to him." I brought the manuscript, saw Nekrasov for a minute, and we shook hands. I was embarrassed at the thought that I had come with my work and left quickly. . . . I thought little of success and was afraid of that "party from *The Fatherland Notes*," as people then used to call it. For some years I had been reading Belinsky with great interest, but he seemed to me to be an awesome and terrible person. "He will laugh at my *Poor Folk*," I thought. But I also thought sometimes: "I had written the work with passion, almost with tears. 'Can it be,' I said to myself, 'that all this, all those moments I lived through with pen in hand while writing this story—can it be that all this is a lie, a mirage, a falsity?'" But such thoughts, of course, came only in moments, and my sense of apprehension quickly returned.

On the evening of the same day . . . I went off to visit an old friend who lived some distance away.[155] We spent the entire night talking about *Dead Souls* and reading the work—I cannot remember how many times we had read it previously. That is what young people did in those days; two or three got together: "Why don't we read Gogol, gentlemen!" someone would say; and then sat down and read, perhaps all night long. Many, many of the young people of the day seemed to be filled with a spirit of some sort and seemed to be waiting for something. When I came home it was already four o'clock on Petersburg "white night," as white and bright as day. The weather was fine and warm, and when I arrived at my apartment, I did not go to bed but opened the window and sat by it. Suddenly, the bell rang, giving me a great start, and then Grigorovich and Nekrasov, in utter rapture and both almost in tears, burst in to embrace me. They had come home early the evening before, taken up my manuscript, and begun to read to see what it was like: "We'll be able to tell from the first ten pages." But when they had read ten pages, they decided to read ten more; and then, without putting it down, they sat up the entire night reading aloud, taking turns as one grew tired.

"When Nekrasov was reading about the death of the student," Grigorovich told me later when we were alone, "I suddenly noticed that at the point where the father was running after the coffin, Nekrasov's voice broke; it happened once, and again, and suddenly he could not restrain himself; he smacked the manuscript with the palm of his hand and exclaimed, 'Ah, this so-and-so!' He meant you, of course. And so we kept on all night." When they had finished . . . they both decided to see me at once. "Who cares if he's asleep," they said, "*this* is more important than sleep!" . . .

Nekrasov and Grigorovich spent about a half hour with me, and during that time we discussed God knows how many things, one understanding the other with only half a word, speaking hastily and with exclamations. We spoke of poetry and of truth and of the "current situation," and of Gogol too, of course, quoting from *The Inspector General* and *Dead Souls*; but mainly we spoke of Belinsky. "I'll take him your story this very day, and you'll see: what a man he is, such a man he is! You will meet him and you will see: what a splendid soul he is!" Nekrasov said with delight, both his hands shaking me by the shoulders. "Now, get some sleep, we are leaving; you will come see us in the morning!" As if I could have slept after their visit! What delight, what success, and the main thing, I clearly remember a cherished feeling: "Others have success; people praise them, greet them, and congratulate them; but these two came running here in tears, at four o'clock in the morning, to wake me up because this matters more than sleep. . . . Ah, how fine!" That is what I was thinking; how could I sleep!"

Nekrasov took the manuscript to Belinsky that same day. . . .

"A new Gogol has appeared!" Nekrasov cried out as he came to Belinsky with *Poor Folk*.

"You find Gogols springing up like mushrooms," Belinsky replied sternly, but he took the manuscript. When Nekrasov visited him again in the evening, Belinsky greeted him "plainly excited": "Bring him here, bring him as soon as you can!"

Late May 1845.
Dmitri Grigorovich, from his memoirs.

At Nekrasov's home, I was the one who did the reading of *Poor Folk*. On the last page when the old man Devushkin bids farewell to Varinka, I could not restrain myself any longer and begin to sob openly. I also glanced at Nekrasov on the sly. Tears were rolling down his face, too. Passionately I began to convince him that such a good turn of events could not be postponed, and that we had to set out to Dostoevsky's place right away, despite the fact that it was late (it was around four a.m.), to tell him about the success of his work and to come to some agreement about the publication of his work.

Nekrasov, very much aroused [by what he had read], dressed quickly, and we headed out.

I must confess that . . . I had acted without thinking very clearly. Knowing well the character of my roommate, his lack of sociability, his morbid impressionability, his reserved nature, I should have told him about what had happened on the following day, and not awakened him, not distressed him with unexpected joy, and further, not brought to him at night a person whom he hardly knew. I myself, though, was in such an excited state and did not act like calmer individuals in such moments.

Having opened the door and seeing an unfamiliar face next to me, Dostoevsky paled and frowned. For a long time, he could not answer a word to what Nekrasov was telling him. After Nekrasov left, I expected that Dostoevsky would begin to scold me for my immoderate zeal and superfluous enthusiasm; but this did not happen. He limited his response only by entering his room and locking the door behind him. For a long time, I lay on my couch, listening to his steps, which told me about the distressed state of his soul.

Late May 1845.
Sofia Kovalevskaya, from her memoirs.

Having sent off his manuscript [to Nekrasov], Dostoevsky regretted immediately what he had done. . . . Suddenly he was seized by doubt and despair. All the weaknesses of the novel appeared before him in a bright light; everything seemed to him insignificant and pale. He even felt repulsion and shame for his child. . . .

"Belinsky will laugh at my *Poor Folk*," he said to himself almost in tears. . . .

"All night long," Dostoevsky told his friends, "I spent in a debauchery that was dirty, cheap, and without pleasure. It was so simple, from grief and bitterness. It was already four o'clock in the morning when I returned home. It was May, and outside was a Petersburg white night. I could not endure these nights. They always irritated my nerves and brought on a special, some kind of 'vile,' angst. . . . I could not sleep. So I sat alongside an open window. My soul was vile and base. I felt like running off and drowning myself somewhere. . . . Suddenly, I heard a knock at the door. I thought: 'Who could this be at this time of night?' I went to open the door. Good Lord! . . . Without saying a word, Nekrasov and Grigorovich rushed to hug me. I had not been on familiar terms with either one;[156] I knew them only by their faces.

"It turned out that during the evening they had set about to read my manuscript, seeking to glance through 'the first ten pages to see what it will be like.' But after the first ten, came still another ten, and still more after so that, in an unnoticed way, they read it all in one sitting. When they came to the place where the old father runs to Pokrovsky's grave, Nekrasov hit his palm on the manuscripts and said: 'Oh, poor soul.' They both immediately decided to see me: 'So what if he is asleep, we will wake him. This is more important than sleep.' . . .

"I went to Belinsky's with such a beating heart," Dostoevsky told me, "and he met me in such an extremely significant and restrained way. For a long time he started at me silently, as if to study me. Then he said suddenly: 'Do you yourself understand what you have written?'"

"He questioned me so severely that for the first minutes, I became perplexed, not understanding a thing. After that, there followed such an enthusiastic tirade that I became confused and thought: 'Good Lord, I am really as great as all that?'"

Circa June 1, 1845.
Fyodor Dostoevsky, from *A Writer's Diary*.

I recall that at first glance, I was greatly struck by Belinsky's appearance, his nose, his forehead. For some reason I had imagined him quite differently—"this awesome, this terrible critic." Belinsky greeted me in an extremely solemn and restrained way. "Well, I suppose that's the way it should be," I thought; but I think that not more than a minute passed before everything changed: the solemnity was not that of a great personage, or that of a great critic meeting a twenty-two-year-old[157] beginning writer; it came, so to speak, from respect for those sentiments that he wished to instill in me as quickly as possible, a respect for those important words that he so hastened to say to me.

Belinsky spoke ardently, with burning eyes: "Do you, your very self, realize what it is you have written?" he repeated several times, crying out, as was his custom. He always did so when speaking with strong emotion. "You, as an artist, could have written this only via a spontaneous instinct; but have you yourself comprehended all the terrible truth you have shown to us? It cannot be that you, with your twenty years, have understood such a thing. This wretched clerk of yours[158]—why, he has served for so long and has brought himself to the point where, from humility, he does not even dare to acknowledge his own wretchedness; or consider even the slightest complaint as freethinking; or claim even the right to his own unhappiness. When a good man, his general, gives him those hundred rubles, [the clerk] is shattered, destroyed from the amazement that 'their Excellency,' as he tells us, not even his Excellency, but their Excellency, could pity someone like himself. The time when the button that fell off or when he kissed the general's hand—why, this is not a matter of compassion for the poor fellow, but horror, genuine horror! The horror is that he is grateful! It is a tragedy. You have touched the very essence of the matter; straightaway you have shown the most significant thing. We critics and journalists only talk about such things, we try to explain them in words, but you, an artist, immediately and in one stroke, reveal the very essence in an image that you can feel with your hands, so that the most unthinking reader understands everything immediately! That is the secret of art; that is the truth in art! That is how the artist serves the truth! To you, an artist, the truth has been revealed and proclaimed; it has come to you as a gift. Cherish your gift, remain faithful to it, and be a great writer!"

Circa June 2, 1845.
Pavel Annenkov, from his memoirs.

> I saw Belinsky sitting by a window with a huge notebook in his hands. His face was greatly excited. When he saw me, he cried out: "Come over here right away. I have news for you...."
>
> Belinsky continued: "I have had this manuscript for two days, and I cannot tear myself away from it. It is a novel by a new writer. Who this individual is and what are his views on life, I still do not know, but his work discloses the secrets of Russia and its people in a way that no one has done previously. Just think, here is a first attempt at a social novel in our country.... The plot is a simple one: two good-natured eccentrics who think that to love the world is both an unusual pleasantness and the duty of everyone. They cannot understand anything, especially when the wheel of life, with all its rules and regulations, runs over them and silently crushes their limbs and bones. That is all—but what drama, what types! ... The name of this artist is Dostoevsky."
>
> With unusual feeling and in a nervous way, Belinsky began to read selections from the work that had impressed him.

June 7, 1845.
Nikolai Nekrasov, from a letter to Alexander Nikitenko.

> In 1846 I am assembling an almanac ... and may I ask that you serve as the censor for the work.... Among the pieces ... is Dostoevsky's *Poor Folk* (a novel that is extremely remarkable as you yourself will see).

Circa June 10, 1845.
Vissarion Belinsky, from a letter to Fyodor Dostoevsky.

> Dostoevsky, my soul (immortal) thirsts for you. Please come and visit us. The man who brought this note will take you. All of us will be here. Do not fear the host. He will be very glad to see you.

Summer 1845.
Fyodor Dostoevsky, from *A Writer's Diary*.

> In the summer of 1845 I began—after meeting with Belinsky—this second tale of mine, *The Double: The Adventures of Mr. Golyadkin*.

September 3, 1845.
Fyodor Dostoevsky, from a letter to Mikhail Dostoevsky.

As we agreed, I'm writing to you immediately after my arrival [from Revel]. It's beyond my pen to tell you, my beloved friend, how much unpleasantness, boredom, sadness, vileness, and vulgarity I endured on the road, as well as on my first day back in Petersburg. In the first place, having bid farewell to you and dear Emilia Fyodorovna, I boarded the ship in the most unbearable frame of mind. The crush was terrible, and my angst unbearable.... The ship crawled rather than sailed. The wind was against us, the waves lashed across the entire deck. Unbearably chilled and frozen through, I spent an indescribable night, sitting up and almost deprived of both my senses and my ability to think. The only thing I recall was that I threw up about three times. On the next day, at exactly four o'clock in the afternoon, we arrived at Kronstadt, i.e., in 28 hours. After waiting there for about three hours, when it was already twilight, we set out on a most miserable and vile little steamer, *Olga*, which sailed for about three and a half hours in the night and fog. How sad I felt when we sailed into Petersburg! In those deathly three hours before our arrival, I experienced my entire future in a dim way. Especially after I had gotten used to being with you and getting so accustomed to our time together that it seemed as though I had spent my entire existence in Revel, Petersburg and my future life in that city seemed to me to be so terrible, lonely, and joyless. Necessity also seemed so severe that if, in that moment, my life had ended, I seemingly would have died with joy. Truly, I'm not exaggerating. This entire show is absolutely not worth the candles. You, Brother, want to spend time in Petersburg. But if you do come, come by land, because there is nothing sadder or drearier than arriving in the city from the Neva and especially at night. At least, so it seemed to me. You can probably see now that even now my thoughts are still marked by the shaking of the boat.

When I arrived at my apartment at midnight, my servant was not at home. For a time he was working at another place, and the yard keeper, rejoicing over God knows what, handed me the orphaned key of my six hundred rubles of an apartment (in debts). I could not even drink some tea; so I went to bed in an absolutely apathetic state. Today, after waking up at eight o'clock, I saw my servant before me. I questioned him a bit. Everything is just as it was, the same as before. My apartment has been renovated slightly. Grigorovich and Nekrasov are still not in Petersburg, and rumor has it that they will perhaps turn up in the city by September 15th. Even that is doubtful, though. After giving a very short but extremely decisive audience to my creditors, I set off on business and did absolutely nothing. I acquainted myself with the journals, ate something, and bought some paper and pens; that was all. I didn't go to see Belinsky. I intend to go out tomorrow, but today I'm terribly out of sorts. In the evening I sat down to write this letter, which is already almost finished; but the letter is dull and depressed. It echoes perfectly my present burdensome state: "It is sad in this world, gentlemen!"[159]

I'm writing this letter to you, in the first place, as a result of my promise to write soon, and in the second, because of my depression and because the letter begged to be written. Oh, Brother, what a sad business this being alone is, and I am beginning to envy you now. Without you yourself being aware of it, you are lucky, really lucky.... I'm a little bit distracted by the fact that (until the 15th), I'm almost completely without resources, but only a little because at the present time I cannot even think of anything. Anyway, it is all nonsense. I have grown terribly weak and I want to go to bed now, because it is already night outside. The future will say something. What a pity that one has to work harder in order to live. My work cannot bear compulsion.

Oh, Brother, you would not believe how I would like to spend if only another hour or two with you right now. What is going to happen? What lies ahead? I am a genuine Golyadkin[160] now, on whom, by the way, I will get down to work tomorrow.... Does [your son] little Fedya still remember me or is he showing indifference? Goodbye, my dearest friend.

P.S. Golyadkin has profited from my spleen. Two ideas have been born and one new situation. Well, goodbye, my dear. What will happen to us in twenty years? I do not know what will happen to me. I only know that I feel things in a tormenting way.... Petersburg is still empty. Everything is quite dull.

Early fall 1845.
Fyodor Dostoevsky, from *A Writer's Diary*.

I recall that Nekrasov and I somehow went our separate ways, and rather quickly, and that our closeness lasted no longer than several months. There were misunderstandings, external events, and good people.

Early fall 1845.
Fyodor Dostoevsky, from *A Writer's Diary*.

From the very beginning of the fall of 1845, Belinsky took a great interest in [*The Double*], this new work of mine. Even before reading it, he informed Andrei Alexandrovich Kraevsky (whose journal Belinsky worked for). Belinsky introduced me to Kraevsky; and he and I agreed that *The Double* would appear in *The Fatherland Notes* in the first months of 1846.[161]

Early fall 1845.
Fyodor Dostoevsky, from *A Writer's Diary*.

"But do you know," Belinsky screeched one evening (sometimes if he was very excited, he would screech), as he turned to me, "Do you know that man's sins cannot be counted against him and that he cannot be laden down with obligations and with turning the other cheek when society is set up in such a mean fashion that a man cannot help but do wrong; economic factors alone lead him to do wrong, and it is absurd and cruel to demand from a man something which the very laws of nature make it impossible for him to carry out, even if he wanted to. . . ."

We were not alone that evening; one of Belinsky's friends, a man whom he highly respected and whose advice he often followed, was present, as was a certain young novice writer who later won fame in literature.[162]

"It is touching just to look at him," Belinsky said, suddenly breaking off his furious exclamations and turning to his friend as he pointed to me. "I no sooner mention the name of Christ than his whole face changes, just as if he were going to cry. . . . But believe me, you naive fellow," he said, attacking me again, "Believe me, that your Christ, were he born in our time, would be the most undistinguished and ordinary of men; he would be utterly eclipsed by today's science and by those forces that now advance humanity."

"Oh. I think not," Belinsky's friend interrupted. (I recall that we were sitting, while Belinsky was pacing back and forth around the room). "I think not. If Christ appeared now he would join the socialist movement and take his place at its head. . . ."

"He would indeed," Belinsky agreed suddenly, with surprising haste. "He would certainly join the socialist movement and take his place at its head."[163]

October 8, 1845.
Fyodor Dostoevsky, from a letter to Mikhail Dostoevsky.

Until now I have had neither the time nor disposition to inform you about anything concerning me. Everything was so vile and repulsive that it was nauseating to look about God's world. In the first place, my dearest and only friend, all this time I was without a copeck and was living on credit, itself quite a vile thing. In the second place, everything was somehow sad so that one loses heart unwittingly. You do not take care of yourself and become brainlessly indifferent. But worse than that, you cross the border and become angry and furious to the extreme. At the beginning of this month, Nekrasov appeared and repaid my part of the debt. I will receive the other part in a few days. You should know that about two weeks ago Belinsky gave me complete instructions on how to get along in the literary world; and he told me that I definitely, for the salvation of my soul, must demand no less than 200 paper rubles per signature sheet. Thus my Golyadkin will be sold for at least 1,500 rubles. Tormented by pangs of conscience, Nekrasov ran ahead like a hare and promised me 100 silver rubles by January 15 for the novel he bought from me, *Poor Folk*. He himself confessed frankly that 150 rubles is not a Christian payment. For that reason, from repentance, he is adding an additional 100 silver rubles. So far, so good. But here is what is vile. Absolutely nothing has been heard from the censors bout *Poor Folk*. They are dragging about such an innocent novel; and I do not know how it will all end. What if they forbid it from being published? Will they cross it out from top to bottom? That would be a catastrophe, pure and simple. Further, Nekrasov says that he will not have time to publish the almanac, and that he has already spent 4,000 paper rubles on it.[164]

Yakov Petrovich Golyadkin is holding up his character fully. He is a terrible scoundrel; he is unapproachable. In no way does he wish to move forward, pretending that he is not yet ready, and that for the time being, he is fine just as things are, that is he is all right. He also claims that he is not drunk, and that perhaps, if it came to that, he could do that too. Why not, why shouldn't he? After all, he is so-so, like everyone else. What does he care? A scoundrel, a terrible scoundrel! He absolutely refuses to end his career earlier than mid-November. He has already explained things to his Excellency now, and perhaps (why not) he is ready to tender his resignation. He is putting me, his creator, in an extremely difficult situation.[165]

I visit Belinsky quite often.[166] He is so incredibly well-disposed toward me and sees me as serious *proof to the public* and the validation of his opinions.... Generally speaking, the future (and none-too-distant) may be good, and it may be awfully bad. Belinsky is urging me to finish Golyadkin. After all, he has trumpeted the work to the entire literary world and practically sold it to Kraevsky. Further, half of Petersburg is already talking about *Poor Folk*. What is Grigorovich worth? He himself tells me: "I am your publicity agent!"

By nature, Nekrasov is a shady dealer; otherwise he could not exist. He was born that way. The other day he arrived at my place and suggested a project: a *breezy little almanac* to be created by all our literary people writing to the best of their ability; but with the main editors being Grigorovich, Nekrasov, and myself. Nekrasov will bear the expenses for the work. The almanac will take up two signature pages and will come out once every two weeks, on the 7th and 21st of each month. It will be called *The Scoffer*. Its goal is to make jokes and laugh at everything, to have mercy on no one, and to take a poke at the theater, journals, society, literature, happenings on the street, an exhibition, newspaper reports, foreign news, in a word, everything, all in the same spirit, and same direction. It will start on November 7th. It has turned out splendidly. In the first place, it will have illustrations. For the epigraph, he will take Bulgarin's famous words from a feuilleton from *The Northern Bee* that "we are prepared to die for the truth, we cannot be but with the truth," and the like, and it will be signed "Faddei Bulgarin."[167] The announcement that will come on November 1st will say the same thing. The articles for the first issue will be Nekrasov's "*About Certain Incidents of Baseness in Petersburg*" (which happened a few days earlier, of course); a future novel by Eugène Sue, titled *The Seven Deadly Sins* (the entire novel will take up three little pages);[168] a survey of all the journals; a lecture by *Shevyryov* with this claim: Pushkin's verse is so harmonious that when Shevyrov was in the Colosseum and read a few stanzas from *Pushkin* to the two ladies who were there with him, *all the frogs and lizards came crawling out from there to hear him*. (Shevyryov said such a thing at Moscow University.)[169] It will also take in the last meeting of the *Slavophiles* in which it will be proven solemnly that Adam was a Slav and lived in Russia, and that on this occasion, there will also be shown all the extraordinary importance and utility of the resolution of such an important social question for the prosperity and good of the entire Russian nation. Then in the section on art and the arts *The Scoffer* will do full justice to Kukolnik's *Illlustration*,[170] and in that connection, it will even cite the following point in the work where it says "iisktgezl-dtoom-dudurn" and so on, several lines in that way. (It is well known that *Illustration* is quite careless in proofreading; the transposition of words, words backward mean nothing at all to it.) Grigorovich will write *The History of a Week* and put several of his observations there.[171] I will write *A Servant's Notes About His Master*[172] and so on. You can see that the journal will be quite a merry affair, rather like Karr's *Guêpes*.[173] It is a good business because, the minimum income for me alone may be 100–150 rubles a month. The booklet will sell. Nekrasov will publish his poems there too.

Well, goodbye. I will write more next time. I am terrible busy now, but you see, by the way, I have penned you an entire letter, but you will not write me half a line with a letter from me. You count on visits. You are such a lazybones, a Fetyuk, simply a Fetyuk.[174]

Read *Teverino*.[175] (George Sand in *The Fatherland Notes*. There has been nothing like it in our century.) There are people for you. . . . prototypes. I am trying to sniff out a translation for you now. But also, at *The Fatherland Notes*, there are three official translators. Perhaps you and I, Brother, can work out something together. Everything is in the future, however. If I make it, so will *Schiller's Theatrical Works*—that's all I know.

October 8, 1845.
Konstantin Aksakov, from a letter to Ivan Aksakov.

In *The Double*, Dostoevsky has moved to something very close to self-parody.

November–December 1845.
Valerian Maikov, from his memoirs.

> Already in November and December 1845, all the literary dilettantes . . . were tossing about the joyous news of the appearance of a great new literary talent. Some cry out that he is "not worse than Gogol"; others counter that he is "better than Gogol"; still others, that "Gogol has been killed."

Circa early November 1845.
Ivan Turgenev, from his memoirs.

> "Yes," Belinsky said proudly, as if he had accomplished a great feat. "Yes, my friend, I will show you! This small bird is not tall"—and here he raised his hand almost an *arshin*[176] from the floor! . . .
>
> You can imagine my surprise when I met Mr. Dostoevsky soon later. I saw an individual who was more than middle height—but in any case taller than Belinsky himself! In a fit of fatherly tenderness to this newly born talent, Belinsky acted like a father to a son, as if it were his own "small child". . . .
>
> One must also confess that unrestrained praise of *Poor Folk* was one of Belinsky's first blunders and served as proof of the incipient weakening of his organism. Here his democratic streak won over him.

November 15, 1845.
Avdotya Panaeva, from her memoirs.

> Dostoevsky came to our home for the first time in the evening along with Nekrasov and Grigorovich. . . . From the outset one could see that he was a strangely nervous and impressionable young man. He was somewhat thin, small in stature, blond, and with a sickly pallor to his face. His small eyes seemed to dart anxiously from object to object; his pale lips moved about nervously. Almost everyone there had already become acquainted with Dostoevsky, but he, apparently, was restrained and did not take part in the general conversation. Everyone tried to engage him so as to mitigate his shyness and to show that he was a member of the circle.

November 16, 1845.
Fyodor Dostoevsky, from a letter to Mikhail Dostoevsky.

> I am writing to you in haste, all the more since time is so short. Golyadkin is still not done, but I must finish it without fail by the 25th of this month. You took such a long time to answer me that I was beginning to get very worried about you. Write more often; your attempts to convince me of a lack of time, I see as complete nonsense. . . .

Provincial laziness is destroying you in the flower of your youth, dear Brother; that is all there is to it.

Well, Brother, I think that my fame will never reach such heights as now. Everywhere there is an unbelievable admiration, as well as a terrible curiosity about me. I have met with a great many of the most respectable people. Prince Odoevsky is asking me to pay him the honor of a visit,[177] and Count Sollogub is tearing his hair out from despair [over meeting me]. . . . Panaev told him there has appeared a talent that will trample all of them into the mud. Sollogub ran around to see everyone and, stopping in at Kraevsky's, asked him suddenly: "Who is this Dostoevsky? Where can I *get hold of this Dostoevsky*?"[178] Kraevsky, who does not give a damn about anyone and who cuts everyone to the quick regardless of the consequences, answered him: "Dostoevsky will not wish to do you the honor of delighting you with a visit. That is really the way it is." That horrid little aristocrat is now going about on stilts and thinks that he will destroy me with the grandeur of his kindness. Everyone is receiving me like a miracle. I cannot even open my mouth without having it repeated everywhere that Dostoevsky said such-and-such, or that Dostoevsky wants to do such-and-such. Belinsky could not love me any more than he does. A few days ago the poet Turgenev returned from Paris (you probably have heard) and from the very first meeting he bound himself to me with such an attachment, with such a friendship, that Belinsky explains it as Turgenev's having fallen in love with me. But, Brother, what kind of person is he? I also have almost fallen in love with him. He is a poet, a talent, an aristocrat, a handsome fellow, wealthy, educated, bright, 25 years old.[179] I do not know what nature has denied him. Finally, he is an inexhaustibly direct and splendid personality, formed in the best school. Read his story "Andrei Kolosov" in *The Fatherland Notes*. It is he himself, although he did not think to show himself there.

At the present I am still not rich in money, but I am not in need. A few days ago I did not have even a copeck to my name. Meanwhile Nekrasov has started up *The Scoffer*—a charming humorous almanac for which I wrote the announcement. The announcement raised a storm because it was the first announcement of such lightness and humor in things of this sort. It reminded me of Lucien de Rubempré's first feuilleton.[180] My announcement has already been published in the section "Miscellaneous News" in *The Fatherland Notes*. For it I took 20 silver rubles. A few days ago, I dropped in on Nekrasov. While I was at his place, the idea for a novel in 9 letters came to me. After I arrived home, I wrote the novel in a single night. . . . The next morning I took it to Nekrasov and received 125 paper rubles for it, i.e., my page in *The Scoffer* is valued at 250 paper rubles. That evening my novel was read to our entire circle at Turgenev's place and it raised a furor. It will be published in the first issue of *The Scoffer*.[181] I will send the book to you by December 1st and you will see for yourself if it is any worse than, for example, Gogol's *The Lawsuit*.[182] Belinsky said that he is absolutely certain of me because I can take up completely different elements. The other day Kraevsky, having heard that I was without money, implored me most humbly to take a loan of 500 rubles from him. I think that I will sell him my signature sheet for 200 paper rubles.

I have a heap of ideas, but I cannot tell any of them even to Turgenev, without the next day people in almost all corners of Petersburg knowing that Dostoevsky is writing such-and-such and such-and-such. Well, Brother, if I were to begin to enumerate to you all my successes, there would not be enough paper for them. I think that I will have money, Golyadkin is turning out splendidly; it will be my chef d'oeuvre. Yesterday I was at Panaev's for the first time, and it seems that I have fallen in love with his wife.[183] She is intelligent and very good-looking; in addition, she is kind and incredibly direct. I spent the time there in a merry way. Our circle is very large. But I keep writing about myself. Forgive me, dear Brother. I will tell you openly that I am quite intoxicated with my own fame. With my next letter, I will send you a copy of *The Scoffer*. Belinsky, though, says I am profaning myself by publishing my pieces in such a work....

P.S. Belinsky is protecting me from entrepreneurs. I have read over my letter to you and have found that in the first place I am illiterate, and in the second I am a braggart.

Goodbye, and for God's sake, write.

Our Schiller will work out without fail. Belinsky praises the undertaking of a *complete edition*. I think that in time we will be able to sell it profitably, at least to Nekrasov....

The Minushkas, Klarushkas, Mariannas, and the like have become beautiful beyond words, but they cost a terrible amount of money.[184] The other day Turgenev and Belinsky let me have it over my disorderly life. These gentlemen do not have the slightest idea how to love me, but they are all in love with me, every last one of them. My debts are where they were formerly.

November 16, 1845, and after.
Anna Dostoevskaya, from her memoirs.

Dostoevsky's attraction for Panaeva was fleeting,[185] but just the same it was the single attraction of Dostoevsky [for a woman] in these years. When, at her home, people treated Fyodor Mikhailovich in a mocking way, the intelligent and perceptive Panaeva took pity on him and for this she received his heartfelt gratitude and the tenderness of sincere attraction.

November 16, 1845, and after.
Avdotya Panaeva, from her memoirs.

From that evening on, Dostoevsky often came to visit us. His shyness passed, and he showed a certain passion. He entered into arguments with everyone; apparently from a certain stubbornness he contradicted others. Because of his youth and nerves, he was not able to control himself and way too clearly showed his authorial pride and opinion about his writer's talent.

Stunned by the unexpected and brilliant result of his first step into fiction and showered with praises by competent people in literature, Dostoevsky was an impressionable individual. He could not hide his pride before our young writers who had stepped modestly into the literary field. When such individuals appeared in our circle, it was their misfortune to be torn to pieces. Dostoevsky himself responded with an annoyed and arrogant manner, saying that with his talent, he was incomparably better than anyone else. The members of the group took to teasing him, to irritate him with jibes in their conversations.

November 16, 1845, and after.
Dmitri Grigorovich, from his memoirs.

I can say with assurance: the success of *Poor Folk* and, perhaps even more importantly, the unrestrained and ecstatic praises of Belinsky affected Dostoevsky in an extremely harmful way, since until that time he had lived isolated within himself, and meeting, on an infrequent basis, only a few friends who had nothing in common with literature. How could such an individual preserve a normal condition of spirit when, with his very first step into literature, such an authority as Belinsky bowed before him, loudly proclaiming that there had appeared a new light in Russian literature?

November 27, 1845.
Nikolai Nekrasov, from a letter to Vladimir Odoevsky.

I saw Dostoevsky. He is very busy now and has asked me that you excuse him, since he cannot visit you until after December 1st.

November 27, 1845.
Alexander Kraevsky, from a letter to Vladimir Odoevsky.

I have just received *Poor Folk*. I am giving it to you only *for a night* and I ask that you show it to *no one*; tomorrow *morning* return it to me.

Circa December 1845.
Fyodor Dostoevsky, from *A Writer's Diary*.

I must have used this word [*stushevat'sia*—to disappear, perish, to descend to *nothingness*] successfully in the first three chapters of *The Double*, which I read at Belinsky's, when I described how one annoying and sly little fellow managed to disappear from the scenes at appropriate times (or something like that, I forget). I say that because the new term did not surprise any of the listeners. On the contrary, it was at once understood and noted by everyone. Belinsky interrupted me specifically to compliment me on the expression. All those who were there at the time (they are all still alive) also praised me . . . including Ivan Turgenev . . . (most likely, he has forgotten it now). Later, Alexander Kraevsky also had many nice things to say.

Early December 1845.
Fyodor Dostoevsky, from his notebooks.

At Belinsky's, highly well-known writers were in raves [over what I had written].

Early December 1845.
Apollon Maikov, from a letter to Alexei Pisemsky.

> Did you see a comet in the sky? . . .
> Did you see how one well-known general
> Hitched his carriage to its tail? . . .
> No, you did not, and neither did I.
> But Grigorovich did.

December 2, 1845.
Nikolai Nekrasov, from a letter to Nikolai Ketcher.

The Scoffer . . . will not come to be. Why? *The editors are not at fault.*

Circa December 3, 1845.
Fyodor Dostoevsky, from *A Writer's Diary*.

In the beginning of December 1845, Belinsky insisted that I read two or three chapters from my story *The Double*. For this he even arranged a gathering (something he almost never did) and invited his closest friends. At that evening, I recall, was Ivan Sergeevich [Turgenev].[186] He listened attentively to about half of what I was reading. He praised it but then left, very much in a hurry to rush off somewhere. The three or four chapters that I had read, Belinsky liked in an extreme way. . . . But he did not know the end of the story and was still under the fascination of *Poor Folk*.

Circa December 3, 1845.
Pavel Annenkov, from his memoirs.

In Belinsky's home, Dostoevsky read a second story: *The Double*, his sensational portrait of an individual who lives between two worlds, real and fantastic, and who, in the end, never decides between the two. Belinsky liked the work for its full and forceful treatment of an original and strange theme . . . but it also seemed to me that the critic had something else in mind [about the work] which he did not consider it necessary to say right away. Belinsky constantly called Dostoevsky's attention to the necessity of *becoming a practiced hand* . . . to render one's thoughts deftly . . . free from the difficulties of exposition.

Belinsky, apparently, could not feel at home with the then fashionable, if vague, manner of storytellers who return constantly to old phrases, repeating and changing them endlessly. Such failings he ascribed to the inexperience of the young writer. . . . But here Belinsky was wrong: He had met not a novice, but an author who was formed completely. . . .

Dostoevsky heard out the exhortations of the critic in a gracious but indifferent way.

Circa December 3, 1845.
Dmitri Grigorovich, from his memoirs.

Belinsky sat across from the author, latching onto his words in a greedy way. In places, he was unable to restrain his enthusiasm, repeating that only Dostoevsky could discover such remarkable psychological subtleties.

After December 3, 1845.
Dmitri Grigorovich, from his memoirs.

Rumors reached me that Dostoevsky had asked that *Poor Folk* be published in a special font and that a border frame every page. I was not present at any of these conversations; so I do not know if such an assertion was justified or not. If there was something to these stories, they most likely suffered from exaggeration.

After December 3, 1845.
Nikolai Blagoveshchensky, from a letter to Alexander Sheller-Mikhailov.

Turgenev began to recall the past. . . . [He remembered] Dostoevsky during the time of Belinsky; his distrustfulness and suspiciousness; his demands that his articles in an almanac be printed with a border on each page so as to distinguish them from the rest.

After December 3, 1845.
Ivan Turgenev, as told to Konstantin Leontiev.

When the *unfortunate* Dostoevsky . . . gave his story to Belinsky for publication, he was so carried away by what he had written that he told him: "*You should surround my story with some kind of small border!*"

After December 3, 1845.
Ivan Panaev, from an 1855 article.

> Our little idol demanded that his work be published without fail at the beginning or the end of the book . . . [he also requested] that it be set off from the others with a golden border or edge . . . so that it would catch everyone's eyes. The editor agreed to everything, and having patted the man's shoulder, began to sing:
>
> I will make a fuss over you
> I will set forth, a scoundrel on the mend
> I will surround you with a border
> And put you at the end.[187]

After December 3, 1845.
Anna Dostoevskaya, from her memoirs.

> In April [1880] people were telling Fyodor Mikhailovich about an article by P. V. Annenkov titled "A Remarkable Decade," published in *Messenger of Europe*, in which the author discussed Dostoevsky. Fyodor Mikhailovich was very interested in this piece and asked me to get the April issue of the journal from the library. I managed to get it from friends just before our departure from Russia, and took it with us.
>
> Having read the article, my husband was outraged. In his memoirs, Annenkov alleged that Dostoevsky had such a high opinion of his own literary talent that he demanded that his first novel, *Poor Folk*, be printed . . . "with a border about the edges."
>
> Fyodor Mikhalovich was disturbed deeply by this slander and immediately wrote a letter to Suvorin asking, in his own name, to announce in *New Time* that "*what Annenkov said in* Messenger of Europe *about a 'border' did not happen, nor could it have happened.*"
>
> Many of Fyodor Mikhailovich's contemporaries (Apollon Maikov, for example) who had an excellent recollection of the period, were also angered by Annenkov's article. Suvorin, based on Fyodor Mikhailovich's letter and the testimonies of colleagues who were with him at the time, wrote two excellent paragraphs (on May 2 and 16, 1880) on the subject of the "border," publishing them in *New Time*.
>
> In answer to my husband's refutation, Annenkov stated . . . that an error had occurred and that Fyodor Mikhailovich's demand for a "border" was for a work titled "Plismylkov's Story" (which Fyodor Mikhailovich never wrote).[188] My husband was so infuriated by Annenkov's [latest] slander that he resolved that, at the memorial activities for Pushkin,[189] he would not recognize Annenkov

if he met him . . . and that if Annenkov approached him, he would refuse to shake hands.

After December 3, 1845.
Pavel Annenkov, from an 1880 article.

> The sudden success of *Poor Folk* gave Dostoevsky a very high opinion of himself. . . . It also freed him from the typical wavering and doubt which accompanied the first steps of a writer.[190] Indeed, Dostoevsky understood the success of *Poor Folk* as a prophetic dream, portending laurels and crowns. In fact, when he decided to publish his novel in an upcoming almanac, Dostoevsky demanded calmly, as a condition and a right . . . that his book be distinguished from all the other pieces in the work with special typographical distinction, for example a border. And his work was in fact, surrounded by a venerable border in [Nekrasov's] almanac.[191]

After December 3, 1845.
Orest Miller, from his biography of Dostoevsky.

> The rumor [about the border around *Poor Folk*] sustained itself easily, since *The Petersburg Miscellany* had long been a bibliographical rarity. But what did it cost someone to ask for a copy of it in the Public Library and see if was really so?

After December 3, 1845.
Alexander Suvorin, from an 1880 article.

> Having gotten hold of *The Petersburg Miscellany*, we saw that . . . *Poor Folk* was published without any borders and in the same font as the other works in the collection.

After December 3, 1845.
Pavel Annenkov, from an 1880 letter to Mikhail Stasyulevich.

> My memory has not deceived me, nor could it deceive me. The entire literary world at that time knew about the lengthy negotiations between Dostoevsky and Nekrasov, the former's demand that his novel be set apart from the other pieces in the work with some kind of honored mark.
> An outraged Nekrasov agreed to all the demands of the author, and took revenge with an epigram that circulated from hand to hand.[192] I also ask that you seek out Turgenev for further information, since he knows of the entire affair and even now remembers the epigram by heart. . . .
> *I myself saw the first copies of* The Petersburg Miscellany *with borders*.[193]

After December 1845.
Mikhail Stasyulevich, from an 1880 article.

[Mr. Annenkov], the author of "Recollections," is abroad, but we need not expect any explanations from him, as we ourselves can get the [requisite] information. The essential story about a "border" is beyond a doubt. The author of "Recollections" has referred to a "circumstance" regarding *Poor Folk* that was well-known at the time, but the matter concerned another of Mr. Dostoevsky's stories, "Plismylkov's Story," or something in that nature, which had been designated for Belinsky's anthology, *Leviathan*.

After December 3, 1845.
Alexander Suvorin, from a letter to Fyodor Dostoevsky.

I am sending you a copy of *Messenger of Europe* in case you do not subscribe to it. On page 412, you will find an answer to my note as to the "border." Will you respond to it or not? . . . You can also answer me directly. . . .

Messenger of Europe . . . did not include my remarks . . . on the border about Turgenev's story and Panaev's essay, that it was their works that were illustrated. Instead, the people there came up with nonsense-gossip, for which there was no evidence. . . .

If you choose not to respond, scribble two words. I myself will answer [in your place] and repeat that there is nothing convincing in the story in *Messenger of Europe*, and most likely that of Turgenev too.

P.S. Did you ever write a story, titled, "Plismylkov's Story"?[194]

After December 3, 1845.
Victor Burenin, from an 1880 article.

To support this vile gossip made up by some idle journalist almost half a century ago, and also to ascertain it in such a serious and important way as do the honored editors of *Messenger of Europe*—truly, this is an unworthy thing. It is bad enough that Mr. Annenkov . . . [claimed borders around Dostoevsky's *Poor Folk*] in his memoirs, but it is also completely foolish that Mr. Stasyulevich [the editor of *Messenger of Europe*], by means of false wiles and tricks, seeks to assert the truth of such journalistic rubbish.[195]

After December 3, 1845.
Alexei Suvorin, from an 1880 letter to Fyodor Dostoevsky.

Are you satisfied with what Burenin wrote about the border [about *Poor Folk* in *New Time*] or would you have wanted in your own name to assert that [Annenkov's] story was a lie?[196]

After December 3, 1845.
Fyodor Dostoevsky, from an 1880 letter to Alexei Suvorin.

> As regards that stupid "border," I do not know what to tell you. I am, of course, pleased with what was written in *New Time* (about it). If I myself write something about this, it will be sometime later when I begin my *Literary Remembrances* (which I will do without fail). But if you would, for example, as the publisher of a newspaper, write just *five* lines saying something like this: "We have received from Mr. Dostoevsky a formal declaration that what the *Messenger* said about the border never and in no way happened, nor could it happen," and so on and so forth. (However you want to do this is up to you). For such a thing I will be extremely grateful.[197]

After December 3, 1845.
Alexei Surovin, from an 1880 article.

> F. M. Dostoevsky, now residing in Staraya Russa,[198] where he is taking a cure, has asked me to assert in his name that "what has been put forth in *Herald of Europe* by P. B. Annenkov regarding the 'border' [about *Poor Folk*] did not occur, nor could it occur."[199]

After December 3, 1845.
Fyodor Dostoevsky, from an 1880 letter to Konstantin Pobedonostsev.

> Turgenev is acting as my personal enemy in a decisive way. *Messenger of Europe* has let loose some kind of trivial gossip about some legendary event that happened thirty-five years ago.[200]

After December 3, 1845.
Fyodor Dostoevsky, from a draft of *A Writer's Diary*.

> There is one thing I have been avoiding for a long time, namely the personal squabbles arising from attacks ... on me personally. ... But last year (1880) I was assailed by one journal [*Messenger of Europe*] which, upon first glance, was very insignificant.
>
> I was on the verge of wanting to show my scorn by not answering [the people involved], but they had discussed my biography, and not to correct them ... and raise objections would seem to say that what they were saying was something that I agreed with and that all of it was just.
>
> In *Messenger of Europe* Annenkov [charged] that I was arrogant even then. ...
> I was surprised [by such an allegation] ...

> To demand a border (about my work)—this I was not on such terms [with Nekrasov] as to do....
>
> Panaev has harmed me in a thing or two, but all the same I will not accuse him of inventing the anecdote about the border [about *Poor Folk*].... But how could Mr. Annenkov have heard [about the border]... and from whom did he hear such a thing?
>
> *Messenger of Europe* is asserting [the story] primarily in verse, but that is all the evidence the people there have. As I see it, such lines should open the eyes of my most passionate detractors (though I do not understand why they are so fervid) and convince them *beyond a doubt* that they were not written about me....
>
> All this is, perhaps, nonsense, and of course is not worth getting mixed up with. But I myself have written about Belinsky and my meeting with him [over *Poor Folk*]....
>
> Maybe I should have said something funny?... Let it go....
>
> I also cannot help but note that once someone has told an untruth, he will tell another, and that is what I expect from the organs of Mr. Stasyulevich, all kinds of future untruths.[201]

After December 3, 1845.
Fyodor Dostoevsky, from his diary.

> Is the journal *Messenger of Europe* acting morally when they slander me like that?

December 15, 1845.
Ivan Aksakov, from a letter to a friend.

> What a business! A number of almanacs are to come out this winter, including one, published by *The Fatherland Notes*.... The people there have found a new star, some Dostoevsky, who they are elevating almost as high as Gogol.... Good Lord, this is all so repulsive and vile, but here in Moscow, everything is so empty and dead that one does not know what to do or where to bow your head!

Late 1845.
Valerian Panaev, from his memoirs.

> At this time Nekrasov was preparing an edition titled *Petersburg Miscellany*, which was to include Dostoevsky's first novel, *Poor Folk*. Belinsky, Nekrasov, and Grigorovich already knew this novel from manuscripts, and Ivan Panaev arranged a reading [of it] for other writers and acquaintances.

I attended the gathering. Dostoevsky read his work. At that time he was a shy individual, but his rendition [of *Poor Folk*] made a shattering impression on everyone there....

One should also note that even in this short time, when Dostoevsky visited Ivan Ivanovich [Panaev], he was very irritable and sensitive.

Late 1845.
Pavel Sokolov, from his memoirs.

Nekrasov began to walk about the room in a nervous way, rubbing his hands feverishly. He said: "Well, Mr. Sokolov, the main piece in this Almanac will be the most outstanding story of Dostoevsky, *Poor Folk*. [In your illustrations] please try to capture these matchless types.[202]

Late 1845.
Dmitri Grigorovich, from his memoirs.

After Dostoevsky had met Nekrasov ... and Belinsky ... he underwent a noticeable change. When *Poor Folk* was being published, he was in a constant state of nervous excitability. As was his wont, he did not tell me about what had transpired between him and Nekrasov, or what happened in further encounters between them.

Conclusion

By the end of 1845, the twenty-four-year old Dostoevsky was not unlike the heroes of both his early and mature fiction. He, too, showed duality: a searing, and potentially self-defeating, mix of strengths and weaknesses.

Regarding strengths, the young Dostoevsky was a child of privilege. Throughout his early years, he knew only stability, love, and peace. His parents, Mikhail and Maria Dostoevsky, were the salt of the Russian earth who wanted the very best for their second son, and who did everything in their power to ensure his personal and professional success. Under their loving care, the young Dostoevsky enjoyed an embarrassment of riches, a life brimming with sensibility and sense. Mikhail and Maria taught young Fyodor to be loyal and loving, independent and industrious. They incurred in him a love of learning: classical and experiential, Russian and European, with a particular emphasis on literature. Indeed, poetry and prose were the cornerstones of the young Fyodor's life. With their second son, Mikhail and Maria also stressed *pro Deo et patria*, a faith in Russia and Orthodoxy. Above all, they raised young Fyodor in love and reverence for an all-caring God.

Most important, Mikhail and Maria taught to young Fyodor three life-lessons: When windows close, doors open; the things that do not kill people make them stronger; and, most crucially, perhaps, no matter what the joy or sorrow, the triumph or tragedy, life must go on.

Such instruction came into play with the death of Maria. Painful as her passing was, young Fyodor came to see that there was life after death. When he arrived in St. Petersburg, there were new adventures and experiences, new schools and studies, new mentors and friends. There were also new obstacles and challenges, most of which he cleared handily. Injustice and failure floored him only momentarily. Indeed, like father Mikhail, they fired in him a wish for success and, more importantly, the desire to live life on his own terms.

In St. Petersburg, young Fyodor was initially a model. If he was seen as a monk-mystic-saint, it was because he was seemingly without sin. By every measure, young Fyodor was not one of the guys. He did not drink or smoke; he did not play pranks or pluck "hazel hens"; he did not chase after titles and ranks. He gave to the poor; he protected the humiliated and injured. Most notably, he did not look for love in all the right or wrong places. Indeed, young Fyodor did not look for love at all.

Like father Mikhail, the young Fyodor went his own way, physically and mentally. He was happiest when alone, thinking, studying, reading, and writing. Indeed, young Fyodor relished his time under the radar. Surrounded by books, papers, and pens, he seemed mesmerized by books and study, heedless of everyone and everything around him. The lad came to life only when he talked about literature, when he declaimed poetry and prose, and (a portent of the future) when he told others what to read and do. He avoided the spotlight, but he relished moments when all eyes and ears were focused on him.

In truth, though, the young Dostoevsky was like a simmering volcano that bubbled and boiled, a tight spring that buckled and bent. On one hand, the energy was positive. The young Dostoevsky sought not to explore the world so much as to dissect it, even to tear it apart. As much as he reveled in the ethers, sputtering idealist philosophy, he raced madly through physical and spiritual undergrounds, embracing-enduring harsh life. From the gardens of the Mariinsky Hospital in Moscow to the nooks and crannies—the "corners"—of St. Petersburg, the young Fyodor sought out the downtrodden and deranged. Quickly, he came to see that if his life was a blessing, the life of others—sadly, the majority of humankind—was a curse.

On the negative side, the energy within the volcano-spring that was the young Fyodor threatened to destroy him utterly. Like many geniuses, he had not learned how to control-direct the creative tension-flow. Rather, he watched, often helplessly, as his gifts were consuming him alive. At times, the demise was passive; more often, though, it was active. Indeed, if anybody was guilty for the young Fyodor's pain and suffering it was he. Unwittingly, he had become archetype-exemplar of the teeming masses that he had sought out so earnestly.

The young Fyodor withdrew from kith and kin. He wrote so few letters to his father and brother that they thought him dead. Even more seriously, he forsook his formation. Once a saint, he was now a sinner. The young Fyodor was no longer loyal and loving, industrious and independent; rather, he was selfish and egotistical, needy and inert. He abused his body; he ceded to anxiety and angst; he let his head rule his heart. The young Fyodor not only saw the wolves at the door, but in his disordered life, he also let them into the house. He treated everyone badly, especially the ones who loved him most. Most seriously, he had forgotten God. The young Dostoevsky no longer noted the Deity in his letters. As he saw it, God, if existing at all, cared little for him or humanity. Indeed, just as the young Dostoevsky moved to the dregs of humanity in life, so did he enter into the company of the losers of his early fiction. He was Makar Devushkin in *Poor Folk*, complaining of his life and fate; he was Golyadkin Senior and Junior, neurotically unsure if he was to be in life or out.

Three things saved the young Dostoevsky from catastrophe. The first was his love for literature. He continued to read voraciously. To everyone, he talked of writers and works. The second was his wish to be a writer. Come hell or high water, the young Fyodor was determined to enter the Russian literary world. Translations of European fiction, plans for anthologies and editions, sojourns to booksellers and censors, filled his day and gave him purpose and meaning. The third was the writing-success of *Poor Folk*, which temporarily released the tension-flow of his gifts and imbued him with the recognition-attention he craved so desperately.

In retrospect, with *Poor Folk*, the young Dostoevsky should have been more careful about what he had wished for. His elation over the applause for his first work was only momentary. Old demons returned, new ones appeared. Success had not only come too soon, but it also went to his head. The young Fyodor started to believe that he had saved Russian literature, if not the world. Very soon, however, he found himself wobbling from the heights. Indeed, the young Dostoevsky was soon caught in the same dilemma that would trap many of the alleged "extraordinary men" in his mature fiction. He wondered if he could repeat the success of *Poor Folk*. He was not sure if his new acquaintances were genuine friends who wanted him to enhance the national written expression; or craven opportunists who, sought the "little idol" for their own political, social, and economic ends.

Again with hindsight, such anxiety-angst proved to be a blessing. With the young Dostoevsky, everything happened for the right reason, even if it took years for him (and investigators of his life and literature) to piece together the shard-like fragments of his puzzle-existence. Indeed, it was only in writing his major fiction that Dostoevsky would come to see that without mistakes, there was no learning; that without darkness, there was no light; and most importantly, that without doubt, there was no faith in God and life or return to the values he had learned as a child, adolescent, and youth.

In 1845, though, the young Dostoevsky was far from such knowledge; but (with apologies to George Bernard Shaw), he would later take satisfaction that his youth had not been wasted on the young.

Directory of Prominent Names

Aksakov, Ivan Sergeevich (1823–1886), publicist, poet, journalist, publisher, and social figure.
Aksakov, Konstantin Sergeevich (1817–1860), writer, critic, Slavophile, and brother of Ivan Aksakov.
Alexander I (1777–1825), tsar of Russia from 1801 to 1825.
Alexandra Fyodorovna (1798–1860), wife of Nicholas I.
Alexandrova, Ekaterina Alexandrovna (1821–1845), servant and consort of Mikhail Andreevich Dostoevsky.
Alexei Petrovich (1690–1718), son of Peter the Great.
Alighieri, Dante (1265–1321), Italian poet.
Andreyanova, Elena Ivanova (1819–1857), dancer.
Annenkov, Pavel Vasilievich (1811?–1887), critic, memoirist, and prose-writer.
Ariosto, Ludovico (1474–1533), Italian poet.
Asenkova, Varvara Nikolaevna (1817–1841), actress.
Auber, Daniel (1782–1871), French composer.
Balzac, Honoré de (1799–1850), French writer.
Bantysh-Kamensky, Nikolai Nikolaevich (1788–1850), Latinist and historian.
Baratynsky, Evgeni Abramovich (1800–1844), poet.
Barkov, Ivan Semyonovich (1732–1763), poet, translator, and diplomat.
Barshev, Ioann (Ivan Vasilievich) (1778–1858), priest and friend of the Dostoevsky family.
Barshev, Sergei Ivanovich (1808–1882), professor and son of Ioann Barshev.
Barshev, Yakov Ivanovich (1807–1894), son of Ioann Barshev.
Beck, Karl (1817–1879), German poet.
Begichev, Dmitri Nikitch (1786–1855), writer.
Beketov, Alexei Nikolaevich (1823–?), classmate of Fyodor Dostoevsky.
Belinsky, Vissarion Grigorievich (1811–1848), critic.
Bellini, Vincenzo (1801–1835), Italian composer.
Bely, Andrei (1880–1934), novelist, poet, theorist, and literary critic.
(von) Benkendorf, Alexander Khristoforovich (1781?–1783), general and statesman.
(von) Bennigsen, Leonti Leontievich (1745–1826), general.
Bentham, Jeremy (1748–1832), English jurist, philosopher, and political and social reformer.
(de) Béranger, Pierre-Jean (1780–1857), French poet and songwriter.
Berezhetsky, Ivan Ignatovich (1820–?), friend of Fyodor Dostoevsky.
Bilevich, Nikolai Ivanovich (1812–1860), teacher.
Blaes, Arnold (1814–1892), Belgian clarinettist.
Blagoveshchensky, Nikolai Alexandrovich (1837–1889), writer.
Bonaparte, Napoleon (1769–1821), French politician and general.
Botkin, Vasili Petrovich (1811–1869), literary critic, essayist, and translator.
Bryanchikov, Ignaty (n.d.), classmate of Fyodor Dostoevsky at the Main Engineering Academy.
Bulgarin, Faddei Venediktovich (1789–1859), editor and journalist.

Bunin, Ivan Alexeevich (1870–1953), writer.
Burenin, Viktor Petorvich (1841–1926), critic, poet, and dramatist.
Bürger, Gottfried (1748–1794), German poet.
Byron, George (Lord) (1788–1824), English poet.
Caesar, Julius (100–44 BC), Roman military and political leader
Catherine II (the Great) (1729–1796), empress of Russia from 1762 to 1796.
(de) Cervantes, Miguel Saavedra (1547–1616), Spanish novelist.
(de) Chateaubriand, Francois-René (1768–1848), French writer, politician, and diplomat.
Chatterton, Thomas (1752–1770), English poet.
Chermak, Avgusta Frantsevna (n.d.), wife of Leonti Chermak.
Chermak, Karl Leontievich (1809–1888), son of Leonti Chermak.
Chermak, Leonti (Leopold) Ivanovich (1770?–1840s?), teacher and administrator.
Chernoglazov (n.d.), translator.
Chrysostom, John (347–407), Greek archbishop of Constantinople and early Church Father.
Clairville (1811–1879), French actor and playwright.
Cooper, James Fenimore (1789–1851), American writer.
Corneille, Pierre (1606–1684), French dramatist.
Cournant, Josèphe (n.d.), teacher at the Main Engineering Academy.
(de) Custine, Astolphe-Louis-Léonor (1790–1857), French aristocrat, writer, diplomat, and traveler.
Dal, Valdimir Ivanovich (1801–1872), writer and lexicographer.
D'Anthès, Georges-Charles de Heeckeren (1812–1895), French baron.
Davydov, Ivan Ivanovich (1792?–1863), teacher, philosopher, linguist, and aesthete.
Defoe, Daniel (1661?–1731), English journalist, writer, and pamphleteer.
Derzhavin, Gavriil Romanovich (1743–1816), poet.
(von) Ditmar-Dostoevskaya, Emilia Fyodorovna (1822–1879), wife of Mikhail Fyodorovich Dostoevsky.
Dmitri Ioannovich ("False Dmitri") (dates unknown), tsar of Russia from 1605 to 1606.
Dmitri of Rostov (1651–1709), metropolitan and saint.
Donskoi, Dmitri Ivanovich (1350–1389), prince of Moscow.
Dostoevskaya, Anastasia (patronymic unknown) (1763?–1805?), grandmother of Fyodor Dostoevsky.
Dostoevskaya, Anna Grigorievna (1845–1918), second wife of Fyodor Dostoevsky.
Dostoevskaya, Ekaterina Mikhailovna (1853–1932), niece of Fyodor Dostoevsky.
Dostoevskaya, Lyubov Fyodorovna (1869–1926), daughter of Fyodor Dostoevsky.
Dostoevskaya, Maria Fyodorovna (1800–1837), mother of Fyodor Dostoevsky.
Dostoevskaya, Maria Mikhailovna (1843–1880), pianist and daughter of Andrei Mikhailovich Dostoevsky.
Dostoevskaya-Golenovskaya, Alexandra Mikhailovna (1835–1889), sister of Fyodor Dosteovsky.
Dostoevskaya-Ivanova, Vera Mikhailovna (1829–1896), sister of Fyodor Dostoevsky.
Dostoevskaya-Karepina, Varvara Mikhailovna (1822–1893), sister of Fyodor Dostoevsky.
Dostoevskaya-Savostyanova, Varvara Andreevna (1858–1935), daughter of Andrei Dostoevsky.
Dostoevsky, Alexander Andreevich (1857–1894), nephew of Fyodor Dostoevsky.
Dostoevsky, Andrei Andreevich (1863–1933), nephew of Fyodor Dostoevsky.
Dostoevsky, Andrei Grigorievich (1756–1819?), grandfather of Fyodor Dostoevsky.
Dostoevsky, Andrei Mikhailovich (1825–1897), engineer, architect, and brother of Fyodor Dostoevsky.

Dostoevsky, Fyodor Mikhailovich (1821–1881), writer.
Dostoevsky, Mikhail Andreevich (1788–1839), father of Fyodor Dostoevsky.
Dostoevsky, Mikhail Mikhailovich (1820–1864), writer, critic, journalist, translator, and brother of Fyodor Dostoevsky.
Dostoevsky, Nikolai Mikhailovich (1831–1883), brother of Fyodor Dostoevsky.
Drashusov-Sushard, Alexander Nikolaevich (1816–1890), teacher, agronomist, and son of Nikolai Drashusov-Sushard.
Drashusov-Sushard, Nikolai Ivanovich (1783–1851), teacher.
Drashusov-Sushard, Vladimir Nikolaevich (1819–1883), teacher, editor, publisher, and son of Nikolai Drashusov-Sushard.
Drashusova-Sushard, Evgenya Antonovna (1796–1874), teacher and wife of Nikolai Drashushov-Sushard.
Drozdov, Andrei (n.d.), peasant.
Dumas-père, Alexander (1802–1870), French writer.
Efimov (n.d.), peasant.
Efremov, Marko (1787–?), peasant.
Elagin, N. P. (n.d.), police chief.
Elsner, Ludwig Fyodorovich (n.d.), university lecturer.
Evstafi (n.d.), servant of Fyodor Dostoevsky.
Fet, Afanasi Afanasievich (1820–1892), poet.
Filipov, Danila (circa 1700), alleged founder of the Khlysty.
Filosova, Anna Pavlovna (1837–1912), social activist.
Fouqué, Baron (Friedrich Heinrich Karl de la Motte) (1777–1843), German writer.
Gartong, Vasili Andreevich (n.d.), translator, officer, and friend of Dostoevsky.
Godunov, Boris Fyodorovich (1551–1605), tsar of Russia from 1598 to 1605.
Goering (n.d.), teacher at Chermak's school
(von) Goethe, Johann Wolfgang (1749–1832), German writer.
Gogol, Nikolai Vasilievich (1809–1852), novelist and dramatist.
Golenishchev-Kutuzov, Mikhail Illarionovich (1745–1815), prince and general.
Golenovsky, Nikolai Ivanovich (?–1872), colonel and first husband of Alexandra Dostoevskaya.
Goncharov, Ivan Alexandrovich (1812–1891), writer.
Grabbe, Christian (1801–1836), German dramatist.
Grebenka, Evgeni Pavlovich (1812–1848), Ukrainian writer.
Grech, Nikolai Ivanovich (1787–1867), novelist and journalist.
Grigoriev, Apollon Alexandrovich (1822–1864), poet, critic, translator, memoirist, and songwriter.
Grigorovich, Dmitri Vasilievich (1822–1899), writer.
Heine, Heinrich (1797–1856), German poet, journalist, and critic.
Heine, Maximilian (1805–1879), doctor and brother of Heinrich Heine.
Herzen, Alexander Ivanovich (1812–1870), writer and thinker.
Hoffman, E.T.A. (1776–1822), German writer, composer, critic.
Holty, Ludwig (1748–1776), German poet.
Homer (circa 850 BCE?), Greek poet.
Hugo, Victor-Marie (1802–1885), French writer.
Igumnov (n.d.), clerk at the Main Engineering Academy.
Ioganson, Christian Petrovich (1817–1903), dancer.
Isaev (n.d.), peasant.

Isaeva, Akulina (n.d.), daughter of Isaev.
Isaeva, Marfa (n.d.), peasant.
Ivanov, Alexander Pavlovich (1813–1868), husband of Vera Dostoevskaya.
Ivanov, Savin (n.d.), peasant
Ivanova, Maria Alexandrovna (1848–1929), niece of Fyodor Dostoevsky.
Ivanova, Olga Alexandrovna (1863–1926), niece of Fyodor Dostoevsky.
Ivanova, Sofia Alexandrovna (1846–1907), niece of Fyodor Dostoevsky.
Joan of Arc (1412–1431), warrior and saint.
Jodelle, Étienne (1532–1573), French dramatist and poet.
Kachenovsky, Mikhail Trofimovich (1775–1842), journalist, professor, and historian.
Kachenovsky, Vladimir Mikhailovich (1826–1892), writer, memoirs, classmate of Fyodor Dostoevsky, and son of Mikhail Kachenovsky.
Kamensky, Pavel Pavlovich (1810–1870), writer.
Karamzin, Nikolai Mikhailovich (1766–1826), historian and writer.
Karatygin, Vasili Andreevich (1802–1853), actor.
Karepin, Pyotr Andreevich (1796–1850), husband of Varvara Dostoevskaya and guardian of the Dostoevsky children after the death of Mikhail Andreevich Dostoevsky.
Karr, Jean-Baptiste Alphonse (1808–1890), French critic, journalist, and novelist.
(von) Kaufman, Konstantin Petrovich (1818–1882), general.
Ketcher, Nikolai Khristoforovich (1806–1866), translator and publisher.
Khinkovsky, Ilya Vasilievich (1788?–1859), deacon, teacher, and tutor of Fyodor Dostoevsky.
Khlebnikov, Konstantin Dmitrievich (1822–1894), engineer and classmate of Fyodor Dostoevsky.
Khotyaintsev, Alexander Fyodorovich (?–1851), neighbor of Mikhail Andreevich Dostoevsky.
Khotyaintsev, Pyotr Petrovich (n.d.), neighbor of Mikhail Andreevich Dostoevsky.
Khotyaintsev, Vladimir Fyodorovich (1794–1857), collegiate assessor and relative of Pavel Khotyaintsev.
(von) Kleist, Bernd (1771–1811), German novelist, poet, dramatist, and short-story writer.
Klopstock, Freidrich (1724–1803), German poet.
Köhler, Ioann-Melchior (1806–1864), financial broker.
Köhler, Louis (1820–1886), German composer, conductor, piano teacher, and brother of Ioann Köhler.
Koni, Fyodor Alexeevich (1809–1879), publisher and dramatist.
Kotelnitsky, Vasili Mikhailovich (1769–1844), doctor, professor, state councillor, dean, and great-uncle of Fyodor Dostoevsky.
Kostomarov, Koronad Filippovich (1804–1873), engineer, captain, and teacher of Fyodor Dostoevsky.
Kovalevskaya, Sofia Vasilievna (1850–1891), mathematician, dramatist, prose-writer, and memoirist.
Kraevsky, Andrei Alexandrovich (1810–1889), publicist, journalist, editor, and public figure.
Krivopishin, Ivan Grigorievich (1796–1867), general-lieutenant and vice-director of the Department of Inspection for the Russian Ministry of War.
Krylov, Ivan Andreevich (1769–1844), fabulist.
Kryukova, Alyona (Elena) Frolovna (1780?–1850)?, childhood nurse of Fyodor Dostoevsky.
Kubaryov, Alexei Mikhailovich (1796–1881), specialist in Latin literature.
Kukolnik, Nikolai Vasilievich (1809–1868), writer, poet, and musician.
Kumanin, Alexander Alexeevich (1792–1863), uncle of Fyodor Dostoevsky.
Kumanina, Alexandra Fyodorovna (1796–1871), aunt of Fyodor Dostoevsky.

DIRECTORY OF PROMINENT NAMES   231

Kvitka-Osnovyanenko, Hryhory (1778–1843), Ukrainian writer, journalist, and playwright.
Lagvenova, Alexandra Dmitrievna (n.d.), alleged fiancé of Mikhail Andreevich Dostoevsky.
(de) Lamartine, Alphonse (1790–1869), French writer, poet, and politician.
Lavrentieva, Agrafena Timofeevna (1810–?), peasant.
Lazhechnikov, Ivan Ivanovich (1790?–1869), writer.
Ledru-Rollin, Alexandre (1807–1874), French politician.
Leibrecht, A. I. (n.d.), neighbor of Mikhail Andreevich Dostoevsky.
Lenau, Nikolaus (1802–1850), German poet.
Lenin, Vladimir Ilyich (1870–1924), revolutionary, theorist, and politician
Lenz, Jakob (1751–1792), German writer.
Leontiev, Konstantin Nikolaevich (1831–1891), philosopher.
Lermontov, Mikhail Yurevich (1814–1841), writer and poet.
Lesage, Alain-René (1688–1747), French novelist.
Leskov, Nikolai Semyonovich (1831–1895), novelist, journalist, and short-story writer.
Lessing, Gotthold (1729–1781), German writer, philosopher, dramatist, publicist, and art critic.
Lessmann, Daniel (1794–1831), German writer.
Livy (59 BCE–17 CE), Roman historian.
Lizst, Franz (1811–1886), Hungarian composer, pianist, and teacher.
Lomonosov, Mikhail Vasilievich (1711–1765), writer.
Lugansky. See Dal.
Lukeria (n.d.), peasant.
Maikov, Apollon Nikolaevich (1821–1897), poet.
Maikov, Valerian Nikolaevich (1823–1847), critic and brother of Apollon Maikov.
Makarov, Danila Savinovich (1841 to after 1925), peasant.
Makarov, Kharlam (1797–?), peasant.
Makarov, Savin (from 1790 to after 1877), village elder.
(de) Malherbe, Francois (1855–1628), French poet, critic, and translator.
Marcus, Fyodor Antonovich (n.d.), brother of Mikhail Marcus and neighbor of Fyodor Dostoevsky.
Marcus, Mikhail Antonovich (1790–1895), doctor.
Maria Fyodorovna (1758–1828), empress and second wife of Paul I.
Marlinsky. See Bestuzhev-Marlinsky.
Marryat, Frederick (1792–1848), English novelist.
Masalsky, Konstantin Petrovich (1802–1861), writer.
Maturin, Charles Robert (1782–1824), Irish novelist and playwright.
Melikhov, Ivan Vasilievich (1856–?), peasant.
(von) Metternich, Klemens (1773–1859), Austrian politician and statesman.
Mezhevich, Vasili Stepanovich (1813–1849), writer and journalist.
Mickiewicz, Adam (1798–1855), Polish poet, playwright, writer, and activist.
Mikhailov, Alexei (n.d.), peasant.
Mikhail Fyodorovich (1596–1645), tsar of Russia from 1613 to 1645.
Mikhail Pavlovich (1789–1849), grand duke and brother of Nicholas I.
Miller, Orest Fyodorovich (1833–1889), folklorist, professor of Russian literature, and Fyodor Dostoevsky's first biographer.
Mironov, Andrei (1792–?), peasant.
Molière (1673), French playwright and actor.

(de) Montesquieu, Charles-Louis (1689–1755), French commentator and thinker.
Montigny, Joseph-Nicholas (1792–1845), Belgian engineer.
Mozart, Wolfgang Amadeus (1756–1791), Austrian composer.
Narezhny, Vasili Trofimovich (1780–1825), writer.
Nechaev, Fyodor Timofeevich (1769–1832), merchant and grandfather of Fyodor Dostoevsky.
Nechaev, Mikhail Fyodorovich (1801–1838), uncle of Fyodor Dostoevsky.
Nechaeva, Olga Yakovlevna (1794–1870), grandmother of Fyodor Dostoevsky.
Nekrasov, Nikolai Alexeevich (1821–1878), poet, writer, critic, and publisher.
Nicholas I (1796–1855), emperor of Russia from 1825 to 1855.
Nikitenko, Alexander Vasilievich (1805–1877), professor and censor.
Nikitin, Vasili (n.d.), peasant.
Obodovsky, Platon Grigorievich (1805–1864), translator.
Odoevsky, Vladimir Fyodorovich (1803–1869), philosopher, writer, critic, and philanthropist.
Orlova-Chesmenskaya, Anna Alexeevna (1785–1848), princess and philanthropist.
Ostrogradsky, Mikhail Vasilievich (1801–1862), Ukrainian mathematician and physicist.
Owen, Robert (1771–1858), Welsh reformer and socialist.
Ozerov, Vladimir Alexandrovich (1769–1816), dramatist.
Ozmidov, Nikolai Lukich (1844–1908), professor.
Panaev, Ivan Ivanovich (1812–1862), writer and journalist.
Panaev, Valerian Alexandrovich (1824–1899), writer.
Panaeva, Avdotya Yakovlevna (1819–1893), writer and wife of Ivan Panaev.
Pascal, Blaise (1623–1662), French mathematician, physicist, and philosopher.
Patton, Oscar Petrovich (1823–1869?), translator and friend of Fyodor Dostoevsky.
Paul I (1754–1801), emperor of Russia from 1796 to 1801.
Perevoshikov, Dmitri Matveeevich (1788–1880), professor and scientist.
Perlov, Ivan (n.d.), peasant.
Perrault, Charles (1628–1703), French writer.
Pesotsky, Ivan Petrovich (?–1849), editor.
Peter I (the Great) (1672–1725), tsar of Russia from 1682 to 1725.
Petipa, Jean-Antoine (1787–1855), French-Russian ballet dancer and father of Maurius Petipa.
Petipa, Marius Ivanovich (1818–1910), French teacher, choreographer, and ballet dancer.
Petrarch, Francesco (1304–1374), Italian scholar, poet, and humanist.
Petrov, Fedot (n.d.), peasant.
Photius the Great (810?–893?) saint and patriarch of Constantinople.
Pirandello, Luigi (1867–1936), Italian dramatist, novelist, poet, and short-story writer.
Pisemsky, Alexei Feofilaktovich (1821–1881), novelist and dramatist.
Plaksin, Vasili Timofeevich (1796–1869), critic and teacher at the Main Engineering Academy.
Plekhanov, Georgi Valentinovich (1857–1918), Russian revolutionary and Marxist theoretician.
Polevoi, Ksefont Alexeevich (1801–1867), biographer and brother of Nikolai Polevoi.
Polevoi, Nikolai Alexeevich (1796–1846), editor, writer, and historian.
Polonsky, Yakov Petrovich (1819–1898), poet.
Pushkin, Alexander Sergeevich (1799–1837), writer.
Pushkina, Natalia Nikolaevna (1812–1863), wife of Alexander Pushkin.
(de) Quincey, Thomas (1785–1859), English author and intellectual.
Racine, Jean (1639–1699), French dramatist.
Radcliffe, Anne (1764–1823), English writer.

DIRECTORY OF PROMINENT NAMES 233

Radetsky, Fyodor Fyodorovich (1820–1890), general.
Radonezhsky, Sergei (1314?–1392), spiritual leader and saint.
Raphael (1483–1530), Italian painter.
Rasputin, Grigori Yefimovich (1869–1916), monk and intriguer.
Ratkova-Rozhnova, Zinaida Vladimirovna (1870–1966), daughter of Anna Filosova.
Renan, Ernest (1823–1892), French philosopher and writer.
Reshetov, Nikolai (n.d.), writer, landowner, and teacher.
Rizenkampf, Alexander Egorovich (1821–1895), doctor and friend of Fyodor Dostoevsky.
Rochefort, Edmond (1790–1871), French writer, dramatist, and songwriter.
(de) Ronsard, Pierre (1524–1585), French poet.
Rossini, Gioachino (1792–1868), Italian composer.
Rubini, Giovanni (1794–1854), Italian tenor.
Sand, George (1804–1876), French writer.
Saltykov-Shchedrin, Mikhail Evgrafovich (1826–1889), writer.
Saveliev, David (?–after 1856), coachman.
Savushkin, Andrei (n.d.), peasant.
Schelling, Freidrich (1755–1854), philosopher.
(von) Schiller, Johann (1759–1805), German writer and poet.
Schlegel, August Wilhelm (1767–1845), German poet, translator, and critic.
Schonknecht (n.d.), doctor.
Schronrock, I. M (n.d.), doctor.
Scott, Walter (1771–1832), English novelist.
Sechyonov, Ivan Mikhailov (1829–1905), physiologist.
Semyonov-Tyan-Shansky, Pyotr Pyotrovich (1823–1904), writer, translator, explorer, geographer, and natural scientist.
Seneca (the Younger), Lucius Annaeus (4 BCE–65 CE), Roman philosopher, statesman, dramatist, and humorist.
Senkovsky, Osip Ivanovich (1800–1858), writer, critic, editor, scholar, and publisher.
Shakespeare, William (1564–1616), English dramatist.
Shaw, George Bernard (1856–1950), Irish playwright and critic.
Sheller-Mikhailov, Alexander Konstantinovich (1838–1900), writer, poet, and critic.
Sherwood, John (1796–1867), government official.
Shevyakov, Vladimir Vasilievich (?–1889), bureaucrat and second husband of Alexandra Golenovskaya-Dostoevskaya.
Shevyryov, Stepan Petrovich (1806–1864), literary historian, critic, and poet.
Shidlovskaya, L. (n.d.), sister-in-law of Ivan Shidlovsky.
Shidlovsky, Ivan Nikolaevich (1816–1872), friend of Fyodor Dostoevsky.
Shirokov, Ivan Semyonovich (n.d.), peasant.
Shlefakht, Olga Timofeevna (1822–1845), dancer.
Smirnova, Tatyana Petrovna (1821–1871), dancer.
Sokolov, Pavel Petrovich (1826–1905), illustrator.
Sollogub, Vladimir Alexandrovich (1813–1882), writer.
Soloviev, Vladimir Sergeevich (1853–1900), philosopher, writer, poet, and teacher.
Soloviev, Vsevelod Sergeevich (1849–1903), writer, memoirist, and brother of Vladimir Soloviev.
Soulié, Frédéric (1800–1847), French novelist and playwright.

Spassky, Peter Nikitich (1792–1838), archimandrite.
Spiridonova, Avdotya (n.d.), peasant.
Stasyulevich, Mikhail Matveevich (1826–1911), historian, journalist, publisher, and social figure.
Sterne, Laurence (1713–1768), Irish novelist.
Strakhov, Nikolai Nikolaevich (1828–1896), critic, philosopher, and publicist.
Stravinsky, Igor Fyodorovich (1882–1971), composer.
Strugovshchikov, Alexander Nikolaevich (1808–1878), poet and translator.
Stuart, Mary (1542–1587), Scottish queen from 1542 to 1587.
Sue, Eugène (1804–1857), French novelist.
Suvorin, Alexei Sergeevich (1834–1912), journalist and dramatist.
Taglioni, Maria (1804–1884), Italian-Swedish ballerina.
Tasso, Torquato (1544–1595), Italian poet.
Tatarinova, Ekaterina Filipovna (1783–1856), spiritual leader.
Thackeray, William (1811–1863), English writer.
Timofeev, Alexei Vasilievich (1812–1883), poet and prose writer.
Totleben, Adolf-Gustav Ivanovich (1824–1869), count and friend of Fyodor Dostoevsky.
Totleben, Eduard Ivanovich (1818–1884), engineer, general, and brother of Adolf Totleben.
Tolstoy, Lev (Leo) Nikolaevich (1828–1910), writer.
Tredyakovsky, Vasili Kirillovich (1703–1768), poet.
Trubetskaya, Zinaida Alexandrovna (1908–1973), princess and granddaughter of Anna Filosova.
Trutovsky, Konstantin Alexandrovich (1826–1893), painter and friend of Fyodor Dostoevsky.
Turgenev, Alexander Ivanovich (1784–1846), statesman and historian.
Turgenev, Ivan Sergeevich (1818–1883), writer.
Turunov, Mikhail Nikolaevich (1813–1890), teacher at the Main Engineering Academy.
Vasiliev, Grigori (1787–?), servant of the Dostoevsky family.
Vasilisa (n.d.), servant of the Dostoevsky family.
Vasnetsov, Viktor Mikhailovich (1824–1896), painter.
Veltman, Alexander Fomich (1800–1870), writer.
Vernet, Horace (1789–1863), French painter.
Viardot, Pauline (1821–1910), French mezza-soprano, pedagogue, and composer.
Vigel, Filipp Filippovich (1786–1856), memoirist.
Vitkovsky, Nikolai Ivanovich (1820?–1892), archeologist and classmate of Fyodor Dostoevsky.
Vizard, Yakov Ivanovich (1796–1854), teacher.
Voekov, Alexander Fyodorovich (1778–1839), poet.
Voltaire (1694–1778), French philosopher and writer.
Voronikhin, Nikoforovich (1759–1814), architect and painter.
Vrangel, Alexander Yegorovich (1833–1912?), count, diplomat, lawyer, and archeologist.
Vyazemsky, Pyotr Andreevich (1792–1878), poet.
(von) Wallenstein, Albrecht (1583–1634), Bohemian general and politician.
Wollstonecraft, Mary (1759–1797), English writer, philosopher, and advocate of women's rights.
Yanovsky, Stepan Dmitrievich (1815–1887), doctor.
Yershov, Pyotr Pavlovich (1815–1869), poet.
Zagoskin, Mikhail Nikolaevich (1789–1852), writer.
Zhdan-Pushkin, Ivan Vikentevich (1813–1872), mayor and general.
Zhemchuzhnikov, Lev Mikhailovich (1828–1912), artist.

Zhukovsky, Vasili Andreevich (1793–1816), poet.
Zotov, Vladimir Rafailovich (1821–1896), critic, dramatist, poet, and prose writer.
Zschokke, Johann (1771–1848), German writer and reformer.
Zubov, Nikolai Alexandrovich, statesman and brother of Platon Zubov
Zubov, Platon Alexandrovich (1767–1822), statesman.

Notes

Preface

1. See T. Marullo, *Ivan Bunin: Russian Requiem, 1885–1920*; *Ivan Bunin: From the Other Shore, 1920–1933*; and *Ivan Bunin: Twilight of Emigré Russia, 1934–1953*, published by Ivan R. Dee Press in 1993, 1995, and 2002, respectively. Also see T. G. Marullo, *Cursed Days: Ivan Bunin*, published by Dee in 1998.
2. T. G. Marullo, *Ivan Bunin: The Liberation of Tolstoy* (Evanston: Northwestern University Press, 2001).
3. T. G. Marullo, *Ivan Bunin: Anton Chekhov: An Unfinished Symphony* (Evanston: Northwestern University Press, 2007).
4. T. G. Marullo, *Petersburg: The Physiology of a City* (Evanston: Northwestern University Press, 2009).

Introduction

1. Nowhere in these years is there any evidence for Konstantin Mochulsky's claim that the domestic life of the young Dostoevsky "conforms completely to the designation of a 'haphazard household'"; and that "in his father's house, under the respected forms of a strictly ordered existence, the boy began to detect falsehood and insecurity." See K. Mochulsky, *Dostoevsky: His Life and Work*, translated by Michael Minihan (Princeton: Princeton University Press, 1967), 7–8.
2. Mikhail Dostoevsky, a year old than Fyodor, became a publisher, critic, and short-story writer. Andrei Dostoevsky, four years younger than his illustrious brother, was an architect, engineer, restorer of buildings, memoirist, and father of the renowned histologist Alexander Dostoevsky. Nikolai, ten years younger, was also an engineer.

Varvara married Pyotr Karepin, a successful bureaucrat. Vera wedded Alexander Ivanov, who was a doctor, state councilor, and a teacher of physics and the natural sciences. Alexandra was espoused twice, to Nikolai Golenovsky, a colonel and military inspector, and to Vladimir Shevyakov, a bureaucrat.

3. See Mochulsky, *Dostoevsky*, 11.

Part One: All in the Family

1. Mochusky writes: "A man of extremely difficult temperament, sullen, contentious, suspicious, the elder Dostoevsky . . . was a fusion of cruelty and sensibility, piety and avarice." See Mochulsky, *Dostoevsky*, 3.
2. Frank, *Dostoevsky: The Seeds of Revolt*, 83.
3. Open to question is the claim by Frank that "the astonishing conviction that he was one of God's elect, this unshakable self-assurance that he was among the chosen, constituted the very core of

Dr. Dostoevsky's being ... [and] made him so self-righteous and pharisaical, so intolerant of the smallest fault, so persuaded that only perfect obedience from his family to all his wishes could compensate for all his toil and labor on their behalf." See Frank, *Dostoevsky: The Seeds of Revolt*, 17.

4. Frank, *Dostoevsky: The Seeds of Revolt*, 90.

5. Ibid., 85.

6. Ibid., 87 and 88.

7. Also lacking evidence is Mochulsky's assertion that Dostoevsky's "imagination was deeply shaken not only by the dramatic circumstances of the old man's death, but also by a feeling of guilt before Mikhail Andreevich. He did not love him; he used to complain about his stinginess; shortly before his death he had written him an irritating letter; and now he felt himself to a degree responsible for his death."

Even more unfounded is Mochulsky's avowal that the "problems of fathers and children, of crime and punishment, of guilt and responsibility met Dostoevsky at the very threshold of his life. This was a psychological and moral trauma to his being." See Mochulsky, *Dostoevsky*, 7.

8. The memoirs of Andrei Dostoevsky are the only reliable source of the writer's early years.

9. Dostoevsky's grandfather, Andrei Grigorievich Dostoevsky, was a Uniate priest in Bratislava in present-day Slovakia; thus, he celebrated the rites of Orthodoxy but also accepted the authority of the pope. Since the nonmonastic clergy in Russia was a caste, rather than a calling, Mikhail Andreevich Dostoevsky was expected to follow in the footsteps of his father.

10. Having left the seminary in Kamenets-Podolsk (in western Ukraine, roughly seven hundred miles southwest of Moscow), Mikhail Dostoevsky came to Moscow in 1802 and entered the Moscow Imperial Medical-Surgical Academy on October 15, 1809. He was twenty-one years old.

11. There are two Mikhail Dostoevskys in the text: Mikhail Andreevich Dostoevsky (Fyodor's father), and his son Mikhail Mikhailovich Dostoevsky (Fyodor's brother). Until the time of Mikhail Andreevich's death in 1839, they appear in the text as Mikhail Dostoevsyky *père* and Mikhail Dostoevsky *fils*, respectively.

12. Anastasia Dostoevskaya is thought to have died in 1805; Andrei Dostoevsky in 1819. The family was indeed at the bottom of the social scale. As already noted, Andrei was a humble priest. One son was also a cleric. Of Andrei's six daughters, three married provincial clergy, and three wed Ukrainian minor officials for the state.

13. Dostoevskaya is referring to the French invasion of Russia (also known as the Patriotic War of 1812 and the First Fatherland War) on June 24, 1812.

14. On March 15, 1813, Maria's sister, Alexandra, married Alexander Kumanin, a wealthy Muscovite merchant. Although the two had furnished Mikhail Dostoevsky with contacts to build his medical practice (and possibly to secure his appointment at the Mariinsky Hospital), they were the objects of his envy at their vaunted wealth and his scorn for what Mikhail saw as their lack of culture and sophistication.

Alexander Kumanin visited the Dostoevskys regularly until a quarrel with Mikhail ended such encounters. Allegedly, the two men reconciled at the deathbed of their father-in-law, but Alexander no longer visited the family when Mikhail was at home. Alexandra, though, continued as godmother to all of the Dostoevsky children.

15. Fyodor was baptized five days later at the hospital chapel of Saints Peter and Paul. Most likely he was named after his maternal grandfather, Fyodor Nechaev, who was also his godfather. (A statue of the writer now graces the Mariinsky Hospital where he was born.)

16. Beginning in the sixteenth century, the Dostoevskys are mentioned in various documents in southwestern Russia. Over time, the family lived in lands claimed by Lithuania, Belarus, Poland, Russia, and Ukraine.

17. As will be seen, David Saveliev is a key figure in stories of the alleged murder of Dostoevsky's father.

18. Alyona Frolovna entered service into the Dostoevsky family in December 1822.

19. Like many languages, Russian has a formal "you" (*vy*), and an informal "you" (*ty*).

20. In Russia, doves were revered as symbols of the Holy Spirit and, according to tradition, the populace was forbidden kill them.

Various legends about doves were also popular in Russia. One was that doves sought to relieve the sufferings of the crucified Christ. A second was that doves, as bearers of good news, avoided unkind people. A third was that doves were angels and/or the souls of dead relatives who had been loved greatly in life. A fourth was that the devil, wizards, and witches assumed the form of any bird but a dove.

It was also a folk belief that people who ate doves during times of hunger or war gave birth to children who became drug users and alcoholics.

21. In Slavic folklore, the Firebird is a magical bird with glowing red, orange, and yellow plumage, like a bonfire just past its peak. Typically the Firebird is an object of capture by a young man, who secures his prize with the help of magical helpers and other good people.

Alyosha Popovich (literally, son of a priest) is the youngest of the three *bogatyri* or "wandering knights-errant" who, together with Dobrynya Nikitich and Ilya Muromets, appear in Russian *byliny* or "oral epics." (The three can be seen in Victor Vasnetsov's famous 1898 painting, *Bogatyrs*). Fun-loving, agile, and sly, Alyosha outsmarts his foes with cunning and trickery. He is also known as a liar, a cheat, and a "mocker of woman."

Bluebeard is the 1697 French tale written by Charles Perrault in his *Stories or Fairytales from Bygone Eras: The Tales of Mother Goose*. It concerns a nobleman who murders his wives and the attempt of one spouse to avoid such a fate. The work also included such stories as "Sleeping Beauty," "Little Red Riding Hood," "Cinderella," and "The Master Cat, or Puss in Boots."

22. *One Thousand and One Nights* is a compendium of folk tales collected over many centuries by various authors, translators, and scholars from the Middle East and North Africa. Common to all editions of *The Nights* is the ruler Shahryar, his wife Scheherazade, and a framing device in which stories proceed from an original tale.

Some of the best-known stories in *The Nights* are "Aladdin's Wonderful Lamp," "Ali-Baba and the Forty Thieves," and "The Seven Voyages of Sinbad the Sailor."

23. Vasili Kotelnitsky, the brother of Dostoevsky's maternal grandmother, was both professor of medical toxicology, or pharmacology as it was known at that time, and dean of the medical school at Moscow University. Kotelnitsky was also a member of the Society of the History of Russian Antiquities at Moscow University, which was founded in 1804 and which, from 1849 to 1901, published primary and secondary materials on Russian history.

24. *Balagany* were temporary, unheated, and highly flammable wooden theaters erected for the Russian carnivals of Shrovetide and Easter week. Accommodating as many as fifteen hundred spectators, *balagany* typically featured lavish productions constructed on three or four raised platforms with scores of participants, with interludes of single scenes with several characters.

25. Petrushka is stock character of Russian folk puppetry, a jester distinguished by a red dress and hat and often a long nose, made famous by Igor Stravinsky's 1911 ballet of the same name. (Compare English Punch, Italian Pulcinella, and French Polichinelle.)

26. The Troitsky-Sergiev Lavra Monastery, located about forty miles northeast of Moscow, was founded in the mid-fourteenth century by Sergei Radonezhsky, one of the most honored Russian saints.

The Troitsky-Sergiev Lavra was seminal to the unification of Russia. According to legend, it was there that Sergei blessed Dmitri Donskoi, the grand duke of Moscow, for the battle against the

Mongols at Kulikovo in 1380. Strategically, the Troitsky-Sergiev Lavra protected Moscow in the north. It was also where national books and chronicles were written and preserved.

Today the Troitsky-Sergiev Lavra is one of Russia's most hallowed sites and also one of four Russian Orthodox complexes to be called a "Lavra"—a monastery under the direct aegis of the Russian Patriarch. One of its treasures is the Troitsky Sobor (Trinity Cathedral), built in 1422–1423. The Troitsky-Sergiev Lavra was also home to Andrei Rublyov, one of Russia's greatest icon painters.

27. Mikhail, almost exactly a year older than Fyodor, was born on October 25, 1820.

28. The French two-act melodrama *Jocko, or the Brazilian Monkey*, was written by Edmond Rochefort in 1825. In it a rich Portuguese man traveling to Brazil captures a monkey, which, during a crossing on the Atlantic, saves the man's child from shipwreck but perishes in the process. (In later productions, the public demanded that the monkey survive).

The play also gave rise to a ballet of the same name, one rendition of which was staged by Jean-Antoine-Nicolas Petipa (the father of the famous teacher, choreographer, and ballet dancer, Maurius Petipa). *Jocko* is also seen as the precursor for the humanized monkeys in *King Kong* and *Planet of the Apes*.

The seven-year-old Dostoevsky saw *Jocko* in Moscow on February 1, 1828.

29. The reference is to a legend by the Roman historian Livy, in which the sacred geese of the Temple of Juno clapped their wings to alert the Romans to an attack by the Gauls in 390 BCE. Mikhail Dostoevsky might also be referring to Krylov's 1811 story about the same, titled "Geese."

30. Ann Radcliffe's *The Mysteries of Udolpho*, published in four volumes in 1794, was a parental favorite.

31. Don Pedro is a character in William Shakespeare's 1660 play *Much Ado About Nothing*; and Dona Clara, in Miguel Cervantes's 1605 novel, *Don Quixote*.

32. Such advice was in vain. Mikhail Nechaev died at age thirty-seven in December 1839.

33. *The Monthly Readings* or *Menologian* was the ambitious project of Saint Dmitri of Rostov, who, from 1684 to 1705, integrated all the lives of Russian saints into a single work. Until the twentieth century, *The Monthly Readings* was the main source from which Russians learned about the holy men and women among them.

34. More accurately, the book in question is Joseph Hubner's *Four Hundred Sacred Stories, Chosen from the Old and New Testament for the Benefit of Youth with Noble Reflections*, which was published throughout the last three decades of the eighteenth century.

Four Hundred Stories, which children were supposed to learn by heart, contained many Bible stories that later played a role in Dostoevsky's major works, such as the fall of Adam and Eve, the trials of Job, and the raising of Lazarus.

35. Dostoevsky is referring to Nikolai Karamzin's *History of the Russian State*, which was published in twelve volumes from 1816 to 1829, and which was the first work to disinter the Russian past from monkish chronicles and poetic legend. Most likely, the family was reading either the third or fourth edition of the work, published in 1830–1831 and 1833–1834.

36. Vladimir Kachenovsky was the son of Mikhail Kachenovsky, a chaired professor of Russian history at the University of Moscow, who gave birth to the so-called skeptical school of imperial historiography—he claimed that the Russian Primary Chronicles was a falsification from Mongol times, and that ancient Russians "lived like mice or birds . . . without money or books."

37. Dostoevsky wrote *Devils* in 1872. Trubetskaya's claim has been challenged by one Vitali Svintsov, who asserts that the above passage is a memory-within-a-memory—that is, what Trubetskaya recalled to the Dostoevsky scholar Sergei Belov, regarding Filosova's recollection. Svinstov also notes that Dostoevsky never mentioned the incident again.

Belov also notes that Trubetskaya was still a very young girl when her grandmother died, and that, conceivably, the story was a family legend preserved by Trubetkskaya's mother, Zinaida Ratkova-Rozhnova.

Adding to the doubts of Svintsov and Belov is Dostoevsky's claim that he used such an event to put an end to Stavrogin in his famed novel.

See V. Svinstov, "Dostoevskii i otnosheniia mezhdu polami," *Novyi mir* 5 (1999), 197–200; and S. Belov, "Z. A. Trubetskaia," in Belov, *F. M. Dostoevskii*, 23–24.

38. Friedrich Schiller's *The Robbers* premiered in 1782.

39. Restoration of noble status allowed Mikhail Dostoevsky to own property with serfs. In summer 1831 Mikhail Dostoevsky bought the estate of Darovoe from one Alexander Khotyaintsev. The purchase was in Maria's name, most likely because the funds for the sale came from her family. (At that time, Mikhail's salary at the hospital was between six hundred and a thousand rubles yearly—accounts differ—supplemented by equally modest sums from his private practice.)

The village of Darovoe included between 300 and 1,300 acres of land (accounts again vary) and 40 male serfs with their wives and children (for a total of 95 serfs and 9 household servants). All was not peaceful at Darovoe. A key difficulty was quarrels between Mikhail and a neighbor, Pyotr Petrovich Khotyaintsev, a cousin of Alexander's, who was also a retired decorated major, a veteran of the Russian campaign against Napoleon, and a much wealthier landowner with 500 serfs.

One problem was the lack of formal boundaries between the properties of the two men. Strips of Pyotr's village, Monogarovo, encroached on Mikhail's domain; six houses occupied by Alexander's serfs actually stood on Darovoe. A second problem was a threat by Alexander to keep Mikhail in line by purchasing the village of Cheremoshnya, located three miles from Darovoe with approximately 200 acres, 74 serfs, and 5 house serfs. In response, Mikhail went heavily into debt to buy Cheremoshnya for 12,000 silver rubles in winter 1833. (In the 1930s, Darovoe became a collective farm named after Dostoevsky.)

Mikhail and Alexander's dispute over the lines between Darovoe and Monogarovo dragged on in the courts for some fifteen years. (The suit was initiated by Maria in April 1832; it was settled only in 1847, eight years after Mikhail's death.) According to Andrei Dostoevsky, though, relations between Mikhail and Alexander were often cordial and even included frequent visits between the two families. Trouble with Pyotr, though, would flare up again with Mikhail's passing in 1839 (see below).

40. Marey actually was named Marko Efremov.

41. In truth, Dostoevsky was eleven years old at the time.

42. The fire had occurred five days earlier, on April 7.

43. The family did not take the money.

44. In truth, the mud-walled house of the Dostoevskys survived the blaze. Arkhip perished in the disaster; his daughter, Arisha, was taken in by Maria as a house servant.

45. This was the first time Fyodor Dostoevsky traveled to Darovoe.

46. Fyodor and Mikhail spent four months with their mother at Darovoe annually for the next four years. After they entered school, the two came to the village only for July and August. (Like the annex at the Mariinsky Hospital in Moscow, the place is now a museum.)

47. Mikhail and Maria Dostoevsky had agreed that she would spend six months at Darovoe, managing the estate. The journey of roughly one hundred miles, always preceded by a religious service and a priestly blessing, took two days to complete.

48. The visits to Darovoe remained with Dostoevsky throughout his life. In *A Writer's Diary*, he wrote in July 1877: "I happened to mention to an acquaintance [in Moscow] . . . that I wanted to make a small detour of some hundred miles to visit a place of my childhood and youth—the village that had once belonged to my parents, but that long ago had become the property of another member

of the family. I had not been there for forty years and had wanted to see it so many times but had not been able to do so, despite the fact that this little, unremarkable spot had left a most deep and profound impression on my entire life and that everything there was filled with the most cherished memories." See Dostoevskii, *Dnevnik pisatelia za 1877 god*, 271.

Immediately thereafter, Anna Dostoevskaya recalled, of her husband's visit: "In recent years Fyodor Mikhailovich has often expressed regret that he has not been able to visit Darovoe, the estate of his late mother, where he spent his summers as a child.

"Since he was feeling quite well that summer, I persuaded him . . . to make the trip there. So he did, and stayed two days with his sister Vera [who had inherited the estate].

"Later his family told me that during his stay, my husband visited the various places in the park and outskirts dear to his memory. He even walked to the grove he had loved as a child. . . . He also went to visit the huts of the peasants he had known as a boy, many of whom he still remembered. The old men and women and also those of his own age . . . were very happy to see him, invited him into their homes, and treated him to tea.

"The trip to Darovoe gave rise to many memories, which, after his return home, my husband recounted to us with great enthusiasm. Without fail, he promised to take the children to Darovoe and to show them all his favorite spots in the park.

"[In 1884, three years after Dostoevsky's death] I fulfilled his wish and took the children to the places . . . where he had spent his childhood . . . with his family, pointing out everywhere my husband had walked for the last time." See Dostoevskaia, *Vospominaniia* (1971), 313–314.

49. Daniel Defoe wrote *The Life and Strange Surprising Adventures of Robinson Crusoe* in 1719.

50. For such shenanigans, the two boys received a severe scolding from their mother.

51. Dostoevsky wrote *The Brothers Karamazov* between 1878 and 1880. Again, Dostoevsky is not alone in such a claim. "The idiot Agrafena," Mochulsky writes, "this is an indirect confirmation of the bond between Fyodor Pavlovich Karamazov and Dostoevsky's father." See Mochulsky, *Dostoevsky*, 8.

52. At Darovoe, Maria Dostoevskaya had installed a huge pond in the dried-up river bed behind Bryukovo, from which she banned the peasants by having the local priest circle the place with icons and holy banners, the idea being to impose a curse on would-be poachers of the fish Maria had stocked there.

53. Located some twenty miles from Darovoe, Zaraisk was founded in the thirteenth century as one of the fortresses of the Great Abatis Border, a line of ditches, felled trees, and barricades intended to protect Russians from Tartars in both Kazan and the Crimea. The six-towered stone kremlin in Zaraisk, allegedly the smallest in Russia, was built in 1531 and exists to this day.

54. Most likely, Maria is referring to the ruined estate at Darovoe.

55. This is the first known letter of Fyodor Dostoevsky.

56. The first tutor was Ilya Khinkovsky, who taught theology, mathematics, and Russian language and literature at the Catherine Institute in Moscow (a fashionable school for daughters of the aristocracy); the second was Nikolai Drashusov-Sushard, a teacher at both the Alexander and Catherine Institutes, who taught French to the Dostoevsky brothers and who, within the year, accepted both Mikhail and Fyodor into his school.

57. Andrei has in mind Metropolitan Filaret's *An Outline of Church-Biblical History for the Benefit of Spiritual Youth*, which was first published in St. Petersburg in 1816 and was reprinted numerous times throughout the nineteenth century.

58. Russians celebrate their "name day" (also knows as "Angel day")—the feast day of the saint after whom they were named. Typically, such a celebration begins with divine services followed by a festive party. Before the Revolution, name days were considered as important as birthdays, if not more so.

59. Voltaire published *The Henriade*, an epic poem on religious fanaticism and civic discord in later sixteenth-century France, in 1723.

60. As will be seen, Dostoevskaya's claim is as outrageous as it is untrue.

61. Indeed, the sacrifice was considerable. Since tuition at [Drashusov]-Sushard's school was literally twice what Mikhail made as a doctor at the Mariinsky Hospital, he struggled to make up the difference with his private practice.

62. Both Yakov and Sergei Barshev were professors of criminal law at Moscow University.

63. Scott published both *The Edinburgh Dungeon* (also known as *The Heart of Midlothian*) and *Rob Roy* in 1818.

64. Charles Dickens wrote *Oliver Twist* in 1838; *Nicholas Nickleby* in 1838–1839; and *The Old Curiosity Stop* in 1840–1841.

65. Mikhail Dostoevsky was forty-five years old at the time.

66. Most likely, Mikhail's children.

67. The person in question is the peasant Kharlam Makarov, who is conceivably the grandfather or a relative of Danila Makarov, who will report later on the events surrounding the death of Mikhail Dostoevsky.

68. Dostoevsky is referring to his then two-year-old brother, Nikolai.

69. Andrei Dostoevsky is referring to the False Dmitri (also know as Dmitri Ioannovich), who was tsar of Russia from 1605–1606, and one of the three imposters to the Russian throne during the Time of Troubles, a period of interregnum from the death of Ivan the Terrible in 1584 to the accession to the throne of Mikhail Romanov in 1613.

70. Ksefont Polevoi published his two-volume work on Lomonosov in 1836.

71. Gavrila Derzhavin's poem "God" appeared in 1794.

72. Karamzin wrote *Poor Liza* in 1792; *Letters of a Russian Pilgrim* between 1792 and 1801; and *Marfa, the Boyar's Daughter* in 1803.

73. Mikhail Zagoskin wrote *Yury Miloslavsky, or the Russians in 1612* in 1829. Konstantin Masalsky published *Streltsy* in 1832. (*Streltsy*, or "Shooters," were Muscovite infantrymen in the sixteenth and seventeenth centuries); and in that same year, Dmitry Begichev penned *The Khomsky Family: Particular Mores and the Way of Life, Family and Personal, of the Russian Nobility*. Ivan Lazhechnikov's *The Ice House* appeared in 1835.

74. Vasili Narezhnyi wrote *The Seminarian* in 1825.

75. Alexander Veltman's *Heart and Pillow: Adventures; A Novel in Four Parts* appeared in 1838.

76. Vasili Zhukovsky's "The Count from Hapsburg," written in 1818, was a translation of Schiller's 1798 ballad of the same name.

77. More accurately, Pushkin wrote "The Song of the Prophetic Oleg," in 1822.

78. It was a German teacher at Chermak's school, an individual by the name of Goering, who, in his blind admiration of Pushkin, influenced Dostoevsky's own love for the writer. With tremendous enthusiasm (and an equally atrocious German accent), Goering recited Pushkin's poems for his students. He also kept them spellbound with stories of a personal meeting with the famed poet, as well as the (untrue) claim that Pushkin had granted to Goering permission to translate his works into German.

79. Andrei Dostoevsky is again referring to Mikhail Nechaev, a draper's shop assistant, who was roughly thirty-three years old at the time.

80. Having opened on January 22, 1819, Chermak's school was also rated among the top five private institutions in Moscow. For whatever reason, Chermak was forced to close the school in the late 1840s; he himself died in poverty.

81. Tuition and board at Chermak's school was eight hundred rubles per student, or roughly Mikhail Dostoevsky's yearly salary at the hospital.

82. More accurately, when the Dostoevsky brothers entered Chermak's school, there were sixty-eight students, fifty of whom were from the nobility.

83. Lacking evidence, therefore, is Frank's assertion that "the transition from home to [Chermak's] school, and particularly to boarding school, came as a rude shock to Fyodor." See *Dostoevsky: The Seeds of Revolt*, 34.

84. Lessons at Chermak's school began at 8 a.m. with breaks at 10 and 12. After lunch there were lessons from 2 to 6 o'clock with a break at 4 p.m. From 6 to 9 p.m. students did their homework, after which they had supper and went to bed.

So much, also, for Mochulsky's claim that the young Dostoevsky "lacked a systematic education." See Mochulsky, *Dostoevsky*, 17.

85. John Sherwood was the son of a mechanic who had come to Russia in 1800. Having received a good education, fluent in French, German, Latin, and English, Sherwood served as a teacher in the household of a general until he eloped with one of his pupils. The couple were soon parted—she to a convent, he to the army.

Eventually, Sherwood was promoted to lieutenant and served at Kherson, where he chanced to hear officers plotting to assassinate Nicholas I, a conspiracy that culminated in Decembrist Revolt of 1825.

Sherwood wrote a letter of warning to Nicholas, for which he was promoted to captain and, together with his father, awarded a pension. (He was given a bodyguard.) Sherwood was also renamed Ivan Vasilievich, and given a coat of arms with the imperial eagle at the center.

Known as Sherwood-*Vernyi*, or "the Faithful," the man set aside recommendations by Nicholas that he, for his continued safety, retire in England. For this final act of loyalty to the tsar, Sherwood was reunited with his wife.

Sadly, Sherwood did not detail his objections to Chermak's school.

86. Dostoevsky wrote this letter almost three months before his death.

87. As will be seen, Dostoevsky behaved similarly as a student at the Main Engineering Academy in St. Petersburg.

88. This is not true. During the years Fyodor and Mikhail Dostoevsky attended Chermak's school, Latin was taught by an individual named Yakov Ivanovich Vizard.

89. Nikolai Bantysh-Kamensky's *Grammatica Latina* had gone through numerous printings since its first publication in 1779.

Interestingly, Mikhail's facility with Latin was one reason why he was awarded a scholarship to the Moscow Medical-Surgical Academy.

90. Alexander Voekov completed "The Insane Asylum," a spoof on all the Russian writers of the time, in 1838 and published it 1841.

91. *The Library for Reading* was a conservative monthly of literature, science, the arts, industry, news, and fashion published in St. Petersburg from 1834 to 1865. (Osip Senkovsky was its first editor.) It published works by Alexander Pushkin, Nikolai Gogol, Mikhail Lermontov, Vasili Zhukovsky, Ivan Krylov, Vladimir Odoevsky, Evgeni Baratynsky, and Pyotr Vyazemsky.

The Library for Reading also reviewed and/or published in translation the works of such French writers as Honoré de Balzac, Victor Hugo, George Sand, and Eugène Scribe.

92. A red cap was a distinguishing characteristic of privates in Russian penal regiments in Siberia, recruited, in part, from convicts who had finished their prison terms there. The remark was prophetic; Dostoevsky served in such a regiment after his release from prison in Siberia in 1854.

Unfounded is Mochulsky's claim that "Dostoevsky's childhood was hardly serene.... The conflicts with his father, his fear of him, and a latent ill-will borne toward him developed a reticence and lack of straightforwardness early in the boy's life."

Also without basis is Mochulsky's avowal that "by his very nature, [the young] Dostoevsky was an introspective, withdrawn individual. The interior always prevailed in his personality over the exterior." See Mochulsky, *Dostoevsky*, 4 and 9.

93. Tsarskoe Selo, located fifteen miles south of St. Petersburg, was the summer residence of the tsars, specifically, the famous Alexander and Catherine Palaces. It is now part of the town of Pushkin. The first railway in Russia, connecting Tsarskoe Selo and St. Petersburg, was built in 1837.

Saint Isaac's Cathedral, the largest Russian Orthodox Church, in St. Petersburg, was constructed between 1818 and 1858.

94. To Mikhail's apparent surprise, Maria was pregnant with Dostoevsky's sister, Alexandra.

95. The individual in question is Nikolai Bilevich, who was an instructor at Chermak's school from the second half of 1835 to the first half of 1837. In 1830 Bilevich graduated from the Nezhinsky Gymnasium of Advanced Science; his schoolmates included Gogol, Evgeni Grebenka, and Nikolai Kukolnik. (Several years later in Moscow, he attended a reading of *Dead Souls* by Gogol.)

Bilevich also wrote poems and satire, his most famous works being two anthologies, *A Picture Gallery of Societal Life, or the Mores of the Nineteenth Century* in 1836; and three years later, *Christmas Evenings, or Stories of My Aunt*.

96. In an article, titled "The Strange Confessions of George Sand," an anonymous author noted: "[Sand] dresses in men's clothes, carouses with young people throughout the streets of Paris, dines with them in coffeehouses and taverns, and with them visits places where women never go."

The author continued: "George Sand was born with *masculine inclinations*; she is consumed by boundless pride; she is in despair that she is a woman and regrets bitterly that having been born a poet, a free woman, she is destined to lead a *nomadic* life." See "Strannye priznaniia Zhorzha Sanda," *Biblioteka dlia chteniia*, vol. 17 (1836), 6 and 9.

97. Yegor is a peasant first name.

98. "The great Yegor Sand," Senkovsky wrote "has produced a great drama, titled *Cosima*, which, by nature, is very boring . . . but with the most immoral philosophizings." See S. Senkovsky, "Frantsuzskii teatr v Parizhe," *Biblioteka dlia chteniia*, vol. 41 (1840), otd. 7, 27. (Sand's *Cosima* premiered on April 29, 1840.)

99. In a letter to the editors of *Northern Bee*, an alleged and anonymous "French correspondent" wrote that Alexandre Ledru-Rollin, minister of the provisional government, "has become the friend and patron of all capricious women, using his position to satisfy their strange and depraved desires. During the past two years, a wild orgy has been going on in the Ministry of Internal Affairs. In Ledru-Rollin's circle are Citizen Sand and actresses who are known more for their adventures than their talent, and who feast and make merry at the expense of the Republic." See "Frantsiia," *Severnaia pchela* 109 (May 17, 1848), 435.

100. Pauline Viardot wrote to Sand on February 27, 1847, that in Russia "all your works are translated as they appear; everyone, from the top to the bottom of the social scale, reads them. Men adore you, women idolize you; and you reign over Russia more absolutely than the tsar." See E. Semenoff, "1830 et le romantisme russe," *Mercure de France* 224 (December 15, 1930), 578–579.

101. Specifically, Sand's *Indiana*, published in Russian in 1838.

102. Interestingly, early in his career, Belinsky also disapproved of Sand. "Indeed, what does French literature have to offer," he wrote in 1838. "The reflection of small and worthless systems, ephemeral parties, momentary questions. Dudevant, or George Sand, so well-known but not at all celebrated, is writing an entire series of novels, one more absurd and scandalous than the next, so as to promote Saint-Simonian ideas of society. And what are those ideas? O, matchless ones. Exactly this, that the industrial trend should prevail over the ideal and spiritual ones."

Two years later, Belinsky did an abrupt about-face. "In George Sand," he wrote, "there is neither love nor hate for the privileged classes, and neither reverence nor disdain for the lower classes of society. For her there are neither aristocrats nor plebeians; for her there are only human beings. George Sand finds human beings in all levels of society. She loves them, pities them, takes pride in them, cries over them.... With such a stance, is it not surprising that Mrs. Dudevant is so hailed by the blind rabble, by the savage and ignorant mob, as an immoral writer?"

In a more balanced frame of mind, Belinsky continued in 1842: "Without a doubt, George Sand is the foremost poetic glory of the contemporary world.... One can choose to disagree with her principles; one can find them false or unacceptable; but it is impossible not to respect her as a human being for whom every conviction is a belief of her heart and soul. That is why she never leaves our memory and mind. It is also why her talent never diminishes... but strengthens and grows." See Belinskii, *Polnoe sobranie sochinenii v tridnadtsati tomakh*, vol. 3 (Moscow: Akademiia Nauk, 1953), 398; vol. 5 (1954), 175; and vol. 5 (1955), 279.

103. Dostoevsky is off by a year. Sand's *Uscoque* was published in *The Library for Reading* in 1838.

104. During the 1830s and 1840s, Russians, particularly youth, formed a veritable cult around George Sand; so much so that the term *Zhorzhsandism* was used to describe Russian novels of the time with themes similar to those of the writer. Readers relished Sand's political engagement, as well as her revulsion for repressive social institutions, particularly the exploitation of women by men, both of which she, in her fiction, cloaked in impassioned correspondences, indiscreet encounters, threatened suicides, and highly charged, often Gothic situations and events.

105. Translations of Dickens's works appeared in Russia at the end of 1838, although excerpts from his works, such as *The Pickwick Papers*, appeared several years earlier.

106. Balzac spent three months in St. Petersburg in 1843.

107. In her memoirs, Anna Dostoevskaya recalled that Dostoevsky particularly liked *Père Goriot*. See Dostoevskaya, *Vospominaniia* (1971), 167.

108. "Balzac lives like some kind of prince," Belinsky wrote in 1835, "with gold buttons on his tails and a cane with a gold knob (the height of capricious luxury), but his pictures of poverty and need freeze the soul with their terrible truth."

Three years later, he continued: "Balzac teaches that to be poor is better than to wind up alive in hell, and that to be blessed and content means to have a pile of money and a *de* before your name."

In 1841, Belinsky intoned: "M. *de* Balzac's dukes and duchesses, his counts and countesses, and his marquises are as genuine and true-to-life as M. De Balzac is to being a great writer or genius."

A year later, he continued: "Balzac is a great story-teller, and if he would not swim off into the watery and extended verbiage that he sees as the precise analysis of dresses, rooms, hearts, souls, passions, and feelings... [and] if he did not invent counts and marquises who exist only in his imagination, chained as it is to lobby-salons... he would be a most remarkable writer of the second or third rank, he would not be forgotten and laughed out of Paris, and he would have not written himself out so quickly and published such poor articles [as he does now]."

Even more irritating to the great critic was Balzac's popularity among Russian and Western European readers and reviewers at the expense of writers Belinsky believed to be more talented and worthy. Consider his 1836 complaint that society "will enrich Balzac, but will allow Schiller to die in hunger."

Compare also this, noted in 1839 by Custine: "I attempted to carry on a conversation about our newest [French] literature, but I saw that in Russia, people knew only Balzac. They worshiped him endlessly and had rather accurate opinions of his writing. Almost all the writings of contemporary French writers were forbidden in Russia, proof of the importance [that the officials there] ascribed to them. Most likely, Russians knew of other French writers from encounters at the customs-house, but they were afraid to speak about them."

See Belinskii, *Polnoe sobranie sochinenii*, vol. 1, 279; vol. 2, 157 and 469; vol. 5, 175; and vol. 6 (1956), 61–62; and Custine, *Rossiia*, 378.

109. Dostoevsky has his facts wrong. As noted by an anonymous reviewer in *The Library for Reading* in 1834, it was not George Sand but Mary Wollstonecraft who "propounded . . . 'the rights of woman' and was taking it upon herself to revive a human entity vis-à-vis the 'free wife.'" See "Slovesnost' vo Frantsii," *Biblioteka dla chteniia*, vol. 6 (1834), 73–74.

110. As will be seen, Dostoevsky would later translate Sand's 1839 Venetian novel, *The Last Aldini*, but would not publish his work.

111. George Sand wrote *Jeanne* in 1844.

112. Compare Turgenev's remark in a letter, written to Alexei Suvorin and published in his newspaper *New Time* on June 21, 1876, that George Sand "is one of our saints." See Turgenev, *Polnoe sobranie sochinenii i pisem v dvadtsati tomakh*, vol. 14 (Moscow: Akademiia nauk, 1967), 234.

Also consider Belinsky's comment in a letter to Nikolai Bakunin, dated November 7, 1842, that George Sand "is the Joan of Arc of our times." See Belinskii, *Polnoe sobranie sochinenii*, vol. 12 (1956), 112.

113. Maria Dostoevsky was suffering from tuberculosis, which eventually claimed her life.

114. Father Barshev conducted the funeral for Maria Dostoevskaya on March 1, 1837. The service was held at the Church of the Holy Spirit in Moscow, known for its impressive painting of the rising of Lazarus.

115. It should be noted that Dostoevsky made such comments immediately after the death of his seven-month-old, daughter, Maria, in 1862.

116. Claims as to epilepsy—or as it was known at the time, falling sickness—is a frequent, if unfounded motif of Dostoevsky's early years. According to I. Iakubovich, Lyubov Dostoevskaya avowed that it was a quarrel between Dostoevsky's parents that brought on young Fyodor's first attack of the affliction. Nowhere in the editions of Dostoevskaya's memoirs, though, is there any mention of such an occurrence. See Iakubovich et al., *Letopis'*, 29.

117. The Lazarevskoe Cemetery is located roughly three miles north of the Kremlin.

118. In fact, Mikhail Dostoevsky was forty-nine years old at the time.

119. The orphan Katerina, or, more formally, Ekaterina Alexandrovna Alexandrova, had been taken into the household as a chambermaid two years earlier. At this time, she was sixteen years old.

120. Akulina Isaeva was a fourteen-year-old peasant who, having entered the household at age ten or eleven, remained with Mikhail Dostoevsky after Maria's death to assist him in his medical practice.

121. Andrei Dostoevsky is referring to the death of Pushkin at the hands of Georges D'Anthès, a dashing Frenchman whom Pushkin had met in 1834 and who, a year later, was paying court to his wife, Natalya. Although it has never been proven that Natalya was unfaithful to her husband, Pushkin had little choice but to believe she was. When the poet received an anonymous letter, claiming his election to "The Most Serene Order of Cuckolds," he challenged D'Anthès to a duel and died on January 29, 1837.

National grief over Pushkin's death was so great that, at the last moment, the authorities moved his funeral to a small church. They also sought to minimize public mourning. Newspapers were forbidden to print anything but brief, dispassionate reports of Pushkin's passing, with no mention of the duel.

After a requiem mass at a small church near Pushkin's apartment on February 1—the service was initially planned for St. Isaac's Cathedral—the poet's remains were whisked away in the dead of night and under police escort to the poet's family estate near Pskov, roughly 175 miles southwest of St. Petersburg. Only Pushkin's friend Alexander Turgenev was allowed to accompany him on this final journey. Here the poet was buried in a low-key ceremony attended by only a few mourners.

The news of Pushkin's death reached the Dostoevsky brothers after the death of their mother. Most likely the source was an article titled "Pushkin," written by Nikolai Polevoi in an issue of *The Library for Reading* published on March 3.

122. The citation is from Nikolai Karamzin's 1792 "Epitaph." It was prefaced by "To my unforgettable friend, tender spouse, and most guardian mother." The other side of the marker was inscribed: "Lord, into Your hands I commend my spirit."

Part Two: To Petersburg

1. Frank, *Dostoevsky: The Seeds of Revolt*, 91.
2. Consider, for example, two of Hoffman's stories on Venice, "The Lost Reflection" (1814) and "Doge and Dogaressa" (1817); as well as Sand's novels on the city, *Mattea* (1833), *Leone Leoni* (1834), *The Private Secretary* (1834), and *Letters of a Voyager* (1834–1836).
3. Similarly, the Marquis de Custine wrote in 1839: "A little further on I saw a mounted courier . . . or some other infamous employee of the government, get out of his carriage, run up to one of the two polite coachmen and strike him brutally with his whip, a stick, and his fists." See Astolphe Marquis de Custine, *Rossiia v 1839 godu v dvukh tomakh*, vol. 1 (Moscow: Izdatel'stvo imeni Sabashnikovykh, 1996), 286.
4. The individual in question is Nikolai I.
5. Mikhail Dostoevsky had been offered the position as senior physician at the Mariinsky Hospital.
6. Mikhail Dostoevsky was released formally from state service on July 1, 1837.
7. Having retired from service at the relatively early age of forty-eight, Mikhail Dostoevsky moved permanently to Darovoe in August 1837 with Vera, Alexandra, and Nikolai, as well as with Alyona Frolovna.
8. In May 1837 Mikhail Dostoevsky enrolled his two sons in a boarding school run by Koronad Kostomarov to prepare them for the entrance examination into the Main Engineering Academy.
9. Mikhail Pavlovich was the brother of Nicholas I and also the Inspector General for Engineering Affairs.
10. Andrei Dostoevsky was a student at Chermak's school from 1837 to 1841.
11. Dostoevskaya has erred in her chronology. The seventeen-year-old Varvara Dostoevskaya married the forty-four-year-old widower Pyotr Karepin on April 21, 1840. Karepin also had a four-year-old daughter from his first marriage. The story is that Karepin had never seen Varvara and was marrying her for her dowry.

In truth, though, Karepin was doing quite well on his own, both as the director of the Moscow Governor-General's office and as the honorary secretary to several charitable societies. He also enjoyed a large income from serving as the chief manager of the estates of Count Dmitri Golitsyn, the town governor of Moscow.

Andrei Dostoevsky recalls, of the initial meeting between Karepin and Varvara: "My sister Varen'ka was made to sit down on the right of her fiancé. After the second deal, Karepin fanned out his cards and showed them to my sister. But at that moment, she, poor thing, could hardly distinguish between a king and a knave. And, indeed, to see a man for the first time in her life and to be conscious of the fact that his man was her fiancé, her future husband!" See Dostoevskii, *Vospominaniia*, 113.

12. Lacking basis, therefore, is Mochulsky's insistence that "Fyodor did not have any friends at [Chermak's] school; he was unable to get along with his contemporaries." See Mochulsky, *Dostoevsky*, 10.

13. Sometime between September 3 and 15, 1837, the doctors had examined Mikhail Dostoevsky and claimed that he showed signs of consumption.

14. In truth, there were already two brothers who were studying at the Main Engineering Academy at state expense. One pair were the Totlebens: Adolf became a roommate of Dostoevsky (see below). Eduard achieved fame as a defender of Sevastopol in the Crimean War; he also was instrumental in obtaining for Dostoevsky a full pardon after the writer's release from prison in Siberia.

Also at the Main Engineering Academy at this time was Ivan Sechyonov, who would be known as father of Russian physiology; Konstantin von Kaufman, who, in the early 1870s, enabled Russians to expand into Central Asia; Fyodor Radetsky, who helped Russia to win the Russo-Turkish War of 1877–1878 (and is considered a national hero in Bulgaria); and Konstantin Trutovsky, who achieved fame as a Realist in art in the 1860s and 1870s (see below).

15. Mikhail Antonovich Markus was appointed personal physician to Empress Alexandra Fyodorovna in 1837. His brother Fyodor was not only a close friend of the Dostoevsky family but also came to their rescue after the death of Dostoevsky's mother.

About Fyodor Markus, Andrei Dostoevsky recalled: "As our closest neighbor . . . [Fyodor Markus] . . . often spent evenings, talking to Mama and Papa. He always spoke in such a way that I . . . fixed my eyes on his and listened to what he was saying. On my childhood, he left the most joyous impression. . . .

"When Mama died, it was Fyodor Antonovich who, at Father's request, arranged for the funeral. After that, he also visited Father almost every day, entertaining him with his stories. At that time Fyodor Antonovich became even closer to us children, too. When, after Mama's death, Father retired and left for the village, Fyodor Antonovich . . . looked after us . . . and gave us money for provisions. . . . He also took me from Chermak's school to spend the holidays with him." See Dostoevsky, *Vospominaniia*, 32–33 and 81.

16. A grade of ten was the highest possible score a student could earn on examinations.

17. In truth, Dostoevsky came in eleventh out of twenty-three applicants in the competition. See Iakubovich, "Dostoevskii," 181.

18. Auntie is Alexandra Kumanina.

19. This letter of Mikhail to his sons has not survived.

20. Mikhail Dostoevsky had paid Kostomarov an additional 300 rubles for both sons to take lessons in fencing and fortification.

21. The Mikhailovsky Castle, also known as St. Michael's Castle and the Engineering Castle, was built as a residence for Tsar Paul I in 1779–1801. Located opposite the famed Summer Gardens, the Mikhailovsky Castle featured a massive pseudo-Gothic style but, in the 1820s, was redone in a more Neoclassical taste. Thick walls and huge portals attended oversized obelisks and a gilded spire. Also, because of Paul's interest in medieval knights (and his fear of assassination), the Mikhailovsky Castle was surrounded by the Moika and Fontanka Rivers, as well as by two specially dug waterways (the Church and Sunday Canals), transforming the place into an artificial island, accessible only by drawbridges that were raised at night.

The interior of the Mikhailovsky Castle was particularly grim. The cellars and first floor were made from hewn granite; the upper levels were done in brick and covered in marble and bronze. Impassive statues and somber historical canvases took their place amid vast chambers, long drafty corridors, and dark reddish walls, a lady of the court having sent her evening glove to Paul to suggest the forbidding bloody color. The Mikhailovsky Castle was also a labyrinth of dark staircases and gloomy corridors, which, lighted by lamps that burned day and night, led to new mazes of secret passages and rooms. By the time the young Fyodor had entered the Main Engineering Academy in January 1837, the building had been remodeled to include rooms and hallways that were conducive to study but that also failed hide the place's sinister allure.

After Dostoevsky graduated from the Main Engineering Academy in 1844, the Mikhailovsky Castle continued to house military schools, and after the Revolution, various Soviet institutions. During World War II, the Mikhailovsky Castle served as a hospital for soldiers wounded at the front. In 1994 a third of the building became a branch of the Russian Museum, and it now houses the Portrait Gallery, featuring official portraits of Russian emperors and empresses and other dignitaries and celebrities from the late seventeenth to the early twentieth century. It also hosts the Central Navy Library, an immense collection of books, magazines, and documents on the Russian fleet.

22. Custine is referring to Emperor Paul I, who ascended the throne in 1796. Plots to assassinate Paul—one including the British ambassador—had been in the making at least a year before his actual murder.

On the night of March 12, 1801, Count Pyotr Pahlen, the head of the Secret Police, Count Leonyi Benningsen, Count Platon Zubov, the last lover of Catherine the Great, and Zubov's brother Nikolai entered the Mikhailovsky Castle. Having found the tsar hiding behind a screen in his bedchamber—Paul had lived in the Castle only eleven days, engaged in quasi-religious orgies with friends of both sexes—the conspirators sought to force his abdication from the throne. When Paul resisted, he was first struck with a sword, and then beaten (or strangled) and trampled to death. The gruesome event was the last palace revolution in Russian history. Revealingly, the murder was never investigated.

Further, the complicity of Paul's son Alexander Pavlovich (and soon-to-be tsar Alexander I) in the murder is not known completely, since Pahlen destroyed many of the documents tied to the affair. The story goes that it was Nikolai Zubov who informed Alexander (who was in the palace at the time of this father's death) of his accession to the throne with the admonition: "Time to grow up! Go and rule!"

Paul's bedroom was later turned into a chapel, but the events within it served as the catalyst for Pushkin's famed 1817 work "Freedom: An Ode." Also, even into the 1990s, the room was closed to visitors.

23. The Marquis de Custine visited Russia in 1839, spending most of his time in St. Petersburg, but also visiting Moscow and Yaroslavl. Four years later, he published an account of his experiences in the country widely in Europe.

Lost to obscurity for a time, Custine's work became a favorite text for disgruntled American diplomats who, stationed in Moscow during Stalin's rule, plundered the work for the writer's insights into the national despotism—for example, Russians as "voluntary automata" who, among other things, surrendered to "the police of the imagination."

24. The Khlysts or *Khlysty* were an underground religious sect allegedly founded by Danila Filipov, a peasant from Kostroma (roughly two hundred miles east of Moscow), and existing in Russia from the late seventeenth to the early twentieth centuries.

Initially, the members of the sect were called *Khristovery* or *Khristy* ("Christ-believers"). Later, though, they were cited by critics as *Khlysty*, from the Russian word for "whip" (*khlyst*), which they allegedly used for self-flagellation.

Like many Eastern mystics, the Khlysts divided the world into spirit and flesh, good and evil. They believed that in the beginning, Primordial Man was androgynous and spiritual but that, after the Fall, he had become physical, mortal, and gendered. For the Khlysty, also, Primordial Man was not alone in his demise; Earth itself, also initially spiritual, became dense, material, corrupt, and subject to decay and death.

The Khylsty rejected holy books, the priesthood, and the veneration of the saints. Rather, the restoration of both androgynous man and virgin earth were key to their doctrine and ritual. The Khlysty sought direct communication with the Holy Spirit, who, they asserted, was embodied in living people. They also attempted divine grace via asceticism and ecstatic rites, which were rumored to have turned into sexual orgies. (Grigory Rasputin is said, falsely, to have been a khlyst.)

Typically, the Khlysty formed communities called "Arks," which were headed by male *and* female individuals, called the "Christ" and the "Mother of God," respectively. The distinction of the former underscored the Khlysts' belief that Christ did not leave earth after the resurrection, but that, like the Holy Spirit, He dwelled in God-realized individuals. The designation of the latter hearkened back to the original virginal state of Mother Earth.

A final note: Having achieved Christhood and oneness with the divine Beloved, the Khlysty saw themselves as akin to the Son of Man, who contravened Mosaic Sabbath Law and disdained self-righteous religious authority. For them political, social, and moral laws and conventions were anathema; only divine illumination and God-realization were needed for life.

The departures from traditional doctrine and ritual notwithstanding, the Khlysts allowed their members to attend Russian Orthodox churches. At their height, they numbered about forty thousand individuals. In the later years of their existence, the Khlysty were found mostly in factories about Perm. After 1917 their numbers dropped precipitously, but communities of Khlysts existed in southeast Russia, the northern Caucasus, and Ukraine.

It is also of interest to note that the Khlysty figure prominently in Andrei Bely's novel *The Silver Dove*, published in 1907.

25. The circle of Baroness Ekaterina Tatarinova, known alternately as the Brethren in Christ, the Union of Brothers and Sisters, and the Ship of Tatarinova (among other names), appeared in St. Petersburg in 1817.

More than seventy members attended gatherings at Tatarinova's apartment regularly, including members of the Russian aristocracy and such notables as the attorney general of the Holy Synod, the minister of education, the general-mayor of St. Petersburg, and the vice presidents of the Russian Academy of Art and of the Russian Bible society. Even Alexander I is said to have visited there.

Services at Tatarinova's apartment were usually held on Sundays and holidays. (She lived at the Mikhailovsky Castle until 1821.) The women wore dresses, often white; the men also wore white clothing. During the proceedings, Tatarinova allegedly prophesied. Forms of worship included praying and singing, as well as ecstatic spinning and dancing. (Although the group was intrigued with native Castrates and Flagellants, none of the men underwent castration.)

When in an 1822 edict, Alexander I banned secret societies in Russia—a measure directed primarily against Masons, Rosicrucians, and other religiously suspect groups—Tatarinova was also prohibited from continuing her spiritual activities. Nonetheless, she sponsored small assemblies at irregular intervals. In 1830 Count Alexander Benckendorff, chief of police, demanded that Tatarinova end such gatherings and ordered that her home be open to official searches. Seven years later, all fifteen or so members of her group were arrested, tried, and banished to distant monasteries. Tatarinova herself was cloistered in a convent and kept under strict surveillance for ten years. In 1847, after she had admitted her guilt formally and promised not to resume her assemblies, Tatarinova was allowed to return to Moscow, where she died in 1856.

26. Fyodor Dostoevsky entered the Main Engineering Academy on January 16, 1838.

27. As will be seen below, there is no other evidence for such a claim.

28. Grigorovich entered the Main Engineering Academy a year before Dostoevsky, on January 2, 1837.

29. From 1839 to 1865, Russian literature at the Main Engineering Academy was taught by Vasili Plaksin, a chaired professor who was also a critic, a student of the theater, and author of an 1835 pedagogical novel titled *The Upbringing of Women*, which, among its chapters, included the title: "How Easy to Ruin the Splendid Soul of a Woman, and Difficult to Correct What Has Been Ruined."

Plaksin knew Pushkin personally; but in a series of textbooks on Russian literature written between 1832 and 1844, he undervalued not only the writer, but also Lermontov and Gogol.

Not surprisingly, such failings earned Plaksin frequent scorn from Belinsky. About Plaksin he wrote in 1836: "As everyone knows, the ingenuous division [of Russian literature] into categories of *high, middle, and low* began in ancient times and continues to our teachers and lawgivers of eloquence, from Lomonosov to Plaksin." See Belinskii, *Polnoe sobranie sochinenii*, vol. 2, 99.

In 1847 Belinsky continued: "It should be added that [Plaksin] is a theorist who has spent his entire life in compiling and teaching all kinds of rhetoric and poetics, which, like all books of this type, have never taught anyone about the art of good writing, but which have succeeded only in confusing many minds.

"That is why [Plaksin] is amazed by the complete freedom and independence of Gogol's works from all school rules and traditions; and why he could not credit Gogol for these qualities, on one hand, and on the other, why he could not but reproach the writer for them. Hence [Plaksin's] claim that Gogol's works feature the 'most repellant errors' and 'an undisguised, chaotic state of art.'"

"And, if you ask [Plaksin] what these errors are, and we are sure that he will first mention the watchman [in *Dead Souls*] who killed vermin with his fingernails; and that he will use this fact to assert with finality that 'Gogol knows no history and has seen no models of art.'" See Belinskii, *Polnoe sobranie sochinenii*, vol. 10 (1956), 292–293.

30. It was from Josephe Cournant, a French instructor at the Engineering Academy, that Dostoevsky came to admire such writers as Jean Racine, Blaise Pascal, Pierre Corneille, Pierre Ronsard, François Malherbe, Honoré de Balzac, Victor Hugo, George Sand, and Eugène Sue.

31. Intriguing as the story is, Saveliev has the facts wrong. At this time, Felix Tol was a student at the Main Engineering Academy, graduating in 1844. He returned there to teach Russian literature and history only in 1848. More interestingly, perhaps, Dostoevsky and Tol later crossed paths as members of the Petrashevsky Circle.

32. Sadly, if Dostoevsky had gone from Chermak's school to Moscow University, he would have studied with such writers as Alexander Ostrovsky, Alexei Pisemsky, Apollon Grigoriev, Afanasi Fet, and Yakov Polonsky, all of whom would become his literary colleagues.

33. Dostoevsky is referring to *The Double*.

34. Not quite. For whatever the reason, the authorities at the Main Engineering Academy submitted a request to the Heraldry Office on May 19, 1838, seeking to find out the "origin of the minor Dostoevsky." It was only a year and a half later, on November 29, 1839, that the Heraldry Office confirmed that "one may consider the minor Fyodor Dostoevsky as belonging to the class of nobility." The designation was reaffirmed on December 23, 1844.

35. Heinrich Zschokke's four-volume work, *Hours of Devotion for the Advancement of Genuine Christianity and Familial DivineWorship*, was published in 1825 and 1831. (There were twenty-seven editions of the work in the writer's lifetime.) It espoused a rationalist approach to religion and morality, one that bypassed dogma in favor of Christian love and social concerns.

36. The reference is either to St. Photius the Great, the patriarch of Constantinople, from 858 to 867 and from 877 to 886, who championed the Eastern Church; or, more tantalizingly, to an eccentric

archimandrite from Novgorod named Peter Spassky, who, upon becoming a monk named Photius, moved to a Rasputin-type figure in the court of Alexander I.

Like his later counterpart, Spassky-Photius regarded himself as the "militant instrument of Providence" and the "Savior of the Church and the Fatherland," his activities including damning heretics, bedding female patron-penitents (most notoriously, Countess Anna Orlova-Chesmenskaya), and making life difficult for the tsar.

Consider these epigrams by Pushkin:

A Conversation between Photius and Countless Orlova (1822–1824)
Please listen to what I say
Body of a eunuch, soul of a man
What have you done to me?
Body into soul, this I can.

To Countess Orlova-Chesmenskaya (1824)
Saintly woman,
To God her soul
But to Archimandrite Photius
Her body, sinfully droll.

On Photius (1824)
Half-fanatic, half-cheat,
A curse, a sword, a cross, a knout
Are his spiritual might.
Send us sinners, O Lord,
Fewer such pastors, half-holy, half-good
Spare us such holy blight.

37. In French, "*Ne dites jamais la vérité aux depens de votre vertu.*" Montesquieu said such words in a farewell speech on the occasion of his retirement from the French parliament in 1725.

38. Ivan Berezhetsky entered the Main Engineering Academy in December 1837.

39. Mochulsky also notes a "secret spirit ... the musician Chikhachyov and Ignati Bryanchikov [who] once they had finished the officers' courses, entered St. Sergius Monastery as novices. Among the students of the school they were known derogatorily as 'Bryanchaninovites.'"

Lacking evidence, though, is Mochulsky's claim that "it is altogether possible that this mystical stream touched even young Dostoevsky." See Mochuksky, *Dostoevsky*, 11.

40. Saveliev's comment is interesting, because Shidlovsky was not a student at the Main Engineering Academy.

41. The Fontanka is a left branch of the river Neva that flows through central St. Petersburg. Its name derives from the fact that it furnishes the fountains of the Summer Garden in the city.

42. Initially at the Main Engineering Academy, Grigorovich was in the class ahead of Dostoevsky, but he had been left back for a year. They were together in the same classes, beginning in 1839.

43. More accurately, the reference is to E.T.A. Hoffman's novel, *The Life Opinions of Tom-Cat Murr, Together with the Fragmentary Biography of Conductor Johannes Kreisler in Accidental Gallery Proofs, Edited by E.T.A. Hofmann*, which appeared in 1819 and 1821.

44. Grigorovich is mistaken here—the author of the work is Thomas de Quincey—but the error is understandable, since the 1834 Russian translation of the work was published under the title "*The Confession of an Englishman, Having Used Opium,*" *a Composition by Maturin, the Author of "Melmoth."* (The reference is to Charles Maturin's novel, *Melmoth the Wanderer: a Tale*, published in 1820).

45. Walter Scott's novel *Guy Mannering or the Astrologer* appeared in 1815.

46. Grigorovich has in mind Fenimore Cooper's 1840 novel *The Pathfinder, or the Inland Sea*.

47. Frédéric Soulié published his novel, *Memories of the Devil* in 1837–1838.

48. Revel is now Tallinn in Estonia.

49. *The Northern Bee* was a conservative newspaper edited by Faddei Bulgarin, who in it attacked such writers as Pushkin, Gogol, and Belinsky.

50. Peterhof (German/Dutch for "Peter's Court") is known as the "Russian Versailles": the site of palaces, fountains, and gardens, ordered by Peter the Great, and located on the southern shore of the Gulf of Finland about twenty miles west of St. Petersburg. Dostoevsky was in summer camp at Peterhof from June 11 until August 2, 1838.

51. The famed Samson Statue, depicting Samson ripping open the jaws of a lion, was installed at Peterhof to celebrate Russia's victory over Sweden in the Great Northern War (1700–1721). (The lion is an element on the Swedish coat of arms; one of the great victories of the struggle was won on St. Samson's day.) The Samson statue was looted by the Germans during the Second World War; a replica of the sculpture was installed in 1947.

52. It will be recalled that Katerina was the orphan chambermaid whom Mikhail Dostoevsky, after the death of his wife, allegedly appealed to for company and support. After the death of Mikhail, Katerina married a thirty-five-year-old widower with whom she bore two sons, both of whom died in infancy.

53. Mikhail Dostoevsky entered the St. Petersburg Military-Engineering Company as a second-year student on January 25, 1838.

54. In fact, Fyodor had been writing to Mikhail, but his letters had not arrived or were lost.

55. Mikhail is quoting from Matthew 11:28.

56. Rizenkampf is mistaken. At the time, Mikhail Dostoevsky was eighteen years old.

57. Rizenkampf dates this reading as June 1837, but it took place a year later.

58. As has been seen, none of Dostoevskaya's statements is true.

59. As will be seen, such a claim is false.

60. With the Polish insurrection of 1831, Nicholas I had become so taken with military engineering that he grew quite fond of the Main Engineering Academy, often gracing it with his presence.

61. At this time, Dostoevsky was roughly five feet six inches tall.

62. Most likely, Dostoevsky knew of Shakespeare's 1599–1601 play, *Hamlet*, from an 1837 translation by Polevoi.

63. Dostoevsky is quoting from Pascal's 1666 work, *Thoughts*, which was known in Russia both in French editions and in an 1843 Russian translation.

64. The works of Hoffman appeared not only in Russian journals of the time but also in an eight-part translated edition of his works in 1836.

In his admiration of Hoffman, Dostoevsky was hardly alone. "I do not understand," Belinsky told Pavel Annenkov, "why Europe has placed Hoffman alongside Shakespeare and Goethe. He is a writer of singular strength and stature." See P. Annenkov, *Literaturnye vospominaniia* (Moscow: Pravda, 1989), 123.

65. The work was translated into Russian in 1840.

66. Goethe published the first part of his dramatic poem, *Faust*, in 1808; the second, in 1832. Although Dostoevsky read such selections from Goethe in the original, the first translation of the writer's works into Russian appeared in 1838.

67. Polevoi penned his six-volume *History of the Russian People* between the years 1829 and 1833. In it he used the ideas of such French Romantic historians as Augustin Thierry and Jules Michelet to challenge Karamzin's idea of morally enlightened despots as integral to the state, and to assert the people as key to national health and well-being. Polevoi's *Ugolino* appeared in 1838.

68. Zhukovsky's *Undina*, a verse adaptation of Baron Fouqué's 1811 *Undine*, appeared in 1837.

69. Hugo wrote his dramas *Cromwell* in 1827 and *Hernani* in 1830.

70. Alban is the hero of Hoffman's 1813 story "The Magnetizer," who, via his occult powers, cedes to the Satanic temptation to rival God as master of the world.

71. The exact nature of the offense or offenses is unknown. Frank notes that young Fyodor, in his letter to Mikhail, neglected to list his abysmally low grade in military drill, a shortcoming that may have caused his failure. See Frank, *Dostoevsky: The Seeds of Revolt*, 83.

72. Byron wrote his narrative poem *The Prisoner of Chillon* in 1816.

73. Dostoevsky is citing from Pushkin's 1830 poem "To the Poet."

74. François-René Chateaubriand's work *The Genius of Christianity* appeared in 1802 and was a major impetus to French romanticism. In it Chateaubriand defends the wisdom and beauty of Christianity against attacks by the philosophers and politicians of both the French Enlightenment and the Revolution.

75. *Son of the Fatherland* was a journal of history, politics, and literature founded by Nikolai Grech and published between 1812 and 1844 and again between 1847 and 1852.

76. Désiré Nisard wrote his article on Hugo and others in the March–April 1838 issue.

77. Nisard was a foremost defender of the Classicists against Romantics.

78. One of Shidlovsky's poems, "The Sky," was to be published in the November 1838 issue of *Son of the Fatherland*.

79. Such a claim is highly unlikely.

80. If Shidlovsky did see Pushkin's remains, he did so in the company of such poets as Vyazemsky and Zhukovsky, as well as of individuals from all segments of society, including students—despite the fact that officials had forbidden administrators at the university to cancel classes.

81. Ivan Barkov wrote humorous, but often pornographic verse.

82. Voronezh is a city located about three hundred miles southeast of Moscow.

83. The Valuisky Assumption Monastery was founded near Voronezh in 1613.

84. Consider also this letter written by Shidlovsky to Fyodor Dostoevsky on December 14, 1864, on the death of his brother Mikhail on July 22 of that year:

"Mikhail Mikhailovich [Dostoevsky] is no longer in this world. It is far too early to feel his absence fully. I have always believed in his warm feelings for me. Despite all the poverty of our earthly worth, the genuine memory of such an individual ennobles our existence. I also kept dreaming of seeing both of you again, but suddenly one of you is no longer there, and so early was his demise. It seems that a large part of my heart has died. . . .

"The deceased had informed me about your intentions to write to me; and I rejoiced and waited, but most likely, the sweet leisure of literary creation did not allow time [for you] to write a line or two. I will not murmur against you, or pick a quarrel, or take you from your work, sensible and sweet.

"But now is a different matter. I appeal to you as a supplicant who is humble, humiliated, and plaintively-passionate. More than likely, you have pictures of Mikhail Mikhailovich. Send me a likeness of him, and if possible, in the most simple pose. I do not feel like buying ones for sale. Perhaps you cannot but believe my love for both of you. But give to me what is mine, just as to Caesar what is Caesar's, and to God, what is God's. Please do this! The matter is not a great or difficult one! . . . Do not refuse my soul!

'I have not forgotten your cherished soul
The song of friendship of youthful days!'

See Lanskii, "Dostoevskii," 398–399.

85. Pushkin wrote *Egyptian Nights* in 1837.

86. More accurately, Zhukovsky published "The Smailholm Tower: A Scottish Tale," in 1824, based on an 1800 ballad written by Walter Scott titled "The Eve of St. John," from legends in the ongoing wars between England and Scotland in the first half of the sixteenth century.

The Smailholm Tower was attacked by the English in 1543, 1544, and 1546, and is now a historic monument and tourist attraction in southeast Scotland.

87. Mikhail is quoting from Pushkin's 1823 poem "The Cart of Life."

88. The young Dostoevsky soon remedied the situation. He progressed steadily through the ranks; for example, on both November 29 and December 27, 1840, he was commended for his "good behavior and knowledge of service at the front." See Iakubovich, *Letopis'*, 70 and 71.

89. Shidlovsky had called upon Polevoi previously.

90. Sometime in December 1838, Shidlovsky attempted suicide by throwing himself through an ice-hole in the Fontanka, the reason being an unsuccessful love affair. He was saved by a soldier and a "coarse woman." See Iakubovich, *Letopis'*, 56.

91. Most likely, Shidlovsky's servant.

92. Shidlovsky is referring to the suicide of the hero in Goethe's *The Sorrows of Young Werther*, published in 1774.

93. The reference is to the English poet Thomas Chatterton who, at age twenty-two, died of arsenic poisoning either from an attempt at suicide or from self-medication for venereal disease.

94. The poem in question is the already cited "A Vision of Mother."

95. More accurately, Mikhail Dostoevsky is referring to Daniel Auber's 1828 opera, *The Mute Girl of Portici*, generally regarded as the first example of French grand opera.

96. The great German romanticist August Schlegel translated Shakespeare's seventeen dramas into German between 1791 and 1801.

97. Wrong therefore is Grossman's assertion that Dostoevsky "never manifested any interest in Latin language or literature and [that] the only old classical Roman poet he ever mentioned was Juvenal—and even then he was quoting someone else." See L. Grossman, *Dostoevsky: A Biography* (Indianapolis: Bobbs-Merrill, 1975), 17.

98. According to a journalist of the time, central Russia in 1839 was host not only to "tropical heat" but also to violent storms, fires, and floods that destroyed both livestock and crops. See Nechaeva, *Rannii Bunin*, 86 and 87.

99. This is the last letter Mikhail Dostoevsky wrote before his death.

100. Although Yanovsky is exaggerating the difficulties of Dostoevsky's childhood, he does affirm the emotional distance between Fyodor and Andrei.

101. Nechaeva, from her 1925 research into the murder of Dostoevsky's father, recalls, of her interview with Makarov and Savushkin: "The peasants had only a vague recollection of Dostoevsky's father, Mikhail Andreevich. They recall that the master was severe and unkind, but that none of the peasants who knew the man personally are still alive. The one thing that did stand out in their recollections was the fact of his violent death.

"Two peasants from Darovoe—Danila Makarov and Andrei Savushkin—could talk about things in detail. The first, between ninety and a hundred years old, was a boy about seven years old when the murder happened. The second knew about it from listening to his father. The two men talked together, correcting each other and adding things." See Nechaeva, "Iz literatury," 131.

102. Nechaeva, from her investigation into the murder of Dostoevsky's father, continued: "On July 8 1925, M. V. Volotskoi, author of the work, *A Chronicle of the Dostoevsky Clan*, and I . . . traveled to Darovoe with the specific goal of talking to the peasants [about the murder of Dostoevsky's father]. The calm and detailed narratives of the elders were devoid of any strivings for effect; they were also neither confusing, nor contradictory. Also true were the names they gave of long departed peasants, which I then checked in the church records in the village of Monogarovo. In so doing, they vindicated the proclamation of a long-covered up crime." See Nechaeva, *Rannii Dostoevskii*, 93.

103. The date for the death of Mikhail Dostoevsky was thought to be May 29, 1839; it has now been established as June 6.

It should also be noted that at the time, Andrei Dostoevsky was a fourteen-year-old student at Chermak's school in Moscow, and that his account of his father's demise was written more than forty years after the events.

104. The peasant Efimov was the uncle of Katerina, who, it will be recalled, was Mikhail Dostoevsky's consort with whom he had fathered a child. Since Katerina had grown up with Efimov's own children, the peasant wanted to avenge his niece for the *droit du seigneur* Mikhail exercised with the girl.

105. The peasant Isaev was the father of the house-serf Akulina Isaeva (noted earlier). His suspicion of an illicit union between Mikhail and his daughter was the reason for his involvement in the murder.

To this Nechaeva adds: "When one considers that two of the murderers, and perhaps all four, had close female relatives among old Dostoevsky's house-serfs, and that the name of Katya's uncle is first among the persons named as murderers (the murder took place in the yard of the house in which Katya was raised), this interpretation seems to be confirmed." See Nechaeva, *V sem'e*, 59.

106. Petrovka is the Russian folk name for the Russian Orthodox holiday of St. Peter celebrated on June 29.

107. The individual in question is David Saveliev.

108. At this time, Alyona Frolovna was looking after Mikhail's two youngest children, Nikolai and Alexandra.

109. Kashira is located about seventy miles to the southeast of Moscow.

110. A heavy drinker, Mikhail Dostoevsky often suffered from delirium tremens and (less likely) from epilepsy.

111. It has been suggested that Dostoevsky was the first in the family to have learned of his father's death.

112. As has been shown throughout this study, Dostoevskaya's statement begs credibility; but she is not alone in such assertions. "The 'idea' of the Karamazov father was doubtlessly inspired by the image of Dostoevsky's father." See Mochulsky, *Dostoevsky*, 7.

113. Such a claim is false. A seizure would not have passed unnoticed by the hundred or so schoolmates with whom Dostoevsky lived on close terms at the Main Engineering Academy. Also, if Dostoevsky had had such an attack, he would have been dismissed immediately by the administrators of the institution.

114. In fact, Andrei Dostoevsky was informed of Mikhail's death only on June 29, 1839, because the family did not wish to distract him from examinations at school.

115. There is no evidence for such a statement.

116. Olga Nechaeva had come from Moscow to take the newly orphaned Alexander, Nikolai, Vera, and Varvara Dostoevsky back with her. The children went to live with the Kumanins.

Incredibly, after the meeting with Olga Nechaeva, Pyotr Khotyaintsev again indicted Dostoevsky's peasants, the charge of murder again returning to the Kashira District Court, and as will be seen, involving Mikhail's children and relatives in Moscow.

117. Such a claim is true. "In cases [of murders of masters by peasants]," de Custine wrote in 1839, "the entire village is sent to Siberia or, as it is called in Petersburg: 'to populate Asia.'" See Custine, *Rossiia*, 135.

118. After the death of Mikhail Dostoevsky, the Kumanins looked after the youngest five Dostoevsky children (Alexandra, Nikolai, Vera, Andrei, and Varvara) but refused to be official guardians for the group. That position was assumed by the local police chief, Nikolai Elagin, in July–August 1839, who, during the next eighteen months, robbed the family blind.

119. According to both Maria and Olga Ivanova, each of Dostoevsky's three sisters received 25,000 rubles as a dowry. See Volotskoi, *Khronika*, 74 and 158–159.

120. This is incorrect. Mikhail was fifty at the time.

121. It was also the case that when the peasants found Mikhail, he was still alive, and that in an effort to save him they sent for a doctor from nearby Zaraisk—one I. M. Schonrock—rather than from the more distant Kashira. Because Schonrock came from another province, he did not have the authority to issue the death certificate. Hence the arrival of another doctor from Kashira by the name of Schonknecht, who confirmed Schonrock's diagnosis. Also, since judges in Kashira stipulated that Mikhail's body be "left in the exact place and position where he died," the corpse lay in the field for two days.

122. With the passing of Mikhail Andreevich Dostoevsky, his son Mikhail Mikhailovich Dostoevsky would no longer be noted as *fils*.

123. At this time, Fyodor Dostoevsky was again in camp at Peterhof, from June 22, 1839, to August 8, 1839.

124. After Elagin, legal guardianship for the five youngest Dostoevsky children moved to Pyotr Karepin, who, as has been already noted, had married Dostoevsky's sister Varvara, and who, in late December 1840, had also become the guardian of the Dostoevsky estate.

125. That is, Alexander Kumanin.

126. It was this Pyotr Khotyaintsev who initiated the rumor as to the murder of Mikhail Dostoevsky by his peasants, his idea being that, if the alleged assassins were deported to Siberia, he could buy the land that had been disputed between himself and Mikhail for a very cheap price.

127. Such an assertion is false. Mikhail Dostoevsky never encouraged his son to renew contact with the Kumanins. More to the truth, Mikhail so disliked the couple that he sought to break all ties between them and his children.

Part Three: Darkness before Dawn

1. I. Kniaz'kin, "Prostitutsiia," in P. Bukharin, ed., *Tri veka Sankt-Peterburga: Entsiklopedia v trekh tomakh*, vol. 2, bk. 5 (St. Petersburg: Filologicheskii fakul'tet Sankt-Peterburgskogo gosudarstvennogo universiteta, 2006), 745.

2. As quoted in W. Bruce Lincoln, *Nicholas I: Emperor and Autocrat of All the Russias* (Bloomington: Indiana University Press, 1978), 152. Also see Lincoln, 130–134.

3. The reference is to Pushkin's *Eugene Onegin*, written between 1823 and 1831. See stanza 33 and ff.

4. Shidlovsky's play *Maria Simonova* has been lost to time.

5. The Catherine Palace, located in the town of Tsarskoe selo (now Pushkin), was completed in 1756. Apparently, Dostoevsky lost contact with Shidlovsky after the latter left Petersburg in 1839.

6. Most likely, Dostoevsky is referring to Berezhetsky.

7. Again, Dostoevsky has Berezhetsky in mind.

8. Don Carlos and the Marquis de Posa are from Schiller's historical drama *Don Carlos* written between 1783 and 1787; Mortimer is from his *Maria Stuart*, penned between 1799 and 1800.

9. Homer wrote *The Iliad* sometime between the ninth and sixth centuries BCE.

10. Jean Racine wrote *Andromaque* in 1667.

11. Racine's *Iphigénie* was first performed in 1674.

12. Achilles is a character in *Iphigénie*.

13. Racine's *Phèdre* made its debut in 1677.

14. The reference is to Gogol's 1834 story "How the Two Ivans Quarreled."

15. Étienne Jodelle's 1552 tragedy *Cleopatra the Captive* was greeted by contemporaries as evidence of the rebirth of ancient Greek and Roman drama.

16. In linking the names of Vasili Tredyakovsky and Pierre Ronsard, Dostoevsky has in mind the epic poems of both men.

17. Pierre Corneille's 1635 play *Medea* follows closely Seneca's circa 54 BCE play of the same name.

18. Corneille wrote *Cinna* in 1642.

19. Karl Moor is the hero in Schiller's 1778 play, *The Robbers*; Fiesco in his 1783 drama, *Fiesco, or The Conspiracy of Genoa* in 1783; and Tell in his 1804 theatrical piece, *Wilhelm Tell*.

20. "Let us be friends, Cinna."

21. Corneille's *Horace* appeared in 1640.

22. Diomedes, Ajax Telamonian, Achilles, Curias, and Patrocles are all characters in *The Iliad*.

23. Corneille wrote *Le Cid* in 1635.

24. Perepenko is another character from Gogol's story, "How the Two Ivans Quarelled."

25. The individual in question is Mikhail Nechaev.

26. Actually, Dostoevsky should mean three years, since his mother died on February 27, 1837.

27. Marfa Isaeva was the thirteen-year-old sister of Akulina Isaeva and the daughter of Isaev, one of Mikhail Dostoevsky's alleged murderers (noted above). Alexei was the twenty-three-year-old son of Mikhailov, another of the purported conspirators. There were no convictions.

The Marshal of the Nobility in Kashira was also ordered to submit information as to "how the deceased Mr. Dostoevsky treated his peasants in his lifetime." Further, he was asked for particulars as to whether Mikhail's "serfs had brought any complaints against him, and if so, the nature of these complaints." No reports of grievances were found.

After still another review of the materials by officials in late October 1840, the case of the "suddenly deceased" father of Fyodor Dostoevsky was closed on November 5, 1840, and relegated to the court archives. See Fëdorov, "K biografii," 19.

28. Emilia Fyodorovna von Dimter married Mikhail Dostoevsky in January1842.

29. Mikhail passed the examination and was promoted to ensign-engineer on January 9, 1841. On May 31, he was named head of the drafting section of the Revel Engineering Brigade.

30. Such a tortuous line of thinking may echo passages in Mikhail Lermontov's novel *A Hero of Our Time*, which had come out as a separate edition in April–May of this year.

31. More reverberations from Lermontov's novel.

32. The work in question is Nekrasov's first (and highly imitative-romantic) 1840 collection, *Dreams and Sounds*. It should be noted that later in life, Nekrasov himself rejected the work.

Dostoevsky was named a noncommissioned officer (*unter-ofitser*) on November 29, 1840, and a sword-carrying cadet (*portupei-iunker*) on December 27.

33. Goethe wrote *Hermann and Dorothea* in 1797. It appeared in Russian in 1842.

34. The Alexander Theater, founded in 1756, is the oldest national theater in Russia. It was also the main imperial theater, the tsars taking an active interest in its operation.

35. Schiller wrote *Mary Stuart* in 1800.

36. In late 1840, Mikhail Dostoevsky had come to St. Petersburg to take an examination for field officer ensign; he entered that rank in January 1841. He left the imperial city on February 17, 1841.

37. Fyodor Dostoevsky was again in camp at Peterhof from June 20 to early August 1841.

38. Dostoevsky lived here until February–March 1842.

39. As has been noted, Dostoevsky and the Totleben brothers were classmates at the Main Engineering Academy.

40. On October 6, 1841 Mikhail Dostoevsky had traveled to Darovoe to collect the furniture and other items that had remained at the estate after the death of his father. Mikhail then continued to Moscow to ask both Alexander Kumanin and Pyotr Karepin for money for his upcoming marriage in January 1842 to Emilia von Ditmar, who hailed from Revel.

On the way back to Revel, Mikhail took Alexander to Fyodor so that he could prepare for entrance examinations for the Main Engineering Academy.

About Mikhail's trip to Darovoe, Andrei writes: "Mikhail took away everything that was of any value and sent it off to his bride in Revel. Some of the things, such as my father's fur coats, he sold in Moscow for next to nothing. All the china and silver was shared by my two elder brothers, and afterward I saw the items in their houses." See Dostoevskii, *Vospominaniia*, 121.

41. Mikhail Dostoevsky left St. Petersburg on October 17, 1841.

42. The paper was to certify Dostoevsky's agreement as to the transferred guardianship of his younger siblings from Elagin to Pyotr Karepin.

43. Andrei continued to live with Dostoevsky.

44. Most likely, Mikhail had complained about the financial difficulties arising from his impending marriage. It should also be noted that in late December 1841, Mikhail Dostoevsky joined Pyotr Karepin as a trustee of the Dostoevsky estate.

45. That is, Andrei Dostoevsky.

46. Dostoevsky has in mind either the Kumanins or the Karepins.

47. Rizenkamp leaves unclear the precise nature of these meetings.

48. Miller's claim is true.

49. The Imperial Academy of Arts, also known as the St. Petersburg Academy of Arts, opened in 1757 and was a bastion of neoclassicism in Russia.

50. Konstantin Trutovsky was also an illustrator for books by Pushkin, Gogol, and Taras Shevchenko.

51. In truth, Grigorovich was a year younger than Dostoevsky, having been born in 1822.

52. In September or December 1842 (sources vary), Andrei Dostoevsky entered the Academy of Civil Engineering in St. Petersburg. (Earlier that year, he had failed the entrance examinations for the Main Engineering Academy.) He left his brother's apartment on November 27, 1842.

53. It should also be noted that Dostoevsky had just completed a month-long ordeal of final examinations, beginning on May 20, 1842.

54. The Kumanins had sent Andrei a hundred rubles to celebrate his acceptance at the Academy of Civil Engineering.

55. Andrei Dostoevsky is not telling the truth here. The relationship between the two brothers was never this close; they often did not see each other for months on end.

56. The person in question is Louis Köhler.

57. Fyodor Privits was Director of the Academy of Civil Engineering, where Andrei had just enrolled, and was also in possession of the money that the Kumanins had sent to Andrei.

58. Alphonse Lamartine wrote "The Dying Poet" in 1832.

59. Rizenkamp is mistaken here. Soulié's *General Confession* came out in 1857.

60. Balzac penned *Two Brown Tales* in 1832.

61. Rizenkampf is again in error. Dostoevsky was reading a French translation of Frederick Marryat's 1836 English novel *Japhet, in Search of a Father*.

62. *The Fatherland Notes* was a literary and sociopolitical journal published in St. Petersburg from 1839 to 1867. It tended toward the ideas of the Westernizers, with Belinsky playing a prominent role as editor of the literary, critical, and bibliographical sections of the publication. At this time, *The Fatherland Notes* had a huge circulation of some 2,500 copies monthly.

63. "To France Were Returning Two Grenadiers" is the first line in Heine's poem, "Two Grenadiers," published in 1822–1823.

64. Karl Beck wrote *Janko, the Hungarian Horse-Herd: A Novel in Verse* in 1841.

65. Dostoevsky was granted a leave to Revel for twenty-eight days, beginning on June 21, 1843.

66. Dostoevsky graduated from the Main Engineering Academy on August 12, 1843.

67. On the next day, July 1, 1843, Dostoevsky left for Revel, where he spent two and a half weeks with his brother Mikhail and his family. Rizenkampf saw him off at the dock.

68. From July 3 to July 18, 1843, Dostoevsky lived in Revel with Mikhail, together with Mikhail's wife, Emilia, and their child, Fedya. He returned to the Main Engineering Academy on July 20.

69. The experiment, in an apartment in one of the poorer quarters of St. Petersburg, was a disaster, lasting only six months, from September 1843 to March 1844.

70. Dostoevsky fails to mention here that, absorbed in literary projects, he had so neglected his studies that he graduated only in the middle of his class, and that instead of being assigned to a first-class fort he was appointed to an exceedingly modest post in the Engineering Corps.

71. Dostoevskaya's claim here is false. As will be seen, Fyodor Dostoevsky retired from service on October 19, 1844, after a little more than a year in the Engineering Department.

72. Grigorovich and Dostoevsky began to live together sometime in fall 1844.

73. The individual is Pyotr Karepin.

74. The figure of 5,000 is overblown. Dostoevsky received an annual allowance of only 1,000 rubles from Karepin, plus his salary as an officer, which was considerably less. In fact, Dostoevsky's salary must have been no more than 2,000 rubles a year.

75. Both items Dostoevsky had bought on credit.

76. Truth be told, the money Dostoevsky slipped to the group came not only from his own pockets but also from Rizenkampf's professional fees.

77. Dostoevsky had been to Revel in summer 1843 for a four-week visit to Mikhail and his new wife, Emilia.

78. Mikhail and Emilia Dostoevsky did as Fyodor wished. Maria Mikhailovna Dostoevskaya was born on March 2, 1844.

79. The translation into Russian of the first part of Eugène Sue's 1841 novel, *Mathilde, or the Notes of a Young Woman*, was published on February 25, 1842, without the name of the translator. (A complete translation of the work did not appear until 1846–1847.)

Dostoevsky admired Sue greatly, borrowing many of the writer's images and ideals as his own. In fact, the childhood of the heroine in his 1849 unfinished novel, *Netochka Nezvanova*, bears a striking affinity to the early years of the main character in *Mathilde*.

80. The project never went beyond the planning stages.

81. Alexander Nikitenko was one of the most liberal censors of the time.

82. Since Kovalevskaya met Dostoevsky when he was forty-three, the alleged incident took place around 1844.

83. It is of interest to note that although critics have discussed rumors of Dostoevsky's misconduct with minors later in life, they do not assess the accuracy of Kovalevskaya's remarks. See V. Svinstov, "Dostoevsky and Stavrogin's Sin," *Russian Studies in Literature* 4 (1998): 37.

84. The plays in question are *The Inheritance*, a reworking of Soulié's 1840 play *Eulalie Pontois*, as well as his translation with Vladimir Zotov of Clairville's 1842 vaudeville *Opium and Champagne, or the War of China*.

85. Patton was translating *A History of the Polish Uprising and War in the Years 1830 and 1831*, by Fyodor Smitt, published in Berlin in 1839.

86. More accurately, *The Store for Instructive and Pleasant Reading for German Readers in Russia* was published by a group of German doctors from 1831 to 1840. As the center for German literary life, it focused on light literature and such popular themes as family, religion, and everyday life.

87. Rizenkampf is referring to the various translations of works that Dostoevsky undertook at this time.

88. Specifically Christmas 1843.

89. Dostoevsky's play *Yankel the Jew* has not survived, though at least one scholar has suggested that the play embraced characters and themes from both Shakespeare's 1603 drama *Measure for Measure* and Gogol's 1835 novella *Taras Bulba*.

90. Dostoevsky did, in fact, publish his translation of Balzac's *Eugénie Grandet* in the journal *Repertoire of Russian and Pantheon of All European Theaters*, in June and July 1844. It was his first publication.

91. Sue wrote his novel *Plik and Plok* in 1832.

92. Alain-René Lesage's 1707 work *The Lame Devil* appeared in Russian in 1832.

93. Murad is a character in Pavel Kamensky's 1830 bildungsroman, *The Seeker of Strong Sensations*. Murad wishes to know and understand everything, but becomes lost amid the vast realms of knowledge.

94. The work is the already noted *The Last Aldini*.

95. Contemporary Russian investigators of Dostoevsky support Miller's claim.

96. The journal in question is *Repertoire of Russian and Pantheon of All European Theaters*, which was published in St. Petersburg from 1842 to 1856 by Fyodor Bulgarin and Fyodor Koni, and which, as the title suggests, focused on a wide range of dramatic literature.

97. Dostoevsky is referring to Schiller's article "About Naive and Sentimental Poetry," penned between 1794 and 1796. It was translated into Russian by Mikhail Dostoevsky and appeared in *The Fatherland Notes* in 1850.

98. *Semela*, written between 1779 and 1780, is an opera libretto written by Schiller; it was translated into Russian in 1842.

99. That is, the Kumanins.

100. Dostoevsky is here a victim of wishful thinking; the decree was issued on October 19, 1844, and on November 7 his name was struck from the lists of the Petersburg Engineering Command.

101. Dostoevsky is citing the French proverb, "*Chacun pour soi et Dieu pour tous*." He also wrote in *Diary of a Writer* in 1880: "Dare we take the liberty to assert that *Chacun pour soi et Dieu pour tous* is not only a proverb, but also a social formula accepted by all in the West, which *everyone* serves and believes." See Dostoevskii, *Polnoe sobranie sochinenii*, vol. 26, 154.

102. Orenburg is roughly 1,100 miles southeast of St. Petersburg. Sevastopol is a port city in Ukraine on the Crimean peninsula, located roughly 800 miles from Moscow and 1,000 from St. Petersburg.

103. The Kamchatka peninsula is approximately 4,000 miles east of the imperial capital.

104. The Kazan Cathedral was fashioned by the architect Andrei Voronikhin. Dedicated to Our Lady of Kazan, whose image is arguably the most venerated icon in Russia, the Kazan Cathedral was to be the main Orthodox Church in Russia.

The Kazan Cathedral was built in 1737, rebuilt from 1801 to 1810, and consecrated in 1811. (To the consternation of some of the Russian Orthodox clergy, the reconstruction of the Kazan Cathedral, with its enormous scale and impressive stone colonnade, was modeled after St. Peter's Basilica in Rome.)

After the defeat of the French by the Russians in 1812, the Kazan Cathedral was deemed a monument to the national victory. Captured banners of the enemy were hung inside the church; Mikhail Golenishchev-Kutuzov, the commander of the Russian troops during the war, was buried there.

The Kazan Cathedral was also the site of the first political demonstration in Russia when on December 6, 1876, some four hundred people, organized by members from workers' associations (one of whom waved a red flag), heard Georgi Plekhanov indict autocracy and what he considered to be other national failings. Thirty-one people were arrested, five of whom would be sentenced to from ten to fifteen years in Siberia. (The flag waver found himself incarcerated for five years in a Russian monastery.)

The Bolsheviks closed the Kazan Cathedral in 1929, but four years later they reopened it as the Museum of the History of Religion and Atheism. After the collapse of communism, religious services in the Kazan Cathedral were resumed in 1992; four years later the church was returned to the Russian Orthodox Church, but it still shares the premises with the Museum (with the word "atheism" omitted).

105. As will be seen, Mikhail vouched to Karepin for his brother twice.

106. Dostoevsky is referring to Jeremy Bentham's 1787 treatise *The Defense of Usury*. Most likely, he became familiar with Bentham's idea with his translation of Balzac's *Eugénie Grandet*, in which the chair of the committee (in Dostoevsky's translation, "president") affirms: "Every thing is a good with its own price. So determined Jeremy Bentham about moneylenders. The famous publicist proved that the prejudices associated with moneylenders were complete nonsense."

107. Perepenko is also a character in Gogol's story "How the Two Ivans Quarreled."

108. Most likely, the reference is to an aphorism from Goethe's 1795 novel, *The Apprenticeship of Wilhelm Meister*. That is, in the beginning of the chapter titled "Thoughts in the Spirit of Pilgrims," Goethe writes: "The most insignificant person can be 'complete' if he functions within the spheres of his capabilities and talents. But if the requisite equilibrium disappears, then the greatest attributes darken . . . and are reduced to dust."

109. Famusov is a character in Alexander Griboyedov's 1825 play *Woe from Wit*; Chichikov, from Gogol's 1842 novel *Dead Souls*; and Falstaff, from Shakespeare's *Henry IV*, parts 1 and 2, written in 1596 and 1599, respectively.

110. Such an assertion is open to question.

111. In another retelling of this story, Trutovsky claims that he was seventeen years old.

112. The work in question is Grigorovich's essay *The Petersburg Organgrinders*, which was published in Nekrasov's almanac, *The Physiology of Petersburg*, in 1845.

113. This letter is unknown.

114. Such an assertion never came to be.

115. Schiller never wrote a play titled *Treachery*. What Dostoevsky may have had in mind is Schiller's 1800 dramatic trilogy *Wallenstein*, about the betrayal and murder of the Bohemian general Albrecht von Wallenstein in 1634.

116. Dostoevsky is referring to Schiller's *Letters about Don Carlos*, written in 1788, and the already mentioned "About Naive and Sentimental Poetry."

117. As noted previously, the projected edition of Schiller did not come to fruition.

118. Dostoevsky is noting the family estates of Darovoe and Cheremoshnya.

119. Dostoevsky's request for retirement arrived at the Military Chancellery on October 5, 1844.

120. The novel in question is *Poor Folk*.

121. Dostoevsky is borrowing a line from scene 5 of Gogol's 1842 play *The Inspector General*.

122. Dostoevsky is again quoting a line from scene 5 of *The Inspector General,* in which the hero, Khlestakov, says: "What if he really drags me off to prison? What of it? If it is done in a noble way, well then, I. . . . No, no, I do not want to go."

123. Not quite. Dostoevsky finished translating *Eugénie Grandet* in late January 1844.

124. Grigorovich is wrong again. As has already been noted, Dostoevsky published his translation of *Eugénie Grandet* in *Repertoire and Pantheon* in June and July 1844.

125. Again, the novel is *Poor Folk*.

126. In the end, Karepin acceded to Dostoevsky's request and sent him 500 silver rubles in late November 1844, for a sum total of 2,412 rubles 50 copecks by the end of the year.

127. This letter is not known.

128. "My religion has never changed in its fundamentals," George Sand was quoted as saying in *Novoe vremia* on June 3, 1876. "The eternal teaching of believers—the God of all blessings, the immortality of the soul, and hopes for another life—all this is above any criticism, any discussion, and even any attempts at hopeless doubt." See Dostoevskii, *Polnoe sobranie sochinenii*, vol. 23, 368.

129. Dostoevsky is quoting from Acts 4:12: "There is no salvation through anyone else, nor is there any other name under heaven given to the human race by which we are to be saved."

130. The ant heap is a key motif in the soliloquy of Dostoevsky's Underground Man.

131. Compare citations from Deuteronomy 8:3: "He therefore let you be afflicted with hunger, and then fed you with manna, a food unknown to you and your fathers, in order to show you that not by bread alone does man live, but by every word that comes forth from the mouth of the Lord"; and from Matthew 4:4: "Jesus said in reply, 'It is written: One does not live by bread alone, but by every word that comes forth from the mouth of God.'"

132. This is not true. George Sand's mother was a peasant; Dostoevsky repeats a mistake in an obituary for the writer published in the Russian newspaper *New Time* on May 29, 1876. In truth, it was Sand's paternal grandmother who claimed the aristocratic tie, she being the illegitimate daughter of the famous general Maurice, Count of Saxony, also known as Marshal Saxe, who in turn was the bastard son of August II, king of Poland and elector of Saxony.

133. The Vyborg side of St. Petersburg is located northeast of the central part of the city and encompasses the entire area along the right bank of the Neva.

134. That is, the Karepins.

135. Again, the work in question is *Poor Folk*.

136. The source for this citation is unknown.

137. That is, *Poor Folk*.

138. The Brocken (or Blocksberg) is the highest peak among the Harz Mountains, located in northern Germany.

139. *The Invalid*, more accurately *The Russian Invalid*, was a military newspaper published from 1813 to 1917 for patriotic and philanthropic purposes (the income from publication was used to help veterans, widows, and orphans).

140. In an article titled "Poets in Germany" published in *The Russian Invalid* on March 22, 1845, the author wrote: "Lessing died in need, cursing the German nation. Schiller never had more than a thousand francs to go and look at Paris and the sea. In all, Mozart received 1,500 francs as salary, leaving, after his death, three thousand rubles in debts. Beethoven also died in extreme need.

Holderlin was forced to be a schoolteacher. Tormented by love and need, he went insane at the age of thirty-two and lived that way until his death forty-four years later.

"For a piece of bread, Holty, the pure poet of love, gave lessons for six francs a month. He died young, having poisoned himself. Burger waged an incessant struggle with need.... Grabbe, author of the brilliant 'Faust and Don Juan,' literally died from hunger at the age of thirty-two. Lenz, the friend of Goethe, died of extreme need at the home of a shoemaker in Moscow.... Kleist shot himself. Lessman hanged himself. Raimund—the actor and poet—shot himself.... Lenau was carried off to a home for lunatics." See A. Veis, "Smes': Poety v Germanii," *Russkii invalid* 64 (March 22, 1845): 3.

Dostoevsky was particularly unnerved by Veis's piece because he had just retired from service to pursue a literary career.

141. Dostoevsky was twenty-four at the time.

142. Chateaubriand's *Atala* was published in 1841; it was not his first work.

143. Laurence Sterne's *A Sentimental Journey Through France and Italy* was first published in 1768.

144. Dostoevsky read *A Sentimental Journey* in French translation published in 1845. Critics of Sterne agree that La Fleur is a fictional character.

145. Plyushkin is a character in Gogol's *Dead Souls*.

146. Walter Scott published *Guy Mannering, or the Astrologer* was translated into Russian in 1824.

147. In truth, Scott was forty-four.

148. The novel in question is *Poor Folk*.

149. The citation is to E. Chapelle's 1834 vaudeville, *My Wife and My Umbrella*, which was staged in France in 1834, and reworked in 1840 by Pyotr Karatygin with the title *The Wife and The Umbrella, or the Distressed Tuner*.

The allusion is obvious. Not unlike Dostoevsky's regard for his apartment, novel, and trip to Revel, Chapelle's hero sees both a wife and an umbrella as necessary facets of a middle-class life.

150. Sue published *The Eternal Jew* in 1844–1845.

151. Most likely, Dostoevsky is referring to the collapse of his plans to publish an edition of Schiller's works.

152. Alexander Veltman's *Emelia, or the Metamorphosis*, a parody of Russian romantic clichés, was published in 1845.

153. Vladimir Sollogub penned *Tarantas*, a satire of a journey from Moscow to Kazan in a dilapidated cart, in 1845.

154. More accurately, Dostoevsky and Nekrasov were both twenty-four years old.

155. The individual in question is thought to be Konstantin Trutovsky.

156. As has been seen, Kovalevskaya is quite wrong about the tie between Dostoevsky and Grigorovich.

157. Again, Dostoevsky was twenty-four.

158. Belinsky is referring to Makar Devushkin, the hero of *Poor Folk*.

159. The citation is again from Gogol's story, "How the Two Ivans Quarreled."

160. Golyadkin is the hero of Dostoevsky's second story, *The Double*, which he had begun to write in summer 1845.

161. At the same time, Belinsky insisted to Dostoevsky that from Kraevsky he should demand two hundred paper rubles per page.

162. The highly respected individual is Pavel Botkin; the young writer is Ivan Turgenev.

163. It should be noted that in his comments about Belinsky, particularly his espousal of socialism and atheism, Dostoevsky is talking not only from hindsight but also with a severe lack of memory. As has been shown, Dostoevsky himself had turned his back on his religious

beliefs; within the next few years, he, too, would flirt with socialism as the answer to the problems of humankind.

164. Dostoevsky's *Poor Folk* came out in Nekrasov's almanac, *The Petersburg Miscellany*, which went on sale to the Russian public on January 12, 1846.

165. By this time, Dostoevsky had sketched the next-to-last chapter of *The Double*.

166. Since Dostoevsky had been in Revel from June 9 to September 9, 1845, he resumed his friendship with Belinsky three months after their first meeting.

167. In his ongoing feuilleton titled "Journalistic Hodgepodge," Bulgarin styled himself as a champion of truth; so much so that Belinsky called Bulgarin's journal *The Northern Bee* the "defender of truth and purity of the Russian language." See Belinskii, *Polnoe sobranie sochinenii*, vol. 9 (1955), 371.

Belinsky continued: "If one is to believe this publication, only *The Bee* loves truth more than anything else in the world—and every minute, it is ready to die for the truth, and for it to suffer the persecution of the entire literary brotherhood." See Belinskii, *Polnoe sobranie sochinenii*, 9:615–616.

168. Here Dostoevsky has in mind a parody of Sue's many-tomed novels, replete with multiple mysteries, horrors, and romantic adventures.

169. The anecdote "Pushkin and the Lizards" poked fun at Stepan Shevyryov, whom the members of Belinsky circle saw as a representative of "official nationality." It was published in the 1846 almanac *The First of April*.

170. *Illustration* was a newspaper published weekly in St. Petersburg from 1845 to 1849; Nikolai Kukolnik was the editor for the first two years of its existence.

171. Grigorovich never wrote the story.

172. Such a work never came to be. Instead, Dostoevsky wrote *A Novel in Nine Letters*.

173. *Les Guêpes* was a satirical journal founded by Alphonse Karr in 1839.

174. The reference is to a line by the character Nozdryov in chapter 4 of Gogol's *Dead Souls* (*Mertvye dushi*).

175. Sand wrote *Teverino* in 1845.

176. An *arshin* is a Russian measure, equivalent to seventy-one centimeters.

177. Dostoevsky first met Odoevsky sometime in late November or early December 1845 (sources vary), most likely on Belinsky's invitation.

178. Vladimir Sollogub paid a surprise visit to Dostoevsky around January 26, 1846.

179. At the time, Ivan Turgenev was twenty-seven (three years Dostoevsky's senior); only a week earlier, he had returned to Russia from a six-month stay in Europe. He was also not wealthy, but not quite so in need until 1850. See P. Annenkov, "Molodost' Turgeneva," in Annenkov, *Literaturnye vospominaniia*, 370.

180. Lucien de Rubempré is the hero of Balzac's novels *Lost Illusions*, written in 1843, and *The Harlot High and Low*, published five years later. As a journalist in *Lost Illusions*, de Rubempré seeks to publish a feuilleton "in a new and unusual manner, bringing about an entire revolution in journalism."

181. In truth, Dostoevsky published *A Novel in Nine Letters* in Nekrasov's *The Contemporary* in 1847.

182. Gogol's *The Lawsuit* was written in 1842 and staged at the Alexander Theater two years later.

183. The woman in question is Avdotya Panaeva, a writer in her own right.

184. So much for Dostoevsky's alleged aloofness from women.

185. Anna Dostoevskaya's statement is true.

186. Grigorovich and Annenkov were also present.

187. In Russian: "Budesh' ty dovolen mnoiu/ Postupliu ia kak podlets/ Obvedu tebia kaimoiu/ Pomeshu tebia v konets."

In truth, the verse is a final stanza of a piece titled "A Greeting from Belinsky to Dostoevsky," which was composed in late January 1846 by Nekrasov, Turgenev, and Panaev, and which reads:

> A knight of mournful cast,
> Dostoevsky, dear, grand, and tall
> Like a new pimple on literature's nose
> Redly do you glow to all.
>
> Although a new writer
> Joyfully you dethrone one and all
> The Emperor praises you
> Even Lichtenberg is enthralled.
>
> For you the Turkish sultan
> Will send his wisest men
> But the grand reception before princes
> No one knows where and when.
>
> Now a myth and question
> You have fallen like a Finnish star
> And sneezed your pug-like nose
> At a red-haired beauty from afar.
>
> How tragically inert
> You looked at the object of your light
> And so close to death.
> Did not perish at your artful height.
>
> From the envious cliffs
> Bend your ear to my request
> Cast your ashen glance
> Cast it at me, your guest.
>
> For the sake of future praise
> (Such extremes, you see, are quirks)
> But separate *The Double*
> From your unpublished works.
>
> I will make a fuss over you
> I will set forth, a scoundrel on the mend
> I will surround you with a border
> And put you at the end.

See I. Nikol'skii, *Turgenev i Dostoevskii: Istoriia odnoi vrazhdy* (Sofia: Rossisko-Bolgarskoe Knigoizdatel'stvo, 1921), 5–6.

188. "Plismylkov's Story," originally titled "Polzunkov," was to be published in the anthology *Illustrated Almanac* in 1848.

189. It was on June 8, 1880, at ceremonies celebrating the unveiling of the Pushkin monument in Moscow that Dostoevsky delivered his famous speech on the writer. (He died eight months later.)

190. Such an assertion was false.

191. Interestingly, Annenkov omitted this last sentence in later editions of his memoirs.

192. The piece has been cited above.

193. Annenkov wrote this letter to Stasyulevich on April 7, 1880.

194. Suvorin wrote this letter to Dostoevsky on May 1, 1880.

195. Burenin defended Dostoevsky in *New Time* on May 2, 1880.

196. Suvorin penned this dispatch to Dostoevsky on May 12, 1880.

197. Dostoevsky wrote this letter to Suvorin on May 14, 1880.

198. Staraya Russa, famous for its mineral springs, is a town in northwest Russia, roughly sixty miles south of Novgorod.

199. Suvorin published this statement in *New Time* on May 18, 1880.

200. Dostoevsky penned this missive to Pobedonostsev on May 19, 1880.

201. Dostoevsky wrote this excerpt sometime in 1881.

202. *Poor Folk* appeared in print on January 21, 1846.

Source Notes

1803.

1803 and after. A. Dostoevskii, *Vospominaniia Andreia Mikhailovicha Dostoevskogo* (Leningrad: Izdatel'stvo pisatelei, 1930), 17.
1803 and after. L. Dostoevskaia, *Dostoevskii v izobrazhenii svoei docheri* (Moscow: Gosudarstvennoe izdatel'stvo, 1922), 10–11.

1812.

Circa 1812 and after. Dostoevskaia, *Dostoevskii*, 12.

1820.

After 1820. Dostoevskii, *Vospominaniia*, 403–404.
After 1820. F. Dostoevskii, *Dnevnik pisatelia za 1873 god* (Berlin: Izdatel'stvo I. P. Ladyzhnikova, 1922), 418.
After 1820. Dostoevskii, *Vospominaniia*, 94.
After 1820. Dostoevskii, *Vospominaniia*, 49.
After 1820. L. Dostoevskaia, *Dostoevskii v izobrazhienii svoei docheri* (St. Petersburg: Andreev i synov'ia, 1992), 34.
After 1820. M. Volotskoi, *Khronika roda Dostoevskogo, 1506–1933* (Moscow: Sever, 1933), 51.
After 1820. Dostoevskii, *Vospominaniia*, 92–93.
After 1820. M. Grossman, *Dostoevskii na zhiznennom puti: Molodost' Dostoevskogo (1821–1850)* (Moscow: Kooperativnoe izdatel'stvo pisatelei: Nikitinskie subbotniki, 1928), 20.
After 1820. Dostoevskii, *Vospominaniia*, 35.

1821.

October 30, 1821. Grossman, *Dostoevskii*, 23.
After October 1821. Dostoevskaia, *Dostoevskii* (1922), 33.

1822.

Circa 1822 and after. Dostoevskii, *Vospominaniia*, 28.
Circa 1822 and after. Dostoevskii, *Vospominaniia*, 29.
December 1822 and after. Dostoevskii, *Vospominaniia*, 24–26.

270   SOURCE NOTES

December 1822 and after. Dostoevskii, *Dnevnik pisatelia za 1876 god*, 182.
December 1822 and after. Dostoevskii, *Vospominaniia*, 27.
December 1822 and after. L. Grossman, *Seminarii po Dostoevskomu: Materialy, biografiia i komentarii* (Moscow: Gosudarstvennoe izdatel'stvo, 1922), 62 and 64.
December 1822 and after. A. Dostoevskaia, "God kak zhizn': Iz zapisnoi knizhki," *Literaturnaia gazeta* (April 16, 1986), 3; and Volotskoi, *Khronika*, 50.

1823.

1823. Grossman, *Seminarii*, 66.

1824.

Circa 1824. P. Bykov, "Vyderzhki iz avtobiografii F. M. Dostoevskogo," *Krasnaia gazeta* (February 24, 1925); as quoted in I. Volgin, *Rodit'sia v Rossii: Dostoevskii i sovremenniki; zhizn' v dokumetakh* (Moscow: Kniga, 1991), 162.
Circa 1824. O. Miller, "Materialy dlia zhizneopisaniia F. M. Dostoevskogo," in F. Dostoevskii, *Biografiia, pis'ma i zametki iz zapisnoi knizhki* (St. Petersburg: Tipografiia A. S. Suvorina, 1883), 5–6.
Mid–late 1820s. Miller, "Materialy," 16.
Mid–late 1820s. Dostoevskii, *Vospominaniia*, 44–45.
Mid–late 1820s. Miller, "Materialy," 9.
Mid–late 1820s. Dostoevskii, *Vospominaniia*, 38–39.
Mid–late 1820s. Dostoevskii, *Vospominaniia*, 48.
Mid–late 1820s. A. Dolinin, ed., *F. M. Dostoevskii: Pis'ma v chetyrekh tomakh*, vol. 2 (Moscow: Gosudarstvennoe izdatel'stvo, 1930), 264.

1825.

1825. Miller, "Materialy," 6.

1826.

Circa 1826 and after. Dostoevskii, *Vospominaniia*, 49–50.
Circa 1826 and after. A. Dostoevskaia, *Vospominaniia* (Moscow: Khudozhestvennaia literatura, 1971), 89.
Circa 1826 and after. Dostoevskaia, "God kak zhizn'," 3.
Circa 1826 and after. "Pis'ma S. D. Ianovskogo," in A. Dolinin, ed., *F. M. Dostoevskii: Stat'i i materialy*, bk. 2 (Moscow: Mysl', 1924), 393.

1828.

Circa 1828. Dostoevskii, *Vospominaniia*, 43.
February 1, 1828, and after. Dostoevskii, *Vospominaniia*, 49.

June 28, 1828. Dostoevskaia, *Dostoevskii* (1922), 13.
After June 1828. Dostoevskii, *Vospominaniia*, 17–18.

1829.

Before 1829. F. Dostoevskii, *Polnoe sobranie sochinenii v tridtsati tomakh*, vol. 5 (Leningrad: Nauka, 1973), 46.
Circa 1829. V. Pereverzev, ed., *F. M. Dostoevskii: Pis'ma k zhene* (Moscow: Gosudarstvennoe izdatel'stvo, 1926), 273.
1829. "Iz snoshenii F. M. i M. M. Dostoevskikh s Ia. P. Polonskim," in A. Dolinin, ed. *F. M. Dostoevskii: Stat'i i materialy*, bk. 1 (St. Petersburg: Mysl', 1922, 454.
1829. Grossman, *Seminarii*, 68.

1830.

Circa 1830 and after. Dostoevskaia, *Dostoevskii* (1992), 30.
Circa 1830 and after. Dostoevskii. *Vospominaniia*, 33.
Circa 1830 and after. Dostoevskii, *Vospominaniia*, 47.
Circa 1830 and after. Dostoevskii, *Vospominaniia*, 46–47; and Miller, "Materialy," 9–10.

1831.

Circa 1831. Dostoevskii, *Dnevnik pisatelia za 1873 god*, 418.
Circa 1831. Dostoevskii, *Dnevnik pisatelia za 1877 god* (Paris: YMCA Press, 1946?), 299.
Circa 1831. Pereverzev, ed., *Pis'ma*, 171.
Circa 1831. Dostoevskii, *Vospominaniia*, 63.
Circa 1831. Dostoevskii, *Dnevnik pisatelia za 1873 god* (1922), 418.
Circa 1831. Dolinin, ed., *F. M. Dostoevskii: Pis'ma*, vol. 2, 300.
Circa 1831. V. Kachenovskii, "Moi vospominaniia o Dostoevskom," *Moskovskie vedomosti* (January 31, 1881), 4.
Circa 1831. S. Belov, ed., *F. M. Dostoevskii v zabytykh i neizvestnykh vospominaniiakh sovremennikov* (St. Petersburg: Andreev i sinov'ia, 1993), 25–26; and Z. Trubetskaia, "Dostoevskii i A. P. Filosofova," *Russkaia literatura* 3 (1973), 117.
Circa August 1831 and after. Dostoevskii, *Polnoe sobranie sochinenii*, vol. 19 (1979), 17.
Circa August 1831. F. Dostoevskii, "Literaturnyi otdel: Dva pis'ma F. M. Dostoevskogo," *Rus'* 30 (June 6, 1881), 22.
August 1831. Dostoevskii, *Dnevnik pisatelia za 1876*, 72–76.
August 1831 and after. Dostoevskii, *Vospominaniia*, 58–59.

1832.

April 12, 1832. Dostoevskii, *Dnevnik pisatelia za 1876 god*, 181–182.
April 12, 1832. Dostoevskii, *Polnoe sobranie sochinenii*, vol. 24 (1982), 181.

April 12, 1832. Dostoevskii, *Vospominaniia*, 60.
Late April 1832. Dostoevskii, *Vospominaniia*, 61.
Late April 1832 and after. Miller, "Materialy," 13.
Late April 1832 and after. Dostoevskaia, *Dostoevskii* (1922), 13.
Late April 1832 and after. Dostoevskii, *Vospominaniia*, 55–58.
Late April 1832 and after. Dostoevskii, *Vospominaniia*, 61–63.
Late April 1832 and after. V. Nechaeva, "Iz literatury o Dostoevskom: Poezdka v Darovoe," *Novyi mir* 3 (1926), 131.
Late April 1832 and after. Dostoevskii, *Vospominaniia*, 56.
Late April 1832 and after. Dostoevskii, *Vospominaniia*, 57.
June 29, 1832. V. Nechaeva, *V sem'e i usad'be Dostoevskikh* (Moscow: Gosudarstvennoe sotsial'no-ekonomicheskoe izdatel'stvo, 1939), 73 and 75.
June 29, 1832. Dolinin, ed., *F. M. Dostoevskii: Pis'ma*, vol. 1 (1928), 39.
Late summer 1832. Dostoevskii, *Vospominaniia*, 61.
Early fall 1832. Dostoevskii, *Vospominaniia*, 64–65.
November 8, 1832 and after. Dostoevskii, *Vospominaniia*, 47–48.

1833.

Circa 1833. Dostoevskii, *Dnevnik pisatelia za 1876 god*, 97.
January 1833–fall 1834. Dostoevskaia, *Dostoevskii* (1922), 13.
January 1833 and after. Dostoevskii, *Vospominaniia*, 30–31.
January 1833 and after. Dostoevskii, *Vospominaniia*, 71.
January 1833 and after. Dostoevskaia, *Dostoevskii* (1922), 35.
Summer 1833 and after. Dostoevskii, "Literaturnyi otdel," 22.
Summer 1833 and after. Dostoevskaia, "God kak zhizn'," 3.
Summer 1833 and after. Dostoevskaia, *Dostoevskii* (1992), 91.
July 9, 1833. Nechaeva, *V sem'e*, 76–78.
August 6, 1833. Nechaeva, *V sem'e*, 81; and D. Magarshack, *Dostoevsky* (New York: Harcourt, Brace, and World, 1962), 9.
August 23, 1833. Nechaeva, *V sem'e*, 81.
August 23, 1833. Dostoevskii, *Vospominaniia*, 358.
August 23, 1833. Nechaeva, *V sem'e*, 83.

1834.

1834–1836. Dostoevskii, *Vospominaniia*, 68–70.
April–May 1834. "Pis'mo Dostoevskogo k materi, ot 1834 goda," in A. Dolinin, ed., *F. M. Dostoevskii: Stat'i i materialy*, bk. 2 (1924), 309.
Late 1834. Dostoevskii, *Vospominaniia*, 33–34.
Early September 1834–spring 1837. Dostoevskii, *Vospominaniiia*, 66 and 95.
Early September 1834–spring 1837. Dostoevskaia, *Dostoevskii* (1922), 13.
Early September 1834–spring 1837. Dostoevskii, *Vospominaniia*, 96.
Early September 1834–spring 1837. Dostoevskii, *Vospominaniia*, 36.
Early September 1834–spring 1837. Dostoevskii, *Vospominaniia*, 97.

Early September 1834–spring 1837. D. Grigorovich, *Literaturnye vospominaniia* (Moscow: Gosudarstvennoe izdatel'stvo khudozhestvennoi literatury, 1961), 47.
Early September 1834–spring 1837. A. Fëdorov, "Pansion L. I. Chermaka v 1834–1837 gg.," i n V. Bazanov et al., *Dostoevskii: Materialy i issledovaniia*, vol. 1 (Leningrad: Nauka, 1974), 251.
Early September 1834–spring 1837. I. Troitskii, "Donos Shervuda (1843)," *Zhizn' Shervuda-Vernogo* (Moscow: Izdatel'stvo vsesoiuznogo obshchestva politkatorzhan i ssyl'no-poselentsev, 1931), 250.
Early September 1834–spring 1837. "Pis'mo F. M. Dostoevskiogo k Kachenovskomu," in A. Dolinin, ed., *F. M. Dostoevskii: Stat'i i materialy*, bk. 1, 71.
Early September 1834–spring 1837. Kachenovskii, "Moi vospominaniia," 4.
Early September 1834–spring 1837. Dostoevskii, *Vospominaniia*, 67–68.
Fall–winter 1834. Dostoevskii, *Vospominaniia*, 65–66.

1835.

Circa 1835 and after. Dostoevskii, *Vospominaniia*, 70–71.
Circa 1835 and after. Miller, "Materialy," 25.
1835 and after. Dostoevskii, *Vospominaniia*, 69.
1835 and after. M. Dostoevskii, "Peterburgskii telegraf: Signaly literaturnye," *Panteon i repertuar russkoi stseny* 5 (1848), 73–74.
1835 and after. Dostoevskii, *Vospominaniia*, 71.
April 26, 1835. Nechaeva, *V sem'e*, 83 and 85.
April 29, 1835. Nechaeva, *V sem'e*, 85–86.
May 1, 1835. Nechaeva, *V sem'e*, 87–88.
May 3, 1835. Nechaeva, *V sem'e*, 88–90.
May 9, 1835. Nechaeca, *V sem'e*, 90–91.
May 16, 1835. Nechaeva, *V sem'e*, 94.
May 19, 1835. Nechaeva, *V sem'e*, 95–96.
Circa mid-May 1845. Dostoevskii, *Vospominaniia*, 48.
Circa mid-May 1845. Dostoevskii, *Vospominaniia*, 81.
Before May 23, 1835. V. Nechaeva, *Rannii Dostoevskii, 1821–1849* (Moscow: Nauka, 1979), 30.
May 23, 1835. Nechaeva, *V sem'e*, 97–98.
May 24, 1835. Nechaeva, *V sem'e*, 99–100.
May 26, 1835. Nechaeva, *V sem'e*, 100–101.
May 29, 1835. Nechaeva, *V sem'e*, 103–104.
May 31, 1835. Nechaeva, *V sem'e*, 105–107.
June 2, 1835. Nechaeva, *V sem'e*, 107–108.
June 8–10, 1835. Nechaeva, *V sem'e*, 109–110.
June 23, 1835. Nechaeva, *V sem'e*, 110–111.
August 19, 1835. Nechaeva, *V sem'e*, 111–112.

1836.

Circa 1836. Dostoevskii, *Vospominaniia*, 68.

1836 and after. Grossman, *Seminarii*, 65.
1836 and after. Volotskoi, *Khronika*, 96.
1836 and after. Volotskoi, *Khronika*, 96.
Early fall 1836 and after. Dostoevskii, *Vospominaniia*, 77.
Early fall 1836 and after. Dostoevskaia, *Dostoevskii* (1922), 14.

1837.

1837 and after. Dostoevskii, *Dnevnik pisatelia za 1876 god*, 264–271.
January 1837. Dostoevskii, *Vospominaniia*, 77.
January 1837. Dostoevskaia, *Dostoevskii* (1922), 14.
Late February 1837. Dostoevskii, *Vospominaniia*, 78.
February 26–27, 1837. Dostoevskii, *Vospominaniia*, 78.
After February 27, 1837. Dostoevskaia, *Vospominaniia* (1971), 179.
After February 27, 1837. Volgin, *Rodit'sia v Rossii*, 184.
After February 27, 1837. Volgin, *Rodit'sia v Rossii*, 184.
March 1837 and after. Dostoevskaia, *Vospominaniia* (1971), 135.
March 1837 and after. Dostoevskii, *Vospominaniia*, 109.
March 1837 and after. Grossman, *Dostoevskii*, 53.
March 1837. Dostoevskii, *Vospominaniia*, 78–79.
March 1837. Dostoevskii, *Vospominaniia*, 80.
April 1837. Dostoevskii, *Vospominaniia*, 78.
April 1837. Dostoevskaia, *Dostoevskii* (1992), 35.
Early May 1837. Dostoevskii, *Vospominaniia*, 79–80.
Early May 1837. Dostoevskii, *Vospominaniia*, 79.
Mid-May 1837. Dostoevskii, *Vospomimaniia*, 80.
Mid-May 1837. Dostoevskii, *Dnevnik pisatelia za 1876 god*, 41–42.
Mid-May 1837. Dostoevskii, *Dnevnik pisatelia za 1876 god*, 555.
Mid-May 1837. Dostoevskii, *Dnevnik pisatelia za 1876 god*, 41–43.
Mid-May 1837. Dostoevskii, *Polnoe sobranie sochinenii*, vol. 7 (1973), 138.
Mid-May 1837. Nechaeva, *V sem'e*, 115.
Early June 1837. Nechaeva, *V sem'e*, 114.
July 1837 and after. Dostoevskii, *Vospominaniia*, 81.
July 1837 and after. Dostoevskaia, *Dostoevskii* (1922), 15–16.
July 3, 1837. Dolinin, ed., *F.M. Dostoevskii: Pis'ma*, vol. 1, 41–43.
July 23, 1837. Dolinin, ed., *F.M. Dostoevskii: Pis'ma*, vol. 1, 43–44.
August 1837 and after. Dostoevskaia, *Dostoevskii* (1922), 16.
August 1837. Dostoevskii, *Vospominaniia*, 97.
August 20, 1837. Dostoevskii, *Vospominaniia*, 365–366.
September 2, 1837. I. Iakubovich, "Dostoevskii v Glavnom Inzhenerom Uchilishche," *Dostoevskii: Materialy i issledovaniia*, vol. 5 (Leningrad: Nauka, 1983), 180.
September 6, 1837. Dolinin, ed., *F. M. Dostoevskii: Pis'ma*, vol. 1, 44–45.
September 27, 1837. Dostoevskii, *Vospominaniia*, 366–368.
October 8, 1837. Dostoevskii, *Vospominaniia*, 368–370.
October 17, 1837. Nechaeva, *V sem'e*, 115–116.

November 6, 1837. Nechaeva, *V sem'e*, 116–117.
November 8, 1837. L. Lanskii, "Dostoevskii v neizdannoi perepiske sovremennikov," in V. Bazanov, ed., *Literaturnoe nasledstvo: F. M. Dostoevskii; Novye materialy i issledovaniia*, vol. 86 (Moscow: Nauka, 1973), 358.
December 3, 1837. Dostoevskii, *Vospominaniia*, 372.
Late December 1837–early January 1838. Dostoevskii, *Vospominaniia*, 372.

1838.

January 1838–June 1843. A. Custine, *Rossiia v 1839 godu v dvukh tomakh*, vol. 1 (Moscow: Izdatel'stvo imeni Sabashnikovykh, 1996), 135.
January 1838–June 1843. Miller, "Materialy," 44.
January 1838–June 1843. N. Leskov, "Prividenie v Inzhernernom Zamke (Iz vospominanii kadetov)," *Sobranie sochinenii v odinnadtsati tomakh*, vol. 7 (Moscow: Khudozhestvennaia literatura, 1958), 110–111.
January 1838–June 1843. Miller, "Materialy," 44.
January 1838–June 1843. F. Vigel', *Zapiski*, vol. 2 (Moscow: Krug, 1928), 170–171.
January 1838–June 1843. Dostoevskii, *Dnevnik pisatelia za 1876 god*, 158–159.
January 1838–June 1843. Miller, "Materialy," 35.
January 1838–June 1843. A. Saveliev, "Pamiati D. V. Grigorovicha (Prebyvanie ego v Glavnom Inzhenerom uchilische)," *Russkaia starina* 8 (1900), 327–328.
January 1838–June 1843. Miller, "Materialy," 42–45.
January 1838–June 1843. Miller, "Materialy," 35–37.
January 1838–June 1843. Grigorovich, *Literaturnye vospominaniia*, 38–41, and 45.
January 1838–June 1843. Grossman, *Dostoevskii*, 62.
January 1838–June 1843. A. Saveliev, "Vospominaniia o F. M. Dostoevskom," *Russkaia starina* 8 (1900), 19.
January 1838–June 1843. Dolinin, ed., *F. M. Dostoevskii: Pis'ma*, vol. 2, 178.
January 1838–June 1843. Dolinin, ed., *F. M. Dostoevskii Pis'ma*, vol. 4 (1959), 267–268.
January 1838–June 1843. Dostoevskii, *Dnevnik pisatelia za 1877 god*, 456–459.
January 1838–June 1843. Dostoevskaia, *Dostoevskii* (1992), 36–37.
January 1838–June 1843. Dostoevskaia, *Dostoevskii* (1922), 35–36.
January 1838–June 1843. Saveliev, "Vospominaniia," 13–14.
January 1838–June 1843. Saveliev, "Vospominaniia," 14.
January 1838–June 1843. Saveliev, "Vospominaniia," 19.
January 1838–June 1843. Miller, "Materialy," 37–38.
January 1838–June 1843. Miller, "Materialy," 45.
January 1838–June 1843. Saveliev, "Vospomaniia," 17–18.
January 1838–June 1843. V. Cheshikhin-Vetrinskii, *Feodor Mikhailovich Dostoevskii v vospominaniiakh sovremennikov v ego pis'makh* (Moscow: V. Dumnov, 1923), 28–30; and Miller, "Materialy," 37–38 and 43.
January 1838–June 1843. Grigorovich, *Literaturnye vospominaniia*, 46–48, and 88.
January 1838–June 1843. Saveliev, "Pamiati," 331–332.
January 1838–June 1843. Saveliev, "Vospominaniia," 17.
January 1838–June 1843. Saveliev, "Vospominaniia," 15–16.

January 1838–June 1843. K. Khlebnikov, "Zapisi Konstantina Dmitrievicha Khlebnikova," *Russkaia arkhiv* 1, 1907, 381.
January 1838–June 1843. Miller, "Materialy," 37–38.
January 1838–June 1843. Saveliev, "Vospominaniia," 18–19.
1838. Nechaeva, *V sem'e*, 58.
January 19, 1838. K. Kumpan, "Pis'ma Mikhaila Dostoevskogo i ottsu," in D. Likhachev et al., eds., *Pamiatniki kul'tury: Pis'mennost'; Iskusstvo; Arkheologiia* (Lenimgrad: Nuaka, 1981), 70.
Late January 1838. Kumpan et al., "Pis'ma," 71–72.
January 29, 1838. Kumpan et al., "Pis'ma," 72–73.
February 4, 1838. Dostoevskii, *Vospominaniia*, 373–375.
February 12, 1838. Nechaeva, *V sem'e*, 117–119.
February 17, 1838. Kumpan et al., "Pis'ma," 73.
February 28, 1838. Kumpan et al., "Pis'ma," 74.
March 1838. I. Iakubovich et al, *Letopis' zhizni i tvorchestva F.M. Dostoevskogo v trekh tomakh, 1821–1881*, vol. 1 (St. Petersburg: Akademicheskii proekt, 1993), 48.
April 15, 1838. Kumpan et al., "Pis'ma," 74–75.
April 15, 1838 and after. Dostoevskaia, *Dostoevskii* (1922), 15.
May 8, 1838. Kumpan et al., "Pis'ma," 76–77.
May 26, 1838. Kumpan et al., "Pis'ma," 77–78.
May 27, 1838. Nechaeva, *V sem'e*, 21–122.
Circa June 1838. A. Rizenkampf, "Vospominaniia o Fyodore Mikhailoviche Dostoevskom," in Bazanov, ed., *Literaturnoe nasledstvo*, 323–325.
June 1838. Rizenkampf, "Vospominaniia," 325–326.
June–September 1838. Rizenkampf, "Vospominaniia," 327.
June 1838 and after. Volotskoi, *Khronika*, 94.
June 1838 and after. Dostoevskaia, *Dostoevskii* (1922), 16.
June 1838 and after. Dostoevskaia, *Dostoevskii* (1922), 40–41.
June 5, 1838. Dostoevskii, *Vospominaniia*, 375–377.
Summer 1838 and after. Dostoevskii, *Vospominaniia*, 109.
June–July 1838. Saveliev, "Vospominaniia," 16.
August 9, 1838. Dolinin, ed., *F. M. Dostoevskii: Pis'ma*, vol. 1, 45–47.
Early October 1838. Kumpan et al. "Pis'ma Dostoevskgo," 78–79; and Lanskii, "Dostoevskii," 362.
October 29, 1938. Iakubovich, *Letopis'*, 53.
October 30, 1838. F. Dostoevskii, "Iz rannikh let Dostoevskogo," *Atenei* (1924), bk. 1–2, 145–147.
October 31, 1838. Dolinin, ed., *F. M. Dostoevskii: Pis'ma*, vol. 1, 49–52.
Late October 1838. Grigorovich, *Literaturnye vospominaniia*, 48–49.
Circa November 1838 and after. V. Soloviev, "Vospominaniia o F. M. Dostoevskom," *Istoricheskii vestnik* 3 (1881), 608.
Circa November 1838 and after. N. Reshetov, "Dela davno minuvshikh dnei," *Russkii arkhiv* 10, 1886, 226–228.
Circa November 1838 and after. M. Alekseev, *Rannii drug F. M. Dostoevskogo* (Odessa: Vseukrainskie gosudarstvennoe izdatel'stvo, 1921), 6.
Circa November 1838. Alekseev, *Rannii drug*, 14.
November 1838 and after. Rizenkampf, "Vospominaniia," 325.
November 1838 and after. Dostoevskaia, *Dostoevskii* (1992), 40.

November 19, 1838. Nechaeva, *V sem'e*, 119–120.
November 28, 1838. Kumpan et al., "Pis'ma," 79–81.
December 16, 1838. Kumpan et al., "Pis'ma," 81–82.

1839.

Circa 1839. Saveliev, "Vospominaniia," 20.
Early 1839. Grigorovich, *Literaturnye vospominaniia*, 48.
January 3, 1839. Iakubovich, "Dostoevskii," 182.
January 17, 1839. G. Prochorov, "Die Brüder Dostoevski und Shidlovski," *Zeitschrift fur Slavische Philologie* 7 (1930), 319–325.
Late January 1839. Kumpan et al., "Pis'ma," 82.
February 2, 1839. Kumpan et al., "Pis'ma," 82–83.
February 24, 1839. Kumpan et al., "Pis'ma," 84.
March 23, 1839. Dostoevskii, *Vospominaniia*, 377–379.
May 5, 1839. Dostoevskii, *Vospominaniia*, 379–381.
May 10, 1839. Dolinin, ed., *F. M. Dostoevskii: Pis'ma*, vol. 1, 52–54.
May 27, 1839. Nechaeva, *V sem'e*, 120–122.
Before June 1839. Volotskoi, *Khronika*, 55.
Before June 1839. S. Ianovskii, "Vospominaniia o Dostoevskom," *Russkii vestnik* 4 (1885), 799–800.
Before June 1839. Volotskoi, *Khronika*, 174.
Before June 1839. Volotskoi, *Khronika*, 174.
Before June 1839. Volotskoi, *Khronika*, 175.
Before June 1839. Volotskoi, *Khronika*, 176.
Before June 1839. Dolinin, ed., *F. M. Dostoevskii: Pis'ma*, vol. 1, 215.
Before June 1839. D. Stonov, "Sel'tso Darovoe," *Krasnaia neva* (1926), 18.
Before June 1839. Volotskoi, *Khronika*, 58; and Nechaeva, "Iz literatury," 131.
Before June 1839. A. Drozdov, "Usad'ba Dostoevskogo: 'Darovoe,'" *Izvestiia* (November 4, 1924), 4.
Before June 1839. Volotskoi, *Khronika*, 55.
Before June 1839. Stonov, "Sel'tso," 18.
June 6, 1839. Dostoevskii, *Vospominaniia*, 109–110.
June 6, 1839. Nechaeva, "Iz literatury," 132.
June 6, 1839. Grossman, *Dostoevskii*, 79.
June 6, 1839. Dostoevskaia, *Dostoevskii* (1922), 16–17.
June 6, 1839. Nechaeva, "Iz literatury," 132.
June 6, 1839. Dostoevskii, *Vospominaniia*, 109.
After June 6, 1839. Nechaeva, *V sem'e*, 60.
June 6–8, 1839. Dostoevskii, *Vospominaniia*, 110.
June 6–8, 1839. Nechaeva, "Iz literatury," 132.
June 6–8, 1839. Dostoevskaia, *Dostoevskii* (1992), 17.
After June 6–8, 1839. Nechaeva, "Iz literatury," 133; and Magarshack, *Dostoevsky*, 11.
After June 8, 1839. Dostoevskii, *Vospominaniia*, 411.
After June 8, 1839. Drozdov, "Usad'ba," 4.
After June 10, 1839. Dostoevskaia, *Dostoevskii* (1992), 17–18.

After June 10, 1839. Dostoevskaia, *Dostoevskii* (1992), 49.
After June 10, 1839. Dostoevskii, *Vospominaniia*, 108.
After June 10, 1839. Volotskoi, *Khronika*, 58.
After June 10, 1839. Nechaeva, *V sem'e*, 60.
Circa June 13, 1839. Dostoevskii, *Vospominaniia*, 110.
After June 13, 1839. Dostoevskii, *Vospominaniia*, 37.
June 16, 1839. G. Fëdorov, "K biografii F. M. Dostoevskogo: Domysli i logika faktov," *Literaturnaia gazeta* (June 18, 1975), 90.
June 30, 1839. Dostoevskii, Vospominaniia, 413–414.
June–July 1839. P. Semenov-Tian-Shanskii, *Detstvo i iunost' (1825–1855 gg.)*, vol. 1 (Petrograd: M. Stasiulevich, 1917), 203.
July 1839. Pereverzev, ed., *Pis'ma*, 41.
July 6, 1839. Fëdorov, "K biografii," 19.
July 6, 1839. Fëdorov, "K biografii," 19.
July 26, 1839. Fëdorov, "K biografii," 19.
August 9–16, 1839. Rizenkampf, "Vospominaniia," 328.
August 16, 1839. Dolinin, ed., *F. M. Dostoevskii: Pis'ma*, vol. 2, 549–551.
September 1, 1839. Lanskii, "Dostoevskii," 363.
September 12, 1839. Fëdorov, "K biografii," 19.
September 29, 1839. Iakubovich, *Letopis'*, 65–66.
October 1839. Fëdorov, "K biografii," 19.
October 6, 1839 and after. K. Trutovskii, "Vospominaniia o Fëdore Mikhailoviche Dostoevskom," *Russkoe obozrenie* 1 (1893), 211–213; and "Vospominaniia o F. M. Dostoevskom K. Trutovskim, 1886 g." *Shchukinskii sbornik* (1902), 90–91.
November 16, 1839. Fëdorov, "K biografii," 19.
December 25, 1839. Dolinin, ed., *F. M. Dostoevskii: Pis'ma*, vol. 2, 551–552.

1840.

January 1, 1840. Dolinin, ed., *F. M. Dostoevskii: Pis'ma*, vol. 1, 54–59.
January 28, 1840. Dostoevskii, *Vospominaniia*, 381–383.
February 9, 1840. Iakubovich, *Letopis'*, 69.
February 13, 1840. Fëdorov, "K biografii," 19.
July 19, 1840. Dolinin, ed., *F. M. Dostoevskii: Pis'ma*, 60–62.
December 1840. Grigorovich, *Literaturnye vospominaniia*, 50.
December 1840. Rizenkampf, "Vospominaniia," 328.

1841.

1841–early 1842. Rizenkampf, "Vospominaniia," 328–329.
1841. Dostoevskaia, *Dostoevskii* (1922), 40.
1841. Dostoevskaia, *Dostoevskii* (1922), 37.
February 16, 1841. Rizenkampf, "Vospominaniia," 328.
February 27, 1841. Dolinin, ed, *F. M. Dostoevskii*, 62–64.
Summer 1841. Volgin, *Rodit'sia v Rossii*, 337.

August 5, 1841. Iakubovich, "Dostoevskii," 185–186.
After August 9, 1841. Miller, "Materialy," 49.
Fall 1841 and after. Trutovskii, "Vospominaniia," 214–215.
Fall 1841 and after. Grossman, *Seminarii*, 55.
Mid–October 1841. Dostoevskii, *Vospominaniia*, 122–123.
December 5, 1841. "Novye materialy: Neizdannye pis'ma k Dostoevskomu," in G. Fridlander, ed., *Dostoevskii: Materialy i issledovaniia*, vol. 8 (Leningrad: Nauka, 1991), 267–268.
December 22, 1841. Dolinin, ed., *F. M. Dostoevskii: Pis'ma*, vol. 1, 64–65.
Late December 1841. Dostoevskii, *Vospominaniia*, 126.

1842.

1842 and after. Rizenkampf, "Vospominaniia," 329.
1842 and after. Miller, "Materialy," 64.
1842 and after. Dostoevskaia, *Vospominaniia*, 89.
1842 and after. Dostoevskaia, *Dostoevskii* (1992), 50.
1842 and after. P. Larina, "Dostoevskii—russkii markiz de Sad," *Labirinty liubvi* (April 29, 2010), 2.
1842. Volgin, *Rodit'sia v Rossii*, 339.
1842. Miller, "Materialy," 41.
February–March 1842 and after. Dostoevskii, *Vospominaniia*, 127–129.
February–March 1842 and after. Dostoevskii, *Vospominaniia*, 127–128.
February–March 1842 and after. Iakubovich, *Letopis'*, 78.
April–May 1842. Rizenkampf, "Vospominaniia," 329.
June 20, 1842. Grossman, *Dostoevskii*, 72.
Late July 1842. Iakubovich, "Dostoevskii," 185.
December 1842. Dolinin, ed., *F. M. Dostoevskii: Pis'ma*, vol. 1, 65.
December 6, 1842. Reshetov, "Dela," 228–229.

1843.

1843 and after. Volgin, *Rodit'sia v Rossii*, 525.
1843. Miller, "Materialy," 52.
January–early February 1843. Dostoevskii, *Vospominaniia*, 159.
March–April 1843 and after. Rizenkampf, "Vospominaniia," 329–330.
March–April 1843 and after. V. Vinogradov, *Problemy avtorstva i teoriia stilei* (Moscow: Khudozhestvennaia literatura, 1961), 596.
March–April 1843 and after. Rizenkampf, "Vospominaniia," 229–230.
March–April 1843 and after. Rizenkampf, "Vospominaniia," 330.
March–April 1843 and after. Rizenkampf, "Vospominaniia," 330–331.
June 8, 1843. Dostoevskii, *Polnoe sobranie sochinenii*, 380.
June 30, 1843. Miller, "Materialy," 50–51.
July 1843. Miller, "Materialy," 51.
August 12, 1843 and after. Miller, "Materialy," 48.
After August 1843. Dostoevskii; *Polnoe sobranie sochinenii*, vol. 27 (1984), 120.

After mid-August 1843 and after. Dostoevskaia, *Dostoevskii* (1922), 20–21.
August 1843–October 1844. Semenov-Tian-Shanskii, *Detstvo*, 203.
September 1843 and after. Miller, "Materialy," 48, and 51–52.
September 1843 and after. Lanskii, "Dostoevskii," 550.
September 1843 and after. Miller, "Materialy," 51.
November 1843. Miller, "Materialy," 52.
November 1843. Dostoevskaia, *Dostoevskii* (1922), 83.
December 1843. Miller, "Materialy," 52–53.
Late December 1843. Dostoevskii, *Vospominaniia*, 384.
Late December 1843. Dostoevskii, *Vospominaniia*, 384.
December 31, 1843. Dolinin, ed., *F. M. Dostoevskii, Pis'ma* vol. 1, 66–67.

1844.

Circa 1844. S. Kovalevskaia, *Vospominaniia i pis'ma* (Moscow: Izdatel'stvo Akademii nauk, 1961), 107.
January–February 1844. Rizenkampf, "Vospominaniia," 331.
Second half of January 1844. Dolinin, ed., *F. M. Dostoevskii: Pis'ma*, vol. 1, 66–69.
Early February 1844 and after. Dostoevskaia, *Dostoevskii* (1992), 48–49.
Early February 1844. Miller, "Materialy," 53.
February 14, 1844. Dolinin, ed., *F. M. Dostoevskii: Pis'ma*, vol, 1, 69–70.
March 1844. Miller, "Materialy," 53.
March–April 1844. Dolinin, ed., *F. M. Dostoevskii: Pis'ma*, vol. 1, 70–71.
Spring 1844. Iakubovich, *Letopis'*, 89–90.
Spring 1844. Iakubovich, *Letopis'*, 117; and Volgin, *Rodit'sia v Rossii*, 358.
Spring 1844. Miller, *Biografiia*, 45.
Spring 1844. Ianovskii, "Vospominaniia," 807.
Spring 1844. Saveliev, "Vospominaniia," 20.
Early April 1844 and after. Dostoevskaia, *Vospominaniia*, (1971), 213–214.
Early April 1844 and after. Grossman, *Seminarii*, 55.
July–August 1844. Dolinin, ed., *F. M. Dostoevskii: Pis'ma*, vol. 2, 553–555.
August 21, 1844. Dostoevskii, *Polnoe sobranie sochinenii*, vol. 30, II (1990), 25.
August 31, 1844. Dostoevskii, *Vospominaniia*, 385–387.
September 5, 1844. Dolinin, ed., *F. M. Dostoevskii: Pis'ma*, vol. 4, 449–450.
September 7, 1844. Dostoevskii, *Vospominaniia*, 387–390.
September 19, 1844. Dostoevskii, *Vospominaniia*, 390–393.
Fall 1844–August 1845. Trutovskii, "Vospominaniia," 215.
Fall 1844. Grigorovich, *Literaturnye vospominaniia*, 84–85.
September 25, 1844. Lanskii, "Dostoevskii," 365–366.
September 30, 1844. Dolinin, ed., *F. M. Dostoevskii: Pis'ma*, vol. 1, 72–74.
September–October 1844. Dostoevskii, *Vospominaniia*, 396.
Circa October 1844. Dostoevskii, *Vospominaniia*, 117.
Circa October 1844. Volgin, *Rodit'sia v Rossii*, 353.
Circa October 1844. L. Grossman, *Zhizn' i trudy F. M. Dostoevskogo: Biografiia v datakh i dokumentakh* (Moscow: Akademiia, 1935), 39.
October 3, 1844. Lanskii, "Dostoevskii," 367–368.

October 19, 1844. Nicholas I, "Vysochaishii prikaz," *Russkii invalid* (October 24, 1844), 1.
After October 19, 1844. Grigorovich, *Literaturnye vospominaniia*, 86–88.
Late October 1844. Dostoevskii, *Vospominaniia*, 393–396.
November 1844. Dostoevskii, *Polnoe sobranie sochinenii*, vol. 28, bk. 1 (1985), 104.
November 28, 1844. Lanskii, "Dostoevskii," 369.

1845.

1845 and after. Dostoevskii, *Polnoe sobranie sochinenii*, vol. 23, p. 37.
Circa January 1845. Dostoevskii, *Polnoe sobranie sochinenii*, vol. 19 (1979), 69.
March 24, 1845. Dolinin, ed., *F. M. Dostoevskii: Pis'ma*, vol. 1, 74–76.
April 5, 1845. N. Bel'chikov, *F.M. Dostoevskii v protsesse petrashevtsev* (Moscow, 1971), 114–115; and Volgin, *Rodit'sia v Rossii*, 359.
May 4, 1845. Dolinin, ed., *F. M. Dostoevskii: Pis'ma*, vol. 1, 77–79.
Late May 1845. Grigorovich, *Literaturnye vospominaniia*, 82–83.
Late May 1845. Dostoevskii, *Dnevnik pisatelia za 1877 god*, 38–43.
Late May 1845. Grigorovich, *Literaturnye vospominaniia*, 89.
Late May 1845. Kovalevskaia, *Vospominaniia*, 125–126.
Circa June 1, 1845. Dostoevskii, *Dnevnik pisatelia za 1877 god*, 41–43.
Circa June 2, 1845. P. Annenkov, *Literaturnye vospominaniia* (Moscow: Pravda, 1989), 258.
June 7, 1845. N. Nekrasov, *Polnoe sobranie sochinenii i pisem v piatnadtsati tomakh*, vol. 14, bk. 1 (St. Petersburg: Nauka, 1998), 51–52.
Circa June 10, 1845. Belinsky, *Polnoe sobranie sochinenii v tridnadtsati tomakh*, vol. 12 (Moscow: Akademiia nauk, 1956), 251.
Summer 1845. Dostoevskii, *Dnevnik pisatelia za 1877 god*, 455–456.
September 3, 1845. Dolinin, ed., *F. M. Dostoevskii: Pis'ma*, vol, 1, 79–80.
Early fall 1845. Dostoevskii, *Dnevnik pisatelia za 1877 god*, 533–534.
Early fall 1845. Dostoevskii, *Dnevnik pisatelia za 1877 god*, 466.
Early fall 1845. Dostoevskii, *Dnevnik pisatelia za 1873 god*, 218–221.
October 8, 1845. Dolinin, ed., *F. M. Dostoevskii: Pis'ma*, vol. 1, 81–83.
October 8, 1845. Volgin, *Rodit'sia v Rossii*, 510.
November–December 1845. V. Maikov, "Nechto o russkoi literature v 1846 godu," in V. Maikov, *Literaturnaia kritika: Stat'i; Retsentsii* (Leningrad: Khudozhestvennaia literatura, 1985), 179.
Circa early November 1845. I. Turgenev, "Vospominaniia o Belinskom," *Polnoe sobranie sochinenii i pisem v dvadtsati vos'mi tomakh* (Moscow: Akademiia nauk, 1967), 52.
November 15, 1845. A. Panaeva, *Vospominaniia* (Moscow: Pravda, 1986), 148.
November 16, 1845. Dolinin, ed., *F. M. Dostoevskii: Pis'ma*, vol. 1, 83–85.
November 16, 1845. L. Grossman, *Put' Dostoevskogo* (Leningrad: Sovremennye problemy, 1928), 121.
November 16, 1845. Panaeva, *Vospominaniia*, 149.
November 16, 1845 and after. Grigorovich, *Literaturnye vospominaniia*, 90–91.
November 27, 1845. N. Nekrasov, *Polnoe sobranie sochinenii*, 55.
November 27, 1845. V. Odoevsky, "Iz perepiski kniazia V. F. Odoevskogo," *Russkaia starina* 6 (1904), 584.
Circa December 1845. Dostoevskii, *Dnevnik pisatelia za 1877 god*, 457.

Early December 1845. Dostoevskii, *Polnoe sobranie sochinenii*, vol. 21 (1980), 264.
Early December 1845. I. Iampol'skii, "A. I. Maikov: Pis'ma" in M. Alekseev et al., eds., *Ezhegodnik rukopisnogo otdela Pushkinskogo doma na 1975 god* (Leningrad: Nauka, 1977), 89–90.
December 2, 1845. Nekrasov, *Polnoe sobranie sochinenii*, vol. 14, bk. 1 (1998), 56.
Circa December 3, 1845. Dostoevskii, *Dnevnik pisatelia za 1877 god*, 456.
Circa December 3, 1845. Annenkov, *Literaturnye vospominaniia*, 259.
Circa December 3, 1845. Grigorovich, *Literaturnye vospominaniia*, 84.
After December 3, 1845. Grigorovich, *Literaturnye vospominaniia*, 83.
After December 3, 1845. N. Blagoveshchenskii, "Vospominaniia N. A. Blagoveshchenskogo o Turgeneve v pis'me k A. K. Shelleru," in N. Brodskii, ed., *I. S. Turgenev: Materialy i isledovanniia* (Orel: Izdatel'svo Orlovskogo Oblastnogo Soveta deputatov trudiashchikhsia, 1940), 53.
After December 3, 1845. K. Leont'ev, *Stranitsy vospominanii* (St. Petersburg: Parfenon, 1922), 27.
After December 3, 1845. I. Panaev, "Literaturnye kumiry, diletanty, i proch.," *Sovremennik* 12 (1855), otd. V, 240.
After December 3, 1845. Dostoevakaia, *Vospominaniia* (1971), 359–360.
After December 3, 1845. P. Annenkov, "Zamechatel'noe desiatiletie," *Vestnik Evropy* 4 (1880), 479.
After December 3, 1845. Miller, "Materialy," 67.
After December 3, 1845. Volgin, *Rodit'sia v Rossii*, 534.
After December 3, 1845. P. Annenkov, *M. M. Stasiulevich i ego sovremenniki v ikh perepiske*, vol. 3 (St. Petersburg: M. Stasiulevich, 1912), vol. 3, 383–384.
After December 1845. Volgin, *Rodit'sia v Rossii*, 535.
After December 3, 1845. Volgin, *Rodit'sia v Rossii*, 535–536.
After December 3, 1845. Volgin, *Rodit'sia v Rossii*, 537.
After December 3, 1845. Volgin, *Rodit'sia v Rossii*, 537.
After December 3, 1845. D. Abramovich, ed., *Pis'ma russkikh pisatelei k A. S. Suvorinu* (Leningrad: Gosudarstvennia publichnaia biblioteka v Leningrade, 1927), 50–51.
After December 1845. Volgin, *Rodit'sia v Rossii*, 538.
After December 3, 1845. "Pis'ma F. M. Dostoevskogo," *Krasnyi arkhiv*, vol. 2, (1922), 247–248.
After December 3, 1845. Dostoevskii, *Polnoe sobranie sochinenii*, vol. 27, 197–198.
After December 3, 1845. Volgin, *Rodit'sia v Rossii*, 536.
December 15, 1845. I. Aksakov, *Ivan Sergeevich Aksakov v ego pis'makh*, vol. 1 (Moscow: Russkaia kniga, 2003), 206.
Late 1845. V. Panaev, "Vospominaniia," *Russkaia starina* 9 (1901), 491.
Late 1845. P. Sokolov, *Vospominaniia* (Leningrad: Komitet populiarizatsii khudozhestvennykh izdanii pri gosudarstvennoi akademii istorii material'noi kul'tury, 1930), 111–112.
Late 1845. Grigorovich, *Literaturnye vospominaniia*, 90.

Index

A

"About Naive and Sentimental Poetry" (Schiller), 262n97
Academy of Civil Engineering, 260n57
Aksakov, Konstantin, 209
Alexander I, 250n22, 251n25, 253n36
Alexander Theater, 145, 259n34
Alexandrova, Ekaterina Alexandrovna, 22, 63, 247n119, 254n52, 257n104
Andromaque (Racine), 139, 259n10
Angel day/name day, 44, 242n58
Annenkov, Pavel Vasilievich: discussed, 216–17; "Recollections," 218; "Remarkable Decade, A," 216
Anonymous: "Strange Confessions of George Sand, The," 245n96
ant heap, 193, 264n130
D'Anthès, Georges, 247n121
appearance, 16, 27, 104, 129–30, 210, 254n61
Apprenticeship of Wilhelm Meister, The (Goethe), 263n108
architecture, 77
Arks, 251n24
Atala (Chateaubriand), 198, 265n142
Auber, Daniel: *Mute Girl of Portici, The,* 256n95

B

Bakunin, Nikolai, 247n112
balagany, 30, 239n24
ballet, 145
Balzac, Honoré de: Belinsky on, 188, 246n108; Custine on, 246n108; discussed, 97, 246n106; *Eugénie Grandet,* 14, 166, 262n90, 264n123, 264n124; *Harlot High and Low, The,* 266n180; *Lost Illusions,* 266n180; *Père Goriot,* 60, 246n107; *Two Brown Tales,* 157, 261n60

Bantysh-Kamensky, Nikolai: *Grammatica Latina,* 244n89
baptism, 238n15
Barkov, Ivan Semyonovich, 102, 255n81
Barshev, Ioann (Ivan Vasilievich), 45, 68
Barshev, Sergei Ivanovich, 243n62
Barshev, Yakov Ivanovich, 243n62
Battle of Borodino, 19
Beck, Karl: *Janko, the Hungarian Horse-Herd,* 157, 261n64
Begichev, Dmitri Nikitch: *Khomsky Family, The,* 48, 243n73
Belinsky, Vissarion Grigorievich: on Balzac, 188, 246n108; discussed, 15, 16, 201, 206–8, 213–14, 261n62; on *The Double,* 206, 214–15; on Hoffman, 254n64; on *The Northern Bee,* 266n167; on Plaksin, 252n29; on *Poor Folk,* 204; on Sand, 245–46n102, 247n112
Belov, Sergei, 37, 240–41n37
Belyi, Andrei: *Silver Dove, The,* 251n24
Benckendorff, Alexander Khristoforovich von, 251n25
Benningsen, Leonyi, 250n22
Bentham, Jeremy: *Defense of Usury, The,* 263n106; discussed, 180
Béranger, Pierre-Jean, 196
Berezhetsky, Ivan Ignatovich, 84, 86–87, 253n38
Bilevich, Nikolai Ivanovich: *Christmas Evenings, or Stories of My Aunt,* 245n95; discussed, 245n95; *Picture Gallery of Societal Life, or the Mores of the Nineteenth Century, A,* 245n95
birth, 27
Blaes, Arnold, 156
Bogatyrs (Vasnetsov), 239n21
Bolsheviks, 263n104
Boris Godunov (F. M. Dostoevsky), 146, 152
Botkin, Pavel, 266n162

Brethren in Christ, 251n25
bride of Christ, 3, 28
Brothers Karamazov, The (F. M. Dostoevsky), 4, 82, 136, 242n51
Bryanchaninovites, 253n39
Bryanchikov, Ignati, 253n39
Bulgarin, Faddei Venediktovich: discussed, 60, 254n49; "Journalistic Hodgepodge," 266n167
Bulgarin, Fyodor, 262n96
byliny, 239n21
Byron, Lord: *Prisoner of Chillon, The*, 100, 255n72

C

career, 12, 14, 159, 261n70
"Cart of Life, The" (Pushkin), 256n87
Catherine Institute, 242n56
Catherine Palace, 259n5
Catherine the Great, 250n22
Cervantes, Miguel de: *Don Quixote*, 240n31
Chapelle, E.: *My Wife and My Umbrella*, 265n149
Chateaubriand, Francois-René de: *Atala*, 198, 265n142; *Genius of Christianity, The*, 100, 255n74
Chatterton, Thomas, 109, 256n93
Chernoglazov (translator), 166
Chikhachyov (musician), 253n39
Christmas Evenings, or Stories of My Aunt (Bilevich), 245n95
Chronicle of the Dostoevsky Clan, A (Volotskoi), 257n102
Church of the Holy Spirit, 247n114
Le Cid (Corneille), 140, 259n23
Cinna (Corneille), 140, 259n18
Clairville: *Opium and Champagne, or the War of China*, 262n84
Cleopatra the Captive (Jodelle), 140, 259n15
Confession of an English Opium Eater, The (Quincey), 85, 254n44
consumption/tuberculosis, 247n113, 249n13
Contemporary, The, 266n181
Cooper, James Fenimore: *Pathfinder, or the Inland Sea, The*, 85, 254n46

Corneille, Pierre: *Le Cid*, 140, 259n23; *Cinna*, 140, 259n18; discussed, 140; *Horace*, 140, 259n21; *Medea*, 259n17
Cosima (Sand), 245n98
"Count from Hapsburg, The" (Zhukovsky), 48, 243n76
Cournant, Josèphe, 252n30
Crime and Punishment (F. M. Dostoevsky), 136
Cromwell (Hugo), 97, 255n69
Custine, Astolphe-Louis-Léonor de: on Balzac, 246n108; discussed, 76–77, 246n108, 250n23, 258n117

D

dark rooms, 4
Davydov, Ivan Ivanovich, 2
Dead Souls (Gogol), 135, 200, 245n95, 252n29
Decembrist Revolt, 244n85
Defense of Usury, The (Bentham), 263n106
Defoe, Daniel: *Robinson Crusoe*, 5, 242n49
delirium tremens, 257n110
Demons (F. M. Dostoevsky), 136
Derzhavin, Gavriil Romanovich: discussed, 139; "God," 48, 243n71
Devils (F. M. Dostoevsky), 37, 240n37
Dickens, Charles: discussed, 60, 246n105; *Nicholas Nickleby*, 46, 243n64; *Old Curiosity Shop, The*, 46, 243n64; *Oliver Twist*, 46, 243n64; *Pickwick Papers, The*, 246n105
Ditmar-Dostoevskaya, Emilia Fyodorovna von, 259n28, 260n40
Dmitri Ioannovich, 243n69
Dmitri of Rostov, Saint: *Monthly Readings, The*, 36, 240n33
"Doge and Dogaressa" (Hoffman), 248n2
dogs, 4
Don Carlos (Schiller): discussed, 144, 168, 169, 172, 183
Don Quixote (Cervantes), 240n31
Donskoi, Dmitri Ivanovich, 239n26
Dostoevskaya, Anastasia, 238n12
Dostoevskaya, Anna Grigorievna, 242n48

Dostoevskaya, Maria Fyodorovna: death, 6, 21, 62, 223, 259n26; discussed, 25, 241n47, 245n94, 247n113; marriage, 20
Dostoevskaya, Maria Mikhailovna, 261n78
Dostoevskaya-Golenovskaya, Alexandra Mikhailovna, 237n2, 245n94
Dostoevskaya-Ivanova, Vera Mikhailovna, 237n2, 242n48
Dostoevskaya-Karepina, Varvara Mikhailovna, 123, 237n2, 248n11, 258n124
Dostoevsky, Alexander Andreevich, 237n2
Dostoevsky, Andrei Grigorievich, 238n9, 238n12
Dostoevsky, Andrei Mikhailovich: discussed, 116, 151, 237n2, 256n100, 257n103, 257n114, 260n52; education, 248n10; relationship with F. M. Dostoevsky, 260n55
Dostoevsky, Mikhail Andreevich: and E. A. Alexandrova, 257n104; autopsy, 121; burial, 121; career, 19–20, 25, 238n9, 248n6; death, 23–24, 119–20, 123, 124, 125–26, 130, 239n17, 256n101, 257n103, 258n121, 258n126; death investigation, 121, 126, 129, 142, 257n102, 259n27; discussed, 19, 254n52, 258n127; L. F. Dostoevskaya on, 24–25, 70; education, 19, 24, 73, 238n10; health, 23, 70, 257n110; honors, 20; Isaeva on, 63; marriage, 20, 25; Miller on, 26; relationship with F. M. Dostoevsky, 20–21; relationship with wife and children, 21; retirement, 21, 23, 70–71, 248n5, 248n7
Dostoevsky, Mikhail Mikhailovich: birth, 240n27; career, 259n29, 260n36; death, 255n84; discussed, 65–67, 237n2, 249n13, 261n68; education, 7, 8, 73, 254n53; health, 8, 73; marriage, 259n28, 260n40; "Morning," 137; poetry, 7, 66, 93–94, 110–11, 144–45; Rizenkampf on, 93–94; "Rose, The," 137; "Steeds of Phoebus, The," 137; "Stroll, The," 137; translation, 262n97; "Vision of Mother, A," 100–101, 137
Dostoevsky, Nikolai Mikhailovich, 72
Dostoevsky family, 3, 32, 238n16
Double, The (F. M. Dostoevsky): Aksakov on, 209; Belinsky on, 206, 214–15; discussed, 16, 156, 204, 213, 214–15, 265n160

doves, 29, 239n20
Dreams and Sounds (Nekrasov), 259n32
"Dying Poet, The" (Lamartine), 157, 261n58

E

Edinburgh Dungeon, The (Scott), 46, 243n63
education. *See also* Main Engineering Academy: advanced study, 22; Bilevich, Nikolai Ivanovich, 245n95; Chermak, Leonti Ivanovich, 2, 49–50, 243n80, 243n81, 244n82, 244n84; Davydov, Ivan Ivanovich, 2; discussed, 223; Drashusov-Sushard, Nikolai Ivanovich, 2, 45, 242n56, 243n61; Father Deacon, 44; Goering (teacher), 243n78; Khinkovsky, Ilya Vasilevich, 44, 242n56; Kostomarov, Koronad Filippovich, 7, 22, 71, 72, 248n8; Kubaryov, Alexei Mikhailovich, 2; languages and literature, 3, 6; liberal arts, 2; Perevoshikov, Dmitri Matveevich, 2; sciences, 2
Efimov (peasant), 119, 257n104
Efremov, Marko. *See* Marey (peasant)
Egor (servant), 149
Egyptian Nights (Pushkin), 104, 256n85
Elagin, Nikolai P., 129, 149, 258n118, 260n42
Elsner, Lyudvig Fyodorovich, 165
Emelia, or the Metamorphosis (Veltman), 199, 265n152
Engineering Castle. *See* Mikhailovsky Castle
epilepsy, 257n110
"Epitaph" (Karamzin), 248n122
Eternal Jew, The (Sue), 199, 265n150
Eugénie Grandet (Balzac): discussed, 14, 166, 262n90, 264n123, 264n124
Eulalie Pontois (Soulié), 262n84
"Eve of St. John, The" (Scott), 256n86

F

False Dmitri, 243n69
Father Deacon, 44
Fatherland Notes, The, 172, 195, 198, 206, 220, 261n62, 262n97

Faust (Goethe), 97, 254n66
Fedot (peasant), 118
Fedya's grove, 41
Fiesco (Schiller), 171, 172
Filaret, Metropolitan: *Outline of Church-Biblical History for the Benefit of Spiritual Youth, An,* 44, 242n57
Filipov, Danila, 250n24
Filosova, Anna Pavlovna, 240n37
fire, 2, 23, 40–41, 44, 241n42, 242n54
Firebird, 30, 239n21
First Fatherland War, 238n13
First of April, The, 266n169
foreigners, 13, 158
Four Hundred Sacred Stories, Chosen from the Old and New Testament for the Benefit of Youth with Noble Reflections (Hubner), 36, 240n34
"Freedom" (Pushkin), 250n22
friends, 3, 12, 52, 65, 72, 85, 249n12

G

games: billiards, 161, 166; cards, 35, 153; dominoes, 167; horsies, 4–5, 43; Robinson, 42; savages, 41–42
Gartong, Vasili Andreevich: "Requiem," 167
geese, 33, 240n29
"Geese" (Krylov), 240n29
General Confession (Soulié), 157, 261n59
Genius of Christianity, The (Chateaubriand), 100, 255n74
"Ghost in the Engineering Castle (From the Memories of Cadets), The" (Leskov), 77
Glinka, Mikhail Ivanovich: *Ruslan and Lyudmila,* 157
"God" (Derzhavin), 48, 243n71
Goering (teacher), 243n78
Goethe, Johann Wolfgang von: *Apprenticeship of Wilhelm Meister, The,* 263n108; discussed, 94; *Faust,* 97, 254n66; *Hermann and Dorothea,* 144, 172, 259n33, 262n98; *Sorrows of Young Werther, The,* 256n92
Gogol, Nikolai Vasilievich: *Dead Souls,* 135, 200, 245n95, 252n29; discussed, 196, 198, 210; *Inspector General, The,* 201, 264n121;

264n122; *Lawsuit, The,* 211, 266n182; *Overcoat, The,* 11, 15, 147; Plaksin on, 252n29; *Tarus Bulba,* 262n89
Golenishchev-Kutuzov, Mikhail Illarionovich, 263n104
Goncharov, Ivan Alexandrovich, 135
Grammatica Latina (Bantysh-Kamensky), 244n89
Great Northern War, 254n51
Grech, Nikolai Ivanovich, 255n75
"Greeting from Belinsky to Dostoevsky, A" (Nekrasov/Panaev/Turgenev), 267n187
Grigorovich, Dmitri Vasilievich: discussed, 15, 153, 164, 260n51; education, 252n28, 253n42; *Inheritance, The,* 262n84; "Petersburg Organgrinders, The," 263n112; on *Poor Folk,* 199–200
Les Guêpes, 209, 266n173
Guy Mannering, or the Astrologer (Scott), 85, 198, 254n45, 265n146

H

Hamlet (Shakespeare), 254n62
Harlot High and Low, The (Balzac), 266n180
hazel hens, 9, 10, 79, 83, 223
health: discussed, 11, 14, 146–47, 158, 165, 188–89; epilepsy/falling illness, 5, 62, 122, 155–56, 247n116; throat illness, 5, 68
Heart and Pillow (Veltman), 48, 243n75
Heart of Midlothian, The (Scott), 243n63
Heine, Heinrich: "Two Grenadiers," 157, 261n63
Heine, Maximilian, 157
The Henriade (Voltaire), 6, 44, 243n59
Heraldry Office, 252n34
Hermann and Dorothea (Goethe), 144, 172, 259n33, 262n98
Hernani (Hugo), 97, 255n69
Hero of Our Time, A (Lermontov), 259n30
Herzen, Alexander Ivanovich: *Who Is To Blame?,* 135
History of the Polish Uprising and War in the Years 1830 and 1831, A (Smitt), 164, 262n85
History of the Russian People (N. A. Polevoi), 97, 255n67

INDEX   287

History of the Russian State (Karamzin), 2, 36, 48, 240n35
Hoffman, E. T. A.: Belinsky on, 254n64; discussed, 97, 254n64; "Doge and Dogaressa," 248n2; *Life Opinions of Tom-Cat Murr, Together with the Fragmentary Biography of Conductor Johannes Kreisler in Accidental Gallery Proofs, Edited by E. T. A. Hoffman,* 85, 97, 254n43, 254n65; "Lost Reflection, The," 248n2; "Magnetizer, The," 255n70
Homer: *Iliad, The,* 139, 259n9, 259n22
homes: apartments, 12, 147, 152–53, 260n38; Darovoe, 1, 241–42n48, 241n39, 241n46, 241n47; with Grigorovich, 159, 188, 261n72; Mariinsky Hospital for the Poor, 1, 4; with Rizenkampf, 159, 261n69; with A. I. Totleben, 148
Horace (Corneille), 140, 259n21
horses, 4
Hours of Devotion for the Advancement of Genuine Christianity and Familial Divine Worship (Zschokke), 83, 253n35
Hubner, Joseph: *Four Hundred Sacred Stories, Chosen from the Old and New Testament for the Benefit of Youth with Noble Reflections,* 36, 240n34
Hugo, Victor: *Cromwell,* 97, 255n69; discussed, 100, 139, 255n76; *Hernani,* 97, 255n69

I

Ice House, The (Lazhechnikov), 48, 243n73
Idiot, The (F. M. Dostoevsky), 136
Igumnov (clerk), 87
Iliad, The (Homer), 139, 259n9, 259n22
Illustration, 209, 266n170
Imperial Academy of Arts, 260n49
Indiana (Sand), 245n101
Inheritance, The (Grigorovich), 262n84
"Insane Asylum, The" (Voekov), 52, 244n90
Inspector General, The (Gogol), 201, 264n121, 264n122
Institute for Tuberculosis, 1
Ioannovich, Dmitri, 243n69
Iphigénie (Racine), 139, 259n11, 259n12
Isaev (peasant), 119, 257n105, 259n27

Isaeva, Akulina, 63, 247n120, 257n105, 259n27
Isaeva, Marfa, 142, 259n27
Italy, 34
Ivan the Terrible, 243n69
Ivanov, Alexander Pavlovich, 237n2
Ivanov, Savin, 142

J

Janko, the Hungarian Horse-Herd (Beck), 157, 261n64
Japhet, in Search of a Father (Marryat), 157, 261n61
Jeanne (Sand), 61, 247n111
Joan of Arc, 61
Jocko, or the Brazilian Monkey (Rochefort), 33, 240n28
Jodelle, Étienne: *Cleopatra the Captive,* 140, 259n15
"Journalistic Hodgepodge" (Bulgarin), 266n167

K

Kachenovsky, Mikhail Trofimovich, 240n36
Kachenovsky, Vladimir Mikhailovich, 36, 50–51, 240n36
Kamensky, Pavel Pavlovich: *Seeker of Strong Sensations, The,* 262n93
Karamzin, Nikolai Mikhailovich: discussed, 6, 36, 64; "Epitaph," 248n122; *History of the Russian State,* 2, 36, 48, 240n35; *Letters of a Russian Pilgrim,* 48, 243n72; *Marfa, the Boyar's Daughter,* 48, 243n72; *Poor Liza,* 48, 243n72
Karatygin, Pyotr: *Wife and The Umbrella, or the Distressed Tuner, The,* 265n149
Karepin, Pyotr Andreevich: discussed, 13–14, 185, 258n124, 260n42; marriage, 237n2 (Introduction), 248n11
Karr, Alphonse, 209, 266n173
Kaufman, Konstantin Petrovich von, 249n14
Kazan Cathedral, 173, 263n104
Kharlashka (peasant), 47, 243n67
Khlysts/Khlysty, 77, 250–51n24
Khomsky Family, The (Begichev), 48, 243n73

288 INDEX

Khotyaintsev, Alexander Fyodorovich, 241n39
Khotyaintsev, Pyotr Petrovich, 126, 241n39, 258n126
Khotyaintsev, Vladimir Fyodorovich, 126, 129
Köhler, Ioann-Melchior, 156
Köhler, Louis, 156
Koni, Fyodor Alexeevich, 262n96
Kotelnitsky, Vasili Mikhailovich, 3, 30, 239n23
Kraevsky, Andrei Alexandrovich, 206, 211–12
Krivopishin, Ivan Grigorievich, 180
Krylov, Ivan Andreevich: discussed, 135; "Geese," 240n29
Kryukova, Alyona (Elena) Frolovna: discussed, 3, 28–29, 40, 120, 239n18, 257n108
Kubaryov, Alexei Mikhailovich: *Theory of Russian Versification, The*, 2
Kukolnik, Nikolai Vasilievich, 209, 266n170
Kumanin, Alexander Alexeevich, 238n14, 260n40
Kumanin, Alexander Andreevich, 123–24
Kumanin, Pyotr Andreevich, 149, 260n42
Kumanina, Alexandra Fyodorovna: discussed, 8, 12, 68, 160, 238n14; A. M. Dostoevsky on, 26–27

L

Lagvenova, Alexandra Dmitrievna, 116
Lamartine, Alphonse de: "Dying Poet, The," 157, 261n58
Lame Devil, The (Lesage), 167, 262n92
Last Aldini, The (Sand), 61
Latin, 3, 21, 51, 114, 244n88
Lavrentieva, Agrafena Timofeevna, 42–43, 242n51
lawsuit, 241n39
Lawsuit, The (Gogol), 211, 266n182
Lazarevskoe Cemetery, 63
Lazhechnikov, Ivan Ivanovich: *Ice House, The*, 48, 243n73
Ledru-Rollin, Alexandre, 245n99
Leibrecht, A. I., 125–26, 129
Leone Leoni (Sand), 248n2
Lermontov, Mikhail: *Hero of Our Time, A*, 259n30
Lermontov, Mikhail Yurievich, 135, 252n29

Lesage, Alain-Réné: *Lame Devil, The*, 167, 262n92
Leskov, Nikolai Semyonovich: "Ghost in the Engineering Castle (From the Memories of Cadets), The," 77
Letters of a Russian Pilgrim (Karamzin), 48, 243n72
Letters of a Voyager (Sand), 248n2
Library for Reading, The: discussed, 6, 52, 244n91
Life Opinions of Tom-Cat Murr, Together with the Fragmentary Biography of Conductor Johannes Kreisler in Accidental Gallery Proofs, Edited by E. T. A. Hoffman (Hoffman), 85, 97, 254n43, 254n65
Livy, 240n29
lizards, 38
Lizst, Franz, 153
Lomonosov, Mikhail Vasilievich, 48, 243n70
Lost Illusions (Balzac), 266n180
"Lost Reflection, The" (Hoffman), 248n2
Lukeria (wet nurse), 30
Lvovna, Anna, 181

M

"*Magnetizer, The*" (Hoffman), 255n70
Maikov, Apollon Nikolaevich, 216
Main Engineering Academy. *See also* education: discussed, 6, 8–9, 70, 78–79, 80–81, 84; F. M. Dostoevsky enters, 251n26; F. M. Dostoevsky graduates, 158, 159, 261n66, 261n70; F. M. Dostoevsky repeats year, 98, 99, 101, 105, 113, 255n71; entrance examinations, 7, 8, 73, 248n8
Makarov, Danila Savinovich, 118, 243n67, 256n101
Makarov, Kharlam. *See* Kharlashka (peasant)
Marcus, Fyodor Antonovich, 249n15
Marcus, Mikhail Antonovich, 73, 249n15
Marey (peasant), 3, 38–39, 241n40
Marfa, the Boyar's Daughter (Karamzin), 48, 243n72
Maria Fyodorovna, Empress, 1
Maria Simonova (Shidlovsky), 138, 259n4
Maria Stuart (F. M. Dostoevsky), 146, 152

Maria's Grove, 54
Marryat, Frederick: *Japhet, in Search of a Father,* 157, 261n61
Mary Stuart (Schiller), 260n35
Masalsky, Konstantin Petrovich: *Streltsy,* 48, 243n73
mathematics, 114
Mathilde, or the Notes of a Young Woman (Sue), 163, 165, 166, 167, 261n79
Mattea (Sand), 248n2
Maturin, Charles Robert: *Melmoth the Wanderer,* 254n44
Measure for Measure (Shakespeare), 262n89
Medea (Corneille), 259n17
Medea (Seneca), 259n17
Melikhov, Ivan Vasilievich, 121
Melmoth the Wanderer (Maturin), 254n44
Memories of the Devil (Soulié), 85, 254n47
Menologian. See Monthly Readings, The (Saint Dmitri of Rostov)
Messenger of Europe, 216, 218, 219–20
Mezhevich, Vasili Stepanovich, 171, 172
Michelet, Jules, 255n67
Mikhailov, Alexei, 119, 142
Mikhailovsky Castle, 9, 76–77, 78, 249–50n21, 250n22, 251n25
Mochulsky, Konstantin, 19, 237n1 (Introduction), 237n1 (Part One), 238n7
money: and billiards, 161, 166; discussed, 10–11, 12–13, 261n74; and dominoes, 167; and M. M. Dostoevsky, 66; and P. A. Karepin, 13; and A. F. Kumanina, 8, 12, 160; and pawnbroker, 161–62; stolen, 161; and women, 212
Montesquieu, Charles-Louis de, 83, 253n37
Monthly Readings, The (Saint Dmitri of Rostov), 36, 240n33
Montigny, Joseph-Nicholas, 157
"Morning" (M. M. Dostoevsky), 137
Moscow Hereditary Gentry, 33
Moscow Imperial Medical-Surgical Academy, 238n10
"Most Serene Order of Cuckolds, The," 247n121
Much Ado About Nothing (Shakespeare), 240n31
Museum of the History of Religion and Atheism, 263n104
music, 34, 153, 157
Mute Girl of Portici, The (Auber), 256n95

My Wife and My Umbrella (Chapelle), 265n149
Mysteries of Udolpho, The (Radcliffe), 240n30

N

Narezhnyi, Vasili Trofimovich: *Seminarian, The,* 48, 243n74
Nechaev, Fyodor Timofeevich, 238n15
Nechaev, Mikhail Fyodorovich, 34, 48–49, 240n32, 243n79
Nechaeva, Olga Yakovlevna, 123, 257n102, 257n105
Nekrasov, Nikolai Alexeevich: discussed, 16, 135, 144, 200–203; *Dreams and Sounds,* 259n32; "Greeting from Belinsky to Dostoevsky, A," 267n187; *Petersburg Miscellany, The,* 15, 217, 220, 266n164; *Physiology of Petersburg, The,* 15, 263n112; on *Poor Folk,* 221
Netochka Nezvanova (F. M. Dostoevsky), 156, 181, 261n79
New Time, 247n112
Nezhinsky Gymnasium of Advanced Science, 245n95
Nicholas I, 12, 13, 244n85, 254n60
Nicholas Nickleby (Dickens), 46, 243n64
Nikitenko, Alexander Vasilievich, 163, 165, 171, 261n81
Nikitin, Vasili, 119–20
Nikolai Pavlovich, Grand Duke, 9
Nisard, Désiré, 100, 255n76, 255n77
Northern Bee, The: Belinsky on, 266n167; discussed, 60, 245n99, 254n49
Notes from the Underground (F. M. Dostoevsky), 136
Notes of the Fatherland, 157, 183
Novel in Nine Letters, A (F. M. Dostoevsky), 266n172, 266n181
Novoe vremia, 264n128

O

Obodovsky, Platon Grigorievich, 172, 183
Odoevsky, Prince, 211, 266n177
Old Curiosity Shop, The (Dickens), 46, 243n64

Olga (boat), 205
Oliver Twist (Dickens), 46, 243n64
One Thousand and One Nights, 30, 239n22
opera, 157
Opium and Champagne, or the War of China (Clairville), 262n84
oral epics, 239n21
Orlova-Chesmenskaya, Anna Alexeevna, 252n36
Ostrogradsky, Mikhail Vasilievich, 147
Ostrovsky (writer), 135
Our Lady of Kazan, 263n104
Outline of Church-Biblical History for the Benefit of Spiritual Youth, An (Filaret), 44, 242n57
Overcoat, The (Gogol), 11, 15, 147

P

Pahlen, Pyotr, 250n22
Panaev, Ivan: "Greeting from Belinsky to Dostoevsky, A," 267n187
Panaeva, Avdotya Yakovlevna, 16, 212–13
parents, 1, 223
Pascal, Blaise: discussed, 96; *Thoughts*, 254n63
Pathfinder, or the Inland Sea, The (Cooper), 85, 254n46
Patriotic War of 1812, 238n13
Patton, Oscar Petrovich, 163, 164, 165, 166, 167–68
Paul I, 1, 76, 249n21, 250n22
Père Goriot (Balzac), 60, 246n107
Perrault, Charles: *Stories or Fairytales from Bygone Eras*, 239n21
Pesotsky, Ivan Petrovich, 171
Peter the Great, 77, 254n50
Peterhof, 86, 254n50, 254n51
Petersburg Miscellany, The (Nekrasov), 15, 217, 220, 266n164
"Petersburg Organgrinders, The" (Grigorovich), 263n112
Petipa, Jean-Antoine-Nicolas, 240n28
Petipa, Marius, 240n28
Petrashevsky Circle, 252n31
Petrovka, 119, 257n106

Phèdre (Racine), 140, 259n13
Photius the Monk, 10, 83, 253n36
Physiology of Petersburg, The (Nekrasov), 15, 135, 263n112
Pickwick Papers, The (Dickens), 246n105
Picture Gallery of Societal Life, or the Mores of the Nineteenth Century, A (Bilevich), 245n95
Plaksin, Vasili Timofeevich: Belinsky on, 252n29; discussed, 86, 147, 252n29; on Gogol, 252n29; on Pushkin, 252n29; *Upbringing of Women, The*, 252n29
Plekhanov, Georgi Valentinovich, 263n104
Plik and Plok (Sue), 167, 262n91
"Poets in Germany" (Veis), 264–65n140
Polevoi, Ksefont Alexeevich, 48, 243n70
Polevoi, Nikolai Alexeevich: discussed, 254n62; *History of the Russian People*, 97, 255n67; "Pushkin," 248n121; *Ugolino*, 97, 255n67
pond, 242n52
Poor Folk (F. M. Dostoevsky): Belinsky on, 204; and border, 17, 215–16, 217, 218–19, 220; and censors, 16; discussed, 15, 136, 170, 213, 225, 266n164, 268n202; Grigorovich on, 199–200; Nekrasov on, 221
Poor Liza (Karamzin), 48, 243n72
Prisoner of Chillon, The (Byron), 100, 255n72
Private Secretary, The (Sand), 248n2
Privits, Fyodor, 156, 260n57
prostitutes, 134, 152
Pushkin, Alexander Sergeevich: "Cart of Life, The," 256n87; death, 6, 63–64, 68–69, 247–48n121; discussed, 5, 48, 85, 102, 135, 196, 198; F. M. Dostoevsky's speech on, 268n189; *Egyptian Nights*, 104, 256n85; "Freedom," 250n22; Goering on, 243n78; Plaksin on, 252n29; "Song of the Prophetic Oleg, The," 243n77
"Pushkin" (N. A. Polevoi), 248n121
"Pushkin and the Lizards," 266n169
Pushkina, Natalia Nikolaevna, 247n121

Q

Quincey, Thomas de: *Confession of an English Opium Eater, The*, 85, 254n44

R

Racine, Jean: *Andromaque*, 139, 259n10; *Iphigénie*, 139, 259n11, 259n12; *Phèdre*, 140, 259n13
Radcliffe, Anne: discussed, 33, 34; *Mysteries of Udolpho, The*, 240n30
Radetsky, Fyodor Fyodorovich, 249n14
Radonezhsky, Sergei, 239n26
rape, 14, 37, 164
Raphael, 196
Rasputin, Grigori Yefimovich, 251n24
reading, 5–6, 10, 11, 14, 36, 46, 48, 107–8, 108, 224, 225
"Recollections" (Annenkov), 218
red cap, 53, 244n92
religion, 2, 26, 35, 224
"Remarkable Decade, A" (Annenkov), 216
Repertoire of Russian and Pantheon of All European Theaters, 183, 262n90, 262n96, 264n124
"Requiem" (Gartong), 167
resignation/retirement: discussed, 172–73, 178, 179, 180–81, 184, 187, 197, 262n100, 264n119
Revel Smelt, The, 86
Rizenkampf, Alexander Egorovich, 93, 158–59
Rob Roy (Scott), 46, 243n63
Robbers, The (Schiller), 5, 37, 171, 241n38
Robinson Crusoe (Defoe), 5, 242n49
Rochefort, Edmond: *Jocko, or the Brazilian Monkey*, 33, 240n28
Romanov, Mikhail, 243n69
"Rose, The" (M. M. Dostoevsky), 137
Rubini, Giovanni, 156
Rublyov, Andrei, 240n26
Ruslan and Lyudmila (Glinka), 156
Russian Invalid, The, 197, 264n139, 264n140
Russian literature, 135–36

S

Saint Isaac's Cathedral, 245n93
St. Michael's Castle. *See* Mikhailovsky Castle
St. Peter's Basilica, 263n104
St. Petersburg, 133–36
St. Petersburg Academy of Arts, 260n49
St. Petersburg Engineering Corps, 12
St. Photius the Great, 252n36
Saltykov-Shchedrin, Mikhail Evgrafovich, 135
Samson Statue, 254n51
Sand, George: Anonymous on, 245n96; Belinsky on, 245–46n102, 247n112; *Cosima*, 245n98; discussed, 6, 60–61, 193–94, 264n132; French correspondent on, 245n99; *Indiana*, 245n101; *Jeanne*, 61, 247n111; *Last Aldini, The*, 61; *Leone Leoni*, 248n2; *Letters of a Voyager*, 248n2; *Mattea*, 248n2; *Private Secretary, The*, 248n2; on religion, 264n128; *Teverino*, 209, 266n175; Turgenev on, 247n112; *Usoque*, 60, 61, 246n103; Zhorzhsandism, 246n104
Saveliev, Arisha, 241n44
Saveliev, Arkhip, 40, 241n44
Saveliev, David, 23, 27, 120, 239n17
Savushkin, Andrei, 118, 256n101
Schiller, Johann von: "About Naive and Sentimental Poetry," 262n97; discussed, 37, 87, 138–39; *Don Carlos*, 144, 168, 169, 172, 183; *Fiesco*, 171, 172; *Mary Stuart*, 260n35; *Robbers, The*, 5, 37, 171, 241n38; *Semela*, 172, 262n98; *Wallenstein*, 263n115
Schlegel, August, 113, 256n96
Schonknecht (doctor), 258n121
Schronrock, I. M., 258n121
Scoffer, The, 208–9, 211, 214
Scott, Walter: *Edinburgh Dungeon, The*, 46, 243n63; "Eve of St. John, The," 256n86; *Guy Mannering, or the Astrologer*, 85, 198, 254n45, 265n146; *Heart of Midlothian, The*, 243n63; *Rob Roy*, 46, 243n63
Sechyonov, Ivan Mikhailov, 249n14
Seeker of Strong Sensations, The (Kamensky), 262n93
Semela (Schiller), 172, 262n98
Seminarian, The (Narezhnyi), 48, 243n74
Semyon (servant), 160
Seneca: *Medea*, 259n17
Senkovsky, Osip Ivanovich, 60, 188, 244n91

Sentimental Journey Through France and Italy, A (Sterne), 198, 265n143, 265n144
Shakespeare, William: discussed, 113, 147, 185, 256n96; *Hamlet,* 254n62; *Measure for Measure,* 262n89; *Much Ado About Nothing,* 240n31
Sherwood, John, 50, 244n85
Shevyakov, Vladimir Vasilievich, 237n2
Shevyryov, Stepan Petrovich, 209, 266n169
Shidlovsky, Ivan Nikolaevich: attempts suicide, 109, 256n90; discussed, 7–8, 88, 101–3, 137–38, 253n40, 259n5; on M. M. Dostoevsky, 255n84; *Maria Simonova,* 138, 259n4; poetry, 103–4; "Sky, The," 255n78
Ship of Tatarinova, 251n25
Shirokov, Ivan Semyonovich, 118–19
Siberia, 258n117, 258n126
Silver Dove, The (Belyi), 251n24
Simeon (E. A. Alexandrova's son), 88
"Sky, The" (Shidlovsky), 255n78
Smailholm Tower, 256n86
"Smailholm Tower, The" (Zhukovsky), 256n86
Smitt, Fyodor: *History of the Polish Uprising and War in the Years 1830 and 1831, A,* 164, 262n85
snakes, 4, 38
Society of the History of Russian Antiquities, 239n23
Sollogub, Vladimir Alexandrovich: discussed, 211, 266n178; *Tarantas,* 199, 265n153
Son of the Fatherland, 100, 255n75, 255n78
"Song of the Prophetic Oleg, The" (Pushkin), 243n77
Sorrows of Young Werther, The (Goethe), 256n92
Soulié, Frédéric: *Eulalie Pontois,* 262n84; *General Confession,* 157, 261n59; *Memories of the Devil,* 85, 254n47
Spassky, Peter Nikitich, 253n36
Stasyulevich, Mikhail Mateevich, 218, 220
statue, 238n15
"Steeds of Phoebus, The" (M. M. Dostoevsky), 137
Sterne, Laurence: *Sentimental Journey Through France and Italy, A,* 198, 265n143, 265n144
Store for Instructive and Pleasant Reading for German Readers in Russia, The, 165, 262n86

Stories or Fairytales from Bygone Eras (Perrault), 239n21
"Strange Confessions of George Sand, The" (Anonymous), 245n96
Streltsy, 243n73
Streltsy (Masalsky), 48, 243n73
"Stroll, The" (M. M. Dostoevsky), 137
Strugovshchikov, Alexander Nikolaevich, 169
stushevat'sia, 10, 81–82, 213
Sue, Eugène: *Eternal Jew, The,* 199, 265n150; *Mathilde, or the Notes of a Young Woman,* 163, 165, 166, 167, 261n79; *Plik and Plok,* 167, 262n91
Summer Gardens, 249n21
Suvorin, Alexei Sergeevich, 216, 247n112
Svintsov, Vitali, 240–41n37

T

Tarantas (Sollogub), 199, 265n153
Tarus Bulba (Gogol), 262n89
Tatarinova, Ekaterina, 78, 251n25
Temple of Juno, 240n29
Teverino (Sand), 209, 266n175
Thackeray, William, 46
Theory of Russian Versification, The (Kubaryov), 2
Thierry, Augustin, 255n67
Thoughts (Pascal), 254n63
Time of Troubles, 243n69
Timofeev, Alexei Vasilievich, 109
Tol, Felix, 81, 252n31
Tolstoy, Leo, 1
Totleben, Adolf-Gustav Ivanovich, 148, 249n14
Totleben, Eduard Ivanovich, 249n14
Trinity Cathedral, 240n26
Troitsky Sobor, 240n26
Troitsky-Sergiev Lavra Monastery, 31, 68, 239–40n26
Trutovsky, Konstantin Alexandrovich, 153, 249n14, 260n50
Tsarskoe Selo, 245n93
Turgenev, Alexander Ivanovich, 248n121
Turgenev, Ivan Sergeevich: discussed, 135, 211, 214, 266n162, 266n179; "Greeting from

Belinsky to Dostoevsky, A," 267n187; on Sand, 247n112
Turunov, Mikhail Nikolaevich, 86
Two Brown Tales (Balzac), 157, 261n60
"Two Grenadiers" (Heine), 157, 261n63

U

Ugolino (N. A. Polevoi), 255n67
Undina (Zhukovsky), 97, 255n68
Union of Brothers and Sisters, 251n25
Upbringing of Women, The (Plaksin), 252n29
Usoque (Sand), 60, 61, 246n103

V

Valuisky Assumption Monastery, 103, 255n83
Vasiliev, Grigori, 40, 142
Vasilisa (laundress), 27, 54
Vasnetsov, Viktor Mikhailovich: *Bogatyrs*, 239n21
Vassilievich, Ivan, 244n85
Veis, A.: "Poets in Germany," 264–65n140
Veltman, Alexander Fomich: *Emelia, or the Metamorphosis*, 199, 265n152; *Heart and Pillow*, 48, 243n75
Venice, 69, 248n2
Vera (maid), 49
Vernet, Horace, 196
Viardot, Pauline, 245n100
"Vision of Mother, A" (M. M. Dostoevsky), 100–101, 137
Vizard, Yakov Ivanovich, 244n88
Voekov, Alexander Fyodorovich: "Insane Asylum, The," 52, 244n90
voice, 5
Volchok (dog), 39
Volotskoi, M. V.: *Chronicle of the Dostoevsky Clan, A*, 257n102
Voltaire: *La Henriade*, 6, 44, 243n59
Voronikhin, Nikoforovich, 263n104
Vyazemsky, Pyotr Andreevich, 255n80

W

Wallenstein (Schiller), 263n115
Wallenstein, Albrecht von, 263n115
weather, 116, 256n98
Who Is To Blame? (Herzen), 135
Wife and The Umbrella, or the Distressed Tuner, The (Karatygin), 265n149
wine, 104
Wollstonecraft, Mary, 247n109
women, 16, 151–52, 212, 266n184

Y

Yankel the Jew (F. M. Dostoevsky), 166, 262n89
Yekaterinhof, 138
Yury Miloslavsky, or the Russians in 1612 (Zagoskin), 48, 243n73

Z

Zagoskin, Mikhail Nikolaevich: *Yury Miloslavsky, or the Russians in 1612*, 48, 243n73
Zaraisk, 43, 242n53
Zhorzhsandism, 246n104
Zhuchka (dog), 4, 41
Zhukovsky, Vasili Andreevich: "Count from Hapsburg, The," 48, 243n76; discussed, 5, 52, 255n80; "Smailholm Tower, The," 256n86; *Undina*, 97, 255n68
Zotov, Vladimir Rafailovich, 262n84
Zschokke, Heinrich: *Hours of Devotion for the Advancement of Genuine Christianity and Familial Divine Worship*, 83, 253n35
Zubov, Nikolai Alexandrovich, 250n22
Zubov, Platon Alexandrovich, 250n22

www.ingramcontent.com/pod-product-compliance
Lightning Source LLC
Chambersburg PA
CBHW032052220426
43664CB00008B/963